An Environmental History of Wildlife in England, 1650–1950

An Environmental History of Wildlife in England, 1650–1950

TOM WILLIAMSON

BLOOMSBURY

LONDON · NEW DELHI · NEW YORK · SYDNEY

Bloomsbury Academic

An imprint of Bloomsbury Publishing Plc

50 Bedford Square	1385 Broadway
London	New York
WC1B 3DP	NY 10018
UK	USA

www.bloomsbury.com

Bloomsbury is a registered trade mark of Bloomsbury Publishing Plc

First published 2013

© Tom Williamson, 2013

British Library Cataloguing-in-Publication Data
A catalogue record for this book is available from the British Library.

ISBN: HB: 978-1-4411-0863-0
PB: 978-1-4411-2486-9
ePDF: 978-1-4725-1456-1
ePUB: 978-1-4725-1305-2

Library of Congress Cataloguing-in-Publication Data
A catalog record for this book is available from the Library of Congress.

Typeset by Deanta Global Publishing Services, Chennai, India
Printed and bound in India

CONTENTS

ACKNOWLEDGEMENTS

This has not been an easy book to research or write, for it has involved excursions into fields of knowledge – ecology, biology and ornithology – which are in part new to me. Producing it would not have been possible without the help, advice and information provided by a large number of people. These include, in particular, members of the Landscape Group within the School of History at the University of East Anglia: academic staff, Jon Gregory, Robert Liddiard and Sarah Spooner; Research fellows, Gerry Barnes and Andrew MacNair; and many past and present students, especially Jane Bevan, Sarah Birtles, Patsy Dallas, John Ebbage, Rory Hart, Sarah Harrison, Adam Stone and Clive Walker. Thanks also to Hadrian Cook, Jon Finch, David Hall, Tracey Partida and Anne Rowe, on whose knowledge I have also extensively drawn. Above all, I would like to thank my wife, Liz Bellamy, for all the support, advice and encouragement she has provided over many years.

The photographs, maps and diagrams are my own, with the exception of 19, by Jon Gregory; 13 and 28, Anne Rowe; 10, D. T. Grewcock/FLPA images; and 22, Tracey Partida. Figures 8 and 9 are redrawn from maps produced by Tracey Partida for a project funded by the AHRC. Figures 13 and 28 are reproduced courtesy of Hertfordshire Archives and Local History; Figure 16, with the permission of Shrewsbury Museum; Figure 7, courtesy of the Museum of English Rural Life at Reading; Figures 4 and 12, with the permission of the Norfolk Record Office; and 26, courtesy of the Norfolk and Norwich Millennium Library and Mrs Flowerdew; Figure 27, courtesy of *Country Life*.

LIST OF FIGURES

CHAPTER ONE

Setting the scene: The nature of nature

The natural landscape?

This book discusses the history of wildlife in England in the three centuries between 1650 and 1950. It examines how the number, and distributions, of different species altered over time, and describes the changing ways in which various wild plants and animals were regarded, controlled and exploited by the human inhabitants of this country. Above all, it explains how the environments in which such creatures made their homes developed over the centuries. Most people today probably think of the countryside as in some sense 'natural', certainly in comparison with the environment of towns. But nature, as Raymond Williams once observed, is the 'most complex word in the language', and problems over its definition underlie many current issues in conservation, and lie at the heart of this book.[1] In truth, rural landscapes as much as urban ones are largely or entirely artificial in character, the creation of particular social, economic and technological circumstances. Heaths, woods and meadows are, in most ways, no more 'natural' than suburban gardens or inner-city waste grounds. Indeed, one indication of how far removed we are from a truly 'natural' landscape in England, uninfluenced by human activity, is the fact that natural scientists argue over what precise form this might have taken.

Following the end of the last Ice Age, around 11,000 BC, England was gradually colonized by plants and animals as the temperature warmed, and as a continued connection with Continental Europe – the English Channel and the southern North Sea were only flooded in the seventh millennium BC – allowed them to move northwards with ease. Until relatively recently it was assumed that the natural vegetation developed through what ecologists call *succession*. Plants colonized in a more or less predictable sequence, each creating conditions which allowed successors to establish and flourish, leading in time to the development of a *climax vegetation* of closed-canopy forest which survived until the arrival of farming soon after 4,000 BC. Following this, most of England was cleared of trees, but if land is abandoned for any length of time succession begins once again, and within a short period, grasses and herbs will give way to scrub, and scrub to woodland.

In the course of the twentieth-century palynology, the study of pollen grains preserved in waterlogged conditions, changed perceptions of the character of the prehistoric 'wildwood'. People had assumed that this had been dominated by oak, understandably given the prominence of this species in surviving examples of ancient woodland. But it now became clear that small leafed lime (*Tilia cordata*) had been the most important component of the post-glacial vegetation across much of lowland England, accompanied by varying mixtures of oak, hazel, ash and elm, and with pine and birch being locally important. In the north and west, lime was rare and pollen cores suggest instead the presence of woodlands comprising diverse mixtures of oak, hazel, birch, pine and elm.[2] But while pollen analysis thus changed our ideas about the composition of the 'wildwood', it did not challenge the basic idea that England had, before man began to make extensive clearances, been more or less continuously wooded. In 1986, however, Oliver Rackham suggested that some areas of more open ground must have existed as part of the country's natural vegetation;[3] while 4 years later such ideas were taken much further by the Dutch ecologist Frans Vera. He drew attention to the importance of oak and hazel in pre-Neolithic pollen cores, noting that these species do not flourish in closed-canopy conditions. The pollen of various trees and shrubs more characteristic of woodland edges, than of continuous woodland, was also prominent, including that of blackthorn, hawthorn, rowan, cherry, apple and pear; so too was that of wood-edge herbs like mugwort (*Artemisia vulgaris*), nettle (*Urtica dioica*) and sorrel (*Rumex acetosa*).[4] Vera suggested that succession to closed-canopy forest had been checked by the grazing of large herbivores such as auroch (wild cattle) and deer. The 'natural' landscape had, in fact, been 'park-like' in character, with areas of open grassland, scattered with trees; patches of scrub; but only sporadic stands of denser woodland. Vera conceded that the pollen evidence superficially indicated a landscape dominated by woodland, rather than by open pasture, but he argued that intensive grazing would have 'limited the flowering of grasses, and thus the pollen emitted by grass into the atmosphere', thus hiding the true character of the vegetation.[5] He also noted that oak and lime emit more pollen when growing in open, park-like conditions than when crowded together in dense woodland.

In addition, Vera suggested that the pre-Neolithic landscape had been more dynamic in character than the conventional concept of the stable, climax 'wildwood'. It included patches of thorny scrub where trees were able to seed and grow, protected from grazing animals. As these reached maturity they eventually shaded out the protective thorns, but by this time they were relatively immune to the herbivores.[6] Eventually, individual trees grew old, or were out-competed by neighbours, and the area became open grassland again: the landscape was thus an ever-changing mosaic. Vera's hypothesis, it must be said, has met with a mixed reception from researchers, one study recently concluding that the contention that 'the bulk of the lowland landscape was half-open and driven by large herbivores . . . is not currently supported by the evidence'.[7] Rackham has argued that the failure of oak to seed and thrive in shade may be the result of the arrival of American oak mildew disease in comparatively recent times, and has pointed out numerous other problems with Vera's model.[8] The landscape of England before the advent of farming was almost certainly more varied and more open than we used to believe, yet much less so than Vera has argued.

Vera's 'dynamic forest' is one aspect of a wider shift in ideas about the way that natural plant communities develop, and in particular over whether vegetation, left to its own devices, will inexorably progress towards a stable 'climax'. The concept of succession, as originally formulated by ecologists like Clements in the early twentieth century, assumes that this development will follow, in effect, a unilinear path to a fixed and predictable end.[9] In the 1940s Tansley and others argued that different plant communities could, in theory, develop in the same environmental circumstances through the influence of minor and random factors – the so-called 'polyclimax theory'.[10] But the very idea of an ordered progression to one, or more, stable 'climax' began to be questioned in the 1970s.[11] By the end of the twentieth century, some ecologists were arguing that natural landscapes are best considered as ever-changing, dynamic systems, comprising habitat 'patches' which are constantly developing, interacting with each other and responding to a myriad of external, especially climatic, influences.[12] No habitat or ecosystem remains 'stable' for long, and its future development is always essentially unpredictable in character.

There are particular problems with applying the idea of 'succession' to England's early post-glacial vegetation, for as this was first developing, humans were already beginning to have a significant environmental impact. Most researchers believe that hunting communities had, in late glacial times, been at least partly responsible for the extinction of mammals like the mammoth and woolly rhinoceros. Levels of predation by post-glacial Mesolithic hunters – armed now with bows and arrows – would likewise have had a significant effect on the large herbivores which Vera believes were the main ecological 'drivers' in the pre-Neolithic landscape. There is certainly evidence that hunting communities had a *direct* effect on the vegetation by burning substantial tracts, probably in order to concentrate game in particular locations, although the extent of the practice remains unclear.[13] More importantly, within a few millennia of the ending of the Ice Age, human societies began to have a far more profound impact, through the introduction of farming.

The 'Neolithic revolution' arrived in England in the fourth millennium. A new way of life, involving the cultivation of crops and – more importantly – the domestication of livestock, was brought by immigrants from Europe, and perhaps emulated by the indigenous population. The principal crops – early varieties of wheat and barley – were introductions from abroad, as were sheep, goats and probably pigs and cattle (although the wild ancestors of both pigs and cattle existed in England, as elsewhere in Europe, the evidence suggests that they were not independently domesticated here).[14] The adoption of farming soon led to the development of tracts of ground which were permanently cleared of trees. The chalk downland around Winchester appears to have been largely deforested by the middle of the fourth millennium BC;[15] in the Peak District blanket bog, which had already begun to form following limited woodland clearances during the Mesolithic, had spread to something like its present extent by 3,000 BC.[16] In the middle Bronze Age, during the second half of the third millennium, a shift away from a mainly pastoral economy to one dominated by mixed farming was associated with an acceleration of deforestation, a process which continued and intensified, albeit with localized phases of regeneration, into the Iron Age.[17] Archaeological surveys suggest that by the Roman period settlement was widespread on almost all soil types, and there may have been as many as two million people living in England.[18] Some ecologists believe that the landscape was already 'something like the present countryside, farmland with small woodlands rather than woodland with small clearings'.[19] But we need to be a little cautious. Large areas of well-wooded terrain still survived, as in Blackdown Forest or the Forest of Dean, and settlement was, in most districts, significantly sparser than it was to become in the Middle Ages.[20] The environment had, nevertheless, unquestionably been drastically modified by human intervention.

The population fell at the end of the Roman period, leading to some localized woodland regeneration.[21] It began to recover again from the seventh century, probably most rapidly after the ninth, and by the time of the Domesday survey in 1086, there were around three million people living in England. With some possible reverses in the early-mid-twelfth century, the population continued to rise thereafter, peaking in the late thirteenth century at between five and seven million.[22] Demographic expansion was then halted by the arrival of the Black Death in 1348/49, which probably reduced the population by around 30–40 per cent. Thereafter, through the later fifteenth and sixteenth centuries, growth resumed. Perhaps more importantly, however, the farming economy became more complex, and more regionally specialized in character.

Farming regions

The medieval landscape, as this crystallized out in the twelfth and thirteenth centuries, already displayed a significant measure of regional variation. There was an obvious contrast between (on the one hand) upland areas, where population levels were generally low, the extent of arable land limited, and large areas of rough grazing survived, and (on the other hand) the more cultivated and populous lowlands. But there was also, within the lowlands, a distinction between what early topographers described as 'champion' and 'woodland' districts.[23] The former, characterized by nucleated villages farming extensive communal open-field systems, occupied a great swathe of central England running from Yorkshire to the Channel coast (Figure 1). Farms comprised numerous separate unhedged strips, each around 7 m wide, which were scattered with varying degrees of regularity through the territory of the township. For the purpose of cropping, the 'lands' or 'selions' were grouped into bundles called 'furlongs', and these in turn into two or three great 'fields', one of which lay fallow each year and was grazed by the village livestock, the dung from which replenished some of the nutrients depleted by repeated cropping.[24] In many places, these highly communal farming systems survived into the eighteenth or nineteenth centuries, when they were removed by large-scale enclosure, often through parliamentary acts. Thus was created the landscape of straight-sided fields which is often referred to – following Rackham – as *planned* countryside.[25]

To the south and east, and to the west, of the champion belt lay the 'woodland' areas, sometimes described as *ancient countryside* by modern

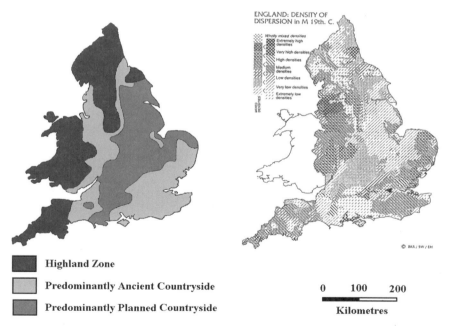

Highland Zone

Predominantly Ancient Countryside

Predominantly Planned Countryside

0   100   200

Kilometres

FIGURE 1 *The principal landscape regions of England. Oliver Rackham's broad distinction between 'Planned' and 'Ancient Countryside'* (left) *is mirrored in the map of nineteenth-century settlement produced by Roberts and Wrathmell* (right), *with strongly nucleated settlement patterns dominating a broad swathe of countryside running through the centre of England.*

scholars. Here settlement was more dispersed in character, with scattered farms and hamlets – many strung around commons and small 'greens' – as well as, or instead of, compact villages. Often some, occasionally the majority, of the land lay in hedged closes. But open fields of a kind usually existed, although their layout was rather different from those found in champion districts. They were 'irregular' in character: the holdings of individual farmers, rather than being scattered throughout the lands of the township, were clustered in particular areas of the fields, usually near their farmstead.[26] Often, although by no means always, communal controls on the organization of agriculture were less pervasive than those in the champion. Such landscapes were often well wooded although the term 'woodland' referred, in fact, to the number of hedges and hedgerow trees they contained, for even where open fields were prominent they were often small, numerous and hedged.

The origins of this broad division in the landscape of lowland England, a matter of continued debate among landscape historians, need not detain us here.[27] What is important to emphasize, however, is that 'woodland' and 'champion' are simplified terms covering a range of landscapes. There were, in particular, two main types of 'champion' countryside.[28] One, found on light, well-drained land, often overlying chalk, boasted extensive tracts of unploughed ground – downland or heath – in addition to the open arable. The individual 'lands' were usually ploughed flat, and separated by narrow, unploughed balks. These were the classic areas of 'sheep-corn' husbandry, in which large flocks were grazed on the extensive pastures by day and close-folded on the arable land by night, the treading of the sheep serving to incorporate their dung and urine effectively within the plough soil.[29] In the Midlands, in contrast, champion landscapes were mainly associated with heavy clays. Here the individual 'lands' were ploughed in broad ridges, to assist drainage. These still survive in places, preserved under grass as the earthworks known to archaeologists as 'ridge and furrow'. Landscapes like these lacked the great open pastures – the nutrient reserves of down or heath – of the sheep-corn lands. Heavy soils retained nutrients better than light, permeable ones, and close-folding would, for much of the year, have damaged the soil structure.[30] The fallows were dunged by the village livestock, but in a less intensive manner.

In highland areas as much as in lowland, in 'woodland' as in 'champion', most of the arable land in medieval England was exploited by peasant proprietors, the majority of whom paid a rent to a manorial lord, in cash or as labour on his *demesne*, or 'home farm'. To such land were appended rights to use the non-arable commons or 'wastes' of the manor, for grazing and as a source of firing and raw materials. Most of the classic 'semi-natural habitats' found in England were then common land, including heaths, moors, fens and chalk downs. By the twelfth century, manorial lords were legally recognized as the owners of such land but their ability to exploit it was limited by the rights enjoyed by their tenants. They did, however, manage to enclose portions as coppiced woods or as deer parks. The connections between habitat and ownership were often close: coppiced woodland was thus always a private land, a part of the lord's demesne.

The broad distinction between 'woodland' and 'champion' regions, never as clear-cut as historians sometimes imply, was eroded through the fifteenth and sixteenth centuries by the progress of enclosure: that is, the conversion of intermixed holdings farmed according to communal routines and regulations, into enclosed fields held as absolute private property.[31] Enclosure was intimately associated with the development of a more commercial system of farming. Specialized livestock production was, in particular, difficult on splintered holdings, scattered through the open fields. Some degree of agrarian specialization had existed in the early Middle Ages, even in the lowlands, and there was always more scope for pastoral than for arable pursuits in upland areas.[32] But most medieval peasants concentrated on the production of the grain upon which, in the last analysis, their survival depended. Even the 'demesnes' of major landowners were often grain factories, supplying hungry urban markets. Agrarian specialization increased after the Black Death, however, as average farm size began to rise, and as the economy generally became more complex and sophisticated.[33] The old forms of customary tenure gradually evolved into a range of 'copyholds', some of which effectively recognized local lords as owners of their manors and their tenants as tenants in the modern sense; others providing farmers with a greater degree of security; and some giving them so many proprietorial rights that they effectively joined the ranks of the small numbers of freeholders who had always existed among the peasant population. Such yeomen farmers, as well as many of the gentry and aristocracy, sought ways to increase their profits, and the size of their properties, as a more complex and market-orientated economy developed.

While many lowland districts continued to focus on grain production, others came to specialize in livestock farming, in dairying, or in fattening sheep and cattle which had often been reared elsewhere, in remote upland regions. The result was the development of a number of discrete farming regions, with their own economies and ways of living, and to some extent their own distinctive ecologies (Figure 2).[34] By the seventeenth century, large parts of both south-eastern and western England were devoted to pastoral farming, with three-quarters or more of their land under grass. They were mainly 'woodland' districts, where much farmland had always taken the form of enclosed fields, or comprised open fields of 'irregular' form which could be enclosed with relative ease in a gradual, piecemeal fashion.[35] In the champion Midlands, in contrast, although the soils were often well suited to livestock farming, the large and complex open fields were more difficult to enclose. Large areas were laid to grass but arable continued to dominate the landscape, at least in the period up to 1650. We should emphasize, however, that not all 'woodland' areas developed pastoral economies. Some, like the Chiltern Hills, remained important cereal-growing districts: there was no neat correspondence of ancient landscape structures and post-medieval farming types.

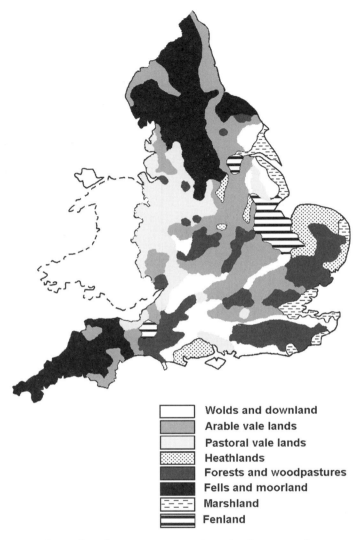

Wolds and downland
Arable vale lands
Pastoral vale lands
Heathlands
Forests and woodpastures
Fells and moorland
Marshland
Fenland

FIGURE 2 *Early-modern farming regions (after Thirsk 1987). This pattern, which emerged in the later Middle Ages, overlay and complicated the more basic structures of settlement and field systems shown in Figure 1.*

Farming and biodiversity

The spread of farmed landscapes from early prehistoric times was bad news for a number of species, especially the large mammals which predated on crops and livestock. The auroch disappeared during the Bronze Age; the bear probably before the Roman period; the lynx not long after it; and while the beaver survived into Anglo-Saxon times it had also probably gone by the time of the Norman Conquest.[36] The wolf hung on into the fourteenth century, but mainly in the counties bordering Wales and Scotland and perhaps in North Yorkshire. Increasing pressure on land probably caused significant declines in other species, especially those associated with woodland. Roe and red deer, in particular, appear to have become fairly scarce, at least in the lowlands. Yalden has noted how the bones of the yellow-necked mouse and of bats like the lesser horseshoe and Bechstein's, species which are now found only in well-wooded parts of south-eastern and western England, have been found on Roman sites in the Midlands and the north.[37] There were likewise changes in the frequency of certain plant species. Small leafed lime, once so common across lowland England, had declined markedly by later Saxon times, probably because it does not withstand grazing pressure very well. The Scots pine, for less obvious reasons, had died out in England by the end of the Roman period.

On the whole, however, the development of farming landscapes in England from the Neolithic times to the Middle Ages was good for biodiversity. Many species, previously confined to liminal niches, flourished as never before. Even if Vera is correct in seeing the natural environment as a largely open one – which, as we have noted, remains improbable – it is unlikely that much of it comprised the kind of close-grazed sward which is created by domesticated sheep and cattle. The kinds of plants which flourish today in such habitats must have been rare before the arrival of farming. Moreover, many species of invertebrate, mammal and bird favour wood-edge habitats, and the steady fragmentation of the forests ensured that these increased, for numerous small pockets of woodland have a higher edge length to area ratio than large, continuous blocks. The proliferation of hedges provided additional 'edge' habitats and also a degree of connectivity between surviving woodlands. Indeed, the patchwork of arable fields, meadows, woods and pastures which emerged as farming developed contained numerous other forms of 'edge' environment which afforded both places in which animals could nest or find cover, and diverse areas over which to forage, in close proximity. More important is the fact that the particular forms of land use adopted by successive human societies – the cutting of meadows at particular times of the year, the intensive cropping of woodland, the grazing of stock on heaths and pastures – tended over time to create particular suites of flora or fauna, more varied than anything which had existed before the advent of farming.

The effects of the fragmentation of the woods, and of the diversification of habitats through the spread of farming, are clearly reflected in the diverse yet often overlapping environmental requirements of our native birds.[38] Around 80 per cent of common farmland birds are woodland or wood-edge species in origin: birds like the blackbird, chaffinch, dunnock, rook, house sparrow, robin, wren, blue and great tit, song thrush, starling, willow warbler and whitethroat. Most of these, the last two being exceptions, are resident all the year round. Some, like the house sparrow and the blackbird, became real generalists, able to live on most kinds of farm and indeed in most conditions, including towns and cities. Others are more selective. Linnets, brambling and corn buntings, for example, are especially associated with arable holdings, often feeding on the fields in great flocks in the winter, while species like dunnock, yellowhammer, common whitethroat, tree pipit, chaffinch and long-tailed tit still need the shelter provided by copses and tall hedgerows, and avoid the more open farms. Such birds shade off into those which never really adapted to more open conditions, and which are still largely restricted to woodland, such as the treecreeper, chiffchaff, wood warbler, pied flycatcher, siskin and redstart.

Rather different are those species, which live in open country, on moors, heaths and downs, and sometimes also on marshes: birds like the partridge, grouse, snipe, golden plover, lapwing, skylark, stone curlew, woodlark, meadow pipit and corncrake. These must have had a fairly restricted distribution before the advent of farming. All are ground-nesting birds, and while some are again limited to particular habitats – such as the black grouse, restricted to heather moors – others are more catholic in their habits, such as the snipe, the redshank or the golden plover, at home on both moors and marshes. Like the woodland species, these open-country birds have, albeit to a lesser and varying degree, adapted to the new conditions of farmland. But many, especially in the lowlands, were only finally obliged to do so in the relatively recent past when – as we shall see – large areas of open 'waste' were enclosed and reclaimed. Birds like the corncrake and skylark gradually became a normal part of farmland bird populations but others, such as the stone curlew or the snipe, have embraced a life in the fields with less enthusiasm or success. Wetland species also benefited initially from human change to the environment, for cutting and grazing served to reduce the amount of alder and willow woodland in waterlogged districts. Some, such as the mallard and reed bunting, are also now found on farmland, if sufficient areas of open water are available. But the majority, like the bearded tit; bittern or the reed warbler; waterfowl like shoveller, wigeon, gadwall and teal; and migratory waders like black- and bar-tailed godwits, remained largely or entirely restricted to wetland habitats and suffered serious declines when these habitats were drained and converted to farmland in the course of the seventeenth, eighteenth and nineteenth centuries.

Indigenous, exotic and naturalized

Agriculture thus served to create, over time, a rich and complex mosaic of habitats. It also increased species diversity in another way. As well as introducing new crops and livestock early agriculturalists brought with them a range of weeds and invertebrates which occupied their fields, as well as a plethora of organisms adapted to dwelling in their homes. The spread of agriculture was a diaspora not only of humans with a particular lifestyle, but of a whole collection of related organisms. A high proportion of the spiders, beetles and other invertebrates regularly found in our homes are thus alien introductions, from the continent or the Near East.[39] Many of our most cherished wild flowers are likewise early interlopers, including poppy and corn-cockle. And further introductions, of both flora and fauna, were soon to follow.

Natural scientists make a broad distinction between 'indigenous' species, present in this country since early post-glacial times; 'naturalized' ones, which have been introduced from abroad but which can reproduce and maintain themselves readily here; and 'exotics' which cannot so do, and which are mainly restricted to parks, gardens and other controlled locations where they are deliberately nurtured.[40] Some of the arrivals from abroad have been introduced intentionally, and others 'hitchhiked' with imported organisms or commodities. Naturalized aliens are an increasing problem throughout this globalized world, for they can cause serious disruption to the ecosystems of their adopted homes. They can act in an 'invasive' manner, altering the character of the environment, displacing indigenous wildlife through competition and predation, spreading pathogens or changing the genetic makeup of natives through hybridization.[41] Yet in practice it is often hard to define or identify what is, and what is not, an introduced species.[42] The development of our indigenous flora and fauna was truncated by the flooding of the English Channel in the later seventh millennium BC, and some species which were unquestionably introduced in historic times had been present in previous interglacials and perhaps *nearly* arrived back under their own steam. This causes problems. A number of wild flowers, thought to be introductions because they fail to be mentioned in early plant lists or herbals, are present in the neighbouring parts of continental Europe and might simply have escaped the notice of early botanists and herbalists, perhaps because their distribution was once more localized. The snowdrop (*Galanthus nivalis*) for example may be native in England, as it certainly is just across the Channel in Brittany. But it is only recorded in the wild from the eighteenth century. Some believe it was introduced as a garden plant as late as the sixteenth century,[43] although Mabey has pointed to the close association of prominent colonies with medieval ecclesiastical sites, and to the plant's role in the celebration of Candlemas in the catholic church.[44] It might be an early introduction, or it might be an indigenous plant, but only in limited areas of south-west England, spreading more widely in recent centuries. The evidence can be interpreted in a number of ways. Similar uncertainties surround other classic wild flowers, including spiked star-of-Bethlehem (*Ornithogalium pyrenaicum*) and, most notably, snakes-head fritillary (*Fritillaria melagris*).[45] This beautiful plant, now rare due to the destruction of its traditional habitats of meadows and pastures, somehow escaped the notice of sixteenth- and seventeenth-century herbalists and others – even those who lived close to what were later to be significant colonies. As the botanist George Claridge Druce put it in 1886, 'It was not a little singular that the Fritillary, so conspicuous a plant of the

Oxford meadows, should have remained unnoticed by the various botanists who resided in or visited Oxford'.[46] Although there are some possible early references to the plant in the wild, the first unequivocal one comes as late as 1736. Native to Europe, it may again have been introduced as a garden plant, later escaping into the wider countryside. Ornamental (and medicinal) gardens have certainly existed in England since at least Roman times and many of the foreign plants which were established within them have unquestionably escaped into the wider countryside. Examples include both relatively uncommon species such as clove pink (*Dianthus caryophyllus*), Jacob's ladder (*Polemonium caeruleum*) and globe thistle (*Echinops sphaerocephalus*), and also more familiar ones like Alexanders (*Smyrnium olusatrum*) and opium poppy (*Papaver somniferum*), both of which like ground elder – the gardener's bane – were probably introduced by the Romans.[47] As we shall see, gardens were to continue to function as important conduits for alien plant species throughout the period covered by this book.

By the middle of the seventeenth century, there had also been a number of important tree introductions. The sweet chestnut, a native of southern Europe, arrived in the Roman period, and a number of magnificent, 'veteran' examples now exist – most notably the great Tortworth chestnut in Gloucestershire, which even in 1800 was thought to be over 600 years old.[48] More problematic is the sycamore. Until recently it was accepted that this had been brought to England in the fifteenth or sixteenth centuries from continental Europe. Its pollen was unrecognized in early cores, and John Gerard in 1597 described the 'Great Maple' as 'a stranger in England'.[49] However, sycamore leaves are unmistakably carved (together with those of maple, with which they might be confused) on the thirteenth-century tomb of St Frideswide in Oxford, and some arboriculturalists have recently argued that sycamore is native to western Britain, where some particularly old specimens exist.[50] But no examples of its distinctive wood have ever been found preserved in archaeological deposits, and the Anglo-Saxons do not seem to have had a word for it. The tree was almost certainly a medieval introduction, of an ornamental character: Evelyn in 1664 refers to its use in 'Gardens and Avenues'.[51] It has since become widely established in the countryside, in part through deliberate planting, in part dispersing under its own steam. Tree introductions continued on an increasing scale in the post-medieval period. The horse chestnut arrived from the Balkans around 1600: the Cedar of Lebanon probably in the 1620s, along with the silver fir, the European larch, false acacia and the American plane.[52] Most of these were to remain in gardens and parks although the larch was to be extensively planted in the wider landscape in the course of the eighteenth, nineteenth and twentieth centuries. Once again, there were to be further introductions in the course of the subsequent centuries.

A surprising number of our common mammals are also introductions. The house mouse was an early arrival, probably in later prehistory, a beneficiary of settled agriculturalism.[53] The black rat came later. A native of southern India, it appears to have spread along trade routes, into the

Roman empire, arriving in England by the third century. Remains have been found in a number of Roman towns, including London, Wroxeter and York.[54] Like the house mouse, the black rat was closely associated with humans, both animals living close to them in towns, villages and farms, consuming their waste and stored cereals. The black rat may have had a more direct impact on human history as the carrier of fleas which were the host of *Yersinia pestis*, if the Black Death was indeed caused by this bacterium. Other relatively common animals, particularly adapted to environments modified by man, may likewise be early immigrants. The bones of the harvest mouse have not been recovered from any prehistoric excavations and from only two Roman sites, and it probably arrived from the Continent, and flourished, only as a largely agricultural landscape developed in England in later prehistory.[55]

Hunting and 'intermediate exploitation'.

Many important additions to our fauna were not accidental but deliberate introductions: they were species brought to these shores to be hunted, or otherwise consumed, by a social elite. In agricultural societies, the exploitation of wild resources is unnecessary for survival and hunting is usually restricted to a powerful minority, and thus expressive of social status.[56] The brown hare was apparently introduced in the Bronze Age and probably as a quarry, for it is hard to see why else it would have been brought from the continent, where it is indigenous.[57] But in addition, by medieval times some animals, especially introduced ones, were managed through what might be called 'intermediate exploitation': forms of livestock management which lay somewhere between the hunting of truly wild animals and the farming of fully domesticated ones.[58]

Deer parks may have existed in pre-Conquest times, but were probably a Norman introduction: either way, by the thirteenth century there was on average one for every three or four parishes in England.[59] They were enclosed areas in which deer were both farmed, as a source of venison, and hunted for pleasure (Figure 3).[60] Deer were high status creatures, symbolic of lordship. Venison could not be bought and sold on the open market but only received as a gift. Most parks were well-wooded environments, enclosed with a stout fence, and they usually contained a specialized building called a 'lodge' which served as a base for the park keeper and as a place for the owner to stay while on hunting trips. Although some parks formed a part of the 'landscapes of lordship' laid out around castles and palaces,[61] most examples in the twelfth and thirteenth centuries lay in remote places, away from the homes of their owners, largely because they had been enclosed from residual areas of waste beyond the margins of cultivated ground. From the later fourteenth century, however, parks began to be more closely associated with major residences, and by the middle of the seventeenth century, most

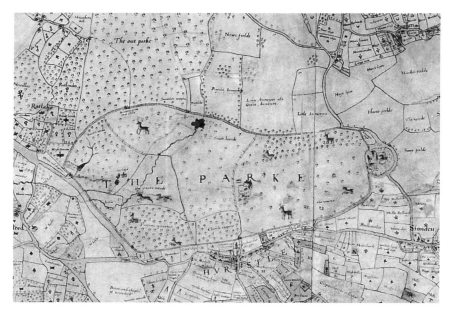

FIGURE 3 *The medieval deer park at Hursley, Hampshire, as shown on an early sixteenth-century map.*

were to be found next to, or even surrounding, mansions.[62] By this stage, as we shall see, they were becoming primarily ornamental landscapes.

Recreational deer hunting made an important impact on the medieval environment in another way. Royal forests were large tracts of the country across which special laws were enforced to encourage deer for the royal hunt, largely by protecting the scrub and woodland in which they found shelter.[63] Most comprised a core of common land, often wooded, owned by the king, but an outer penumbra of ordinary farmland. Many were found in 'woodland' districts, but others were scattered across the 'champion' Midlands, in areas where enough uncultivated ground had survived to make their designation as forests worthwhile. Many could also be found in areas of upland moor, including Dartmoor, a clear enough indication that there was no necessity for forests to be densely timbered.

Deer parks contained the native red and roe deer, but their principal denizens were the fallow deer *Dama dama*, which was more amenable to management. The fallow had become extinct across Europe after the last glaciation, except in a few areas around the Mediterranean, probably as a consequence of human predation. It was possibly reintroduced into Britain shortly before the Norman Conquest, to judge from bones excavated at Hereford, Cheddar and elsewhere, and the evidence – which is contested – of place names.[64] It did not become widespread, however, until after the Conquest, and perhaps only gradually. Fallow deer bones are only thinly represented in the large assemblage excavated from early twelfth-century contexts at Launceston Castle in Cornwall for example, but increase steadily after this time, outnumbering those of red and roe deer by the later thirteenth century.[65] Most fallow deer were kept in parks but they were also introduced, with some success, into royal forests. Even here, however, they were carefully looked after by foresters. The very fact that deer of all kinds were kept in enclosures, or nurtured and protected in other ways, indicates that they were not common in the wider countryside by the twelfth and thirteenth centuries.

The rabbit, like the fallow deer, was present in England in previous interglacials but it did not return. It was reintroduced, probably as a domesticate, in the Roman period, but it did not apparently survive into Anglo-Saxon times: there is no Old English word for the rabbit and no rabbit bones have been recovered from secure archaeological contexts (not one, for example, from among the 45,000-odd excavated from *Hamwih*, the Anglo-Saxon port near Southampton).[66] It was reintroduced for a second time by members of the Norman elite soon after the Conquest. The earliest unambiguous documentary record dates from 1135, when Drake's Island in Plymouth Sound was granted to Plympton Priory *cum cuniculi* ('with the rabbits'),[67] and by the middle of the thirteenth century, colonies had been established throughout England.[68] Coneys (the word rabbit was, until the eighteenth century, reserved for the young) were kept in special areas – originally called "coneygarths", later warrens – for both their flesh and their fur. Before the fourteenth century, most examples were located within deer parks or took the form of small enclosures placed beside elite residences. After the Black Death, however, warrens proliferated and began to be managed on more commercial lines. They were a good way of making money from common heaths and moors, for by a quirk of the law manorial lords holding a grant of free warren – the right to hunt over a defined tract of ground – were allowed to establish a colony of rabbits on common land despite the opposition of commoners, with whose stock they would compete for grass and other herbage. Lords could thus derive an income from manorial wastes without going to the expense and the difficulty of enclosing them.[69] Most warrens contained low oval or rectangular mounds in which the rabbits could dwell and where they could be easily trapped. These were called 'buries' or 'burroughs' by contemporaries, but were christened 'pillow mounds' by twentieth-century archaeologists, who were initially puzzled about their age and purpose. Some were sophisticated structures containing networks of purpose-built tunnels. Warrens also usually contained a lodge; most were provided with enclosures for protecting breeding does, as well as special traps for catching vermin.[70] Not surprisingly, warrens were hated symbols of feudal privilege and were regularly targeted in times of social unrest. During the Peasants' Revolt of 1381, the rebels in St Albans in Hertfordshire placed one of the Abbot's rabbits, liberated from one of his many warrens, in the town pillory.[71] As early as 1388 a survey noted that sixty acres of arable at Wilton in Norfolk were 'worth nothing by the year because of destruction by the coneys of the duke of Lancaster's warren there'.[72] But in the seventeenth century most rabbits still lived in private warrens, rather than in the wild.

Other species were brought into England in medieval times by the landed elite and either hunted or exploited in an 'intermediate' fashion. The pheasant, a native of Central Asia, was probably – like the rabbit and the fallow deer – introduced soon after the Norman Conquest, perhaps via Sicily, and was likewise kept in parks.[73] Here it was hunted with hawks to some extent, but mainly managed to provide food for great feasts. Fish ponds were known in the early Middle Ages, stocked with bream and pike but exploited on a fairly casual basis. Their management appears to have been revolutionized by the introduction of the carp (*Cyprinus carpio*) from central Europe in the fourteenth century.[74] The fish were mainly bred and kept in large ponds, 'great waters', usually created by damming a stream running along a narrow valley: often two, three or more were arranged in sequence, and provided with complex systems of bypass channels. Smaller rectangular ponds called 'stews' or *servatoria* were widely established beside manors houses, abbeys and castles, watery larders where the fish were stored prior to consumption.[75]

Another form of 'intermediate exploitation' common in the Middle Ages was the keeping of pigeons or doves in dovecotes, some of which contained more than a thousand nesting holes.[76] Each pair of pigeons produced two chicks, between eight and ten times a year. The young birds were culled when around four weeks old, before the pin feathers had developed, and the tender meat was usually treated as 'spatchcock' and baked in pies. Unlike rabbit, carp, pheasant and fallow deer, the pigeon was an indigenous creature, descendant of the wild rock dove: but as that bird only ever had a limited distribution, largely restricted to rocky shores, the situation was perhaps broadly similar. Pigeons battened freely on the crops of local farmers and dovecotes thus represented, in effect, machines for turning other people's labour into the owner's meat protein. Not surprisingly, they were by law restricted to the manorial gentry. In the words of one seventeenth-century commentator, they were a 'power and libertye wch in reason and policye of state ought to belonge to great estates and persons of qualitye and commission'.[77]

Conclusion

The environment of England in 1650 had been shaped by thousands of years of human activity. Farming had completely transformed the landscape, creating habitats – often extending over vast tracts of land – with no real parallels in the natural world, and plants and animals once rare were widely established. The emergence and crystallization of distinct farming regions in the course of the fifteenth, sixteenth and seventeenth centuries may have marked a peak in biodiversity. Some animals, it is true, had become extinct over the centuries, but they were outnumbered by the extensive range of flora and fauna intentionally, or inadvertently, introduced by man. From rabbits to rats, poppies to sycamores, the countryside was, and indeed still is, full of creatures which, in the views of some, should simply not be here. Quite how we have come to think of these, and the hedged fields, heaths, moors, meadows and woods which make up our traditional rural landscape, as our 'natural heritage' is one of the themes of this book. But a more important concern is the particular character of these habitats: how they were created and sustained; how they were radically transformed and replaced in subsequent centuries by industrialization, demographic growth, and agricultural change; and what effects all this has had upon the nation's biodiversity.

Investigating these matters is by no means straightforward. It requires a degree of expertise spanning a range of disciplines, in both the sciences and the humanities, that nobody alive really possesses. Moreover, much of the documentary evidence which is available for the study of our past environments is meagre or misleading or both. Although from the eighteenth century an expanding interest in natural history provides us with a variety of observations of flora and fauna, it is usually difficult to convert these into a reliable picture of the actual frequency of different species in the landscape. In particular, as recent experience shows, variations over time in the numbers of particular plants or animals, and even their apparent extinction in a locality, can simply result from differences in levels of observation and recording.[78] To an extent it is possible to model past populations of plants and animals by examining the kinds of flora or fauna found in similar habitats today. But this too can be a hazardous procedure for – as the recent development of the fox as an urban species attests – animals and plants can change their habits and preferences over time.

On top of this there are theoretical problems. Words like 'rarity', 'extinction' and 'biodiversity' are slippery and problematic, especially in terms of how they relate to different geographical scales of analysis. A species can become extinct in one area but flourish elsewhere; 'biodiversity', while usually employed to mean the maintenance of natural variety through the conservation of the range of organisms characteristic of particular districts, is sometimes used more loosely, simply to mean the total number of different plant and animal species found in any area, which is not quite the same thing. Such caveats should always be borne in mind in the pages that follow. What remains certain, and underlies all the arguments presented in this book, is that nature has never existed outside of or independent from the activities of men. The natural lies embedded in the social and the economic: its history is largely, though not entirely, that of successive forms of social, economic, and agrarian organization.

CHAPTER TWO

Seventeenth-century environments: Woodland and waste

Introduction

England in the seventeenth century teemed with wildlife. Plants now rare were then common; the polecat and pine marten were probably present in every county; the great bustard was still a frequent sight on open land. In part, this abundance was due to the fact that while most of the country was occupied by farmland a much higher proportion than today comprised various kinds of woodland and 'waste' – unreclaimed wetlands, moors and heaths, downs and other forms of marginal grazing land. Versions of such habitats existed which have now vanished; intermediate types, where these neat categories merged, were in particular more frequent than today. While the particular character of these varied environments was in part a consequence of soils, drainage and topography, it was largely a result of the ways they had been managed, often over many centuries, for grazing and fodder, or as a source of raw materials and especially fuel. The use of coal was expanding rapidly in the sixteenth and seventeenth centuries, with extensive coal fields developing, in particular, in the north-east of England. Production rose from around 20,000 tons *per annum* in 1560 to two or perhaps even three million by 1700.[1] By the end of the seventeenth century, coal had probably become the main provider of thermal energy in England.[2] But it was not economic to transport coal very far from the coast or navigable rivers, and most domestic firing was still supplied by organic materials. Firewood was cut, not only from woodlands, but also from hedges and free-standing trees; gorse, heather and turf were systematically cropped from heaths and moors; and peat was dug from moors and fens.

Woodland

There was relatively little woodland in seventeenth-century England. Even at the time of Domesday probably only around 15 per cent of the country was tree-covered, and by 1350 this had fallen to around 10 per cent, partly through deliberate clearance and partly through gradual wastage.[3] There was some regeneration following the demographic collapse of the later Middle Ages, but renewed clearances in the fifteenth and sixteenth centuries perhaps reduced woodland cover to around 8 per cent of the country's land area, something which needs to be set against the modern figure, of around 10 per cent.[4] Most of this, however, represents plantations of eighteenth, nineteenth or twentieth-century date, for much of the woodland existing in c.1600 was grubbed out over the following four centuries, and now comprises only around 30 per cent of this total.[5] These remnants are usually referred to as 'ancient woodland' by ecologists. Indeed, the accepted definition of this term is that the woodland in question must have been in continuous existence since 1600.[6] It represented either areas which had never been cleared and cultivated ('primary' ancient woodland) or ones where trees had regenerated over agricultural land in the immediate post-Roman period, or in the demographic decline in the late Middle Ages ('secondary' ancient woodland). It is probable that this distinction obscures the dynamic character of woodland and the extent of deliberate planting in the course of the sixteenth century or earlier. But either way, woodland of this kind took two main forms.

Some comprised *wood-pasture*, areas containing trees which were sufficiently widely spaced to allow grass and other herbage to grow beneath them, which was grazed by cattle, sheep or deer. The majority of the trees were *pollarded*: that is, repeatedly cut at a height of 1.5–2 metres (out of the range of browsing stock) every 10 years or so to provide a supply of 'poles' suitable for fencing, for using as the minor timbers in buildings, for making tools, and above all for fuel (Figure 4). Pollarding (and *shredding*, a related form of management) was also used to produce 'leafy hay' for winter fodder. The trees regenerated rapidly from their cut trunks, or *boles*.[7] Some wood-pastures were private, but in the early Middle Ages most were common land. The lord of the manor – or the King, in the case of royal forests, where wood-pasture commons were extensive – owned the trunk, just as he owned the soil of the common itself, but the commoners usually had the right to crop the poles.

Wood-pastures were inherently unstable environments. Trees could be damaged by livestock, and when they were felled, died or were blown down, could not easily be re-established in the face of continuous grazing pressure. Woodland of this kind thus tended to degenerate over time to open pasture. Indeed, there was no neat dividing line between wood-pasture and open pasture, but instead a continuum, with at one end pasture or heathland

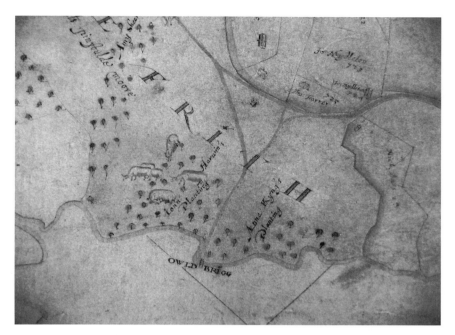

FIGURE 4 *A wood-pasture common shown on a map of Gressenhall, Norfolk, surveyed in 1624. The pollards are divided into named 'plantings', bearing the name of the tenant who maintained and exploited them.*

thinly scattered with trees and at the other dense and continuous stands of pollards. According to some writers, by late medieval times wood-pastures survived best where portions had been enclosed by manorial lords, and managed more intensively as deer parks – the private venison farms and hunting grounds briefly described in the previous chapter. Where they continued to be exploited as common 'waste', in contrast, they tended to degenerate more rapidly because young planting could not be protected by fences, which would have reduced the amount of grazing available to other commoners.[8] But in some areas at least custom allowed commoners to erect temporary enclosures for planting, usually in locations around the margins of a common, close to the farms that often existed there.[9] Wood-pasture also survived well where there was a good market for firewood, as in the hinterland of London, and where manorial control was particularly strong, in a few cases giving the lord the right to the poles from pollards, so that tenants could only crop them at a price. Both circumstances appear to have applied to the vast tracts of wooded common on the heavy clay soils of south-east Hertfordshire. In 1695 it was said that there were 24,000 pollards, mostly hornbeams, on the 1,186 acre-Cheshunt Common: that is, a density of around 50/hectare.[10] All this said, while wood-pastures were still extensive in some districts in the seventeenth century, especially in royal forests, in others they were becoming increasingly open ground, denuded by poorly regulated cropping, felling and grazing.

More stable in character were those woods which were managed as *coppice-with-standards*. In these, the majority of trees and bushes were cut down to at or near ground level on a rotation of between 7 and 15 years, in order to provide a regular crop of poles: like pollards, in effect, but at ground level. The plants regenerated vigorously from the stump or *stool*, or suckered from the rootstock (Figure 5). Such woods contained relatively few standard trees – ones allowed to grow naturally, and harvested for timber – for if these had been numerous, the canopy shade would have suppressed the growth of the underwood beneath.[11] Coppices were vulnerable to grazing livestock, which were thus rigorously excluded – at least for the early stages of the rotation – by substantial boundary banks and ditches, topped by fence or hedge, although these may also have had a symbolic function, emphasizing that the areas in question had been privatized from the wastes by a local lord and were now out of bounds to commoners.

Woods were factories for producing wood and timber, and their species composition was in some ways only loosely related to that of the local 'wildwood'. The majority of standard trees were oaks, the most valued material for constructing ships and timber-framed buildings. The coppiced understorey displayed more variation, related in part to soil type and in part to management history. Hazel, ash and maple were well represented; hornbeam was a major component in areas of heavy soil in the south east and East Anglia; while oak, small-leafed lime, alder, elm holly and sweet chestnut were all locally important.[12]

FIGURE 5 *Wayland Wood, Norfolk: outgrown coppice of ash and hornbeam in a typical ancient wood.*

Coppiced woods were and are important and diverse habitats – around 250 species of flowers, sedges and grasses occur mainly or only within them[13] – but this is largely a consequence of their essential artificiality. Portions of a wood were usually felled in turn, on rotation, creating a mosaic of blocks of coppice in different stages of regrowth – a most unnatural arrangement. Coppicing opens up the floor of the wood to light, yet at the same time leaves the ground flora undisturbed, a regime which favours species such as wood anemone (*Anemone nemorosa*).[14] Other species (such as water avens (*Geum rivale*) and pignut (*Conopodium majus*) are largely restricted to ancient woods simply because they cannot survive grazing pressure well: woods were the only environments in the early modern world neither intensively grazed nor regularly ploughed.[15] In addition, many of these species remained in ancient woods because they are slow to colonize new ones, although as we shall see the extent of this is often exaggerated in the scientific literature. The flower-rich coppices were and are ideal for sustaining a wide range of insects, especially butterflies like the pearl-bordered fritillary, the high brown fritillary, and the Duke of Burgundy. Indeed, the decline of coppicing over the last century or so has been a major factor in the fall in butterfly numbers in England.[16]

The abundant supplies of food afforded by such a diverse and continually changing environment attracted a wide range of birds and mammals, although the former in particular were also directly encouraged by the structural diversity afforded by traditional management. Bird species display much variation in terms of their preferences for different stages of coppice regrowth, and thus the mosaic of fells served to rack up the scale of diversity. Finches, buntings and the *Sylvia* warblers will have been more common in young coppice but tits and thrushes probably increased as they matured. As the canopy closed after 7–10 years, the number of birds would decline, but soon after the compartment would be cut, beginning the whole process anew.[17]

Large numbers of birds and mammals were attracted to the margins of woods, for as already emphasized 'edge' environments are of critical importance, animals benefiting from the opportunities to forage for food in adjacent fields or pastures, but also enjoying the cover, and further sources of food, provided by the wood itself. Garden warbler, blackcap, willow warbler and chaffinch are characteristic birds of the woodland edge, together with chiffchaff and nightingale in places where the wood has a scrubby margin. Hedgehog, the common shrew and other small mammals are also at home here. Some species, such as pygmy shrews, are largely restricted to the wood edge, and are seldom found in the interior. Conversely, red squirrels preferred to live towards the centres of large blocks of woodland, while tawny owls are today absent from some 90 per cent of woods smaller than 100 hectares, but from only c.18 per cent of those larger than this.[18] In terms of birds especially, the interiors of large woods were and are home to woodland 'specialists', while their margins, and smaller woods, are occupied by the more generalist species characteristic of farmland.[19]

On the face of it, seventeenth-century wood-pastures might appear to have had a closer relationship to the natural pre-Neolithic vegetation, at least as envisaged by Vera, than coppiced woods. But in most examples small-leafed lime was rare – it does not withstand grazing pressure well – and oak was again the dominant tree, although elm, beech, ash and hornbeam, alone or in various combinations, could also be found. The few wood-pastures which survive today have usually not been managed for decades and thus lack the regular cycles of change, from light to shade, experienced by coppices. They thus tend to have high levels of humidity and shade, ensuring that they are rich in lichens and bryophytes. This, while sometimes posited as an essential difference between the two types of woodland,[20] is in reality a reflection of recent developments. There are, however, two more important differences between them. First, regular grazing in wood-pastures would have suppressed the range of plants common in coppices: they were floristically poorer. Secondly, while coppiced woods often contained ancient stools, there were few full-grown trees of any great age, as most were felled when they reached economic maturity at around 80–100 years, when their growth rate tended to slow and they were large enough to be used for building houses and ships. The pollards in wood-pastures, in contrast, continued to be cropped into old age, and these environments thus contained a high proportion of ancient or 'veteran' trees, that is, examples old for their particular species.[21] These were, and are, important habitats, containing rotting wood, cavities, cracks and crevices which are home to a range of rare lichens, fungi, and beetles.[22] It has been estimated that there are no less than 1,700 different species of invertebrates in Britain which depend, directly or indirectly, on decayed wood for some, at least, of their life cycle.[23] Snails and slugs, such as the tree snail (*Balera perversa*), also flourish, feeding on both fungi, mosses and ferns. Larger fauna, especially bats, also make their homes in ancient trees; while birds, especially owls like the Barn Owl, nest in the numerous holes created as the trees decay.

Heaths and moors

One important difference between the landscape of the seventeenth century and that of today was the far greater extent of heathland. Between 1800 and 1950 the area of heathland in Dorset, for example, decreased by 67%, and large tracts had already been lost to agriculture in the course of the eighteenth century.[24] Heaths are treeless environments formed in poor, infertile soils overlying porous and acid sands and gravels. Many boast a characteristic soil called a *podzol*, which has a grey upper level, leached of humus and iron, overlying hard layers of 'pan' where these have been re-deposited. Their vegetation features a distinctive range of dwarf shrubs, principally heather or ling (*Calluna vulgaris*), bell heather (*Erica cinera*), gorse or furze (*Ulex europaeus*) and broom (*Sarothamnus scoparius*), together with characteristic grasses such as sheep's fescue (*Festuca ovina*), wavy hair grass (*Deschampsia flexuosa*) and common bent (*Agrostis tenuis*) (Figure 6).[25] Some heaths may always have been open environments, never very extensively colonized by trees: the vegetation of parts of the East Anglian Breckland, for example, includes plants like sand catchfly (*Silene conica*) and yellow medick (*Medicago falcate*), which are characteristic of steppe conditions and which must always have existed in an open landscape. Most, however, developed from woodland, often in remote antiquity but sometimes during the Anglo-Saxon period (as with many of the heaths on the Suffolk coast), sometimes in the course of the Middle Ages (as with Mousehold Heath near Norwich), occasionally even later.[26] Whatever their origins, all heaths rapidly become colonized by woodland if they are not intensively managed. In this sense, at least, they are highly artificial environments.

Most heaths were common land and were intensively exploited by local populations. They were grazed, by cattle but especially by sheep. Many were managed as part of a 'sheep-corn husbandry' system, with the sheep being taken down to the arable fields at night, where they were close-folded on the fallows, in the manner described in the last chapter, treading in urine and dung and providing a much-needed injection of nitrogen and other nutrients to the poor local soils.[27] The heaths, in other words, acted as nutrient reservoirs and the sheep as 'mobile muck-spreaders', continuously removing nutrients and relocating them elsewhere. In addition, from the fifteenth century (and in the East Anglian Breckland probably earlier) manorial lords often established rabbit warrens in heathlands.[28] But as well as being grazed,

FIGURE 6 *Typical heathland on the east Suffolk coast near Sutton.*

heaths were also regularly cut, for a variety of materials. Bracken and heather were used for thatch, as animal litter, and sometimes to cover domestic floors; gorse was employed for fencing and (in the words of John Norden) 'to stoppe a little gap in a hedge'.[29] All these materials were also used as fuel. Heather was harvested for this purpose in the form of turves dug to a depth of at least 2.5 cm, which thus included both the vegetation and a square of combustible matted roots. Crabbe, writing in the late eighteenth century about east Suffolk, refers to the local heaths as a source of 'the light turf that warms the neighbouring poor'.[30] Gorse was simply cropped above ground level, and was sometimes cultivated in special enclosures, especially where there were brick kilns, which were often fired with heathland vegetation. When Blickling Hall in Norfolk was constructed in 1617–21, for example, over a million bricks were made in kilns entirely fuelled with gorse and broom faggots brought from the heaths at nearby Cawston and Saxthorpe (although Blickling also appears to have had its own 'Furze Closes', to judge from an estate map of 1729).[31] Well into the nineteenth century, most of the kilns on the Bedfordshire brick fields were similarly fired using heathland vegetation.[32] The vitrified bricks so common in seventeenth-, eighteenth- and even some nineteenth-century buildings throughout England, and often used in a decorative fashion, may be the consequence of using heather or gorse as fuel, both rich in potash.[33] The significance of heaths as a source of thermal energy, as well as grazing, was seldom lost on contemporaries. In the early seventeenth century, Thomas Blenerhasset, writing about Horsford Heath in Norfolk, described how 'This heathe is to Norwich and the Countrye heare as Newcastle coales are to London'.[34] In short, heaths were both cut and cropped very intensively, ensuring that they were degraded landscapes, continuously depleted of nutrients, deficient in biomass and organic matter.

Today, heaths are most common in East Anglia, mainly overlying glacial sands and gravels, and in the south and south-east of England, mainly on Tertiary sands and gravels although sporadically on the Cretaceous Greensand and Wealden sands. They can also be found in Staffordshire and other west Midland and north-western counties, overlying Triassic sandstone and Carboniferous coal measures, and often shading without clear demarcation into the moors of the uplands. Extensive areas also occur in Devon and Cornwall, often close to the coast. But these are mere fragments of what existed in the seventeenth century for vast areas of heathland, as we shall see, were reclaimed, afforested, or urbanized in the course of the eighteenth, nineteenth and twentieth centuries, or else have degenerated to secondary woodland. Even in the period since 1830, heathland has declined by around 80 per cent[35]: a great deal more than this, possibly three times as much, disappeared during the previous century through enclosure and 'improvement'. What survives is important not only in national but also in international terms, for while heaths were once a common element of the landscape in many European countries, including France and Denmark, they have been eradicated even more systematically there. Yet heaths as we see them today are not only far fewer in number, but also less varied in character than those of the seventeenth century. While most heaths were even then completely open landscapes, some appear to have carried significant numbers of pollards – they were, at least in part, heathland wood-pastures.[36] Moreover, the character and the intensity of grazing displayed much variation. In Lincolnshire and East Anglia heaths often lay remote from settlements and were mainly grazed by the folding flocks. But in southern England they were more likely to be encircled by houses, like other commons: here they were grazed by a wider range of livestock, including donkeys, cattle and deer.[37] In many cases, intensive grazing and cutting would have ensured that heaths were much smoother than those of today, closer in appearance to downland. Grasses were often more abundant, and bracken less so. Indeed, in the sixteenth century the manorial court of Thetford in the East Anglian Breckland ruled to restrict the amount of bracken which could be cut by commoners because it was in short supply.[38] Some heaths were so intensively grazed by sheep and by rabbits that the heather and turf was removed, mosses formed a major part of the ground cover and in extreme cases bare sand was exposed. But elsewhere grazing was less intense. John Norden described in 1618 how gorse was widely used as a fuel in Devon and Cornwall, where it grew 'very high, and the stalke great, whereof the people make faggots', but was less important in this respect in east Suffolk, where the local inhabitants 'suffer their sheep and cattell to browse and crop them when they be young, and so they grow too scrubbed and lowe tufts, seldom to that perfection that they might be' – presumably because alternative sources of fuel were available locally.[39] And while many heaths were permanent habitats, others were sporadically ploughed up, either on a casual basis – when grain prices were high – or on a long but regular rotation, as in the case of the East Anglian 'brecks'.[40] Intense grazing, regular stripping of turf for fuel, and this kind of temporary cultivation together provided a particularly valuable range of ruderal habitats, especially in the case of the eastern heaths, in which plants characteristic of the early stages of succession on such acid soils could be found.[41] Heaths, in short, were a very mixed bag, displaying a variety not always fully recognized today by those involved in their conservation or restoration.

Variations in the character of heaths were in part a function of complex social and economic factors: population density, the relative balance of power between lords and commoners, the extent to which they were managed as part of 'sheep-corn' systems, and the character of the resources available from other local environments. But they were also a consequence of purely natural influences. In southern and eastern England, 'chalk-heaths' were more common than they are today. These are distinctive habitats which are formed where thin layer of acidic topsoil, usually sandy drift, overlie chalk. These boasted an unusual collection of shallow-rooted calcifuge plants, such as heather and tormentil (*Potentilla*), and deeper-rooted plants characteristic of chalkland, such as Cock's Foot (*Dactylis glomerata*) or salad burnet (*Poterium sanguisorba*).[42] Because the layers of acid sand overlying the chalk were thin, they were more easily reclaimed than heaths of more conventional form, which overlay deeper deposits of sand or gravel. Therfield Heath in Hertfordshire and Newmarket Heath in Cambridgeshire lie some 30 kilometres apart but both are fragments of what was, until the nineteenth century, a continuous tract of chalk heath extending all along the scarp of the East Anglian Heights.[43]

Heaths are important not so much because they host a wide range of plants and animals – most are relatively species-poor – but because they are home to species which are rare elsewhere, such as the natterjack toad. Dry, open land with few trees to impede sunlight, their soils are warmer than those of neighbouring habitats, allowing species to flourish which are not normally found this far north, such as smooth snakes and sand lizards; heaths provide the principal English home for the adder.[44] Loose, sandy soils, and the low-growing gorse and heather also afford shelter for invertebrates rarely found elsewhere, such as the silver-studded blue moth. The very openness of the landscape, moreover, is and was attractive to a number of bird species, such as the stone curlew and the Dartford warbler. Nightjar and woodlark are heathland birds, although they also favour woodland edges and may have been a particular feature of wood-pasture heaths. In the seventeenth and early eighteenth centuries, the great bustard and red-backed shrike would also have been common – the former now extinct and the latter hovering on the edge of extinction in England. Those heaths in which the amount of soil disturbance was greatest – either because they boasted high densities of rabbits, or because they were regularly dug for heather turfs or sporadically cultivated – displayed a distinctive flora, including spiked and fingered speedwell (*Veronica spicata* and *V. triphyllus*), perennial knawel (*Scleranthus perennis*) and field wormwood (*Artemisia campestris*), and were particularly favoured by invertebrates like the tawny wave moth.

The most extensive tracts of unploughed ground in the seventeenth century were the moors which were to be found in the higher, wetter areas of northern and western England, above c.300 metres. Like heaths, moors were more extensive then than today. Even in 1773 Arthur Young was able to assert, admittedly with some exaggeration, that 'you may draw a line from the north point of Derbyshire to the extremity of Northumberland of 150 miles as the crow flies, which shall be entirely across wastelands; the exceptions of small cultivated plots, very trifling'.[45] And like heaths, moors were (and are) of varied character. Those on lower ground, and towards the drier east of the country, shade almost imperceptibly into lowland heaths. They are formed over podzols or brown earths, and are largely dominated by heather, only locally out-competed by coarse grasses such as *Nardus stricta*.[46] Bilberry and bracken are also widespread. Many moors, however, occur on higher or wetter land, on broad and poorly draining plateaux. Here deposits of peat, many metres deep, have formed, as plant debris cannot fully decay in such permanently waterlogged ground and accumulates *in situ* over the centuries. While heather is an important component of the vegetation, it is often out-competed by vigorous grasses such as cotton grass (*Eriophorum angustifolium*) and purple moor-grass (*Molinia caerulia*). As with heaths, eighteenth- and nineteenth-century 'improvements' have served not only to reduce the extent of moorland, but also to destroy certain kinds more than others. In general, the lower, heath-like moors were more susceptible to reclamation than those occupying the higher, peat-covered plateaux.

The extent to which moors were originally tree-covered remains unclear and those lying at high levels, and furthest north, were perhaps only ever thinly timbered. Nevertheless, it is probable that most English moors are essentially anthropogenic environments. The lower moors especially were densely settled in prehistory. On Dartmoor, for example, remains of planned field systems of Bronze Age date divide up much of the land surface.[47] The retreat from the uplands came at various times – here in the later Bronze Age, elsewhere as the climate deteriorated in the Iron Age. The removal of trees increased waterlogging and thus peat formation and by the early Middle Ages moors were generally exploited as summer grazing by communities principally based on lower ground, or by specialized grazing establishments called 'vaccaries', the property of major landowners. As we have seen, many were also used for hunting and designated as 'forests' in spite of their open, treeless character. Dartmoor and Exmoor were forests, and there were originally at least 39 named forests in the Pennines and the Lake District, including the Peak Forest in Derbyshire, and Bowland and Rossendale in Lancashire.[48]

Moors were, in the seventeenth century, intensively exploited: had they not been those lying at lower altitudes, at least, would soon have reverted to woodland. They were grazed, both by sheep and by cattle, tough upland breeds which were mainly sent to the lowlands for fattening.[49] They were, like heaths, cut for bracken, heather and gorse, and for rough *molinia* hay in the spring;[50] while peat was extensively dug for fuel, on a vast scale where minerals were smelted, as in the southern Pennines.[51] Already some areas of heather moor were being managed by burning, to judge from a statute of 1607, which attempted to restrict the practice to the winter. The purpose was to destroy old, woody growth, unpalatable to sheep, and encourage new shoots: heather is remarkably fire resistant.[52]

Heather moors, in particular, would have been rich in wildlife. The taller heather provided nesting grounds for the merlin and red grouse, while curlew, golden plover and lapwing preferred areas where it was shorter.[53] Moorland provides homes for fewer mammals and reptiles than heaths, however, owing to the cooler and wetter conditions. Voles and mice are thus often numerous but the range of reptiles was more restricted, although adders would have been common on the heather moors especially.

Common pastures

There was much permanent grassland in the seventeenth-century landscape. It took a range of forms, some now rare, but the most important distinction was between meadow and pasture. Meadows were cut in mid-summer to produce hay, used as fodder to keep livestock through the winter when the grass does not grow.[54] Pastures, in contrast, were directly grazed by stock. In reality, this distinction was always somewhat blurred. Meadows were opened to grazing after the hay had been cut in June or July; while in post-medieval times, when meadows became less restricted to alluvial soils, fields were often used alternately as meadow and pasture. Meadows were usually individually occupied, rather than exploited in common, and so for convenience are treated as farmland and discussed in the next chapter. There were also, even in the Middle Ages, some areas of enclosed private pasture, occupied in severalty, and these increased steadily from the fifteenth century, as England's agriculture became more complex and regionally specialized. But common pastures remained far more extensive, often shading off, without clear demarcation, into heaths, wood-pastures and other varieties of unploughed ground. Most examples occupied thin, acidic, waterlogged or infertile soils unsuitable for arable farming.

Common pastures were permanent and long-lived, and most were rich in species which survived being destroyed by grazing livestock because they are low-growing – like hoary plantain (*Plantago media*) and wild thyme (*Thymus praecox*) – or because they are unpalatable, such as mat grass (*Nardus stricta*).[55] Variations in soils and climate ensured innumerable differences in their composition. Dwarf sedge (*Carex humilis*), for example, is characteristic of limestones in south-west England: Somerset hair-grass (*Koeleria vallesiana*) of south-facing slopes in the Mendips.[56] In general terms, acid grass lands – which shade off gradually into heath – were and are less botanically diverse than calcareous ones, probably because acid substrates are a relatively rare and recent environment, looked at across the scale of evolutionary time, so that fewer plants have evolved to flourish on them.[57] The most diverse grasslands are thus found on limestone uplands and escarpments in Yorkshire, Derbyshire, Cumbria and Durham, and in the Cotswolds, or on chalk. Some areas of common grassland also existed on neutral soils, especially on poorly draining clays – the numerous greens and commons of 'woodland' countryside, but also scattered among the furlongs of 'champion' country in the Midland 'shires'. These tended to carry a less floristically rich sward, although varied enough compared with modern commercial grassland.

Chalk downland still covers extensive areas of southern England, especially in Wiltshire, on Salisbury Plain and Cranbourne Chase. Significant areas also remain on the North and South Downs; in Berkshire; and along the escarpment of the Chilterns running through Oxfordshire, Buckinghamshire and Hertfordshire. Small areas survive on the Wolds of Lincolnshire and Yorkshire. But vast tracts were ploughed up in the course of the eighteenth, nineteenth and twentieth centuries, especially in the east of England. Much of what remained was subsequently compromised by neglect, followed by the adoption of modern management practices. We do not know for certain how much chalk grassland there may have been in the mid-seventeenth century, still in pristine condition, but it must have been at least three times and quite possibly five times the amount which remains today. Like many heathlands, most downs were managed as part of sheep-corn systems, with flocks being moved on a daily basis from upland pasture to the night fold on the arable, constantly depleting them of nutrients.[58] This together with the thin, dry character of the soils and intensive grazing by sheep and, increasingly in the post-medieval period, rabbits created a distinctive, close-cropped turf characterized by low-growing calcicole herbs like cowslip (*Primula veris*), sheep's fescue (*Festuca ovina*), kidney vetch (*Anthyllis vulnerana*), the pasqueflower (*Pulsatilla vulgaris*), as well as many species of orchid. Areas of downland commonly support as many as 40 different plant species per square metre, sometimes more.[59] These in turn provide food and shelter for a phenomenal range of invertebrates, including crickets, grasshoppers and butterflies like the Adonis blue, gatekeeper, silver-spotted skipper, chalkhill blue and Duke of Burgundy fritillary. Snails, too, form an important part of the fauna, including such species as the heath snail, moss snail and large chrysalis snail. The range of mammals, amphibians and reptiles is more limited in these dry and open landscapes, but the bird life was diverse, including – as well as numerous common farmland types – open-country species like the stone curlew, bustard, buzzard, skylark, stonechat, corn bunting and lapwing.

Wetlands

In the seventeenth century, there were vast areas of unreclaimed wetland in England. They fell into three main categories, only one of which constituted a truly natural environment. This was salt marsh, which developed along the coast where silt and marine alluvium had accumulated in estuaries or behind shingle spits or sandbanks, to such a depth that extensive areas were only inundated by the highest tides, and could thus be colonized by salt-tolerant vegetation such as sea fern-grass (*Catapodium marinum*) and red fescue (*Festuca rubra*). The marsh surface was dissected by creeks which filled and emptied with the tides. Such areas graded almost imperceptibly into mudflats, inundated by tides twice a day, rich in sediments and with large numbers (but relatively few different species of) invertebrates, such as lugworm (*Arenicola marina*) and ragworm (*Nereis diversicula*), upon which migratory waders came to feed.[60] Curlew, bar-tailed godwit, dunlin, oystercatcher, shelduck, redshank, ringed plover, turnstone and avocet were trapped or shot in vast numbers by local people. Richard Reyce described in the seventeenth century how 'those we call seapies, coots, pewits, curlews, teal, wiggeon, brents, duck, mallard, wild goose, heron, crane, and barnacle' were regularly trapped on the Suffolk coastal marshes.[61] The drier areas of salt marsh were grazed by sheep during the summer months, and shellfish were frequently collected. Whatever the value of such land, however, it could be greatly increased if 'inned' from the sea and converted to 'fresh' or grazing marsh, a process already under way by the twelfth century in parts of southern and eastern England.[62] Portions were surrounded with embankments to prevent the ingress of salt water, and drainage within assisted by the provision of surface drains (often adapted from the natural creek pattern) leading to 'flap sluices' which were held shut by water pressure at high tide, but which opened to allow the egress of water at low.[63]

Many reclaimed marshes, like those in Essex or on the eastern side of the Norfolk Broads, were used for grazing – for sheep in the Middle Ages, but increasingly for cattle from the fifteenth century – and they were managed from isolated marsh farms. But their rich soils also made good arable land, and the more extensive areas, such as Romney Marsh in Kent, the 'Marshland' of the northern Fens in Norfolk, or the Lincolnshire 'Townlands', had large areas under cultivation in the Middle Ages and contained, not just scattered farms, but sizeable villages. By the seventeenth century, however, with the development of a more regionally specialized farming economy, most marshes were under grass. By this time most of the largest tracts of salt marsh had been reclaimed but smaller areas continued to be drained into the eighteenth, nineteenth and even twentieth centuries.

Embanking radically changed the character of marshes, even if they remained unploughed. Marine animals were immediately destroyed and the vegetation rapidly altered as the salt was washed out of the soil by the rain. Petch, describing the recently embanked lands in the Wash in the 1920s, noted that 'the most striking feature of these lands is the rapidity with which the salt marsh species disappear. Within a year or two of the exclusion of salt water, they have been replaced by the common pasture grasses, and the docks, nettles, thistles, buttercups and daisies of arable fields'.[64] Nevertheless, grazing marshes acquired a range of other distinctive plants, such as marsh lousewort (*Pedicularis palustris*) and marsh valerian (*Valeriana dioica*). Moreover, because the dykes functioned both as a source of drinking water for stock and as 'watery fences' to keep them within particular areas, water levels were maintained almost to the height of the adjacent pasture, even to the point of allowing fresh water to flow *into* the marsh from streams or rivers in summer. Waders thus continued to be attracted to such areas, for a high water table ensured that worms and other invertebrates were concentrated in the upper levels of the soil, and could thus be easily reached by the birds.[65] The rather tall grass sward maintained by cattle grazing, in particular, was also attractive to ground nesting birds like lapwing, redshank, black-tailed godwit and avocet. In addition, the plants and invertebrates found within the drainage ditches or 'dykes' were highly diverse because, although the water was mainly fresh (and thus suitable for cattle to drink), it often became more brackish towards the sea 'wall'.[66] Maintenance of a high water table also ensured that the margins of dykes were poorly defined, trampled and muddy, providing a wide diversity of niches occupied by a range of invertebrates including the *anopheles* mosquito, host for the parasite *Plasmodium* which is responsible for malaria. Indeed, marshes were generally regarded as dangerous, disease-ridden places in the past: but less so than fens.

These, our third main type of wetland, were formed over areas of low-lying peat, many of which lay immediately inland from coastal marshes, occupying the flood plains in the lower reaches of slow-moving rivers. Indeed, most of our more extensive English wetlands (such as the Somerset Levels or the Norfolk Broads) comprised both kinds of landscape, merging and in immediate proximity. In some places in the north of England, fens developed into raised 'mires', with up to ten metres of peat, as on the Thorne and Hatfield Moors south of the river Humber.[67] Relatively few fens were reclaimed and improved in the Middle Ages, or even brought into private ownership, and they were generally devoid of settlements. Instead they were exploited as common land by communities living around their margins.[68] Depending on local circumstances they would be grazed during the drier summer months; mown for rough marsh hay or litter; or cut for thatching materials in the form of reed and saw sedge (*Cladium mariscus*). In the latter case, regular cutting in the right season for one species tended to suppress the growth of the other, leading in time to increasingly pure reed- or sedge-beds. In addition, peat was dug on a huge scale for domestic fuel, usually in shallow excavations a spade or two spade's depth but occasionally from pits up to two metres deep, such as those which, excavated in the early Middle Ages, were then flooded to produce the 'broads' of east Norfolk and north-east Suffolk, or the 'deeps' of the Lincolnshire fens.[69]

Many people in the seventeenth century regarded fens with horror and nobody of wealth would live anywhere near them, in part because of the dangers of malaria. Dugdale in 1662 typically described how the fen air was 'for the most part cloudy, gross, and full of rotten harrs [fogs]; the water putrid and muddy, yea full of loathsome vermin'.[70] Such attitudes have, to some extent, clouded our own perception of fen landscapes, which by the seventeenth century were in general less wild, and often less waterlogged, than we sometimes assume. Areas like the Fenlands of East Anglia, or the Isle of Axholme, were characterized more by grass than by reeds, and managed more by grazing than by cutting. Michael Drayton in 1622 described livestock on the fens near Ely 'hid over head in grass',[71] and some of the attempts currently under way to 'restore' the fens of eastern England arguably place too much emphasis on water and wildness.[72] Nevertheless, most fens did include areas of standing water (either natural, like the great 'meres' at Whittlesey and Soham in Cambridgeshire, or the consequence of peat digging) and extensive reed and sedge beds. Many contained a range of other habitats including areas of wet woodland, although the spread of alder and other trees was kept in check by the intensity of grazing and cutting, while the numerous watercourses contained a diverse range of fish, including vast numbers of eels. Diversity was also encouraged by the regular disturbance of the surface by peat digging and the subsequent, gradual terrestrialization of the resultant pools. Indeed, some of the rarer wetland plants, such as the Fen Violet (*Viola persicifolia*), are still closely associated with former peat diggings.[73] Fens teemed with invertebrates, including butterflies like the black hairstreak, the swallowtail – now confined to a few locations on the Norfolk Broads – and the now extinct large copper. All provided food for birds like the coot, moorhen, little grebe, mallard and teal, water rail and spotted crake, redshank, godwit, lapwing and bittern, all present in vast numbers. These in turn were predated by hobbies, sparrowhawks and red kites. In Newbold's words, 'the local population unwittingly sustained and managed the fens in what would be regarded today as a large nature reserve'.[74]

By the 1630s major attempts to drain the fenlands of eastern England were under way, the result in part of major legal changes. The General Drainage Act of 1600 allowed local common rights to be overturned and investors in major land improvement schemes to be rewarded with a share of the lands reclaimed.[75] The most important project was the draining of the southern Fens of East Anglia, or the 'Great Level', by a consortium of 'Adventurers' (investors) headed by the Duke of Bedford, who employed the Dutch Engineer Cornelius Vermyden. This project culminated in the construction of the two parallel artificial watercourses, the Old Bedford and New Bedford Rivers, which ran for some 25 kilometres, but never more than a kilometre apart. They were designed to speed up the flow of water coming down the river Ouse into the Wash. The two watercourses were embanked, the strip of land between them acting as a linear reservoir for the winter floods.[76] Today, much of this long, narrow area of unimproved and seasonally flooded grassland forms the Welney bird reserve.

The 'Great Level' was finally declared drained, after many difficulties and much opposition from local commoners, in 1653. Some of the land was allotted to the adventurers and major landowners but much remained as common land, albeit now better drained, and divided between the parishes which had formerly shared it. But Vermyden and his associates underestimated the extent to which the drying peat would shrink and, when ploughed within the enclosed parcels, would degrade through microbial action and blow away. The land surface began to fall, and the Fens were subject once more to seasonal flooding. Hundreds of drainage windmills were erected by private owners to improve their land, but with limited effect. Pastures had been improved, and the area under reeds reduced, but the final draining of the fens, both in East Anglia and elsewhere, had to wait until the nineteenth century.

The management of commons

With the exception of coppiced woods and many marshes, most of the environments discussed in this chapter were common land, exploited in diverse ways, potentially in conflict. Areas of low-lying fen, for example, once dug for peat, could not easily be used for grazing, for the resultant pools took several generations to 'terrestrialize'. It was also important to prevent different users from taking more than their share of the resources the commons provided. The intensity of grazing was usually regulated by *stinting* – that is, by laying down the numbers and types of stock which different tenants could graze on the common – or through the rules of *levancy and couchancy*, which related the numbers of stock which could be grazed to the amount of arable land each farmer held, or to the quantity of animals which could be over-wintered on their farmstead.[77] With materials cut from the common, the situation was more difficult. In the Middle Ages there was a general idea that commoners could take what they required to sustain their households, and no more, but sometimes, and probably increasingly in the course of the sixteenth and seventeenth centuries, portions were 'doled': that is, allocated in the form of strips to individual commoners, who could then harvest whatever they required. The entire area of the common, however, continued to be open for grazing. Pressure on the commons was particularly acute by the middle of the seventeenth century because the population had been rising steadily through the previous century and a half. Many were in a poor state. Large areas in royal forests, especially in southern England, lost their tree cover in this period and degenerated to open heathland. Problems were exacerbated by the breakdown of traditional forms of management and regulation, by manorial courts and forest authorities, as a more commercial, market-orientated economy developed. In the early seventeenth century, Thomas Blenerhasset, writing about Horsford heath in Norfolk, complained that the old practice of allowing each commoner a 'dole' from which to take firing was being abused – people sold what they cut from their dole and then illegally took whatever they needed from other parts of the heath.[78] Lords and commoners were frequently at loggerheads; neighbouring communities argued over rights and access where commons were shared. Those in Cawston in Norfolk, the subject of a long-running dispute during Elizabeth's reign over the conflicting claims of warreners and commoners, were described as having 'Sand and gravel . . . cast upp in such great heapes upon the playne ground . . . that ther will noe grasse growe upon the said grownde in a verie long tyme'.[79]

Conclusion

Across much of seventeenth-century England, high levels of biodiversity were associated with a range of habitats which are today often referred to as 'semi-natural', but which were all largely artificial in character, in the sense that they were both created and sustained by human activity. In some cases diversity arose from use in one main way, without change, over long periods of time – as for example with the grazing of chalk downland. But more usually it was associated with repeated *cycles* of use, extending over years or even decades, which endlessly reset the clock of succession, but at different points on adjoining pieces of land – as with the coppicing and re-growth of woodland, or the excavation and subsequent terrestrialization of peat cuttings. Of particular importance is the fact that the countryside was used not just to grow crops and graze livestock, but also to produce raw materials, and above all fuel. It is hard to exaggerate the intensity with which the landscape was exploited: almost every inch was used to produce something useful. Yet this served, for the most part, to enhance biodiversity, rather than to reduce it.

CHAPTER THREE

Seventeenth-century environments: Farmland

Meadows and pastures

Woods, moors, heaths, common pastures and wetlands occupied vast tracts of England in the seventeenth century, well over a third of the total land area. But the rest of the country comprised farmland, divided into fields of various kinds. In the Middle Ages most such land had been farmed as arable, with livestock pastured mainly on commons, but in the more complex economy of the early modern period there was a steady increase in the area occupied by private pastures.

Some of this enclosed grassland comprised short-term leys which alternated with periods of arable use, a system which contemporaries referred to as 'up-and-down' husbandry. But most was permanent or at least long-term in character because it took a long time to establish a rich sward. In the words of the old adage, 'To make a pasture breaks a man; to break a pasture makes a man', the latter a reference to the high yields expected from arable land broken in from grassland, rich in accumulated nutrients and with high levels of organic matter. Not surprisingly, post-medieval farm leases, drawn up to maintain the value of the landowner's assets, frequently laid down restrictions on the ploughing of pasture. Enclosed grassland, usually on clay soils of a moderately fertile, neutral character, often gained a significant range of plants, although seldom acquiring the extreme diversity displayed by downland and other types of ancient calcareous pasture.

Pastures, as noted in the previous chapter, need to be distinguished from meadows. These were cut in mid-summer to produce hay, which was used to keep livestock alive through the winter when the grass does not grow. Meadows had existed in England since at least the seventh century but they increased in numbers and extent during the early Middle Ages, presumably because the expansion of cultivation reduced the amount of winter grazing and fodder available in wood-pastures.[1] Most were located on damp alluvial soils, where a high water table ensured lush grass growth in dry summer conditions.[2] They were often divided into strips, either held as private property or, in some districts, reallocated amongst villagers every year or so.[3] In late medieval and post-medieval times, meadows became more widely distributed, with fields well away from water courses sometimes being managed to produce a hay crop, although they were still generally located on damper ground, such as that afforded by clay soils.

Flood-plain meadows were managed continuously for centuries in a manner that crucially shaped their ecology. They were closed to livestock during the late spring and summer, allowing plants intolerant of grazing and trampling to flourish, flower and set seed without disturbance, many of them tall, bulky species like meadowsweet (*Filipendula ulmaria*), globe-flower (*Trollius europaeus*) or oxeye daisy (*Chrysanthemum leucanthemum*).[4] Depending on soil conditions, they would provide striking displays of cowslips and orchids; they also contained a wide range of grasses, such as Timothy, tottering and sweet vernal.

In the seventeenth century many meadows were managed more intensively, as *water* meadows in the strict sense. These were inundated during the winter months with continually flowing water, so that the ground temperature was raised above 5 degrees Centigrade, stimulating early growth of grass and thus reducing the length of time during which livestock had to be fed on hay and other fodder. Irrigation began before Christmas and stock were put onto the fresh grass in early March. After they had been moved on to summer pastures – in May – the meadows would again be irrigated and substantial crops of hay taken in June or July.[5] Irrigation thus served to raise the numbers of animals which could be kept on farms in two main ways, and this in turn increased the amounts of manure produced, and thus cereal yields: such meadows were especially important in 'sheep-corn' districts of southern England, where the fortunes of arable farming depended so heavily upon the manure supplied by the folding flocks. Forms of 'floating' had existed since at least the late Middle Ages but in the seventeenth century they became more common and more sophisticated.[6] 'Catchwork' floating involved cutting channels along the contours of a valley side, the uppermost being fed from a leat taken off the river at a higher level, or from nearby springs or watercourses: the water simply flowed down the natural slope from one ditch or 'gutter' to the next.[7] More sophisticated were 'bedworks', which were employed wherever valley floors were wide and flat and water could not otherwise be induced to flow continuously (which was essential: stagnant water damaged the grass). A leet taken off the river some distance upstream fed water into channels ('carriers' or 'carriages') which ran along the tops of parallel ridges, superficially resembling the 'ridge and furrow' of former arable fields. The water flowed down their sides and into the 'furrows', which returned it to the river (Figure 7).[8]

Floating was quintessentially a practice of the Wessex chalklands, and by 1750 almost all the main river valleys in this region were managed in this way. By the end of the eighteenth century there were said to be between 15,000 and 20,000 acres (6,000–8,000 hectares) of watered meadow in south Wiltshire alone;[9] while in Hampshire it has been suggested that 'during the eighteenth century, in particular, water meadows must have been pushed to the limits of areas where it was possible to construct them'.[10] The elaborate systems then established – mostly 'bedworks' – remained in widespread use into the nineteenth and, in many cases, into the twentieth century. They have left impressive archaeological traces over many thousands of hectares of valley floor. Only a handful of examples, including that at Britford near Salisbury, are still in use. Floating was also common in parts of Shropshire and Herefordshire, in Devon, and the Cotswolds.[11] It was more sporadically employed, and generally with less success, in the central, northern and eastern parts of the country.[12]

Modern historians studying water meadows tend to emphasize the warming effects of the water in winter, and its irrigating properties (counteracting any soil water deficiency) in the summer. But contemporaries also emphasized the improvements that lime and suspended nutrients brought to the quality of the sward, while recent studies have suggested that floating also altered its composition. It favoured plants which are

FIGURE 7 *A water meadow being 'drowned' at Charlton-all-Saints, Wiltshire, in the 1930s.*

able to grow in aerobic conditions by stimulating the development of stolons (i.e. aerial shoots with the ability to produce adventitious roots which may then become independent of the original plant), while at the same time adversely affecting species unable to cope with a rapid depletion of oxygen.[13] A range of broad-leaved plants, less nutritious for sheep and cattle, were thus suppressed, and the inundated areas came to be characterized by a relatively species-poor grassland community of the kind classified by the National Vegetation Classification scheme (NVC) as type MG11 *Festuca rubra – Agrostis stolonifera – Potentilla anserine*. Some flowering plants, such as the cowslip (*Primula veris*), were adversely affected by spring drowning but others such as the fritillary (*Fritillaria meleagris*) flourished.[14] In winter and early spring the meadows, with their areas of water and early growth of grass, attracted a range of mammals and birds from the surrounding arable and downland, still often frozen hard.[15] In addition, Marshall described how large numbers of rats took up residence in the drains and carriers, feeding off the 'roots and sweet herbage'.[16] But the high stocking densities in spring – as many as 400 ewes and lambs per acre – probably ensured that water meadows were of little use to ground-nesting birds, although they would have provided useful feeding and wintering sites for the more common wildfowl, snipe and thrushes.[17]

Fields: Woodland and Champion

In the seventeenth century, as today, large areas of the land surface were occupied by alien crops, grown either for human consumption or to feed livestock. Wheat and barley were the main cereals, although oats and rye were much more widely cultivated than they are today, especially on poorer, more acidic soils. Beans and peas were widely cultivated as field crops, and turnips were just beginning to appear in the fields in parts of southern and eastern England, joining the red and white clover and sainfoin (probably grown from the sixteenth century), buckwheat, vetches and other fodder crops. Industrial crops like coleseed, woad and hemp were also sporadically cultivated. Seventeenth-century arable land, in terms of appearance and conservation value, differed in a number of key ways from the chemical-soaked, intensively cultivated fields of today.

In particular, the crops themselves would have been infested with a phenomenal ranges of weeds and pests or – to put it another way – arable fields would have had far higher levels of biodiversity. There were no herbicides or pesticides, and as crops were usually sown broadcast rather than in rows it was hard to weed effectively. Numerous plants now uncommon or rare – such as the corn buttercup (*Ranunculus arvensis*), red hemp-nettle (*Galeopsis angustifolia*), broad-leaved cudweed (*Filago pyramidata*), pheasants eye (*Adonis annua*), cornflower (*Centaurea cyanus*), shepherd's needle (*Scandix pectin-veneris*) and Venus' looking-glass (*Legousia hybrida*) – all thrived. Arable weeds are worthy of more attention than they usually receive. Only around thirty of the more than 150 species characteristic of arable fields are actually indigenous. Most are aliens, mainly introduced in prehistory although with some later recruits from the Americas, such as pineappleweed (*Matricaria matioides*), or from Asia, such as common field speedwell (*Vernica persica*). Weeds survived repeated ploughing and harrowing by employing a variety of strategies. Some produced seeds with similar dimensions to cereal grains, and were thus winnowed and stored with these, a proportion returning to the soil with the seed crop. Others, like couch grass (*Elymus repens*), can regenerate from tiny fragments of stem or root. Most, however, produce seed that can lie dormant in the soil, sometimes for years, so that species which germinate in the spring and emerge with the spring crop are able to survive years when fields are sown in the autumn, and *vice versa*: they can also often remain dormant for longer periods, where, for example, land is laid to grass for several years.[18] Such plants often produce vast quantities of seed – over 15,000 per plant, *per annum*, in the case of the poppy. Whatever their particular *modus operandi*, the wealth of weeds growing in the fields provided sustenance for large numbers of invertebrates, and also for birds and mammals, feeding on these or on the seeds or leaves of the plants themselves. Others of course fed off the grain itself, generally when spilled on the ground at harvest.

Weeds were abundant in crops but they really flourished when the fields lay uncultivated or 'fallow', and fallow fields also gave opportunities for ground-nesting birds like the skylark, although most such species would also take their chances in fields under grain. In clayland areas especially the land was often ploughed and harrowed for much of the fallow year (a 'bare fallow'), but even so there was usually an extended period in the winter during which weeds could grow undisturbed. It was usual to spread the work of ploughing and sowing evenly between the autumn and spring, with wheat especially being autumn-sown, ensuring that weeds also had a chance to flourish for a while on spring-sown land, during late autumn and early spring, something which further increased the range and numbers of invertebrates. In addition to all this, crops harvested by hand left longer stubbles than those cut by modern machines. These remained standing in the spring-sown fields as well as on the fallows over winter, providing cover for ground-nesting birds such as the song thrush, skylark, yellowhammer and lapwing.

Arable fields thus provided an abundance of food for birds and mammals. This said, their importance to biodiversity increased considerably if adjacent habitats, providing shelter from the activities of cultivators and additional sources of food, also existed: in the seventeenth century, the character and density of such habitats displayed marked variations from district to district. I noted in Chapter 1 the broad distinction between 'woodland' and 'champion' countryside: the former the landscapes of nucleated villages, and of extensive open fields; the latter characterized by more dispersed patterns of settlement, 'irregular' field systems and early enclosure, as well as by larger amounts of woodland.[19] Many writers on historical ecology, like many landscape historians, have emphasized this distinction. In Lovegrove's words, the champion landscape was rich in 'weeds, invertebrates and flowering plants', but poor in cover. The wide, empty fields, while providing rich feeding grounds, 'except for open-ground species such as brown hare, skylark, corncrake, quail, and grey partridge . . . presented limited scope for supporting a wider range of breeding species'.[20] They were landscapes 'where trees and woodland were scarce'.[21] The densely hedged and well-wooded landscapes of 'woodland' districts, in contrast, provided a much wider range of opportunities for wildlife. To some extent all this was true. But the difference between the two types of countryside can be exaggerated.

To begin with, champion landscapes were seldom as bare and as uniformly arable in character as some writers suggest. The villages themselves contained hedged closes and pollarded trees. More importantly, on lighter land, easily leached of nutrients, large areas of grazing land were usually retained, beyond the margins of the cultivated area, in the form of the heaths and downs already described, to provid feed for the folding flocks. There were, moreover, grassy access ways within the fields which, together with the narrow unploughed 'baulks' which separated the individual strips, provided a place where species characteristic of the adjacent heaths and downs could survive.[22] In chalkland areas the steeper slopes often developed as steps or terraces, partly a natural side effect of ploughing strips parallel with the contours but in some cases, perhaps, the result of deliberate excavation, intended to facilitate ploughing in these circumstances. The sheer banks, which could be six metres or more in height, provided some shelter for mammals and nesting sites for birds while shrubs such as hawthorn often seeded both here and in some cases on the unploughed baulks, providing further cover.

Even on heavier and more fertile soils, in the Midlands, champion landscapes were never entirely under the plough. In some districts, as on the Lias clays in Northamptonshire and Leicestershire, for example, much of the land was so badly affected by seasonal waterlogging that numerous ribbons and pockets of pasture survived within the fields. In western Northamptonshire, for example, a third or more of the land might thus consist of unhedged parcels of grassland, managed for hay or grazed under the supervision of shepherds when the surrounding furlongs were under crops (Figure 8). The documents drawn up when the open fields here were enclosed in the eighteenth century imply that some also grew gorse, thorns and other shrubs.[23] Hedges were also more common in these landscapes than we usually assume. Parish boundaries were often hedged, as at East Farndon in Northamptonshire in 1684;[24] hedges sometimes surrounded the open fields, as at Upper Boddington in the same county, or the meadows;[25] while early maps sometimes show short or discontinuous fragments of

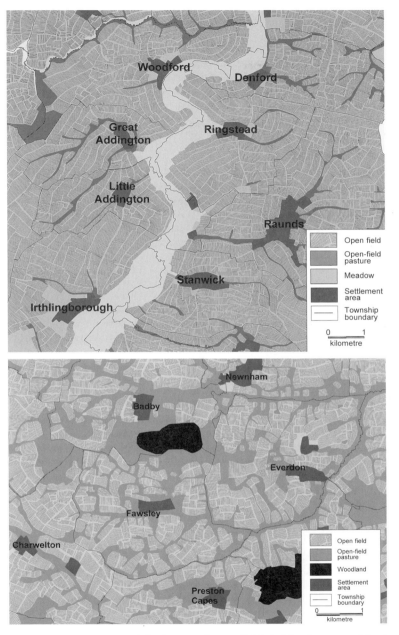

FIGURE 8 *Reconstructions of the layout of open fields in Northamptonshire before enclosure, based primarily on archaeological evidence (see Williamson et al. 2013). Top: open fields on moderately well-drained land in the east of the county, with extensive flood-plain meadows in the valley of the Nene. The ploughed land is almost continuous across extensive areas. Bottom: open fields on heavy Jurassic clays in the west of the county, showing numerous wide ribbons of pasture.*

hedge within the fields themselves, of uncertain function or origin, as at Murcott and Wollaston.[26] Field ponds for watering stock, long-lived and stable features of the landscape existed in some numbers, although they admittedly became more numerous following enclosure.[27] In short, although 'champion' landscapes did feature large areas of very open ground, they were different from the great arable prairies found in many eastern parts of England today. A survey of Brixworth in Northamptonshire, made in 1688 by Richard Richardson, the local vicar, shows the position of numerous individual shrubs and trees and also contains such comments as 'wild thyme grows here'.[28]

We should also note that 'woodland' and 'champion' are broad generalizations, and in reality lowland England displayed a complex range of local field systems and settlement patterns, largely related to environmental factors, some of which fit rather uneasily into any simple binary system of classification. Many districts, such as western East Anglia or the Wessex chalklands, exhibited intermediate characteristics, and both modern historians, and early topographers, have differed over how precisely they should be characterized.[29] Moreover, deep within the conventionally mapped 'champion' zone there were districts which displayed many of the characteristics of 'woodland' countryside, with extensive woods, scattered settlements and irregular field systems. Some lay within royal forests, but not all. Much of north Bedfordshire, for example, was characterized by scattered hamlets, isolated farms and complex field systems: Thurleigh thus had eleven distinct open fields when enclosed in 1805, farmed from a multiplicity of hamlets and isolated farms.[30]

But perhaps the most important misunderstanding about the character of champion landscapes concerns the date of their disappearance, for not all were enclosed through parliamentary acts in the period after 1750, as some ecologists seem to assume. No English county had more than half its land area enclosed in this way, for the removal of open fields had been continuing steadily for three centuries or more, especially on the heavy Midland clays, so that land could be laid to pasture.[31] Equally striking was the extent to which the area under grass increased through the post-medieval centuries even where parishes remained unenclosed, extending the ribbons of unploughed ground which, as we have noted, often existed within the open fields in areas of heavy soil. By the early eighteenth century, many townships contained 'cow pastures'. Morton, writing about Northamptonshire in 1712, described how:

Many of the lordships, and especially the larger ones, have a common or uninclosed pasture for their cattel in the outskirts of the fields. Most of these have formerly been plowed, but being generally their worst sort of ground, and at so great a distance from the towns, the manuring and culture of them were found so inconvenient that they have been laid down for greensward.[32]

030

P100SMUED

BRESCIA UNIVERSITY COLLEGE LIBRARY

5

JT 2135A02 F

Ship To:
BRESCIA UNIVERSITY COLLEG
1285 WESTERN ROAD
LONDON ON N6G 1H2

Routing	1
SORTING	
Processing	
F01A01X	
Shipping	

MiL Alt Available

Volume:
Edition:
Year: 2013.
Pagination: 240 pages
Size:

ISBN	Qty	Sales Order
9781441124869	1	F 18098751 1

Customer P/O No
050113318

Title: An environmental history of wildlife in
England 1650 – 1950 / by Tom

Format: P (Paperback)
Author: Williamson, Tom, 1955 – author.
Publisher: Bloomsbury Academic
Fund: ahism
Location: ustk
Loan Type:
Coutts CN: 23043696

Order Specific Instructions

COUTTS INFORMATION SERVICES:

In addition, smaller groups of strips were often turned over to pasture by neighbours, and 'ends' of furlongs frequently laid down for grazing and the production of hay. All this ensured that, certainly by the early eighteenth century, the landscape of a county like Northamptonshire – a quintessential 'champion' district – was in fact considerably more diverse than we usually assume (Figure 9).[33]

Enclosure, and the expansion of pasture, in the Midlands were in turn part of a much wider development, providing a second important context within which we need to examine wildlife and habitats. This was the emergence in the course of the fifteenth and sixteenth centuries, in the manner described in the previous chapter, of increasingly specialized farming regions. Regional farming economies were not static, of course. The particular emphasis of agricultural production tended to change in response to market conditions, influenced above all by population pressure. The later fifteenth, sixteenth and early seventeenth centuries had been periods of demographic expansion and rising food prices. But between c.1650, and c.1750 population growth was sluggish, or even reversed, and arable farming in particular was in a depressed state, encouraging a greater concentration on livestock production, and thus enclosure and the expansion of pasture. Variations in

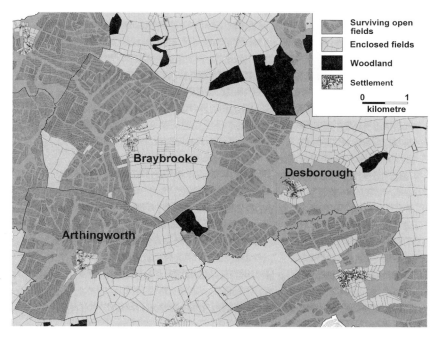

FIGURE 9 *Typical Midland landscape in the early eighteenth century: the area around Desborough and Braybrooke in north-central Northamptonshire. Note the complex mixture of open fields and enclosed land (for sources, see Williamson et al. 2013).*

farming economy, especially the emergence of specialized pastoral districts, had major impacts on England's ecology which to some extent overlay and further confused any simple woodland/champion dichotomy.

Hedges and farmland trees

Although the open, biologically degraded condition of 'champion' regions may be exaggerated in some accounts, it nevertheless remains true that, in general terms, 'woodland' landscapes provided a more diverse range of habitats. Their intricate mixtures of arable and pasture, numerous hedges, and patches of woodland afforded an ideal combination of cover and feeding grounds for mammals and birds. Hedges formed a dense and intricate mesh across the landscape. They were sometimes planted with a single species – usually hawthorn or blackthorn, sometimes elm – but more often with several.[34] Ash, maple and hazel were particularly common components. Pehr Kalm, a Finn who visited England in 1748, noted how in the Chiltern Hills hedges were planted with a mixture of hawthorn and blackthorn but that in addition the farmers 'planted – either at regular intervals or more casually – small saplings of *Salicibus* [willow], beech, ash, rowan, lime, elm and other deciduous trees.'[35] Multi-species planting was usual partly because it was hard to obtain large amounts of hedging thorn but mainly because small farmers regarded hedges not merely as a form of stock-proof barrier, but as a source of fuel, fencing materials and perhaps fruit. At the end of the eighteenth century, William Marshall was still able to describe how the hedges in north-east Norfolk 'abound with oak, ash and maple stubs, off which the wood is cut every time the hedge is felled; also with pollards, whose heads are another source of firewood', adding that the entire supply of wood in the district 'may be said, with little latitude, to be from hedge-rows'.[36] Arthur Young noted how, even in the early nineteenth century, the need for firewood had induced farmers in Hertfordshire 'to fill the old hedges everywhere with oak, ash, sallow and with all sorts of plants more generally calculated for fuel than fences'.[37]

Max Hooper in the 1960s noted that older hedges tend to contain more shrub species than recent examples. He suggested that hedges, once planted, were colonized by new species at a steady rate, and could therefore be approximately dated by counting the number of different kinds of shrub they contained within a standard thirty-metre length, one new species becoming established, on average, every century or so.[38] But even if new colonists arrived with the required punctuality hedges could only be dated in this way if, as Hooper assumed, most had begun life with a single species. This, to judge from a mass of evidence, was not the case, and his dating method is thus largely mythical.[39] Hedges in old-enclosed districts were botanically diverse for other reasons. Many small woods existed, a rich seed source for woody shrubs; while hedges and the banks on which they grew sometimes represented direct intakes from ancient woodland, preserving the slow-colonizing plants like wood anemone characteristic of this environment.

Hedges were often managed by *plashing* or *laying*. This occurred at intervals of 10–15 years and took a number of local and regional forms, all in essence involving the drastic cutting back of the hedge with a billhook and the removal of lateral suckers, dead material, thick old trunks and unwanted species (such as elder, which provides a poor barrier to stock). The principal stems, or 'pleachers', were then cut three-quarters of the way through at an angle of 45–60 degrees, at around 5–10 cm above the ground, and bent downwards so that each overlapped with its neighbour. As growth resumed in the spring, a thick wall of vegetation was formed. In some forms of the practice the pleachers were woven through upright stakes ('stabbers'), and both held in place by 'hethers' or 'binders' – twisted rods of elm or hazel which formed a kind of continuous 'cable' along the top of the hedge (Figure 10).[40] Modern conservation groups sometimes assume that plashing was the universal mode of management in the past but in many districts hedges were managed by coppicing, like the understorey of woods.[41] Their constituent shrubs were simply cut back to within a few inches of the ground at intervals of between 10 and 20 years (Figure 11). Coppicing required less skill than laying and produced more useable firewood, although it caused

FIGURE 10 *Typical laid hedge, showing stabbers (vertical stakes) and hethers (the 'cable' running along the top of the hedge).*

FIGURE 11 *In early modern England hedges were often coppiced, rather than laid. This modern example is being brought back into management after several years of neglect. Note the large amounts of fuel logs and (in the distance) brushwood produced by the process. The upright posts are for the erection of a fence to protect the regenerating stools on the right from grazing livestock. Traditionally, staked brushwood would have been employed for this purpose.*

problems for farmers because the new growth required protection from browsing livestock for 2 or 3 years. Where substantial ditches accompanied a hedge, as was usual on heavier ground, animals were simply excluded from the unditched side for the necessary period. Alternatively, or in addition, the hedge might be temporarily protected with hurdles or lines of staked brushwood. Whatever the precise mode of management, leases often included detailed stipulations regarding the frequency of coppicing or laying, especially where fuel was in short supply and farmers were tempted to over-crop, one for a farm at Harpenden in Hertfordshire in 1723, for example, instructing that the tenant 'shall not new make or plaish [sic] any of the hedges under or above 12 years growth and then onely at seasonable times in the yeare'.[42]

The benefits of hedges in terms of wildlife conservation are well documented. They provide habitats for the same kinds of flora and fauna evolved to thrive on the margins of wooded ground, although with the additional benefit that in many cases they were located beside an arable field, providing particularly rich pickings for small mammals such as field voles. They provide shelter, that is, for animals which would otherwise find no place to live in these endlessly disturbed, yet food-rich, environments.[43] Hedges also serve as corridors, linking wooded areas and other uncultivated pockets, which are used by invertebrates and small mammals, and to a lesser extent by birds and plants, although their precise importance in this respect remains debated.[44] They certainly provide a prime habitat in their own right for bird species like dunnock, yellowhammer and common whitethroat. The importance of hedges for wildlife in the early modern landscape was particularly great because, as already noted, most were planted with a range of species. This provided a diverse structure, and thus a wide range of niches, but also a variety of food sources: modern research has demonstrated that the number of bird species and the number of individual birds present in a hedge both rise as the variety of shrubs increases.[45] Regular management also increased biodiversity for, as with woodland coppices, the changing structure as the hedge re-grew provided a rapid succession of habitats. In old-enclosed areas, moreover, hedges were commonly accompanied by substantial banks and ditches which afforded cover for shrews, voles, mice and other mammals. In addition, many hedges were considerably wider than the majority surviving today, in part because species like blackthorn tended to sucker sideways, especially where fields lay under pasture. Sir John Parnell, writing in 1769, described how Hertfordshire hedges appeared 'rather the work of Nature than Plantations generally Extending 30 or 40 feet Broad growing Irregularly in these stripes and giving the fields the air of being Reclaim'd from a general tract of woodland'.[46] Indeed, in some 'woodland' districts, fields were often bordered by strips of coppiced woodland, like the 'shaws' of Kent.

The density of hedges in 'woodland' districts displayed much variation. On larger holdings fields commonly covered 5, 10 or 20 hectares, but in general they were between two and four hectares in area, and sometimes considerably less, in part because of the importance of hedges as a source of firewood. A 'Particular of Mr Rodwell's Farm' in Diss in Norfolk, made in 1771, describes 21 fields with an average size of less than three acres (1.2 hectares).[47] We should not, however, assume that such very densely hedged landscapes were necessarily the best for wildlife. Research suggests that the number of bird species present in hedges does not increase in a linear manner with increasing density of hedges but instead peaks at around 7–11 kilometres of hedge per square kilometre, due to competition for food and territory.[48]

Hedgerow trees were usually abundant and provided important song-posts for species like whitethroat, wren and robin: hedges with trees support a significantly more diverse avifauna than those without. Free-standing trees were also usually numerous in woodland landscapes, scattered across pasture closes or grouped around the margins of fields in 'rows' two or three deep; for even where land was under cultivation hedges were often accompanied by 'hedge greens', unploughed strips similar in character to modern 'conservation headlands', on which hay was cut or cattle tethered, and which provided a convenient area on which ploughs could be turned.[49] Data from farms in Essex, Suffolk and Norfolk suggest an average of around 25 farmland trees per hectare in the seventeenth and eighteenth centuries.[50] But on some farms the figure was much higher, one at Denham in Suffolk in 1651 boasting an average of 38 trees per hectare, while at Thorndon in the same county there were apparently no less than 72 per hectare in 1742.[51] As late as 1784, a survey of West End Farm in Wormley in south-east Hertfordshire recorded an incredible 1,496 trees scattered through 28 fields covering a mere 38 hectares.[52]

Surviving farmland trees from the seventeenth century or earlier are overwhelmingly oaks, a fortunate circumstance given that this tree can provide sustenance for more than 400 invertebrate species.[53] But this dominance in part results from the greater longevity of this species compared with others, as well as the wholesale loss of elm from the countryside as a consequence of Dutch elm disease in the 1960s and 70s. Seventeenth- and eighteenth-century surveys suggest that while in most districts oak was indeed the most common tree, ash and elm might be close rivals. There was much variation, even within the same district. At Langley in Norfolk 70 per cent of the trees recorded in a mid-seventeenth-century survey were oak and 30 per cent ash;[54] but less than fifteen kilometres away at Buckenham in the 1690s 49 per cent were oak and 44 per cent ash, together with 6.6 per cent elm (as well as six poplars and 'young' trees of unspecified species);[55] while on a farm at Beeston in the middle of the same county in 1761 there were actually more ash than oak trees recorded in the fields and hedges – 47 per cent and 41 per cent, respectively, with 12 per cent elm.[56] Other species were also present in many districts, such as hornbeam on heavy clay soils and beech occasionally on lighter clays and chalk, and these too could be locally dominant. John Norden commented in 1618 on the abundance of fruit trees in the hedges of Devon, Gloucestershire, Kent, Shropshire, Somerset and Worcestershire, as well as in many parts of Wales, and lamented the fact that they were gradually disappearing from the hedges of Middlesex and Hertfordshire due to a failure to replace ageing specimens.[57] He was perhaps over-pessimistic. An undated early eighteenth-century map of a small farm (49 acres or 20 hectares) in Flaunden, on the Chiltern dipslope in west Hertfordshire, details 27 oak, 9 ash and 18 elm, together with 15 'asps' – probably aspen – growing in the hedges.[58] But these were outnumbered by 59 apple trees and no less than 165 cherries, growing not only in the hedges close to the farmhouse but also in those scattered more generally through the farm.

Most trees surviving in the countryside today which were planted before c.1700 are former pollards. It is sometimes suggested that this is because pollarding served to prolong the life of trees, ensuring that they have survived well into senescence.[59] While there may be some truth in this suggestion, the dominance of pollards among our stock of veteran trees has a more straightforward economic explanation. Standard trees in farmland, like those in woods, would not normally have been allowed to reach any great age. For most purposes, timber merchants required oaks aged between 80 and 120 years: beyond this a tree's rate of growth began to slow, so that it made more sense to have it down, and replace it with another. Pollards, in contrast, continued to produce reasonable crops of wood well into old age. More importantly, most farmland trees in this fuel-hungry world were pollarded, so it is hardly surprising that most old trees in the landscape today are former pollards. On a farm in Beeston near Mileham in Norfolk in 1761, there were 413 pollards, but only 104 timber trees: that is, 80 per cent of the trees were pollards (Figure 12).[60] Timber surveys from elsewhere suggest very similar ratios, in the 70–80 per cent range: on a farm at Stanfield in the same county in c.1798, there were 192 pollards but only 66 timber trees (74 per cent pollards): on a farm at nearby Whissonset at the same time, 131 pollards and 59 timber trees (70 per cent pollards) and, a few years earlier, 309–133 (again, 70 per cent); while at Thorndon in Suffolk in 1742, 80 per cent of the trees recorded were pollards.[61] Occasionally the proportion was even higher: 91 per cent at West End, Wormley, in Hertfordshire in 1784.[62] Hedgerow pollards were usually cropped at the same times as the hedge was plashed or otherwise 'new made'. An agreement from 1693 concerning a farm in Aldenham in Hertfordshire thus stipulated that the tenant 'shall not lopp or cutt or cause to be lopped or cut any of the pollards growing upon the premises but when the hedges shall be new made and ditches scoured where the sayd pollards do grow'.[63] Another, drawn up in 1657 for a farm in Ridge in the same county, allowed the tenant 'to lopp all the pollard hasells maples sallows willows hawthorns & hornebeame trees growing in the severall hedges, fields, dells & hedgrows' provided that he 'lopp and cutt but one tenth part of all the pollards hasells, maples sallowes willowes hawthorns & hornbeams every year for and during the last nyne yeres' of the term.[64] Both hedges, and the trees they contained, were thus ever-changing environments,

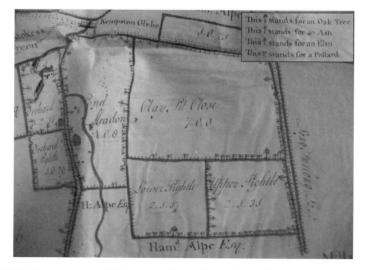

FIGURE 12 *Beeston-next-Mileham in Norfolk, as depicted on a map of 1761 which – unusually – shows the position and character of every hedgerow tree.*

subject to regular cycles of cropping and regrowth, but they also, like many of the other environments I have discussed, displayed elements of stability and continuity. Shrubb, among others, has suggested that old timber was 'rather scarce in farmland' in the period before the agricultural revolution,[65] but this is probably incorrect, in 'woodland' areas at least. Because pollards continued to be cropped into senescence, a high proportion were already, in the seventeenth century, probably 'veteran' specimens, for many of these districts had been well hedged since medieval times.

Village and farmstead

The homes of humans, as much as the land they cultivated or otherwise exploited, were habitats and feeding grounds for a wide range of fauna. Within the mainly timber-framed or stone-built houses, a distinctive invertebrate fauna would have been found, just as it can in our own homes, although then probably more extensive. Many were aliens which had come to England in remote prehistory with the first farming communities. What their original habitats may have been is often unknown: a significant proportion are no longer found in the wild anywhere in the world.[66] Large numbers of birds were attracted to houses, gardens and outbuildings, especially perhaps in champion areas where there was often relatively little cover in the surrounding fields. The situation may have been similar to that which today pertains in the more intensively farmed arable districts of England. Wyllie in 1976 found that bird densities in one Cambridgeshire village were seven times greater than those in the surrounding fields.[67] In most champion districts, the majority of trees were to be found in the village 'envelope' – a situation again paralleled in modern arable districts, although with the difference that in the seventeenth century most would have been pollarded – and in general terms those farmland birds with a clear preference for woodland and wood-edge habitats – wren, blackbird, robin, tits and chaffinch – will have predominated.[68] Some birds also roosted, or nested, in houses and farm buildings: most obviously swallow, house martin and barn owl, but also robin, blackbird, wren, jackdaw, starling, and tawny owl, seeking out spaces in roofs and lofts, and holes in walls and thatch.[69] But food as well as shelter made villages and hamlets magnets for birds. Unlike most rural settlements today, early-modern examples contained numerous working farms, and birds fed freely on spilt grain, weed seeds and threshing residues, as well as on the hay, oats and other foodstuffs intended for stalled cattle and horses. Muck heaps and middens would have ensured high densities of invertebrates; kites, ravens, carrions crows and buzzards would have been drawn to lambing sheds; and bullfinches to orchards (Gilbert White described in 1777 how 'the scenes around the village are beautifully diversified by the bloom of the pear-trees, plums and cherries').[70] Mammal residents were more limited, although rats and mice would have been numerous, in houses as well as outside them, not least because much threshed grain was still stored indoors, in first floor chambers or attics. Grain was either consumed entirely by them or badly damaged: even today as much as 10 per cent of the grain in mills is rendered unsuitable for milling by being 'kibbled', or partially eaten, by the common house mouse.[71] Other mammal species tended to be visitors or raiders: the fox and especially the polecat, savagely persecuted in large measure because of its 'great ravages in hen houses and poultry yards where it destroys great numbers not only of chickens and ducklings but also full-grown poultry'.[72]

Seventeenth-century settlements, in short, offered a measure of cover in the more open environments of England, and also a wide variety of food sources. Villages and hamlets also had a distinctive flora, besides the concentrations of fruits trees and vegetables in orchards and gardens. Unpaved roads, middens and yards provided niches for the kinds of fast-growing and often nitrogen-hungry weeds which, as we shall see, constituted the principal flora of towns – plants like good king Henry (*Chenopodium bonus-henricus*), fat hen (*Chenopodium album*), knotgrass (*Polygonum aviculare*), fumitory (*Fumaria officinalis*), enchanters nightshade and the like. How far seventeenth- and early eighteenth-century farms and cottages possessed ornamental gardens, perhaps featuring some of the exotic plants found in the more extensive grounds of the gentry and aristocracy, remains unclear. A drawing on a map surveyed in c.1720 of Upper Broomhall Farm in Kempsey (Worcestershire) shows a garden with parterres and simple topiary.[73] One of the items mentioned in the probate inventory of the farmer Loye Aggas of Wymondham in Norfolk, who died in 1614, was a pair of 'gardine sheres'.[74]

The distribution of fauna

I have described variations in the environmental character of seventeenth-century England in rather vague terms, extrapolating from what we know of the wildlife found in similar circumstances today. This is risky, not least because species can alter their habits over time to adapt to changed circumstances. There is, however, one source which might provide direct evidence of the varying distributions of certain species in the seventeenth and eighteenth centuries: the records of the bounties paid by churchwardens for particular species killed in their parishes under the terms of the 1566 'Acte for the Preservation of Grayne', a somewhat misleadingly named piece of legislation as many of the animals targeted were not, in fact, primarily grain eaters, but were instead problematic in other ways to farming.[75] The most frequently targeted bird – the house sparrow – did indeed consume much grain, but the most commonly targeted mammal – the hedgehog – suffered in part because it fed off hens' eggs, but mainly because of an erroneous belief that it sucked the milk from sleeping cattle. The act listed a total of thirty species, including other fairly innocuous ones like the kingfisher, for which bounties were to be paid, although in practice most attention was directed towards a more restricted range: the hedgehog, fox, badger, polecat, stoat, weasel, otter, pine marten, wild cat and mole among the mammals; and sparrow, bullfinch, crow, rook, jackdaw, raven, magpie, jay, red kite, and unspecified 'hawks' among the birds.[76]

Large numbers of churchwarden's accounts were meticulously examined by Roger Lovegrove as part of the research undertaken for his excellent book, *Silent Fields: the long decline of a nation's wildlife*. Although not his central concern, Lovegrove examined regional variations in the frequency with which different species were killed, explaining these largely in terms of the character of the local environment. There are, however (as he himself emphasized), a number of problems in using this source in any spatial way. Relatively few parishes have surviving churchwardens' accounts, and where they do these often run for only short periods of time. A surprising number, rather curiously, contain no record of payments for bounties under the act. It is possible that payments were made through some other separate parish account, now lost, for although the terms of the act laid the responsibility for administration on churchwardens, payments also sporadically turn up in the accounts maintained by local constables and the overseers of the poor, while vermin was sometimes controlled by making yearly payments to professionals, especially 'mole men'. But it is also probable that in some places the churchwardens, reflecting the wishes of the local community or its leading members, were simply not prepared to pay for pest control out of the hard-pressed parish rates. In the words of E. L. Jones, 'the chief local agriculturists who would figure disproportionately among the churchwardens or could influence them . . . were, in effect, securing themselves a subsidy out of the public purse. All ratepayers would have to contribute to the cost of the campaign but the farmers would benefit most'.[77] This means, as Lovegrove noted, that 'the decision as to which vermin, if any, were to be allowed for payment in a particular parish was determined by the vestry committee, and not by the prescriptions of the original statute. Parishes themselves decided what to kill and what payments to make for targeted species'. In 1703 the vestry at Great Budworth in Cheshire thus declared that 'for the time to come' they would not make payments 'out of the Parish Purse for any Crows Heds, ffox Heds or urchin [hedgehog] Heds'.[78]

All this means that as well as reflecting the frequency of particular species within the wider environment, the appearance of particular animals within the accounts also reflects the economic interests of the communities in question, and the kinds of eradications that they thought worth funding. Geographical variations might thus reflect the configuration of regional farming economies, as well as the suitability of the countryside for particular kinds of animal. There may well have been other complicating factors. By the early decades of the eighteenth century, the fox was being actively preserved in some districts, to provide sport for the gentry, and reductions in the numbers of payments for fox heads in the churchwardens' accounts might not, therefore, necessarily reflect any reduction in the actual numbers of foxes: indeed, the inverse might be the case. Poaching, moreover, was a major issue, and where a parish was dominated by a powerful squire, he might well have been uneasy about parish officers encouraging people to trap the local wildlife, something which might provide excellent cover for other activities, as Lovegrove notes. In short, the numbers of animals and birds of different species recorded in particular churchwardens accounts must be the consequence of a wide range of factors, rather than being a direct reflection of the character of the local environment.

Lovegrove explained much of the variation in the proportion of parishes making payments, in the level of these payments, and in the kinds of species targeted as a reflection of the dichotomy between 'woodland' and champion districts. The paucity of parishes making payment in Essex, East Anglia and Lincolnshire, and in the east Midland counties lying to the north of the Thames, and the limited range of species targeted – overwhelmingly house sparrows – he attributed to the fact that 'open field systems, apparently poor in wildlife diversity', dominated the landscape.[79] But in fact south and east Norfolk, most of Suffolk, and virtually all of Essex, Hertfordshire and Middlesex were 'woodland' landscapes, characterized by often dense meshes of hedgerows and by an abundance of woodland. In reality, a lack of interest in paying for the control of animals like the polecat, and an emphasis on the house sparrow, across this extensive district probably reflects in part the fact that their economies were based on grain production rather than on livestock rearing. It is true that in some of the 'woodland' districts, in Suffolk and Norfolk especially, cattle formed a major element in the economy. But many were actually reared elsewhere, in the north and west of the country, and only fattened here; while in many of the champion areas of East Anglia the sheep flocks – with their lambs vulnerable to attack by corvids, foxes and mustelids – were the property of manorial lords and great sheep masters, exploiting the ancient privileges of the fold-course system. The peasant grain-producers who constituted and elected the vestry would have little interest in paying for their protection. Conversely, it was mainly in the west of the country – in Devon, Cornwall, and Somerset, the Marcher Counties – and in the north, that much higher proportions of parishes paid bounties, and for a wider range of animals, especially foxes and mustelids – and conversely, displayed less interest in persecuting sparrows.[80] These were communities of small farmers, a substantial proportion of whom were primarily involved in livestock husbandry, and especially in the rearing of sheep and cattle. Lambs, and to a much lesser extent young calves, were vulnerable to carnivores. While to some extent the appearance of particular animals recorded in the churchwardens' accounts may reflect their frequency in the environment, it was also thus a function of human decision-making, contingent upon a complex range of social and agrarian factors.

This said, Lovegrove's carefully collected figures tell us much that is important about seventeenth- and eighteenth-century wildlife. The absences are particularly noteworthy. There are no payments for rabbits, partly perhaps because they did not feature in the original act but also because they were still, even in the eighteenth century, rare in most parts of England.[81] Wood pigeons, now present in vast numbers in the countryside, were likewise not mentioned in the act and do not appear in the payments made by churchwardens: they were still relatively rare, and restricted – as their name implies – to woodland.[82] The polecat, pine marten and wild cat, in contrast, were widespread. Indeed, 'apart from the fox, no mammal was killed in more parishes in England and Wales between the seventeenth and the nineteenth centuries than the unfortunate polecat'.[83] The fact that payments for polecats and pine martens were less frequently recorded in the arable lowlands, as noted, reflects a complex mixture of environmental factors but also economic ones – the extent to which the livelihoods of local communities were threatened by their presence. The county of Northamptonshire illustrates this well. Lovegrove notes a total of 717 payments for dead polecats here in the course of the seventeenth, eighteenth and nineteenth centuries, low by the standards of northern and western counties; and no examples of pine martens, both of which doubtless reflect the paucity of trees and woods in this champion countryside.[84] But both figures are almost certainly further lowered by the lack of interest in persecuting these animals in a countryside dominated by grain growing and cattle fattening. The complete absence of references to pine martens certainly needs to be compared with the fact that Thomas Isham of Lamport caught four in a fortnight in December 1673, and another two months later.[85] The majority of the records for polecats come from places within a few miles of the royal forests of Whittlewood or Rockingham, another reminder that the Midlands was not, in reality, a sea of unrelieved arable but contained many extensive 'islands' of wooded ground. Yet polecats were also killed at Braunceston, on the western edge of the county and far from the forests. So too is Lamport, in the north of the county, where Isham caught his pine martens. Even away from the forests, 'champion' districts were, by the seventeenth century at least, more diversified environments than we often assume.

Conclusion

While it was the extent and biological diversity of the woods and wastes discussed in the previous chapter which would most have impressed a modern visitor to seventeenth-century England, farmland also boasted a vast range of wildlife. These two broad categories of land have, of course, been artificially separated, for ease of description and discussion. In reality they usually lay intermingled, a circumstance which would have further increased diversity. 'Woodland' districts, with their abundance of hedges and hedgerow trees, were particularly rich in wildlife, but we should not underestimate the extent to which 'champion' areas also boasted diverse environments, and this was increasingly the case as enclosure proceeded. But 'woodland' and 'champion' are problematic terms and concepts whose simplicity can obscure the rich variety of English landscapes, and much of the diversity of the countryside was related more to the character of the regional farming economies that emerged from the fifteenth century than to these older and more basic variations in field systems and settlement patterns.

CHAPTER FOUR

The social contexts of wildlife, c.1650–1750

The nature of towns

So far I have discussed the seventeenth and early eighteenth-century environment entirely in terms of farming communities and the practice of agriculture. But this is only part of the story. Already, a significant proportion of the population was not directly involved in farming. Some lived in towns or industrial areas. Others were members of the social elite, whose involvement with agriculture, while often close, was only a part of their interaction with the natural world. Towns, it is true, were relatively minor intrusions in a largely rural landscape in the seventeenth century. Although by 1650 as much as a fifth of the population may have been living in towns and cities they were usually closely packed into them: most people lived within walking distance of their place of work.[1] Few country towns covered more than a square kilometre. Even Norwich, probably England's third largest city in the seventeenth century, was still almost entirely confined within its medieval walls, embracing an area of just over two square kilometres, equivalent to less than five per of the built-up area of the city and its suburbs today. Typically, much of this comprised orchards and market gardens, ensuring that in environmental terms Norwich was more like the villages already discussed than a distinctly urban environment. This would have been truer of smaller towns, some of which contained working farms at no great distance from their central market places. London was more densely and continuously occupied but it remained tiny by modern standards. Although, with its satellite settlements, it is said to have been home to around half a million people, its continuous built-up area covered less than four square kilometres, similar to that of a small country town today like Bicester in Oxfordshire or Wymondham in Norfolk, although it was ringed by separate but swelling villages like Paddington.[2] This said, most of the larger towns would have boasted distinctive ecological features, some no more than the characteristics of rural settlements writ large, but others definably urban.

Before the nineteenth century towns were characterized by low levels of public services, and waste of all kinds tended not to move very far. Moreover, large amounts of food was imported into them, and processed there, including livestock brought in 'on the hoof' and killed in urban slaughterhouses. Bylaws – pioneered in London in the twelfth and thirteenth centuries – were passed in most major towns in an attempt to control the disposal of waste in public places, but all were nevertheless characterized by cess pits which leaked into wells, piles of dung and straw from stables, household middens and refuse from slaughter houses and fish markets. Success in removing the worst waste from the streets, moreover, usually led to it being dumped nearby, or disposed of in watercourses and rivers. In seventeenth-century Bedford the authorities attempted to stop pigs wandering the streets; at Warrington they tried to prevent householders from dumping rubbish in the market place.[3]

Major towns and cities thus attracted large numbers of scavenging birds, especially ravens and kites. In London their contribution to city hygiene – especially in terms of tidying up some of the more unpleasant wastes from butchery – ensured that both were protected by local bylaws, although such protection waned in the course of the eighteenth century.[4] The conditions in towns and cities were well suited to other kinds of wildlife. It is not clear precisely how early pigeons became a standard feature of the urban environment, attracted by vegetable food wastes and grain, but they were well-established in London by the later fourteenth century.[5] Escapees from manorial pigeon houses, they made themselves at home on the churches and other tall buildings which provided nesting places analogous to the cliffs frequented by their ancestor, the wild rock dove. Mice, the common shrew and above all rats were also abundant. The black rat had been in England since at least the third century AD, as we have seen, but the Brown rat only arrived in the early eighteenth century, probably in the 1720s, the consequence of increasing maritime communication.[6] It came from Russia, as part of a general westward expansion of the species, although its popular name, Norway rat, indicates that people thought (possibly rightly) that it had come via that country. *Rattus norvegicus* was soon widespread in rural as well as urban areas, and as early as 1777 Gilbert White considered a black rat killed at Shalden in Hampshire something of a rarity: 'the Norway rats destroy all the indigenous ones'.[7] But rats of both kinds were particularly at home in towns, attracted to refuse tips, middens, grain stores and cess pits, and the larger urban centres like London positively heaved with them.

Urban conditions also favoured particular kinds of plant. Few species could find a foothold in the dirt of unpaved streets, on rubbish tips, and on disturbed ground generally: 'fast-moving, hardy, opportunistic plants'.[8] To succeed in urban conditions they needed to grow rapidly and to spread and survive either by having deep or extensive root systems, or by producing large numbers of seeds which could travel long distances, transported on the wind or by some other vector. An ability to lie dormant in the soil for months or years was also useful. The streets and towns of early-modern England thus probably featured concentrations of plants like groundsel (*Senechio vulgaris*), which can germinate, grow to maturity and set seed within six weeks; fat hen; knotgrass; fumitory; and enchanters nightshade.[9] If left undisturbed for long enough – in the more inaccessible and marginal areas of the early-modern town – these would soon be overwhelmed by perennial plants, thistles, nettles, and docks, and coarse grasses, from which some domestic livestock might derive sustenance, but succession was usually prevented by further disturbance. Once again, however, it is important to emphasize both the limited extent of urban areas and the way in which many towns, like Norwich, featured numerous grazed paddocks and orchards containing the kinds of plants and invertebrates commonly found in the surrounding fields.

Industry too had as yet made relatively little impact on the environment. Only in the north east of England, and in parts of the west Midlands, were extensive and continuous coalfields already a significant feature. There were water mills for grinding corn in many villages, and water also powered iron smelting hammers and a variety of textile machinery, but their small ponds were essentially isolated additions to an existing type of habitat, rather than something new. Extractive industries – clay, sand and gravel pits, stone quarries and the like – similarly formed relatively isolated and discontinuous incidents in the countryside, although in many ways more novel ones. Some quarries resembled upland rock habitats, with vertical cliff faces and steep slopes analogous to scree, habitats rare in most of lowland England. Others produced waste which soon developed as hummocky grassland with distinctive plant communities. The soils which formed gradually over piles of quarry debris usually remained thin, and boasted chemical and physical characteristics different from those of the surrounding landscape, which had developed over longer periods of time, and often in overlying superficial deposits.[10] Barnack 'Hills and Holes' in the old county of Northamptonshire, now a National Nature Reserve, is an extensive area of limestone quarrying which was abandoned in the sixteenth century, and neither cultivated nor, in all probability, very intensively grazed thereafter. It boasts a rich calcareous grassland flora featuring pasque flower (*Pulsatilla vulgaris*), violets (*Viola* sp.), cowslip (*Primula elatior*), a range of orchids and such lime-loving plants as rockrose (*Helianthemum chamaecistus*), and ox-eye daisy (*Chrysanthemum leucanthemum*). More significant, but scattered and limited in area, were the calaminarian grasslands which developed in various parts of northern and western England on waste where lead, silver, zinc, barium, chromium, copper and fluorspar were mined.[11] These, as we shall see, became more significant as the scale of extraction increased through the eighteenth and nineteenth centuries.

Elite landscapes

In the seventeenth and early eighteenth centuries the country's social elite had their own, particular environmental signature. Manor houses and mansions were generally accompanied by ornamental grounds which boasted a flora already radically different from that of the surrounding landscape. Gardens had passed through a series of stylistic changes in the course of the fourteenth, fifteenth and sixteenth centuries, the details of which need not concern us here. In the late seventeenth and early eighteenth centuries their design was shaped by a mixture of influences: elements of indigenous medieval traditions, fused with Renaissance fashions from Italy and more recently, as a consequence of the exile of many royalists during the Civil Wars, with French and Dutch styles.[12] The main garden areas were set within enclosures, fenced or walled, and often included terraces and garden buildings of various kinds. Their design was highly structured and geometric in character, with grass lawns or *plats*, parterres comprising patterns in clipped box or defined by flower beds, as well as box or yew bushes cut as topiary. 'Canals', 'basins' and other small areas of water were a common feature, while beyond the gardens one or more avenues generally ran out through parkland or (more usually) across the surrounding agricultural land. Many gardens also featured 'wildernesses', areas of ornamental shrubbery/woodland, which from the 1680s were increasingly brought up close to the walls of the house, often ranged either side of a central vista. That at Raynham in Norfolk, planted in c.1699, comprised a network of straight paths, hedged 'with hornbeams of two sizes ye Smaller Size of about 2 foot high and Better and ye Larger Size of 4 foot high and Better: the Quarters (i.e. the areas between the hedges) to be planted with ye sevll. Varietys of Flowering Trees Undermentioned ye walkes to be laid all with Sand ye Center places to be planted with Spruce or Silver Firs'.[13] The 'Flowering Trees' were listed as horse chestnut, wild service, laburnum, guelder rose, lilac, bladder senna, wild olive, 'stript' (variegated) sycamore, beech and birch, mixed with 'Silver Firs, Spruce Firs, Scotch Firs, Pine'. The Raynham wilderness thus typically contained a mixture of indigenous plants, some doubtless already modified into more aesthetically appealing forms – wild service, guelder rose, beech – alongside foreign introductions like lilac, laburnum, and bladder senna (*Colutea arborescens*).

New plants continued to arrive through the late seventeenth and early eighteenth century, joining the range of exotics already established in gardens here, including the Tulip tree, Portugal laurel and the weeping willow.[14] The use of trees which, while indigenous to England, were not native to a particular locality also served to distinguish elite grounds from the surrounding landscape. Avenues were thus commonly planted with beech, only really a species of the working countryside in south east England;[15] with common lime *Tilia Vulgaris*, rather than the small-leafed *Tilia cordata*;[16] or with sweet chestnut. The grove of Scots pine planted in the grounds of Somerleyton in Suffolk was such an unusual sight that it could be described in 1662 as one of the place's 'curiosities', and in 1663 as 'the most incomparable piece in the realm of England'.[17]

Garden historians tend to focus on the ornamental aspects of the grounds of great houses, but attention should also be drawn to their more productive and practical areas. Kitchen grounds, and also farmyards, were usually located near the mansion or even interspersed with the ornamental gardens; while many features, such as orchards and nut grounds, were at once ornamental and productive in character.[18] Great gardens not only displayed a knowledge of the latest fashions in architecture and garden design. They also boasted that their owners produced, and consumed, rare and exotic food. This immediately brings us back to wild, or at least semi-wild, creatures, the exploitation of which had, as we have seen, long been a means of displaying social superiority. Deer parks were by now almost invariably located beside – sometimes wrapped around – major residences. In addition, dovecotes were frequently placed close to mansions, and often near or within the main garden areas. This was partly for practical reasons – to protect the birds from theft and to facilitate the movement of the rich dung which they produced. But it was also because such badges of manorial privilege were to be proudly displayed, and seventeenth- and early eighteenth-century dovecotes are often architecturally sophisticated structures, elaborately detailed.[19] Fish ponds were likewise located close to the mansion. Indeed, many if not most canals and basins doubled as 'stews' or holding ponds.[20] Rabbit warrens were perhaps the most surprising elements of these landscapes of lordship. The Catholic recusant Thomas Tresham erected a strange triangular lodge in the 1590s within the warren close to Rushton House in Northamptonshire. This provided both a pun on Tresham's name and a statement of his faith in the tridentine mass: it has three sides, each 33 feet long and with three gables; three storeys; and three-sided chimneys.[21] At Quarrendon in Buckinghamshire the main view from the great house erected by Sir Henry Lee looked out across gardens and onto a large warren which lay some 350 metres to the east. A group of 'pillow mounds', of varied and complex form, still survives here, some carefully placed on the false crest of the hill, and raised higher than most such mounds, to ensure their visibility.[22] Many other large residences, like Sopwell House near St Albans in Hertfordshire, looked out directly across rabbit warrens, which clearly formed an acceptable alternative to deer parks (Figure 13).[23] Such displays, it should be emphasized, were not only to be found at the homes of backwoods squires. Fishponds, warrens and the rest formed important components of designed landscapes at the highest social levels. Chatsworth in Derbyshire was a vast mansion erected

FIGURE 13 *An undated early seventeenth-century map of Sopwell House, near St Albans in Hertfordshire, showing how the rabbit warren formed the principal view from the house.*

by Elizabeth ('Bess') of Hardwick and her husbands in the 1570s. A deer park lay around three sides of the mansion but the main view was across an elaborate complex of fish ponds and out onto an extensive warren featuring a number of pillow mounds. This arrangement survived even after the house was rebuilt in fashionable Baroque style, and at great expense, by the Sixth Earl at the very end of the seventeenth century.[24]

Parks, warrens, and decoys

Parks, warrens and other forms of 'intermediate exploitation', while they frequently served as elements in designed landscapes, were also important economic propositions in the later seventeenth and early eighteenth centuries. In a period of slow or negative population growth, and with agriculture in a depressed state, deer, pigeons, rabbits and the rest formed a useful alternative source of income for hard-pressed landowners. Indeed, while we often think of the exploitation of semi-wild species as an essentially medieval phenomenon the period between 1660 and 1750 was probably its real heyday. The number of parks being created seems to have increased after 1660, following a period of decline in the sixteenth and early seventeenth centuries, and both dovecotes and fish ponds were regarded with renewed interest.[25] The most comprehensive treatise on the latter subject, Roger North's *A Discourse on Fish and Fish Ponds*, was published in 1713.[26] There was, moreover, a new method of exploiting wildlife, introduced from Holland at the start of the seventeenth century. Birds had been driven into tunnel nets in wetland areas since at least the fifteenth century but 'decoys' were more sophisticated. They consisted of a number of curving 'pipes' – tapering channels covered by netting, supported on a framework of hoops of wood or (later) iron – leading off from an area of open water. Each pipe terminated in a long bow-net which could be detached from the rest of the apparatus. Along one side of the pipe was a series of overlapping screens, usually made of wood and reeds, behind which the decoy man would conceal himself.[27] Wildfowl were lured into the net by using a combination of tame decoy ducks and a dog called a 'piper'. The former were trained to enter the pipe in response to a low whistle from the decoy man; at the same time the dog would run around the screens, jumping over the low boards or 'dog jumps' placed between them. The wild fowl gathered near the mouth of the pipe were attracted towards what – to them – must have looked like an appearing and disappearing dog, or fox. Encouraged by the behaviour of the decoy ducks, they swam towards it. When they had proceeded a little way the decoy man would appear, waving his arms or a handkerchief and driving the birds in flight down the tapering pipe, and into the bow net at the end. The earliest known decoy in England was perhaps at Waxham on the north east coast of Norfolk where as early as 1620 Sir William Wodehouse had constructed 'a device for catching DUCKS, known by the foreign name of a koye'.[28] That at Purdis Farm, to the east of Ipswich, must be almost as old for it is mentioned in a lease of 1646.[29] But it was in the period after 1660 that they really proliferated.

While some decoys were intended to supply the needs of great households, and to provide polite recreation, most were commercial ventures, leased to professional decoymen for a rent which was often paid both in money and in specified numbers of wildfowl. A lease for the decoy at Nyland in Somerset, drawn up in 1678, laid down a rent of £55 *per annum* together with 'one hundred cupple of wilde Fowle'.[30] Decoys were mainly located in fens and marshes where wildfowl were numerous, especially in the East Anglian Fens, in the Norfolk Broads, and along the coasts of Suffolk and Essex, but also in wetlands and coastal areas in the west of England. Daniel Defoe remarked of the Fenland decoys how

> It is incredible what quantities of wild-fowl of all sorts, duck, mallard, teal, widgeon &c. they take in these duckoys every week, during the season. It may indeed be guessed at a little by this, that there is a duckoy not far from Ely, from which they assured me at St Ives (a town on the Ouse, where the fowl they took was always brought to be sent to London) that they generally sent up three thousand couple a week.[31]

– a clear enough indication of the true character of the Fenland environment, even after the supposed drainage of the area in the seventeenth century (above, p. 34).

But it is the expansion of rabbit farming that is the most striking feature of this period. In the words of the historian E. P. Thompson, warrens 'became a craze in the early eighteenth century with lords of the manor anxious to improve, not their pastures, but their incomes'.[32] Large commercial warrens, again usually leased to professional operators, now appeared in the Mendip Hills, the Yorkshire and Lincolnshire Wolds and the North York Moors;[33] while on Dartmoor, in Ashdown and St Leonards in Sussex, or in Sherwood Forest in Nottinghamshire, where warrens had been common in the fifteenth and sixteenth centuries, there was a considerable expansion in their area and numbers.[34] By the 1750s 'landscapes of warrening' existed in many areas of downland, heath and moor, in which contiguous rabbit farms extended across many square kilometres, in part because the damage caused by rabbits meant that areas close to warrens could not easily be used for much else. In the later eighteenth century it was typically suggested that land at Allerston on the Yorkshire Wolds 'must by the vicinity of the neighbouring Warrens, lose most of its produce, if not converted into a Warren'.[35]

Like earlier warrens, many of those created in the seventeenth and eighteenth centuries contained pillow mounds or 'buries' for accommodation, vermin traps and lodges or warren houses (Figure 14). But in addition, many were run on more intensive lines than before, and contained enclosures where turnips or other fodder could be cultivated for winter feed. Stocking densities were in consequence higher and rabbits more likely to stray onto adjacent properties, so that boundary walls and banks proliferated. Such was the intensity of rabbit grazing that on the Breckland warrens in East Anglia the turf was stripped and the sand exposed, sometimes forming mobile dunes like that which, originating in Lakenheath Warren in 1688, engulfed the village of Santon Downham in Suffolk and blocked the river Little Ouse. The growth in the extent and numbers of warrens was associated with the expansion of feral colonies, at the same time as genetic mutation was anyway ensuring that the rabbit was becoming better adapted to the English environment. Not surprisingly, as in earlier periods,

FIGURE 14 *A large 'pillow mound' on one of the Dartmoor rabbit warrens. Note the typical moorland scenery in the distance, with the area of heather much reduced by the encroachment of bracken.*

the establishment of warrens aroused strong opposition from local people. In 1749, for example, there was a major riot in Charnwood Forest in Leicestershire when commoners attacked the warrens newly established on the local commons. One rioter was killed, many were arrested and tried, and a contemporary ballad described:

> . . . How they troop from ev'ry Town
> To pull these Upstart Warrens down,
> All praying for the Church and Crown
> And for their Common Right.[36]

The expansion of warrens and parks, and the proliferation of fish ponds and dovecotes, in this period was driven by social and ideological as well as economic factors. Intermediate forms of exploitation had traditionally been reserved, by virtue of their cost or because of legal prohibitions, to the landed elite. Warrens, as we have seen, could be established by lords and squires on manorial waste, regardless of the wishes of commoners, while dovecotes and pigeon houses were reserved by law to the manorial gentry. But during the Civil War and Interregnum in the middle decades of the seventeenth century such rights and privileges had been threatened. The deer parks of the king, and of leading royalists, had been sequestered by the revolutionary government, their timber felled and their deer destroyed. Ponds and dovecotes had been casually trashed by parliamentary troops. Those stationed at Leamington, busy vandalizing the dovecote belonging to Baron Trevor, told their commanding officer that:

> Pigeons were fowls of the air given to the sons of men, and all men had a common right in them that could get them, and they were as much theirs as the barons, and therefore they would kill them . . . and not part from their right: upon which the captain was so convinced by their arguments he could not answer them, and so came away, letting them do as they would.[37]

It is thus hardly surprising that the return of political stability at the Restoration of 1660, in the form of a modified version of the old order, saw a renewed interest in the these traditional symbols of status as ways of making money, as well as their ostentatious display beside great houses.

Hunting

'Intermediate exploitation' shades off, with no clear line of separation, into true hunting, already the central passion of rural life. By the middle of the seventeenth century hawking was going out of fashion, largely due to the availability of sporting firearms, and the great days of deer hunting were also over. The pressure of population on resources ensured that, even in royal forests, deer were becoming rare in the wild. The administration of the forests had collapsed during the Civil War, and was never fully reinstated: the stints on the forest commons were poorly enforced, so that the livestock of local villagers competed with the deer for herbage. Parks continued to be stocked with deer, but while these were still hunted well into the eighteenth century it was on a declining scale.[38] Parks were becoming more ornamental in character, and by the later seventeenth century the numbers of deer kept within them was often reduced, probably to limit the damage they caused to young ornamental plantings in clumps or avenues.[39]

Important acts were passed in 1603 and 1609 for the better protection of deer kept within 'inclosed Ground'. But the most significant piece of game legislation came in 1671. The preamble to the Game Act explained that a new law was necessary because

> Diverse disorderly persons laying aside their lawfull Trades and Imployments doe betake themselves to the stealing, takeing and killing of Conies, Hares, Pheasants, Partridges and other Game, intended to be preserved by former Lawes, with Guns, Dogs, Tramells, Lowbells, Hayes, and other Netts, Snares, Hare-pipes and other Engines, to the great dammage of this Realme, and prejudice of Noblemen, Gentlemen and Lords of Mannours and others Owners of Warrens'.[40]

Lords of manors could now have their gamekeepers search any individual and – with the permission of a local Justice of the Peace – their homes if suspected of possessing equipment which could be used to take game. The right to possess such equipment was restricted to owners of property with a yearly rental value of £100, possessors of leasehold property valued at £150 per annum, the sons and heirs of 'an Esquire, or other person of higher degree', and the owners of parks and warrens and their gamekeepers. The act maintained the penalties laid down in earlier legislation, that is, a fine of 20 shillings per head of game killed or three months imprisonment. But the stakes were subsequently raised higher. An act of 1707 increased the penalty for poaching to a fine of £5, while the Black Act of 1723 prescribed the death penalty for merely being found in the vicinity of a game reserve, suitably disguised or equipped.[41] This was an extraordinary piece of legislation, initially a response to raids carried out by groups of poachers – disguised by having their faces blackened – on parks at Farnham in Surrey and Caversham in Berkshire. It introduced the death penalty for more than fifty offences relating to poaching, vandalism and – in some cases – no more than suspicious behaviour in forests or near parks. It is noticeable that particular legislation was thus required to protect these wild or semi-wild animals. Like the Civil War soldiers, convinced that pigeons were simply 'fowls of the air' given to all men, the rural population evidently regarded these creatures as somehow different in kind to domesticated animals like sheep or cows. Their uncertain, intermediate status between domesticated and wild allowed some moral ambiguity over their status as property, even when restrained within warrens or parks. It is indeed noteworthy that the legislation passed in the late seventeenth and early eighteenth century was essentially concerned with protecting the denizens of rabbit warrens, fish ponds, and deer parks – that is, with forms of 'intermediate exploitation' – rather than with preventing the poaching of birds and animals running freely in the countryside. Only gradually, in the course of the eighteenth century – and especially after 1750 – did legislation come to focus more directly on the preservation of pheasants, partridges, hares and other game in the wider landscapes. This was because it was only in the second half of the eighteenth century that game-shooting, and game preservation, developed in its highly organized modern form.[42]

That development, as we shall see, was dependent on two things: the consolidation of large and continuous landed estates, which meant that it was feasible to breed and preserve game in large numbers; and improvements in firearm technology, which enabled large numbers of game to be shot. In the period with which we are here concerned, between 1650 and 1750, the main firearm employed for recreational shooting was the flintlock. This was more compact and manageable than the earlier matchlock, but still cumbersome enough: anything from 4' 6" to 6' in length, and unreliable in ways that have bequeathed to us a range of common sayings, such as 'flash in the pan' and 'going off at half cock'.[43] Shooting tended to be a casual affair: small groups of legally qualified individuals would go out in the countryside on an informal basis.[44] Often they would hunt across the property of others without hindrance – it was sometimes hard to do otherwise, where properties lay intermingled – taking shots at anything on the ground or near it, especially hares and partridges, but also woodcock and pheasant. This kind of shooting must have made virtually no impact on local wildlife. Only later would more organized shooting, involving the systematic control of vermin with much more effective firearms, take a terrible toll.

Attitudes to wildlife

Whether the kind of hunting and shooting characteristic of the period before c.1750 should be regarded as 'cruel' is not a reasonable subject for historical discussion. Few contemporaries would have so regarded it. Indeed, to modern eyes all social classes in pre-industrial England would have appeared to be routinely cruel and callous to both domestic livestock and wild animals. To some historians, this situation only gradually changed in the course of the eighteenth and nineteenth centuries, as more enlightened attitudes were adopted by the social elite, and gradually spread through society: a view most clearly articulated in Keith Thomas's great book, *Man and the Natural World*. Thomas moreover, while conceding that 'popular taxonomy of plants, birds, beasts and fishes was more elaborate than purely utilitarian considerations required', nevertheless suggested that 'the practical aspect of this popular knowledge of the natural world . . . seems to have been uppermost'.[45] But this is perhaps too simple. The inhabitants of early modern England were intimately immersed in the natural world, in part because there was little else in which to be immersed, and regarded it as a source of beauty and wonder, as well as a resource to be exploited. The nomenclature of wild flowers is especially striking, showing as it does a great store of common knowledge which has now largely, although not entirely, vanished from popular culture. The majority of English wild flowers had traditional names which varied – before attempts at standardization in the eighteenth century – from district to district and from region to region.[46] It is true that some were inventions of sixteenth and seventeenth-century herbalists – indeed, even some eighteenth-century exotic introductions, like Dutchman's breeches (*Dicentra cucullaria*), were given what sound like folk names. But most were not, many for example making allusion to pre-Reformation Catholicism or magical beliefs. Some of these names, since purged by the writers of Victorian wild flower guides, were humorous and/or obscene: naked ladies, pissabed, mare's fart, priests ballacks.[47] Yet ordinary people appreciated the beauty of wild flowers in a world otherwise often drab, as suggested for example in Shakespeare's *A Midsummer Night's Dream*:

> I know a bank where the wild thyme blows,
> Where oxlips and the nodding violet grows,
> Quite over-canopied with luscious woodbine,
> With sweet musk-roses and with eglantine:

There sleeps Titania sometime of the night,
Lull'd in these flowers with dances and delight.[48]

Traditional folksongs, moreover, often suggest an active, intelligent interest in the natural world. The protagonist in *Hanged I shall be* describes how he killed his lover:

'As we were a-walking and talking
Of the things that grew around'.

Numerous references seem to indicate that then, as now, people delighted in such things as the sounds of birdsong ('where the pretty little songbirds do change their voices'). We need to be a little careful here. Shakespeare's audience was probably largely urban, and most traditional folk songs were only first collected in the nineteenth century, by which time, as we shall see, widespread urbanization had removed many people from direct contact with the daily grind of rural life. But wild animals loom large in both folk and 'polite' literature, used as images for human traits, but often reflecting nevertheless behaviour genuinely associated with the animal in question. Both plants and animals were woven into a complex mesh of folk beliefs, partly ancient and indigenous, partly derived from classical mythology. Hares were magical and shape-shifting; hedgehogs, as we have seen, sucked the milk of sleeping kine.

There was certainly a great deal of cruelty to animals, both wild and domestic, in the early modern period. Cockfighting, bear- and badger-baiting were popular pastimes. But in an age of public executions, casual domestic violence, witch trials – and of death sentences for wearing disguise near game reserves – animals were not being singled out for particularly harsh treatment. Moreover, the difference in this respect between our age, and theirs, is not quite as marked as some texts might suggest. Thomas lists the appalling maltreatment sometimes meted out to livestock in the sixteenth, seventeenth and eighteenth centuries, especially domestic poultry, but the fact that most chickens are now kept indoors for their entire lives, in conditions which – even on many 'organic' farms – are cramped, cruel and unnatural, should caution against too optimistic a view of progress.

The scale of slaughter carried out to protect crops and wildlife, as recorded in the bounty payments made by churchwardens under the 1566 act, certainly sounds appalling, and often gratuitous, to modern ears. Lovegrove quotes, for example, the 6,600 bullfinches killed over a period of 36 years in just one Cheshire parish – 452 in 1676 alone; or the 3,344 hedgehogs slaughtered at Sherbourne in Dorset between 1662 and 1799.[49] Reviewers of Lovegrove's book were understandably shocked to read of how millions of 'attractive wild creatures were slaughtered', in an orgy of 'systematic killing on a scale today almost unthinkable'.[50] Yet these were not wanton acts of cruelty but the understandable reactions of people living in a countryside still teeming with wildlife, and who had no choice but to kill in this way, if they and their families were to survive and flourish. Scaring animals away, or fencing them out, would do just as well as killing them: but either way, crops and livestock had to be protected, in both field and garden, from a host of pests and vermin and without the aid of chemical insecticides, automatic bird scarers, or wire netting. Guns, even when people had them, were slow to load and inefficient, but the various traps and techniques listed in books like Mascall's *A Book of Engines and Traps to take Polecats, Buzardes, Rattes, Mice and all other Kindes of Vermine and Beasts whatever* of 1590 – box-traps, the smearing of trees and bushes with sticky 'lime' to trap birds, a wide variety of nets – must have been more effective than they sound, given the scale of killing recorded in the churchwardens' accounts.[51] Yet the most striking feature of this source, perhaps, is the way it suggests that it all made little impact on the numbers of wild animals. The parish of Lezant in Cornwall, for example, killed an average of 32 polecats annually over 86 years, but with no reduction in numbers over the decades. As Lovegrove noted, '. . . during the period of maximum persecution through the parish system, populations of most species remained fairly stable'.[52] At least until the middle of the nineteenth century, but arguably even after that time, it was *environmental* factors, rather than the scale of human predation, that determined the numbers of animals and birds in any locality. It is easy to criticize seventeenth-century pest control, especially its inability to distinguish real from imaginary threats. But a society that seems on the brink of exterminating the hedgehog should be cautious in its criticisms of those who, albeit mistakenly, systematically targeted this creature because they thought it a direct threat to livelihoods, yet made little real impact on its numbers.

Conclusion

It is tempting to examine the environmental impact of man in seventeenth- and early eighteenth-century England entirely in terms of agricultural communities and farming methods. Towns and industry made as yet a relatively small impact on the landscape: the vast majority of the land area was used to grow food or to produce organic raw materials and fuel, shaping the environment and the character of wildlife in complex, intricate ways. Yet urbanization and to some extent industry were already beginning to create distinctive biological communities, which would develop, change and expand over the following centuries. More importantly, the environment was already being shaped by activities like gardening and hunting which were not simply related to the procurement of food. Ideology, status and politics had for centuries helped mould the natural world, and as the economic and technological base of society was transformed by industrialization and agrarian modernization, they were set to do so on an ever grander scale.

CHAPTER FIVE

The industrial revolution

Two 'revolutions'?

The period between c.1750 and c.1860 saw, in many senses, the birth of the modern world. The population of England began to grow rapidly from around 1750, rising with unprecedented speed from around 5½ million to some 9 million by 1800, and to nearly 19 million by 1861 (Figure 15).[1] This had a direct impact on agricultural profitability, especially for cereal growers, reversing the sluggish prices of the previous century. High demand from a burgeoning population was exacerbated by institutional and legal structures – the infamous Corn Laws, brought in by a parliament dominated by landowners, ensured that grain imports were kept to a minimum – and also by political and military factors, principally the French Revolutionary and Napoleonic wars (1793–1815), when blockades, coinciding with a series of poor harvests, led to acute food shortages and the rise of grain prices to unprecedented levels. Perhaps not surprisingly, this was a period of agricultural innovation – of the classic 'agricultural revolution', when the widespread adoption of a range of new techniques boosted production. Even in 1851 imports only accounted for some 16 per cent of foodstuffs consumed in England and Wales. To feed an expanding population the volume of wheat produced more than doubled, while that of barley may have increased by over two thirds, in the course of the later eighteenth and early nineteenth centuries; increases in the production of other foodstuffs were probably of a similar order.[2]

There was, moreover, a dramatic improvement in what economic historians call 'labour productivity', that is, the number of individuals required to produce a given amount of food.[3] In 1760 the output of each agricultural worker could feed around one other person, but by 1841 it could feed another 2.7. This was vital because it was in this period that England also crossed the

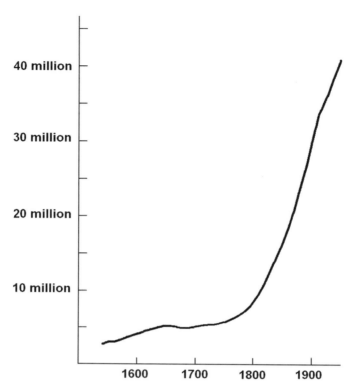

FIGURE 15 *Graph showing the growth of the population of England between 1550 and 1950. Relatively gentle increase up to 1650 was followed by a period of stagnation and decline. From c.1750 population growth resumed, escalating significantly as industrialization intensified in the nineteenth century. The sheer scale of demographic expansion since the sixteenth century and its environmental impact are hard to exaggerate.*

threshold to an economy powered by fossil fuels, experiencing an industrial revolution, so that a higher and higher proportion of the workforce was employed full-time in mines, mills and factories. Growth was based on three key sectors: coal, iron and textiles. Coal production rose from perhaps 2.5 million tons per annum to over 11 million by 1800, reaching more than 22 million by 1830.[4] There were less than twenty blast furnaces in England in 1700; by 1805 there were 177 and by 1852 no less than 665, all now fired with coke rather than charcoal. In 1700 around 30,000 tons of pig iron were produced in England each year. By 1850 the figure was two million. The expansion of textiles was if anything even more dramatic, although it came a little later, following the improvements in spinning machinery made by Hargreaves, Arkwright and Compton in the 1770s.[5]

It is important to emphasize that demographic, industrial and agricultural expansion were intimately interconnected. More reliable food supplies prevented the periodic dearths which had formerly served to check population growth, while the development of a more diversified economy encouraged earlier marriage, and thus higher fertility rates. In addition, although it is true that living conditions in many industrializing and urbanizing areas were poor, encouraging disease, on the whole the population was warmer and healthier than ever before as a consequence of the increased availability of fuel and clothing resulting from the expansion of coal and textile production. More people meant a greater demand for food, and for manufactured products, further stimulating production in both the agricultural and industrial sectors. There were innumerable other connections.

The reasons why this take-off into modernity occurred in England earlier than in any other country are complex, and cannot be discussed in detail here. But some of the key drivers of change need to be highlighted because they have a direct relevance to the principal themes of this book. First, both the agricultural and industrial 'revolutions', although marking a step change, nevertheless had their own 'prehistories'. Not only were major innovations in agriculture made in the sixteenth and seventeenth centuries, as we have seen in the case of water meadows.[6] In addition, the same period witnessed a massive expansion in coal production and the scale of small-scale workshop production – what historians sometimes describe as 'proto-industrialization' – in textiles, metalworking and much else.[7] Approaching Halifax in West Yorkshire in the 1720s Daniel Defoe noted the density of housing:

> This business is the clothing trade, for the convenience of which the houses are thus scattered and spread upon the sides of the hills . . . even from the bottom to the top; the reason is this; such has been the bounty of nature in this otherwise frightful country, that two things essential to the business, as well as to the ease of the people are found here . . . I mean coals and running water upon the tops of the highest hills.[8]

But proto-industrialization was by no means confined to the north and west of England. In the early eighteenth century the Weald of Kent was a major centre for iron working, while East Anglia was one of the main areas of textile weaving, carried on in cottages and small workshops. Both these local industries, like most others, had ancient roots, but they expanded considerably in Tudor and Stuart times.

The two 'revolutions' had prehistories in more important yet more complicated ways. England had long possessed characteristics, shared to some extent with other countries in western Europe, which predisposed it to take-off into the modern world: a society organized around individuals and nuclear families, rather than extended kin groups; one in which private property was established at all social levels; and in which a mercantile and artisan class was numerically and economically important. These characteristics were exacerbated by the political upheavals of the seventeenth century – by the Civil War and Commonwealth. Although this struggle was not, in any real sense, a triumph of the bourgeoisie over a feudal class, as Marxist historians used to argue, it did create conditions under which a market economy could flourish. In spite of the eventual Restoration of the monarchy, the Civil War established a political system which guaranteed the safety of property, under a parliament of the propertied, free from arbitrary royal exactions and in a climate of internal peace. The accumulation of capital could continue at the level of great landowners and merchants, but also among the larger farmers and petty industrialists who made up the 'middling sort' in early modern England. The seventeenth century saw the consolidation of a 'new class of bourgeoisie, intelligent but not always educated, well-to-do but not always wealthy, articulate but not always cultured, who owned property, manipulated money or followed one of the growing professions'.[9] Such men were prepared to invest in new forms of industrial development and also provided a ready market for sophisticated consumer goods, encouraging for example the trades of clock- and instrument-making, and gun-making, all of which utilized techniques – such as precision boring and calibration – essential for the development of industrial machinery, especially steam engines.[10] Also important was the fact that the foreign policy of post-revolutionary governments was focused, not simply on dynastic aggrandisement through European conflict, but on securing advantages for English traders, and ultimately on the acquisition of foreign colonies, particularly in the Americas – a major source of key raw materials for industrialization, most notably cotton. Profits from foreign trade were ploughed back into mining and manufacture to meet an expanding home market.

While all these social, economic, cultural and ideological factors were crucial in the development of the world's first industrial economy, they would have been insufficient in themselves without a key environmental advantage: the availability of large quantities of coal, much of it lying at no great depth. Whatever the importance of what Jacob has termed the 'scientific culture' of early modern England, industrialization was largely the consequence of 'crucial accidents of geography and juxtaposition'.[11] Moreover, the development of efficient steam engines in the middle and later decades of the eighteenth century provided the motive power for the pumps which allowed ever deeper deposits of coal to be reached.[12] It is true that much early industry was not powered by coal at all: textile manufacture was largely dependent on water power well into the nineteenth century, and much contemporary effort was directed towards improving the design of water wheels.[13] Famously, the earliest use of steam engines at Coalbrookdale in Shropshire, a major centre of industrial innovation in the early and middle decades of the eighteenth century, was to pump water to the top of a hill so that it could be used to turn water wheels.[14] Nevertheless, coal had a key role. It provided thermal power for a wide range of industrial processes, from iron smelting to dyeing, which relied on high temperatures rather than on motive power. And it became, in the course of the eighteenth and nineteenth centuries, the main form of domestic fuel in England, replacing wood, peat, gorse and the rest, with major implications for the various habitats which produced these materials. Lastly, coal was a bulk commodity, valuable but expensive to transport, and its gradual adoption as the principal source of heat and energy throughout England would have been impossible without major improvements in transport infrastructure. While it is true that the more general growth of the economy demanded better forms of transport, the development of a more sophisticated communications infrastructure seems largely to have been stimulated by the needs of coal producers.

At the start of the period covered by this book most roads appear to have been in a poor condition, and they deteriorated further as the volume of traffic, resulting from commercial and industrial expansion, steadily increased. Even the most important highways were maintained by the parishes through which they ran. Each was solely responsible for its own section, regardless of its population and resources, and regardless of the amount of traffic the road in question had to bear.[15] This continued to be the case for minor local roads until the later nineteenth century. But from the late seventeenth century major routes began to be improved through the institution of 'turnpike trusts'. Created by individual acts of parliament, these bodies would adopt sections of road, erect toll gates, charge tolls and use the proceeds (after a suitable cut had been taken as profit) to keep the route in adequate repair.[16] Even improved roads, however, were insufficient for moving heavy loads like coal: for this, water transport was required. Navigable rivers had been key arteries of commerce since the Middle Ages, and many were 'improved' in various ways – with the installation of simple staunch locks, for example – in the course of the seventeenth and early eighteenth centuries. But this network was massively extended from the 1750s, beginning with the construction of the Bridgewater canal (designed to serve the coal mines at Worsley), 'the movement reaching a crescendo in the 'mania' of 1789–93'.[17] The need to transport coal also encouraged, as much as powered, the spread of the rail network from the 1830s. Coal thus lay at the heart of the industrial revolution, and industrialization was, above all, a transition to a fossil fuel economy. Indeed, as Wrigley has observed, if coal had not existed England would, by 1815, have required at least 6 million hectares of managed woodland to meet its energy requirements – nearly half its total land area.[18]

Industry and wildlife

On the face of it, the impact of industrialization on England's ecology, and on its wildlife, might appear straightforward. 'Dark Satanic Mills' brought pollution to the atmosphere and watercourses, especially as the spread of the canal network, and the increasing use of coal as the main industrial fuel, encouraged ever-larger concentrations of manufacturing, and associated urban growth.[19] Coal mines, which by the end of the nineteenth century covered around 60,000 hectares of land in Britain as a whole with heaps of waste material, caused extensive pollution to water courses, in part because coals to be used for coking were usually washed of excess dust. Streams in the vicinity of coalfields ran black and meadows downstream were covered in coal dust after floods.[20] Other extractive industries produced heavy metals, toxic to plants and animals alike; while manufacturing processes filled the air with acids (both sulphuric and carbonic) and nitrogen oxide. Although in the course of the eighteenth century conditions in many urban areas improved, as city authorities and 'improvement commissions' provided them with better drainage and street paving, this was less true in the great industrializing towns of the north. Here large areas of rough ground remained unpaved, and standards of sanitation and rubbish disposal poor, not least because many, like Manchester, had developed from rural settlements, and thus had only rudimentary forms of local government. Engels famously described the view from Ducie Bridge in Manchester:

> At the bottom flows, or rather stagnates, the Irk, a narrow, coal-black, foul-smelling stream, full of *debris* and refuse, which it deposits on the shallower right bank. In dry weather, a long string of the most disgusting, blackish-green slime pools are left standing on this bank, from the depths of which miasmatic gas constantly arises and gives forth a stench unendurable even on the bridge forty or fifty feet above the surface of the stream. But besides this, the stream is checked every few paces by high weirs, behind which slime accumulate and rot in thick masses.[21]

Levels of pollution in watercourses downstream from major industrial areas were often appalling: letters could be written with the ink-black water of the river Calder in the West Riding of Yorkshire, while the Bradford Canal actually caught fire on a number of occasions.[22] Even where industrial pollution of watercourses was limited, the sheer scale of population growth ensured unsustainable flows of effluent into water courses. Salmon had disappeared from the Thames by the 1810s and in 1858 the smell of the river was so great Parliament had to be adjourned. Airborne pollution also became a major problem for not only the smoke from factories, but also that from thousands of domestic fires, filled the air. London smog was already a familiar feature of life by the start of the nineteenth century.[23] Sir Charles Napier in 1839 described Manchester as 'the chimney of the world', and the *Manchester Guardian* in 1842 described how in the centre of the city 'flowering shrubs will not grow at all' and trees died.[24] On the Pennines to the east airborne pollution was contributing to the soil acidification which led to 'a change from bog-mosses of the genus *Sphagnum* to the more acid-tolerant cotton-sedge *Eriophorum* . . . over whole stretches of peaty moorland'.[25] The upland bogs ceased to form, instead beginning to erode; plants like bilberry (*Vaccinium myrtillus*) and crowberry (*Empetrum nigrum*) became more important.[26]

Yet, while we must not underestimate the impact of industrialization on the environment, in the period before c.1860 its worst effects were probably localized and limited. It was 'not until well into the nineteenth century that serious pollution occurred' in England's river system.[27] As late as 1900 it could be claimed that 'within the memory of persons still living, salmon still ascended the Mersey every year to spawn in its upper reaches', a river which, by the time this was written, was effectively dead downstream of Stockport.[28] Contemporaries described how palls of smoke visibly hung over Manchester, London and other large cities, but this of course implies that there were cleaner conditions beyond. Although, in the case of the Pennines, significant levels of sulphur dioxide deposition were occurring in the first half of the nineteenth century, they increased significantly thereafter: moreover, in all periods there was a 'steep gradient in the smoke pollution from the city centre to the outskirts'.[29] Even in 1859 Leo Grindon's extensive comments on the flora growing in the area around Manchester contain virtually no references to the effects of pollution: only lichens – particularly sensitive to levels of sulphur dioxide – were declining, even at some distance from the city centre, on the 'high hills beyond Disley, Ramsbottom, Staleybridge and Rochdale'.[30]

The often localized character of pollution is important because, in the period before the 1860s, mines, mills and factories, and associated housing for workers covered relatively small areas and were generally interdigitated with farmland. Many books on the Industrial Revolution feature the famous painting by Phillip de Loutherbourg of 'Coalbrookdale by Night' of 1801, which depicts the flaming furnaces almost as a scene from hell. A different impression is conveyed by William Williams' 'Afternoon' and 'Morning Views of Coalbrookdale' of 1777, which show smoke rising from furnaces set in a resolutely rural, pastoral environment (Figure 16). The Ordnance Survey 6" maps indicate that even in the 1880s the industrial areas in the Ironbridge Gorge were still surrounded by fields and woods. Indeed, in general England's great conurbations did not develop quite as early as we often assume, in part because poor transport facilities meant that people needed to live close to their place of work, and thus at high densities. In the first half of the nineteenth century Manchester's population grew from 88,000 to 400,000: it was the second largest city in the kingdom. Yet in 1850 its built-up area – mills, factories and all – covered less than 18 square kilometres.[31] To the south, the spread of houses ended abruptly at Longsight, and there was a space of some six kilometres, occupied by open countryside, before Stockport (to which the city is now seamlessly connected) began. Oldham was still a completely distinct town, again separated by a belt of open land some eight kilometres wide.[32] At its widest Manchester was less than five kilometres across – an hour's brisk walk – and much of its area comprised, not industrial premises and back-to-back

FIGURE 16 *William Williams' 'Afternoon View of Coalbrookdale' (Shropshire) of 1777, showing smoke rising from furnaces set in a resolutely rural, pastoral environment. The impact of industry on the landscape before the middle decades of the nineteenth century was more limited than we often assume.*

housing, but middle class suburbs.[33] In 1859 Grindon described the view over the city from neighbouring high ground: 'the vastest mass of houses ever heaped together by man is till only an encampment in the fields'. From the train line near Pendleton in Salford it was possible to enjoy views across 'broad, sweet lawns of meadow and pasture, chequered here and there with waving corn fields'.[34] The real expansion of the city, into a continuously built-up area some 30 kilometres north-south, and more than 20 east-west, was a development of the late nineteenth and twentieth centuries. The same was true of other major northern cities, such as Sheffield or Leeds, and also of London. Although the capital's population rose from around half a million in 1650 to some 2.3 million in 1850, its continuously built-up area still extended over less than 50 square kilometres, a fraction of its modern extent (Figure 29).[35] To the south, the villages of Lewisham and Streatham, although suburbanized, were still on the edge of open country. To the north west the continuous streets of houses ended at Highgate; places like Edgware, Harrow and Willesden were separate village surrounded by fields.[36] In all, it is unlikely that truly urban and industrial land exceeded 2 per cent of England's surface area in c.1860. Here, the environment does, indeed, appear to have become significantly degraded by industry, and in particular by the scale of both industrial and domestic coal use. But most of the country was still rural; and most wildlife still lived in the countryside, its fate affected more by farming than by factories.

New habitats: Derelict land and waste tips

The simple view of the Industrial Revolution as necessarily and universally inimical to wildlife also needs to be treated with caution. To some extent, industrialization arguably added significantly to an existing suite of habitats which were themselves, as should by now be clear, largely or entirely artificial in character. I noted earlier the key contribution made by early extractive industry to the environment: its creation of habitats across lowland England which mimicked those encountered in highland areas, such as scree slopes, bare rock or thin soils. The period from 1750 to 1860 saw a significant expansion of these kinds of habitat, through the growth of spoil tips from coal, copper, tin and lead mines, from open-cast extraction of ironstone and building stone, as well as from clay pits dug throughout England, and on a much larger scale after the arrival of the railways encouraged the concentration of brick and tile production at particular spots. Quarries and their waste tips will have provided few niches for wildlife while still being worked. But once extraction and dumping had ceased their sheer rock faces rapidly become breeding places for kestrels, stock doves and jackdaws, and sometimes for peregrines and choughs.[37] Colonization by plants was also rapid, to judge from recent analogies. The quarries at Wingate and Bishop Middleton in Durham, for example, today exhibit a rich flora characteristic of the local magnesium limestone grasslands, a habitat now rare. Abandoned in the 1930s, their importance in this respect was already being recognized in the early 50s.[38] More importantly, the communities which developed on worked-out industrial sites, in the earlier stages of succession especially, often had few local parallels, and sometimes no national ones either.

The characteristics of such communities can be reconstructed in broad terms by considering those which have developed on more recently abandoned sites. Box has described the flora of Stoney Hill, to the west of Telford, where open-cast mining for stone and clay ceased in the 1960s, leaving areas of water interspersed with dumps of acid clay, coal spoil and basic clays which have gradually re-vegetated. Heather, wavy hair-grass (*Deschampsia flexuosa*), with small populations of clubmosses (*Lycopodiella* spp.), lie next to communities with fairy flax (*Linum catharticum*), yellow-wort (*Blackstonia perfoliata*), and common spotted orchid (*Dactylorhiza fuchsii*).[39] Typically, extraction brought to the surface rocks otherwise deeply buried in the locality. Three species of clubmoss were found, all usually associated with upland sites but here at home in a landscape of shallow, recent soil and bare rock. In addition, and again characteristically, diversity was increased by the presence of waste dumped from a variety of local industries. Furnace slag developed a distinctive flora characterized by squirrel-tail fescue (*Vulpia bromoides*), hares-foot clover (*Trifolium arvense*), wall-pepper (*Sedum acre*), and ivy-leaved toadflax (*Cymbalaria muralis*): in early blast furnaces limestone was added to the flux and this, combined with impurities in the iron, produced a lime-rich habitat in an otherwise base-poor area.

Dumped waste, in old quarries or in other contexts, often produced unusual plant communities. Research in the 1970s into the distribution of marsh orchids (*Dactyllorhiza spp*) in south-west Lancashire, Merseyside and Greater Manchester revealed that 25 out of the 35 sites where the plants occurred were 'entirely man-made or grossly modified by man', many in fact being places where highly alkaline waste had been dumped.[40] All are relatively recent sites, of later nineteenth or twentieth-century date, but the patterns of colonization they display will again have been paralleled at earlier periods in areas where lime waste, blast furnace slag with boiler ash, and colliery washery waste and slurry were dumped. Colonization by the orchids, which otherwise occur in the area only on coastal sites, appears to have been rapid – within 15 years in some cases. A number of other rare plants characteristic of coastal locations also occur in these places, such as *Pyrola rotundifolia* subs *Maritima*.

A particularly important form of post-industrial habitat are the so-called calaminarian grasslands which, as already noted, are associated with the extraction of lead, silver, zinc, barium, chromium, copper and fluorspar. The community develops either on old spoil or (more rarely) in river gravels downstream from areas of mineral workings, where heavy metals have been re-deposited. Succession is slowed or even arrested altogether by the high levels of toxicity, and the open-structured plant communities which develop include a range of lichens and bryophytes, and such vascular plants as spring sandwort (*Minuartia verna*), alpine pennycress (*Thlaspi arvense*), and particular varieties of thrift (*Armeria maritime*) and bladder campion (*Silene maritime*) which have adapted genetically to the hostile conditions.[41] In England, such communities are mainly found in the Pennines and western Cumbria. They characteristically occur on networks of pits and spoil heaps crossing the countryside in lines called 'rakes', following the mineral veins. Some are of sixteenth- and seventeenth-century date but most were created in the eighteenth and nineteenth centuries.[42] This is not an entirely anthropogenic community, for where mineral veins lay close to the surface, it would have occurred naturally. But in England at least most extant examples are associated with spoil. Calaminarian grasslands are now subject to their own Biodiversity Action Plan, such is their rarity and importance. Apart from being threatened by 'restoration' to recreational use, the community is inherently unstable because, while soil toxicity reduces the rate of succession, it seldom halts it completely. Many of these plant communities are now being engulfed in birch, gorse and other scrub.

Indeed, in most contexts the distinctive communities created by industrial processes were short-lived. Areas of extraction or dumping did what any abandoned area of land will do if left to its own devices – regenerate to woodland. This is particularly true of the earlier industrial areas, such as Coalbrookdale, which always remained semi-rural in character, and well supplied with coppiced woods which had provided their main fuel before coal came into general use. Benthall Edge Wood, which forms the backdrop to the often-photographed views of the Iron Bridge itself, and which rises to a height of over 500 metres, is a Site of Special Scientific Interest dominated by birch, oak and rowan in its upper sections, and by wych elm and ash lower down. It is crammed with former mineshafts, quarries, and the remains of kilns, inclined planes and former tramways. Nearby Ladywood, beside the road leading from Ironbridge to Broseley, covers an extensive area of former clay, coal and stone extraction, with numerous pits, spoil heaps, shafts and ponds: some of the latter contain, besides a range of newts and frogs, the rare beetle *Haliplus heydenii*.[43]

New habitats: Canals and railways

As already emphasized, the construction of a network of artificial waterways – canals or 'navigations' – was a key feature of the industrial revolution. In 1750 there were around 1,000 miles of navigable waterway in England. By 1850 this had increased to some 4,250 miles (Figure 17).[44] The new network provided a vast area of essentially static water, equivalent to a lake covering something in the region of 50 square kilometres. It might be thought that a canal, regularly disturbed by traffic, would be of little importance to wildlife but narrow boats were drawn by horses and moved at a speed of 3 or 4 MPH, causing much less disturbance than modern motorized boats. The canals thus provided a greatly increased space for aquatic wildlife, and their value in this respect was to some extent enhanced by the way in which they were constructed and maintained. The layers of puddled clay necessary to retain water on permeable soils provided ideal conditions for the establishment of waterweeds and marginal vegetation.[45] But bottom-growing weeds needed to be regularly cut so that they did not impede the passage of boats, while locks needed to be dredged at intervals to prevent silting. These operations served to prevent the commoner and faster-growing weeds from out-competing less vigorous species and ensured that, along the length of a canal, there were always stretches in different stages of succession. Pondweeds, for example, tended to flourish best in the first few years after clearing and dredging.[46]

   The importance of canals for wildlife is perhaps most dramatically illustrated by the case of the Basingstoke canal, which originally ran for nearly 60 kilometres through the Hampshire countryside. It fell derelict in the early part of the twentieth century but has now been partially restored. Today it is considered by many to be 'Britain's best site for aquatic plants, dragonflies and bats'.[47] It was already being noted for its rare plants as early as the 1830s, when still only four decades old; and by the end of the century

FIGURE 17 *Above: navigable waterways in England and Wales in (a) 1760 and (b) 1850. Below: the rail network in England and Wales in (c) 1840 (d) 1850 (c) 1922 (after Cossons 1987).*

it was 'regarded as a "mecca" amongst botanists and entomologists'.[48] It currently supports 102 different species of aquatic plant, more than any natural river in England, 44 of which are rare at a national or regional level. This diversity results in part from the fact that the canal cuts through a range of geological formations, and is thus fed by water sources which are more varied, in terms of their PH especially, than those associated with the tributaries of a natural river.

Where canals crossed watersheds reservoirs needed to be constructed, for some water flowed downhill each time locks were opened. Reservoirs were also needed more generally to compensate for loss of water through leakage and evaporation. These have often developed as important wildlife reserves; now over two centuries old, they have generally lost any artificial appearance and are usually surrounded by reed beds. The four constructed near Tring on the Buckinghamshire/Hertfordshire border to supply the Grand Union (then the Grand Junction) canal have long been one of the most important sites in England for wintering water birds or passing migrants, especially terns and various waders. One of the four, Wilstone reservoir, is famous as the first-recorded nesting site of the black-necked grebe, in 1918, and of the little ringed plover, in 1938. The surrounding reedbeds are now so well developed that they are home to over-wintering bitterns. Again, these great artificial lakes were significant for wildlife almost as soon as they were completed, although their importance in this respect certainly increased over time, especially with the development of marginal vegetation. As early as 1853 one of the reservoirs could be described as the 'the best pike-water near London'.[49] 'The only claim of the Marsh Sandpiper (*Totanus stagnatilis*) to rank as "British" rests upon a single example which was reputed to have been shot by Mr Rothschilde near Tring reservoirs . . . in 1883'.[50] The four reservoirs were declared a National Nature Reserve in 1995.

Canals are, in Richard Mabey's words, 'by definition artificial waterways, cut by man along routes dictated more by economy than geology'.[51] Although they generally follow river valleys, and may in places be no more than tidied-up versions of pre-existing rivers, they usually – as with the Basingstoke canal – track the course of more than one. They connect up several drainage basins by cutting through the watersheds between them, seeking out the lowest passage through a separating range of hills. They thus serve as corridors, linking districts with differing characteristics in terms of hydrology and geology, and allowing the spread of species into new areas, reducing earlier contrasts in the biological character of different districts.[52] Prior to the eighteenth century English rivers draining eastwards, into the North Sea, tended to be richer in species than those draining westwards into the Atlantic – an ancient distinction, originating in early post-glacial times, when the latter watercourses had outfalls into the open sea while the former were connected to the Rhine. Species like bleak and ruffe were thus confined to the east of the country until the creation of the canal network allowed them to spread across the central watershed into western waters.[53] Canals, turning England's separate river systems into a single interconnected network, also provided opportunities for invasive alien species. Canadian Pondweed, introduced as an ornamental plant for garden ponds, was first noted in a canal near Market Harborough in Leicestershire in 1847. Within 10 years it had spread throughout the waterways of Midland and southern England.[54] Macan has shown that some sixteen alien species of freshwater invertebrates have successfully dispersed through the county via the canal network. One example is the American amphipod *Crangonyx pseudogracilis*, which spread rapidly through the canals of central England between 1937 and 1955.[55] The dispersal of some exotics was aided by the fact that in industrial areas discharges of warm water from factories raised the temperature of canals so that, for example, eel grass (*Allerisneria spiralis*) became so profuse in the nineteenth century that it had to be dragged out of canals near Lancashire cotton mills.[56]

Railways had a greater visual impact than canals, because of the cuttings, embankments and tunnels which were constructed to ensure that locomotives had to cope with minimal gradients. The first to be built, in the period before c.1850, were particularly dramatic due to the poor tractive power of the early engines. By that date around 7,000 miles of track had been laid in Britain as a whole, a figure rising to 23,000 by 1914 (Figure 17).[57] Railways could, of course, constitute a threat to wildlife. Although the number of animals killed by trains was relatively low before the introduction of electrified rails, badgers and otters appear to have been particularly vulnerable. But more important were other key characteristics. Like canals, railways provided a network of corridors along which wildlife could move without interruption, including alien introductions. The most famous example of this is the spread of the Oxford ragwort (*Senecio squalidus*), a plant from southern Europe which had been kept in the botanical gardens at Oxford since the eighteenth century. By the start of the nineteenth century, airborne seeds had spread the plant into the city itself, reaching the railway station by the 1850s. From here the species moved rapidly along the Great Western railway, and subsequently along other parts of the rail network. The clinker and chips on which the rails rested provided a close parallel with the Mediterranean mountains which were the plant's original home but in addition (it is alleged) its floating seeds were drawn along in the stripstream of the passing trains, or even transported in the carriages themselves (the Victorian botanist George Claridge Druce described how he was accompanied by one on a train journey from Oxford to Tilehurst in Berkshire).[58] Although Oxford ragwort is now found widely in urban areas, displacing the indigenous ragwort (*Senecio jacobæa*), in rural areas it is still often closely associated with the rail lines. In Herefordshire, for example, it has been observed that it is largely restricted to waste ground lying within a quarter of a mile of the Hereford to Abergaveny railway; beyond, the indigenous ragwort is normally found. Other plants may have benefited in a similar manner, such as rosebay willow herb (*Chamaenerion augustifolium*).[59] Now a familiar plant of waste ground in both town and country, with its tall stems and vivid purple flowers, it was a rare woodland species, scarcely to be seen in many districts, in the eighteenth and early nineteenth centuries. It was described as 'scarce' in Northumberland in 1769, as 'rare' in Herefordshire in the 1840s, and as 'not often met with in a wild state, but common in gardens' in Hampshire in 1853.[60] But in the second half of the nineteenth century it spread rapidly. Again, it has been suggested that the plant's airborne seeds were sucked along the rail network in the slipstream of trains. In reality, as with other radical changes in species distributions, this one was probably the consequence of a number of factors, including the increase in the area of disturbed waste ground, and of thin soils over gravel and scree, that accompanied industrialization and urbanization. In 1867, the Worcestershire botanist Edwin Lees described how the plant was spreading through the Vale of Severn, 'incited to take possession of new-made roads and embankments. I have observed it by the side of a diverted road near Shatterford, and in the cutting of the Birmingham and Gloucester Railway, near Croome Perry Wood'.[61]

Other species may have been spread through the country in part as a consequence of the new rail network, including yellow toadflax (*Linaria vulgaris*) and the garden snapdragon (*Antirrhinum majus*).[62] But railways were as important for the range of new environments they provided – in terms of the steep slopes, thin soils and well-drained conditions of cuttings and embankments, as well as the dry ballast of the 'permanent way' on which sleepers were laid – as for their role as 'wildlife corridors'. Before the widespread use of herbicides to control plant growth, rail tracks were often characterized by displays of spring and summer flowers, species typical of well-drained soil, such as lesser toadflax.[63] A variety of maritime species was also commonly found in these locations, including sand sedge (*Carex arenaria*), possibly because early railways were sometimes laid on ballast brought from the coast, but probably because the new habitat was similar to that favoured naturally by the plant.[64] Embankments produced particularly striking combinations of species. Richard Jeffries described in 1883 how:

> The smooth express to Brighton has scarcely, as it seems, left the metropolis when the banks of the railway become coloured with wild flowers. Seen for a moment in swiftly passing, they border the line like a continuous garden. Driven from the field by plough and hoe, cast out from the pleasure-grounds of modern houses, pulled up and hurled over the wall to wither as accursed things, they have taken refuge on the embankment and the cutting. There they can flourish and ripen their seeds, little harassed even by the scythe and never by grazing cattle. . . Purple heathbells gleam from shrub-like bunches dotted along the slope; purple knapweeds lower down in the grass; blue scabious, yellow hawkweeds where the soil is thinner, and harebells on the very summit. . .[65]

Following the short-sighted contraction of the rail network in the 1960s, a number of abandoned cuttings and embankments have become nature reserves, and even Sites of Special Scientific Interest.[66]

The impact of coal use

The most important impact of the industrial revolution on the environment and wildlife in England in the period before the 1860s was almost certainly an indirect one: the success of canals and railways in ensuring that coal became the main form of domestic fuel in almost every corner of England. As we have seen, before the eighteenth century, many of the key semi-natural habitats in the countryside were in whole or part maintained by regular cutting for firing materials: these included not only ancient woodland but also hedges, heaths, moors and wetlands. The spread of coal use thus had major environmental implications, although the chronology of declines in traditional fuels (and thus of the habitats that provided them) was related in part to their particular characteristics, in terms of calorific value and the ease with which they could be extracted. The cutting of heaths thus declined faster than the coppicing of woodland, which was still continuing on some scale at the end of the nineteenth century.

As I have already emphasized, coal was a high-density material which was difficult and uneconomic to transport. William Harrison, writing at the very end of the sixteenth century, noted how its use was just beginning to spread 'from the forge into the kitchen and hall, as may appear already in most cities and towns *that lie about the coast*, where they have little other fuel except it be turf or hassock' [my italics].[67] This importance of water transport was still being noted by Pehr Kalm in 1748, who observed that coal could be found in London, and was widely burned in villages within a fourteen-mile radius, but 'in places to which they had not any flowing water to carry boats loaded with coals' the population continued to burn wood – mainly from 'trees they had cut down in repairing hedges' – or 'fuel of some other kind, as bracken, furze etc'.[68] The marked improvements in roads which took place in the course of the eighteenth century may well have encouraged the wider use of coal, but it was the creation of the canal network and the spread of railways that ensured the demise of traditional fuels; the longer it took for improved transport to reach an area, the longer traditional fuels were exploited. Well into the nineteenth century most of the kilns on the land-locked Bedfordshire brick fields were fired using heathland vegetation.[69] But coal began to replace gorse and heather here following the arrival of the local rail lines after 1838. The Duke of Bedford's steward, Thomas Bennett, recalled in 1869 how 'Furze used to be grown for a demand for brickmaking, but this fell off some years ago'.[70] Traditional fuel use also persisted longest among the poorer elements of society, and when commons were enclosed by parliamentary acts, especially in the east of England, a 'fuel allotment' or 'poors' allotment' was often created. While the rest of the former common was allotted to individual owners and often 'improved' – converted to arable fields – here the local poor could continue to cut gorse or turf or to dig peat, and in some cases graze livestock, although some allotments were rented out from the start, by the committees of the local worthies who controlled them, to purchase coals for them to burn instead.[71] In the county of Norfolk alone no less than 250 parishes had such allotments, some relatively small in size but others – as at Bridgham or Feltwell – extending over more than 100 hectares.[72] In some upland areas, especially the more inaccessible ones, enclosure commissioners often went further and allocated a 'moss dale' where not only the poor, but also those receiving their own allotment of land – farmers, smallholders and cottagers – could continue to cut peat.[73] Such allotments continued to be made into the middle decades of the nineteenth century, as at Troutbeck in Westmoreland in 1840.[74] Elsewhere, in places where extensive areas of heath, moor or fen survived enclosure, traditional fuels likewise continued to be exploited on a significant scale into the nineteenth century. As late as 1858 a total of six million heather turves were still being cut each year in the New Forest.[75] For the most part, however, the cutting of peat, furze and the rest was in steady decline throughout the late eighteenth and nineteenth centuries. The transition to a fossil fuel economy, as much as new farming methods and a fashionable enthusiasm for 'improvement', sealed the fate of many common wastes, providing further encouragement for their enclosure and reclamation to feed the burgeoning population.

Conclusion

Before the 1860s, the direct impact of industrialization on England's wildlife was probably more limited, and less negative, than sometimes supposed. Towns and industrial areas generally remained small by modern standards, and were often interdigitated with farmland, market gardens and the like. Quarries, waste tips, canals, railways and other industrial areas created new habitats, highly unnatural in character but perhaps no more so than the fields, woods and wastes of the wider rural landscape. Canals and railways also served as corridors for wildlife: they provided a degree of interconnectivity which was the counterpart, in biological terms, of that which allowed industrialization and (as we shall see) agrarian modernization. But these same improvements in communications also ensured that coal became the principal domestic as well as industrial fuel in England. This, together with other social and agrarian changes, rendered vast areas of woodland and 'waste' economically redundant, and thus encouraged their destruction.

CHAPTER SIX

The revolution in agriculture

The character of the 'agricultural revolution'

England's industrial revolution could not have happened without an accompanying improvement in agricultural production. As population soared, and as a higher proportion of the workforce came to be engaged in industry, food shortages would have occurred, rising prices would have choked off home consumption of manufactured products, and food imports would have leached abroad much of the capital required for industrial investment. Most researchers agree that this expansion in food supplies was largely the consequence of the adoption of new crops and rotations. Before the eighteenth century, the yields of cereal crops had been held back by a paucity of nitrogen and other key elements in the soil. These were constantly being depleted by cropping, as well as being leached away by precipitation, especially on lighter land. But the only significant source of fertility was manure, the quantities of which were limited by the fact that relatively few livestock could be kept over the winter. In spite of the spread of 'floating', supplies of hay were still limited in most areas. During the eighteenth century, however, turnips and clover were more widely adopted as field crops, alternating with courses of cereals in a variety of new rotations, of which the 'Norfolk Four Course' – a recurrent cycle of wheat, turnips, barley and clover – is the most famous.[1] The turnips (or other roots) were fed off in the fields by sheep or taken to cattle stalled in yards, while the clover (or similar green fodder crop) was grazed directly or cut for hay, and had the additional benefit of fixing nitrogen in the soil directly from the atmosphere. In reality, many farmers employed some variation on the 'four course', on more fertile soils for example often adding an additional cereal course, but the effects were much the same. More livestock could now be kept, more manure produced, and thus higher yields achieved.[2] The new forms of cropping were hard, although not impossible, to adopt where open fields existed, but these were now enclosed on a large scale using parliamentary enclosure acts. These also allowed vast areas of common land, formerly utilized as rough grazing and for fuel production, to be brought into cultivation. The two developments were often linked, for once fodder crops were grown in the fields and either consumed there, or in neighbouring farmyards, the downs and heaths were no longer required as places to graze the folding flocks: they too could be ploughed up and used to grow crops. Between 1750 and c.1840 production, of cereals especially, was thus increased both by raising the yields on existing arable land *and* by extending the cultivated acreage.

These innovations unquestionably increased production. But the 'agricultural revolution' was, in fact, a more complex process. To varying extents in different regions, small peasant farms were gradually replaced by larger capitalist enterprises, bringing efficiencies of scale to farming. In addition, the new rotations were more important in some districts – those of light, easily-leached land, the traditional 'sheep-corn' areas – than in others, where the soils were more fertile and held nutrients better.[3] Here other innovations were critical, such as the adoption of systematic field drainage, initially using 'bush' drains – trenches cut across fields which were filled with brushwood and/or various other materials, capped with straw or furze, and then backfilled with soil.[4] Even on light land the benefits brought by the new crops should not be exaggerated. In chalkland areas yields of barley increased by perhaps 50–100 per cent between 1750 and c.1840, but those of wheat, the main grain crop consumed by humans, probably rose by only around 25 per cent. It was in areas of heathy, sandy, marginal ground that the greatest increases occurred, with yields of wheat doubling and those of barley tripling: but this was particularly poor land and the increases were from a very low base.[5] It is also worth remembering – for it often seems to be forgotten by historians – that when a farm adopted the 'new' rotations the acreage devoted to grain crops fell: in a traditional course of 'two crops and a fallow', two-thirds of the land was devoted to growing cereals at any one time, but when an 'improved' four-course rotation was adopted this fell to half, offsetting to a significant extent the scale of the 'headline' yield improvement. Indeed, it is arguable that by sowing half their land with fodder crops farmers were in fact mainly trying to satisfy an expanding market for *meat*, especially among better-off town dwellers, rather than trying to enhance cereal yields. The fact that fertility on light land was no longer largely maintained through the use of mobile folding flocks also allowed the development of new sheep breeds, designed to walk little, and to grow fat in the fields of turnips and clover.

An increase in soil fertility resulting from increased manure would not in itself have served to increase yields. It would have benefited weeds as much as cereals: but here the new rotations brought other benefits. The turnips were planted in wide rows, allowing weeding, while the dense foliage produced as they matured shaded out competitors. Grain crops were also increasingly 'dibbled' in rows, rather than being broadcast, likewise allowing a greater intensity of weeding. This required large inputs of labour, and in a host of other ways the 'new husbandry' depended on a pool of flexible, relatively poorly paid workers. Manure produced by stall-fed cattle had to be brought into the fields, while on sandy land turnips would not grow well unless the acidity was reduced by marling – that is, the practice of excavating pits in the fields to reach a more calcareous subsoil, which was then spread on the surface – a particularly arduous and labour-intensive task. Neutralizing soil acidity was also crucial because nitrogen is converted into nitrites by soil bacteria which are highly susceptible to acidity. Without a healthy microbe population, any increased applications of manure would have been pointless: they could simply not have been broken down.

A cheap supply of farm labour was to some extent simply supplied by rapid population growth. But in addition it was an indirect consequence of industrialization, which served to concentrate manufacturing in certain areas of the country – the north and west, where water power was freely available and the principal coal reserves were located – leading in turn to a measure of de-industrialization in the south and east, and thus freeing up cheap labour for often seasonal or casual agricultural work. This was particularly important because of another significant change in economic geography. The complex pattern of agricultural regions which had developed by the seventeenth century, described in the previous chapter, included some mainly arable districts in the centre and west of England and some largely pastoral ones in the east. By the middle of the nineteenth century arable farming was – as today – firmly concentrated in the now de-industrializing east and south of England, where the climate was best suited to the production of cereal crops (Figure 18). The wetter western and Midland areas had been largely laid to grass. This revolution in land use patterns, which was arguably at least as important as any change in raising levels of agricultural production, was partly the consequence of enclosure, and of the adoption of new techniques like marling and under-drainage.[6] But it was mainly the result of improvements in transport infrastructure, which allowed crops to be cultivated in one area and moved with relative ease to another. Once again, we can see the close and intimate connection between the two 'revolutions'.

Moreover, a looming food gap was not only averted by improvements in agriculture. Rising sugar imports provided an alternative source of calories, while a decline in the proportion of people involved in outdoors manual work reduced the need for food: in 1863 the families of agricultural workers consumed almost 50 per cent more calories per adult male equivalent than those of urban workers.[7] Food consumption may also have been reduced simply because the population was warmer, thanks to the increasing availability of coal and the steady decline in the cost of clothing, prices for cotton garments falling in real terms by around 85 per cent between 1750 and 1850.[8] A slow but steady increase in the scale of potato cultivation, again closely connected with progressive improvements in transport systems, also played a part. Acre for acre potatoes yield twice as much nutrition as wheat but 'they are less concentrated as a food source . . . because of their high water content, their storage life is shorter, and the cost of transport much greater'.[9]

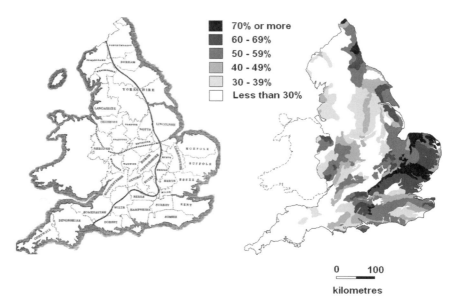

FIGURE 18 *In the course of the 'agricultural revolution' arable farming came to be more and more concentrated in the drier east of England.* Left: *the farming regions of England, as sketched by James Caird in 1851.* Right, *the proportion of land under cultivation in c.1840, based on the information contained in the tithe files (for methodology, see Williamson, 2002). Caird simplified the pattern of farming, but not radically. Both diagrams can be usefully compared with Figure 2.*

Some writers on wildlife employ the term 'high farming' to describe the new agricultural methods of the eighteenth and early nineteenth centuries which I have just described.[10] But this term is more correctly used for the more industrialized forms of agriculture that emerged from the 1840s.[11] 'High farming' was a high-input, high-output system which relied more on manufactured and imported materials, and which substituted durable fixtures and machines for high and regular inputs of labour.[12] One novel feature was the use of imported or manufactured fertilizers. Guano came into widespread use in the 1840s and '50s, together with bone dust, and in the 1840s superphosphates were developed by John Bennett Lawes: by the 1870s four million pounds were being spent each year on this particular commodity.[13] Another key innovation was the use of oil cake, a by-product of the rape and linseed oil extraction industries, as animal fodder. Although turnips, mangold wurzels, and swedes continued to be the main form of winter feed, the national consumption of cake rose from around 24,000 tons in 1825 to 160,000 in 1870.[14] The spread of the rail network helped ensure that by the 1870s, in the arable east of England, few farms lay more than ten miles from a supplier.[15] Livestock numbers rose still further, and the resultant increase in manure would have boosted cereal yields even without the use of the new fertilizers. Equally important were developments in farming infrastructure, with new forms of building; significant levels of mechanization, including the use of steam engines for threshing and, to a more limited extent, ploughing; and new systems of field drainage using earthenware pipes rather than trenches filled with stones or organic materials. Ceramic land drains had been sporadically used in the late eighteenth and early nineteenth century, either in the form of semi-circular tiles laid on flat 'soles', or as hand-made pipes, but pipe drainage was given a major boost by the development of a machine – patented by one Thomas Scraggs in 1842 – which could produce cylindrical clay pipes.[16] Fiscal changes in 1826 exempted drainage pipes from a tax levied on tiles and bricks, and a government loan scheme, allowing estates to borrow substantial sums for drainage and other improvements, were further encouragements.[17] Between 1847 and 1899, just under £5.5 million was advanced by the Land Improvement Companies responsible for administering the loans, but many large estates simply funded drainage programmes and other improvements from their own capital.[18] The practice of agriculture was thus revolutionized in two, overlapping but arguably distinct, phases. Both, not surprisingly, had major impacts on the environment.

Reclaiming the 'wastes': Downs, moors and heaths

The most important environmental effect of the agricultural revolution was unquestionably the enclosure, and the destruction or modification, of most of the great areas of common 'waste' that had previously existed in England. This process was already under way in the middle decades of the eighteenth century, with the ploughing up of many areas of grass heath and chalk downland in the south and east of England. As agricultural prices rose towards the end of the century, and reached dizzying heights during the French Wars, the assault intensified, but at the same time attention turned to the more challenging areas of 'waste', the high moors and the poorer, more acid heaths: a development fuelled as much, perhaps, by fashionable interest in 'improvement' on the part of landowners as by a careful attention to profit and loss.[19] A reduction in the number of small farms in England as agriculture became more commercialized made enclosure easier, for it reduced the number of people who had to agree to the change. The development of enclosure by parliamentary act further facilitated the removal of commons and open fields. The two-third majority required for an enclosure under this system was assessed, not on the basis of individual owners, but on the value of the acres they owned (Figure 19).

The declining importance of commons as a fuel source made them ripe for enclosure, while in many arable areas, as I have noted, the new rotations

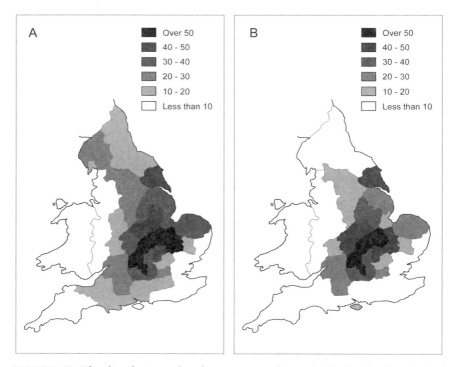

FIGURE 19 *The distribution of parliamentary enclosure in England, after Michael Turner.* Left *percentage of land area in each county enclosed by act: open fields and commons.* Right: *open fields only.*

involved the dissolution of the age-old distinction between permanent arable and permanent pasture, and brought an end to the great mobile folding flocks, making their daily walk from downs and heaths to fallows. Sheep-corn villages had often had between a quarter and a half of their land devoted to permanent grazing, but this was now drastically reduced. Where this had comprised grass heath, in particular, the expansion of arable was usually considerable: the thin deposits of sand were easily ploughed and reclaimed. Arthur Young famously described how in north-west Norfolk:

> All the country from Holkham to Houghton was a wild sheep walk before the spirit of improvement seized the inhabitants . . . Instead of boundless wilds and uncultivated wastes inhabited by scarce anything but sheep, the country is all cut up into enclosures, cultivated in a most husbandlike manner, well peopled, and yielding an hundred times the produce that it did in its former state.[20]

In biological terms the enclosure of heaths, downs and other lowland commons was disastrous, rendering many plants once common locally or even nationally rare. The nineteenth-century botanist George Claridge Druce was told how the soldier and monkey orchids (*Orchis militaris* and *Orchis simia*) had been 'tolerably plentiful about Whitchurch [Oxfordshire] till 1837': the chalk slopes were then pared and burnt, his correspondent describing how he 'actually witnessed the roasting alive of both Soldier and Monkey orchids'.[21] At Burford in the Cotswolds the pasque flower could no longer be found: 'The . . . locality is now brought under cultivation, and the plant is certainly extinct there'.[22] Charles Babbington similarly described in the 1860s how, until the start of the nineteenth century, the chalk hills of south Cambridgeshire had been

Open and covered with a beautiful coating of turf, profusely decorated with *Anemone Pulsatilla* [pasqueflower], *Astragolus hypoglottis* [purple milk-vetch], and other interesting plants. It is now converted into arable land, and its peculiar plants mostly confined to small waste plots by road-sides, pits, and the very few banks which are too steep for the plough. Thus many species that were formerly abundant have become rare. . . Even the tumuli, entrenchments, and other interesting works of the ancient inhabitants have seldom escaped the rapacity of the modern agriculturalist, who too frequently looks upon the native plants of the country as weeds, and its antiquities as deformities.[23]

Some of the land broken up as prices hit record levels during the Napoleonic Wars was abandoned again after a few years: but once the ancient, herb-rich pastures had been destroyed, it was hard to recreate them. In the 1880s, as a more serious downturn in agricultural fortunes set in, James Caird commented that 'there is no doubt that vast areas of poor down and heath land, in the south of England, were converted to arable at the beginning of this century – land that cannot be tilled profitably now, and that cannot be restored to its former condition within any reasonable limit of time, if ever'.[24]

Destruction of downs and heaths on such a scale was also detrimental to the country's fauna. There was, in particular, a significant reduction in the distribution and numbers of open-country, ground-nesting birds. By 1825 the hen harrier had disappeared from Kent, Essex, Wiltshire and the Forest of Dean, all areas in which it had been common before c.1800; and by 1850 it had also been driven from Oxfordshire, East Anglia and Yorkshire.[25] The stone curlew, once a common bird throughout southern and eastern England, declined dramatically in the course of the nineteenth century, although it finally died out in many counties only at the very end of the century (and hung on in Kent until 1909 and Yorkshire until 1937).[26] Such an extended chronology of decline, shared by some other species, suggests that factors other than the ploughing of heaths and downs played their part: the destruction of other habitats favoured by some of the species in question (wetlands in the case of the hen harrier, for example); the more intensive cultivation of arable land; the proliferation of hedges and plantations; and recreational shooting (see below, pp. 122–5). The way in which the effects of reclamation were compounded by other developments is well illustrated by the case of the great bustard. This was the iconic bird of the open downs and heaths – a huge creature with a weight that could reach 18 kilograms, making it an inviting target for sportsmen. J. Swayne reported in the 1780s how he had 'often heard conversations amongst farmers. . . [on Salisbury Plain] about the scarcity of bustards on the Down, which they attributed to the heath, etc., being broken up and converted to tillage, and to the corn being weeded in the spring, whereby the birds were disturbed and prevented making their nests'.[27] In the East Anglian Breckland, similarly, contemporaries reported how the bird had formerly nested in the arable as well as on heathland, in fields which were sown broadcast. Now, as crops were more intensively weeded by gangs of labourers, few nests survived. In addition, the open heaths and common fields were now divided by hawthorn hedges and tree belts:

> Not only entirely changing its aspect but rendering it entirely unsuitable to the wary habits of the bustard, which soon learned to become as jealous as any strategist of what might afford an enemy harbour.[28]

There were occasional later visits from bustards, flying in from abroad – in 1876 one appeared in Hockwold Fen in Norfolk, the first since 1838, and another was shot (and eaten) in the county in 1891[29] – but the species never again bred in England, until it was reintroduced at the start of the present century.

The areas of light land which saw the greatest feats of reclamation had been the main centres of rabbit farming in the seventeenth and early eighteenth centuries. Much of this land could now be made more profitable as arable fields and antipathy to warrens gathered pace. On the chalk Wolds of Yorkshire and Lincolnshire, for example, 'Few of the warrens listed in the early nineteenth century directories were recorded in the 1880s'.[30] Warrens seemed both old-fashioned and unneighbourly. One landowner could hardly invest in expensive 'improvements' if his neighbour continued to stock his land with rabbits, kept uncertainly within the warren banks.[31] Throughout the East Anglian Brecklands, and on the Wolds of Lincolnshire and Yorkshire, the ploughs of the improvers levelled the warren walls and fodder enclosures with peculiar thoroughness, and the land was given over to grain production.[32] The extent to which warrens declined should not, however, be exaggerated. In the sandy Breckland of East Anglia, and sporadically elsewhere, some continued to operate into the twentieth century. But in general, in England at least, the great age of rabbit farming was over.

In the old sheep-corn districts, extensive and continuous areas of heath and down were thus destroyed. In the 'woodland' districts of England innumerable areas of common land, ranging from small 'greens' to larger tracts of wood-pasture, also now disappeared. Enclosure was followed by the improvement of their rough pastures or by ploughing; vast numbers of pollards were felled. George Claridge Druce reported that the buck's-horn plantain (*Plantago coronopus*) could not be found in Ballingdon in the Oxfordshire Chilterns: 'the enclosure of Ballingdon Green has extirpated it'.[33] The northern section of the 2,000-acre Northaw Common in Hertfordshire still had thousands of pollards growing on it when enclosed by an Act of 1803: the work of division was continuing when the Ordnance Survey draft 2" map was made, the surveyor writing the words '?clearing for enclosure' across its area, indicating clearly enough its expected fate.

Enclosure and reclamation also occurred in the uplands, as the frontier of 'improvement' moved onto the moorlands of the north and west. Field drainage, using drains filled with stones, had been practised on a small scale for centuries on lower ground, but it was now more widely adopted.[34] The same was true of liming, a necessary remedy for the acute soil acidity which resulted from the high levels of precipitation on elevated ground.[35] In upland areas, there was nothing like the calcareous marl so useful in some lowland heathland districts, but limestone was often freely available which could be burnt in kilns and converted into lime.[36] Its benefits had long been appreciated: in 1628 the manor of Campsall in Yorkshire was said to contain 'great store of lymestone an excellent compost beinge burned to manure cold grounds'.[37] As inland waterways were improved, however, and as new canals were constructed, it became easier to move not only the limestone but also – more importantly – the coal to fire the kilns. Temporary sod kilns and simple stone-built 'flare kilns' were gradually supplemented by sophisticated 'draw kilns' in which limestone and coal were fed into the kiln continuously, and burnt together. The arrival of the railways ensured the development of larger industrial complexes with kilns arranged in batteries of two, three or more.[38]

Liming and drainage were employed on enclosed pastures, on the lower slopes, but were vital in the reclamation of the open moors. The most extensive and permanent schemes of 'improvement' were in areas below 300 metres OD and towards the south and east of the main upland masses, where moors were largely formed over podzols or acid brown earths and where waterlogging was mainly caused by iron pan at no great depth. Moorlands of this kind had already been reduced by encroachment and enclosure through the sixteenth and seventeenth centuries, but the process now continued on an increasing scale. Paring and burning, draining, liming and re-seeding were all employed to convert the heather and rough grass into improved pastures, often accompanied by deep ploughing to break up the iron pan. Much of the better land was even converted to arable. As prices rose in the 1790s and early 1800s, attention turned to the main blocks of high, peat-covered plateaux, and to the bleak fells, large tracts of which were enclosed by parliamentary acts. John Christian Curwen described in his presidential address to the Workington Agricultural Society in 1812 the recent 'disposition to carry the plough much nearer heaven than what was ever dreamed of a few years ago'.[39] Typical was the transformation of Whinfell in Cumberland after its enclosure in 1826, where John Nicholson obtained a compact allotment of upland moor, rising to 385 metres above sea level, which he surrounded and subdivided with drystone walls, and built a new farmstead called 'Hatteringill'. Stones were cleared, the moors pared and burnt, then harrowed and sown.[40] In such locations, more than anywhere else, ambitious schemes of reclamation were often fuelled mainly by a fashionable enthusiasm for improvement, and many were abandoned as prices fell back either at the end of the Napoleonic Wars, or later in the century.

The more permanent improvements made to the lower moors must have had a serious impact on wildlife. Even where the new fields were only converted to improved pasture the loss of heather, the dominant vegetation, would have led to a reduction in the numbers of characteristic upland birds: the golden plover, the red and black grouse, the hen harrier, the dunlin and the short-eared owl.[41] Improvements in drainage would have had a similar impact on birds like the lapwing, snipe and redshank. Even where moors survived enclosure and improvement, moreover, their character often changed. This was because the late eighteenth and early nineteenth centuries saw higher stocking levels in upland areas, for larger numbers of animals could now be over-wintered on fodder grown on lower ground; there was also an increasing emphasis, from the early eighteenth century, on sheep rather than on cattle, in part due to changes in the agriculture of lowland areas. Sheep tend to be selective grazers and, at high densities, suppress the growth of the more palatable plants and grasses, and of heather, leading to the development of a more uniform, species-poor acidic grassland characterized by *Nardus stricta*, *Molinia caerula* and reeds.[42] The decline in cattle may also have begun the spread of bracken across the uplands, which was to accelerate further from the later nineteenth century.[43]

In some areas, however, heather moors survived in a more robust condition. Landowners often favoured enclosure to allow for the protection, and more intensive management, of grouse. Here heather, the principal habitat for the grouse, was carefully nurtured, although as we shall see game keepers often waged a vicious war on other forms of wildlife. Large areas of 'waste' also survived in other contexts. There were very significant reductions in the area of grass heath, and of chalk grassland in the east of England – especially on the Yorkshire and Lincolnshire Wolds. But on the chalklands of the south many parishes still had 30 per cent, and some over 50 per cent, of their area under pasture in the 1830s.[44] The lower slopes were often brought under the plough but the higher downs were 'near the margin of profitable arable cultivation'.[45] The poorer heaths likewise often survived, in part because the deep sandy soils would never repay profitable cultivation and in part because extensive areas of grazing had to be maintained in order to keep the particularly large numbers of sheep which were needed to coax a reasonable crop from the poor soils of the arable. Indeed, a modified form of the old folding system, with daytime grazing on heaths and night folding on the arable, only declined in parts of Suffolk, for example, in the 1930s.[46] The continuing presence of warrens in some of these districts was a further disincentive to 'improvement', while some heaths survived, in the manner already described, as 'fuel allotments'.

Enclosure, in other words, was not the same as improvement and this, together with the fact that both the total area of common waste enclosed by parliamentary act, and the amount removed by other means, remain matters of debate makes it hard to ascertain the quantity of ancient pasture, moor, heath and fen which was lost in the course of the eighteenth and nineteenth centuries. But it was clearly a very great deal. Probably around 3 million hectares in England were affected by parliamentary enclosure, of which well over half – probably c. 1.8 million hectares – comprised common waste, as opposed to open-field arable.[47] If only a third of this had subsequently been 'improved', it would still amount to an area greater than the counties of Bedfordshire, Hertfordshire, Buckinghamshire and Middlesex combined: an ecological transformation on an awesome scale.[48]

Wetlands destroyed

The ploughing of heaths, downs and other commons, and the improvement of moorland, unquestionably had a significant negative impact on a wide range of wildlife. But it was probably the draining of wetlands which caused the greatest amount of damage. As we have seen, early attempts at draining the Fens of eastern England were only partly successful. Daniel Defoe, crossing the Gog Magog Hills near Cambridge in the 1720s, saw the Fens in the distance 'almost all covered with water like a sea . . . the Michaelmas rains having been very great this year'.[49] The poor state of drainage explains, of course, the vast numbers of birds which continued, throughout the eighteenth century, to be caught in the local decoys, as well as the continuing prevalence of malaria in the district, evidence of the large numbers of mosquitoes still present, carriers of the parasite *Plasmodium*.

As agricultural prices rose in the later eighteenth century, some improvements were made to the waterlogged pastures. The formation of Drainage Commissions allowed local drainage to be better organized, and in the early nineteenth century there were changes to the main arterial channels, with the construction of the Eau Brink Cut in 1821, the Ouse cut between Ely and Littleport in 1827, the North Level Main Drain between 1831 and 1834 and the new outfall to the Nene in the late 1820s.[50] But above all, drainage was radically improved through the employment of steam pumps in place of drainage windmills. Steam pumps could lift more water through a greater vertical distance, and they continued to operate whatever the wind conditions. The first was erected, at Sutton St Edmund in Lincolnshire, in 1817[51]: by 1852 J. A. Clarke estimated that whereas there had once been around 700 drainage windmills between Cambridge and Lincoln, the same area was now served by a mere 17 steam engines, which collectively drained upwards of 222,000 acres (90,000 hectares).[52] Drainage was improved still further in the course of the nineteenth century through further refinements in drainage technology including the adoption of light 'grasshopper' steam engines, and (from the 1850s) of Appold's centrifugal or turbine pump. By the 1870s, around 75 per cent of the East Anglian Fenland was under the plough. Many of the fields were tile-drained, and the 'soak' of acid water in the ditches was permanently kept down to a level which would not injure the growing crops. In place of wet grassland, and ditches brimming with water, the Fens had attained their modern appearance: arable fields, filled with wheat or potatoes, extended to the far horizon. Only scattered fragments of undrained fen survived. Babbington described in 1860 how 'With the water many of the most characteristic plants have disappeared, or are become so exceedingly rare that the discovery of single individuals of them is a subject of wonder and congratulation' among botanists. He believed that with the exception of Wicken Fen – which still survives as an important nature reserve – 'there is scarcely a spot remaining . . . in which the ancient vegetation continues undisturbed'. Even the 'absolutely aquatic' plants had suffered, because many of the drainage ditches now dried out completely in the summer.[53] Such a landscape could not sustain the vast flocks of birds which had once thronged it. Richard Lubbock in 1847 described how 'oats are grown where seven or 8 years back *one hundred and twenty-three* Snipes were killed in one day by the same gun'. Upcher in 1884 voiced similar sentiments, commenting that 'The 'trips' of Dotterell (*Eudromis morinellis*), formerly so regular in their appearance, are now scarcely ever seen in our fen country'.[54] The bittern, thought Stevenson in 1885, was 'another of the birds which drainage and enclosure has driven from their old haunts'.[55] There were similar declines in invertebrates, with the large copper butterfly, once a common sight in the Fens, disappearing entirely from the area by the start of the twentieth century: it now hangs on in only a few places in the Norfolk Broads.

When drained wetlands lay under pasture the height of the water in the dykes, as we have seen, was kept artificially high throughout the year, almost at the level of the adjacent land. The margins of the dykes are thus poorly defined, trampled and muddy. When ploughed, in contrast, water levels are kept lower and the ditches are given a steep-sided 'v' shaped profile and have margins with smaller areas of mud and a less well-developed marginal vegetation. The old form of dyke margins would have been an important resource for a very wide range of invertebrates, including *Anopheles*, the mosquito host of the parasite *Plasmodium*, the carrier of malaria. The loss of this pest from the landscape by the later nineteenth century represented, in a strict sense, a reduction in the nation's biodiversity. The fact that it is never discussed as such is a reminder that very few people really believe that *all* of England's native wildlife should be protected and encouraged in the wild.

In some cases, especially in the north and west of England, the drainage of wetlands was less problematic for wildlife. The vast fens of the Somerset Levels, for example, partly reclaimed in the seventeenth century, were systematically eradicated following a series of parliamentary enclosure acts. In the 1770s, the Brue valley began to be drained and between 1780 and 1800 the valleys of the Axe and Cary were reclaimed. The north levels – between the Mendips and the Severn estuary – were enclosed and largely drained in the first three decades of the nineteenth century, and the south levels – the valleys of the Parret, Tone, and Yeo – between 1810 and 1840.[56] These ambitious programmes involved the construction of a number of new arterial channels, as well as the cutting of many hundreds of minor drainage ditches.[57] The drained land was not put to the plough, however, but instead divided into small pasture fields, bounded by drainage dykes lined with pollarded willows: a landscape which remained attractive to wetland birds, and rich in aquatic plants and invertebrates. Many other western wetlands, such as the carrs of north Shropshire, reclaimed between 1750 and 1850, likewise remained largely under grass. But some of the great mosses of Cheshire and Lancashire, drained in the first 40 years of the nineteenth century, were – like the fenlands of the east – converted to arable.[58] The observations made by Coward and Oldham following the drainage of Carrington Moss, the last major reclamation of this kind, in 1886 provides some indication of what was lost. Previously the area had comprised:

> Six hundred acres of moorland . . . the haunt during the breeding season of the Red Grouse, Short-eared Owl, Curlew, Common Snipe, and Twite. An interesting instance of the change in bird life wrought by cultivation is exhibited in the rapid colonising of Carrington Moss, after its reclamation, by the Common Bunting.

For the most part, as here, wetland drainage in the nineteenth century was an environmental disaster, reflected in the marked declines in the numbers of once common birds like the bittern, marsh harrier, ruff and black-tailed godwit, clearly apparent in nineteenth-century county avifaunas, as well as in the loss of large numbers of wetland plants documented in successive surveys, in Cambridgeshire especially.[59]

New fields and hedges

While large-scale reclamation and 'improvement' clearly had adverse effects on wildlife, it might be thought these were partly offset by the innumerable new hedges planted when the open fields and commons were enclosed. In the 1970s Max Hooper and his colleagues compared the bird life recorded in Laxton (Nottinghamshire) – one of the few places in England where open fields have escaped enclosure – with that found in neighbouring, more conventional parishes. Laxton 'only supported populations of the open field species – mainly skylarks and some grey partridge, red-legged partridge, and lapwing, and one pair of reed bunting was found in a hollow. Most of the ordinary farm birds were entirely absent although common enough in the surrounding countryside'.[60] It is important, however, not to exaggerate the impact of the hedges planted during the agricultural revolution period. By 1750 more than three-quarters of England already lay in hedged or walled fields; more importantly, particular features of the new hedges ensured that their ecological benefits were limited. As we have seen, before the eighteenth century most farmers and landowners had planted mixed-species hedges. With the spread of coal use the importance of hedges as a source of firing declined: they came to be regarded simply as barriers to livestock, and as property boundaries.[61] At the same time, the proliferation of nurseries made it easier to acquire large quantities of hedging thorn. Neat, straight, hawthorn hedges now became the norm, and multi-species hedges on the old pattern were regarded as untidy and old-fashioned. Agricultural writers also urged that hedges should be maintained, not by coppicing or even laying, but instead by regular trimming.[62] In reality, in the Midlands especially many were still regularly laid, but the idea of single-species planting unquestionably triumphed, and rigorous coppicing went into marked decline.

The authors of the various *General Views*, produced in the decades around 1800 to describe the practice of farming in the different counties of England, regularly contrasted 'recent' and 'old' hedges in terms of the shrubs they contained. The Rev St John Priest in the *General View of the Agriculture of the County of Buckinghamshire* of 1813, for example, noted that the hedges 'are of two sorts, old and new. The old fences consist chiefly of a mixture of ash, sallow, and hazel, with some whitethorn . . . The new fences consist of whitethorn. . .'.[63] John Boys, writing about Kent, emphasized the difference between 'old hedges, such as Nature has formed', and the newer 'quickset hedges raised from the berries of the white thorn';[64] while in Cheshire the contrast was between the new enclosures, of 'white, or hawthorn', and the 'ancient fences', consisting of 'hasle, alder, white or blackthorn, witch-elm, holly, dogwood, birch &c &c'.[65] Nor was the principal reason for the change lost on contemporaries. As Young put it, a hedge of thorn, kept neatly trimmed rather than being plashed or coppiced, was 'a mere luxury and ornament, and has nothing profitable to recommend it'. He added, significantly: 'Hedges thus cease to be the collieries of a country' (Figure 20).[66]

Hawthorn was not the only hedging plant favoured by eighteenth- and nineteenth-century 'improvers'. Blackthorn was sporadically employed; in

FIGURE 20 *Typical nineteenth-century hedge, planted with and still largely composed of hawthorn, with sparse oak standards.*

some sandy areas of eastern England, especially Breckland, Scots pine hedges were favoured; while a few hedges were planted with more exotic species, such as the Duke of Argyll's Tea Plant *Lycium barabarum*, introduced from China in the 1730s. Whatever was planted, single-species hedges – especially if trimmed rather than regularly laid or coppiced – will have supported a smaller range of species than more substantial and more intensively managed ones, containing a greater range of shrubs.[67] They provided less food for birds and lacked the diversity of structure provided by the recurrent cycles of cutting and regrowth. Most of the new hedges, moreover, did not have much in the way of an accompanying bank or ditch and in arable districts farmers ploughed close, leaving only narrow lines of unploughed ground, poor substitute for the ribbons of pasture running through the old open fields or (in many areas) the myriad of balks which had formerly divided the individual lands. Babbington in 1860 bemoaned how, as a consequence of enclosure in west Cambridgeshire 'the "balks", with the various plants which grew upon them' had been 'destroyed by the plough. Thus the native plants have suffered . . . Where they were once abundant they are now rarely to be found'.[68] In arable areas, moreover, the new rectangular fields were often very large. Those on the Yorkshire Wolds generally covered between 30 and 70 acres[69]: on the Lincolnshire Wolds they were said to be '30 to 100 acres, presenting to the eye of the stranger the aspect of open-field lands' because the hedges were often concealed by the rolling topography.[70] Not surprisingly, Cobbett in April 1830 complained that the 'one deficiency' of the countryside around Horncastle in the heart of the Wolds was 'the want of singing birds':

> We are just now in the season when they sing most. Here, in all this country, I have seen and heard only about four sky-larks, and not one other singing bird of any description.[71]

The spread of hedges in champion districts has often been discussed. Less attention has been paid to changes in the field boundaries of old-enclosed, 'woodland' districts, especially in south-east England and East Anglia. Most of these areas occupied relatively heavy clay soils, and in the seventeenth century many had been involved to some extent in cattle farming. They contained vast numbers of species-rich hedges and farmland trees, and numerous woods and commons; they were among the most biologically diverse landscapes in England. Considerable effort and investment were now directed towards simplifying and tidying these environments, as the spread of coal and rising population put a premium on producing food rather than fuel, and as the changing geographies of agrarian production encouraged conversion of land from pasture to tilth. Small, irregularly shaped fields were inconvenient for ploughing; tall hedges and hedgerow trees shaded the crops, harboured vermin and took up potentially productive land. Fields were thus amalgamated on a large scale, hedges straightened and replanted with hawthorn (Figure 21). The rector of Rayne in Essex observed in the 1790s how on one farm in his parish 'the fields were over-run with wood', but 'since Mr Rolfe has purchased them, he has improved them by grubbing up the hedgerows and laying the fields together'.[72] In 1791, a government enquiry into the state of the nation's timber supplies was initiated which asked a number of questions, including: 'Whether the Growth of Oak Timber in Hedge Rows is generally encouraged, or whether the grubbing up of Hedge Rows for the enlarging of fields, and improving Arable Ground, is become common in those Counties?'.[73] Grubbing out was reported to be widespread, especially in the south and east of the country. One respondent from Suffolk stated that 'Much Timber and the Improvement of Arable Land are incompatible. Arable land in Suffolk is improved, and therefore timber is lessened'.[74] He added: 'Underwood, particularly Blackthorn Bushes, in Hedge Rows that spread Two or Three Rods wide, is the true nursery of Oak Timber, but such Rows are a dead Loss and Nuisance in a well cultivated Country'.[75]

The density of farmland trees, and especially of pollards, was reduced more generally. Large landowners regarded pollarding as an unsightly and backward practice. 'Let the axe fall with undistinguished severity on all these mutilated heads', urged Thomas Ruggles in 1796 in the *Annals of Agriculture*, while William Marshall declared that pollards were 'unsightly; they encumber and destroy the Hedge they stand in (especially those whose stems are short), and occupy spaces which might, in general, be better filled by timber trees; and, at present, it seems to be the prevailing fashion to clear

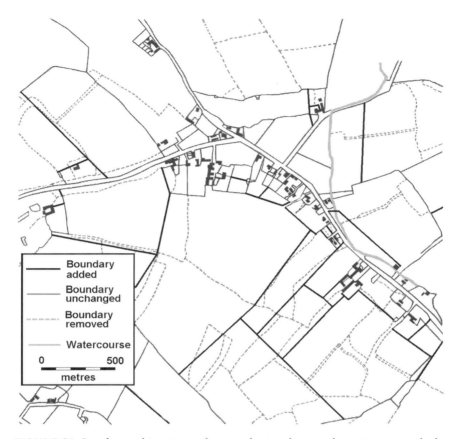

FIGURE 21 *Landscape historians often emphasize the transformation wrought by the enclosure of open fields and commons in the eighteenth and nineteenth centuries, but this period also saw a measure of 'de-enclosure' in many old-enclosed districts. This map, drawn up in 1825, shows how one landowner (George Hall) planned to modernize the landscape at Weston Colville in south eastern Cambridgeshire. The plan was only partially executed.*

them away'.[76] Perhaps of even greater importance was the loss of numerous ancient coppiced woods: the declining value of underwood in many areas encouraged their conversion to farmland, especially as the heavy soils which they often occupied could now be improved by underdrainage. The extent of all these changes varied from parish to parish, with the greatest alterations occurring where large estates, and keen 'improvers', held much of the land. But to some extent they affected all anciently enclosed areas, and in 1801 one observer of the Essex countryside was able to declare: 'what immense quantities of timber have fallen before the axe and mattock to make way for corn'.[77] In general, the countryside in these anciently enclosed districts was neater, tidier, than it had ever been before.

The pattern of farming

Wildlife was affected by developments in the practice of farming as much as by changes in the physical landscape. As Shrubb has emphasized, the most important of these was the way in which arable fields were cropped, under rotations featuring turnips and other roots, and clover.[78] It is often said that these ensured that land was no longer left fallow for a whole year, something which would have had a serious impact on birds like greenfinch, goldfinch, linnet and chaffinch, which fed off fallow weeds like groundsel and thistles, and on those like the corncrake which nested in the stubbles.[79] It is important to note, however, that in most forms of the new rotations a course of wheat, harvested in the late summer, was followed by one of turnips, sown in the middle of the following summer. In some cases, especially in areas of light land, this may have ensured that weeds and stubbles remained intact until at least late spring, although more usually – and especially on heavier ground – the soil was repeatedly ploughed and harrowed from late February, and sometimes during the previous autumn, to prepare the fine tilth required for the turnip seed. In some circumstances, in other words, birds dependent on the fallows may have been less affected by the change in rotations than is usually assumed. But for the most part the new rotations did shorten the duration of fallows, thus reducing their opportunities severely. More importantly, birds of all kinds suffered from the increasing intensity with which crops were now weeded, as we have seen in the case of the great bustard. Turnips were drilled or – more usually – planted in rows, and then regularly hoed until the leaves were large enough to shade out competitors. Wheat was also increasingly 'dibbled' rather than sown broadcast, or even drilled mechanically. It, too, could now be weeded, leading to the destruction of the nests of birds like the skylark, and to a further reduction in feeding opportunities for those which relied on the seeds from cereal weeds or the invertebrates associated with them. Not surprisingly, county avifaunas show that the goldfinch – a bird largely dependent on the seeds from thistles – declined steadily throughout England in the course of the nineteenth century.[80]

Yet at the same time turnips, vetches and other fodder crops provided a much-needed source of nutrition for some species.[81] Turnips were rich in invertebrates, such as the turnip moth *Agrostis* and the turnip sawfly or jigger, now extinct, and these would have been devoured eagerly by birds like plovers and larks.[82] Clover also brought a number of benefits, providing winter food for skylarks and doves, and – in the spring – opportunities for ground-nesting birds like the corncrake and corn bunting.[83] Undersown with the previous barley course, and thus already well grown when this was harvested, clover provided a habitat particularly rich in sawflies and other invertebrates.[84] It is also probable that invertebrate populations were enhanced by the large loads of dung brought into the fields in the spring from the cattle over-wintered in yards. The increased volume of grain produced would itself have benefited birds like the greenfinch and linnet, for a proportion of the crop would always be dropped during harvest, while stacks in rickyards could not easily be protected from birds. In Shrubb's view, supported by a systematic and detailed examination of contemporary avifaunas, the new cropping systems 'were overwhelmingly beneficial to large numbers of farmland birds'.[85] Indeed, some species – such as lapwing, stockdove, corncrake, skylark and yellowhammer – which had formerly nested or lived for much of the time on adjacent areas of waste, but from which they were now displaced by enclosure and reclamation, seem to have adapted (albeit to varying extents) to a life spent largely in the fields.[86]

One bird in particular benefited from the 'new husbandry'. We have already seen how, to judge from the churchwarden's payments for vermin control, the wood pigeon was fairly rare in England in the early eighteenth century. Its numbers rose steadily thereafter, for it feasted on the leaves of turnips and other 'roots', and to some extent on clover: Gilbert White, writing about the Selbourne area in 1780, attributed its recent success to 'the vast increase in turnips'.[87] By 1850 there were said to be so many pigeons in the Cotswolds that in some parishes farmers were ceasing to sow vetches as a fodder crop.[88] The rabbit likewise benefited from the increased winter sustenance afforded by the new crops, although its spread in the course of the eighteenth and early nineteenth century may have also been helped by the increase in hedgerows in former champion districts, and the cover they provided. Either way, by the 1820s, it could be claimed that the rabbit was the most common wild animal in Norfolk.[89]

As noted earlier, across the Midland 'shires' the enclosure of arable open fields was generally followed, not by more intensive forms of arable farming, but by an increase in the area of land under pasture. The responses made by vicars and rectors to a government enquiry into the standard of the harvest of 1801 (the 'Crop Returns') provide some indication of the scale of this development. The vicar of Breedon on the Hill, for example, remarked how in Leicestershire:

> Within the last 30 years almost all the country north-west of Leicester to the extremity of the county has been enclosed: by which means the land is become in a higher state of cultivation than formerly; but on account of a great proportion of it being converted into pasturage much less food is produced than when it was more generally in tillage.[90]

At Twyell in neighbouring Northamptonshire, it was said that 'less corn is grown since the enclosure . . . the land being laid down in grass'; at Ufford, Bainton and Ashton there was 'less corn of all sorts once the enclosure which took place three years ago',[91] while Wilbaston, enclosed in 1798, was still in 1801 in the process of being 'laid or laying down, for grazing'.[92] Across large tracts of ground the weeds of arable fields thus declined sharply, while those associated with permanent pastures increased. Although it would have taken time for a rich and complex sward to develop, certain features of these new pastures immediately encouraged diversity. The fossilized remains of old plough ridges ensured, within a limited area, considerable variation in soil water content (Figure 22). Plants like white clover (*Trifolium repens*) displayed a marked preference for the ridges while spear thistle (*Cirsium vulgare*), ragwort (*Senecio jacobaea*) and nettle (*Urtica dioica*) flourished in the furrows.[93] The number of field ponds increased markedly following enclosure, providing key habitats for a wide range of plants, fish and invertebrates;[94] and not only the rabbit, but other small mammals, benefited from the increase in cover afforded by a landscape of hedged pastures. It is likely that the decline in the cultivation of cereal crops across large swathes of the Midlands and west caused reductions in the numbers of some granivorous birds.[95] On the other hand, more grassland may have increased the numbers of winter visitors, especially lapwings, plovers, thrushes, and starlings, although not perhaps those of ground nesting birds, as evidence suggests that stocking densities in the new fields were high. Local practices had particular effects, although not necessarily immediately. On the Cheshire plain, the pastures were fertilized with 'marl', calcareous mud dug from shallow pits. By 1900 it was said that 'the advance in the manufacture of artificial manures has caused them to be disused, and now they are choked with vegetation. The Moorhen builds among their flags and rushes, and the Sedge Warbler and Reed Bunting sing in the rank herbage and bushes that clothe their margins'.[96] Agricultural change brought winners and losers, although we lack the evidence to assess these in much detail.

The environment of 'high farming'

The high-input, high-output farming systems that began to develop in the 1830s had their own particular impact on the environment. In the eighteenth century field drainage, carried out by means of bush drains, had been largely directed towards arable land. It was now more widely applied, the new ceramic pipes often being installed in order to improve grassland. Phillips has calculated that some 4.6 million acres (1.9 million hectares) must have been drained between c.1840 and 1880, about 35 per cent of the poorly draining land in England: much of it was pasture.[97] This must have removed many of the damp flushes which constitute the more interesting and varied parts of the sward, especially in places where the soil is neutral and moderately fertile. One pasture field at Cheadle near Staffordshire was described, immediately before it was drained, as having 'turf . . . not of an inferior description except that it is full of rushes and other aquatic plants'.[98] Improved systems of land drainage also further encouraged the destruction of further areas of ancient woodland on heavy land in arable districts.[99] Drainage had other effects. Some contemporaries worried about the way in which more rapid run-off from the land led to increased pressure on rivers.

FIGURE 22 *Ridge and furrow in Northamptonshire. The progressive grassing-down of the Midland 'shires' in the course of the post-medieval period served to fossilize under pasture the former plough-ridges of the open fields. The expansion of arable farming in the Midlands since the Second World War, combined with widespread re-seeding of established pastures, has rendered views like this increasingly rare.*

John Bailey Denton, for example, thought that 'floods are more quickly precipitated into the valleys, in proportion to the extent of under-drainage in the various river basins', and urged that if yet more agricultural land was drained, rivers would need to be extensively engineered.[100]

High farming brought a host of other changes. Seed drills came into more widespread use, so too did mechanized hay mowers. The former allowed for a further intensification of weeding, often now carried out with a horse-drawn hoe; both ensured greater disturbance of ground-nesting birds, probably accounting for the marked decline in the numbers of corncrake recorded in nineteenth-century avifaunas in the period after c.1850.[101] Threshing machines, from the 1860s fitted with both winnowing mechanisms and rotary screens, removed weed seeds more effectively from the threshed crop, including that part of it destined for use as seed the following year, something which may have led to declines in cereal weeds like common corncockle (*Agrostemma githago*), thorow wax (*Burpleurum rotundifolium*) and cornflower (*Centaurea cyanus*).[102] Above all, the use of imported or manufactured fertilisers, and of cattle cake, raised the quantities of nitrogen in the farm environment to unprecedented levels. Already there are signs that watercourses were suffering from eutrophication – that is, the build-up of nutrients (nitrogen and phosphorous) which promotes the excessive growth of plants, favouring the development of simple algae and plankton over more complex species. As this proceeds the water becomes cloudy, reducing the amount of light reaching the bottom; as the algae die, moreover, their decomposition by bacteria uses up oxygen in the water, causing problems for fish. Many pondweeds and other plants which float on the surface flourish in these conditions, as does much of the emergent vegetation – that is, plants which are rooted in the bed of the stream or lake but which rise above the surface of the water. But slower-growing waterweeds, which live largely or entirely beneath the surface, fare badly. By the 1850s the Norfolk Broads – the network of East Anglian lakes, largely formed by medieval peat digging, which were already acknowledged as one of the most important areas for wildlife in England – were beginning to suffer. They were largely surrounded by prime arable land which was now receiving ever higher doses of both fertiliser and dung from cake-fed cattle. The waters, once crystal-clear, grew cloudy, and plants such as horned pondweed (*Zanichellia palustris*), water soldier (*Stratiotes aloides*), hornwort (*Ceratophyllum demersum*) and water-lilies were suppressed by the growth of pondweeds such as the stoneworts and bladderworts.[103] Such changes, well documented here, may have been widespread in arable areas. Rapid eutrophication also perhaps provided conditions for certain invasive species to flourish, and the rapid spread of Canadian pondweed through the English waterways in the middle of the nineteenth century (above, p. 85), while certainly facilitated by the new canal network, may have also been a consequence of increased levels of phosphates and nitrates in the water.

Amalgamation of fields and the replanting of hedges in old-enclosed country continued and probably intensified in the 'high farming' period, encouraged in particular by the use of steam engines for ploughing, for the engines and their complicated tackle could only work efficiently in large, and preferably rectangular, fields. Agricultural writers continued to rail against the wastefulness of hedges, the way they harboured vermin and increased the costs of cultivation; Grant in 1845 reported their continued removal in Devon.[104] Hoskyns, writing about his experience of clayland farming in 1865, described them as 'unproductive in themselves of anything that is good' and 'equally an obstacle to the plough that toils for bread, and the eye that wanders for beauty'.

> The waving and extensive Corn-field, the deep rich winter verdure of the turnip-crop, the dark and mellow surface of the fallow, owe little of beauty to the net-work of intersecting barriers that arrest at once the plough and the prospect, and carry a running nest of robbers, like earthworks of the enemy, through the fair fields of human skill'.[105]

But not everyone thought the same. In the 1880s, at the very end of this phase of agricultural expansion and intensification, the vicar of Scarning in Norfolk, Augustus Jessop, bemoaned how:

> The small fields that used to be so picturesque and wasteful are gone or are going; the tall hedges, the high banks, the scrub or the bottoms where a fox or weasel might hope to find a night's lodging . . . all these things have vanished.[106]

Conclusion

In a host of ways, the impact of the agricultural revolution and 'high farming' on wildlife presents an uncertain picture. In part this is because of a lack of reliable evidence. But is also reflects the fact that changes in the fortunes of particular species were seldom the result of one development, but rather of a range of human activities, some of which had little to do with agriculture *per se*. In addition, certain species unquestionably benefited from some at least of the changes I have described. The new crops and rotations, and perhaps the new geographies of agricultural production, increased the numbers and the range of species like rabbit and wood pigeon, and perhaps benefited farmland birds more generally. Yet against this, the dissolution of the age-old distinction between permanent arable and permanent pasture, which lay at the heart of the 'new husbandry', allowed the ploughing up of many thousands of hectares of heath and down, while the reclamation of wetlands destroyed on a significant scale habitats of unparalleled richness. Enclosure was the enemy of biodiversity: although surviving areas of common land are generally impoverished by neglect, they still account for some 20 per cent of Sites of Special Scientific Interest in England and Wales.[107] Those birds, mammals and invertebrates which benefited from enclosure and 'improvement' tended to be generalists, what we now think of as the common fauna of farmland: for agrarian change created a more homogenous countryside, of enclosed fields interspersed with areas of woodland, in place of the more dramatically diversified landscape of earlier centuries, with its great tracts of wetland, heath, wood-pastures and the rest. Specialists like the stone curlew and quail displaced from the wastes but unable to adapt to the food-rich but intensively cultivated farmland thus fared badly. But it is possible that even the more common species of birds and mammals suffered to some extent from the greater intensity of cultivations, and from the general 'tidying up' of the countryside which accompanied agricultural improvement and the transition to a coal-based economy. Most contemporaries certainly thought so. As one commented in 1885: 'The general enclosure of commons and waste lands, the thinning of hedgerows, together with various other farming operations resulting from modern improvements in the system of agriculture, have each, in turn, affected particular classes of birds'.[108]

CHAPTER SEVEN

New roles for nature

Introduction

The fate of England's wildlife in the later eighteenth and nineteenth centuries cannot be understood entirely in terms of the direct impacts of industrialization and agricultural 'improvement'. We need also to consider a number of related social developments. In particular, more people than ever before now lived without any direct involvement in the business of farming, or any practical engagement with the countryside. Large numbers of workers were employed in industry; an industrializing economy required engineers, accountants, surveyors, bankers, as well as factory workers, while the larger and more centralized state which emerged from the late seventeenth century needed a standing army, and a growing cohort of administrators and tax collectors. This new body of town-dwellers required more shops, inns and other facilities than rural ones. In short, the population became steadily more urban, and less rural, in character.

Of particular importance were the lifestyles enjoyed by the upper tiers of society, their interests and attitudes. Members of the established landed elite were fully involved in industrial and colonial expansion and in the eighteenth century forged social links with the upper echelons of the expanding middle classes, the two groups coalescing into a single 'polite society' with shared fashions, tastes and norms.[1] Subsequently, as industrialization gathered pace in the nineteenth century, the middle class as a whole became more economically, culturally and – in time – politically important. But throughout the period most members of these dominant groups shared a similar range of views regarding the 'natural world'. They possessed, in particular, a tendency – present to some extent in the seventeenth century but now more prominent in public discourse – to conflate, or at least to confuse, 'nature' and 'the countryside', to see the rural landscape as something almost independent of human activity. Vicesimus Knox in 1779 typically described the 'natural delights of rural scenery'; William Cowper in 1785 more famously asserted that 'God made the country and man made the town'.[2] Landscapes became objectified: their appearance and visual qualities were discussed and celebrated in a manner that effectively divorced them from the processes of their creation. The countryside became a fitting subject for painting; rural landscapes were described in painterly terms; while the grounds of mansions might, under the supervision of designers like William Kent in the 1730s and 40s, be composed like the paintings of Claude Lorraine, with a carefully contrived foreground, middle ground and distance. But concepts were shifting and uncertain, and in the 1750s and 60s, under Lancelot 'Capability' Brown and his contemporaries, extensive tracts of ground around country houses were shaped along supposedly 'natural' lines which consciously rejected many of the characteristics of normal rural scenery, such as farms and cornfields, comprising instead sweeping panoramas of grazed turf, woods and scattered trees, free of obvious human activity, agrarian or otherwise. The words employed by critics of Brown's style betray further confusion, William Chambers for example asserting that his parklands 'differ little from common fields, so closely is common nature copied in most of them'.[3] Towards the end of the century, and into the nineteenth, there were further developments. 'Picturesque' writers like Uvedale Price and Richard Payne Knight advocated, as Kent had done before them, that landscapes should be designed in the form of paintings, while tourists equipped with the Rev Gilpin's guide books sought out the correct places from which to view a series of rural prospects.[4] Such people favoured more rugged terrain, as opposed to gently pastoral scenery, although in both the design and the appreciation of landscape the 'picturesque' was also about variety and *detail*.[5] Beauty could be found in the lowlands as much as the uplands: in the rutted lane with high hedgebanks, where 'The winter torrents, in some places wash down the mould from the upper grounds and form projections . . . with the most luxuriant vegetation; in other parts they tear the banks into deep hollows, discovering the different strata of earth, and the shaggy roots of trees'.[6] People in the eighteenth and nineteenth centuries thus discussed and appreciated landscapes as never before, and to varying extents considered the countryside as something essentially 'natural' in character. More importantly, they were able to impose their ideas on the environment in an unprecedented way. In spite of escalating demands for food, more and more of the land surface came to be managed for aesthetics and recreation. There were two main aspects to this.

First, towns and cities increased in scale and began to exhibit a measure of social zoning. Areas occupied by the homes of the 'polite' contrasted with central districts increasingly given over to trade and manufacture and, in the case of the larger examples, overcrowded slums.[7] In such working-class districts, conditions were often unsanitary, with closely packed houses and unpaved streets. But in the more salubrious suburbs, gardens filled with 'poorly competitive, slow-growing and crippled plants often living outside their normal climate range' occupied extensive areas of ground.[8] Beyond the suburbs, moreover, there was usually a belt of countryside densely populated by affluent 'villas' – diminutive country houses – with elaborate pleasure grounds or small parks, but often without other attached land.[9] Satellite villages became increasingly gentrified. Defoe in 1722 described the numerous houses lately erected in Stratford, Walthamstow, Woodford, Wansted and West Ham: 'this increase is, generally speaking, of handsome large houses being chiefly for the habitation of the richest citizens'.[10] Proximity to urban centres allowed those with commercial, political or industrial interests to keep a ready eye on business, and made it easier for them to access shops, public spaces, assemblies and other opportunities for fashionable consumption and display. The penumbra of suburbs and mansions, gardens and parks was most marked in the case of London. Directors of city banks, wealthy merchants, and retired army officers all moved *en masse* into the neighbouring counties. Arthur Young commented in 1804 that 'Property in Hertfordshire is much divided: the vicinity of the capital; the goodness of the air and roads; and the beauty of the country' had led 'great numbers of wealthy persons to purchase land for villas'.[11] But other major cities had similar hinterlands, in which gardens, parks and 'lawns' occupied extensive tracts of ground.

Second, and more importantly, this period saw the growth – out beyond the fringes of the towns – of large landed estates, a development associated with the revolutions in agriculture and industry but, like them, with older roots. Landed estates may, for convenience, be defined as extensive and continuous areas owned as absolute private property. At their heart lay a mansion and its grounds, usually accompanied by a 'home farm' which was retained 'in hand'. Beyond lay farms which were leased to tenants, together with a scatter of plantations and game covers likewise retained under the owner's direct control (Figure 23).[12] Aristocratic properties might extend over 10,000 acres (c.4,000 hectares) or more; the estates of the local gentry embraced a parish or two, and ranged from perhaps 1,000 to 10,000 acres (400–4,000 hectares).[13] Whatever the scale of their possessions, landed families vaunted their antiquity, and their own ancient roots. But while some landowners had indeed come over with the Conqueror, rather more could trace their ancestry to individuals who had successful careers in law or royal administration in the sixteenth and seventeenth centuries, or who had more recently grown rich through finance, trade or manufacturing.[14] And while often described as a 'relic of the feudal age', in reality the landed estate was a specifically modern form, for its distinguishing feature was untrammelled power over extensive tracts of countryside. In the Middle Ages estates had seldom comprised continuous, unitary blocks, and rights over land had been complex and diffuse. The customary tenants – villeins and cottars – owed rents and services to a local lord, but farms passed by inheritance within peasant families and in many cases customary land could be bought

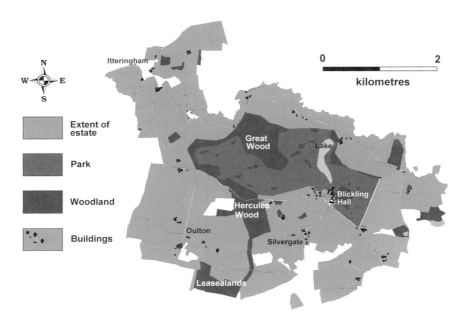

FIGURE 23 *Blickling in north Norfolk, a typical medium-sized landed estate, in c.1840. Note the size of the park relative to the property as a whole, and the extent of woods and plantations. Great Wood is partly medieval in origin: the others were all planted in the eighteenth and nineteenth centuries. Some small, outlying portions of the property are omitted.*

and sold, the rents and obligations attached to it simply passing to the new proprietor. Only the home farm of the manorial lord – the 'demesne' – was his absolute property in the modern sense.

The landed estate began to emerge in the course of the fifteenth and sixteenth centuries, alongside modern concepts of ownership. In some cases, lords managed to convert customary tenancies into forms of tenure – particular types of 'copyhold' – which meant, in effect, that they were freehold owners, and that their tenants were tenants in the modern sense. In addition, large landowners were always on the lookout for new additions to their estate, properties which could be purchased from other freeholders on the fringes of or, in particular, intermixed with their own land. In 1813 the agent of the Blickling estate in Norfolk described how various parcels had been purchased over the previous years 'some of which are so situated as to have been an eye sore from the Mansion house till Lord Suffield became possessed of them'.[15] As an earlier steward put it in 1773, 'If I hear of any uncultivated land or otherwise if adjoining part of your Lordships Estate to dispose of I will apply after it and acquaint your Lordship of it immediately'.[16] Growth of large properties was encouraged by the Dissolution of the Monasteries in 1539, and in the later seventeenth century by legal changes – the development of the entail and the strict settlement, which made the owner of a property in effect a tenant for life, tied by a legal agreement which prevented sale of outlying portions of land so that the estate passed undivided to his heir.[17] It was also assisted by the simple fact that, following the Civil War and the Glorious Revolution of 1688, royal power was limited, political authority resided in a parliament of the propertied, and estates were thus unlikely to be broken up because their owners fell from royal favour, or supported the losing side in dynastic or religious struggles. The stability of the political system, and internal peace, as well as providing the conditions for industrial expansion, thus also created the circumstances in which landed estates could grow. Lastly, large landowners benefited from the enclosure of common land, not only receiving their own allotment in lieu of manorial rights but also often purchasing, within a short space of time, many of the diminutive parcels allotted to the smaller freeholders.[18]

The development of landed estates is central to any understanding the history of wildlife because their owners had the ability to transform, without the hindrance of planning authorities or other constraint, the character of the environment across large areas.[19] But they did not develop to the same extent everywhere.[20] They tended to be most numerous and extensive in the more remote districts, and especially in areas of poor, light soil characterized by arable farming, such as the Lincolnshire Wolds. In such areas small owner-occupiers found it hard to make a living as a national market in grain developed in the course of the post-medieval period, especially in times of depression.[21] They were also characteristic of some upland areas, again where land was relatively cheap but could be made more valuable through investment in the necessary 'improvements'.

The 'great replanting'

One of the most important environmental consequences of the emergence of large estates was a marked upsurge in planting which served to reverse the long-term decline of tree cover in England. Some writers have suggested that the eighteenth century was a period in which continuing deforestation brought problems to many of England's larger animals.[22] Yet while it is true that many coppiced woods were grubbed out to make way for farmland, and large tracts of wood-pastures felled when commons were enclosed, many new areas of woodland were also established, more than compensating – in area at least – for such losses. In Norfolk, for example, around half the area of woodland existing at the end of the eighteenth century was probably less than a century old.[23] The greatest amount of new planting occurred in districts which had formerly carried relatively little tree cover – champion areas and uplands especially. Here, afforestation often formed part of wider programmes of estate 'improvement': examples include the huge plantations established by the Sykes family in the Wolds of Yorkshire; the 150,000 trees planted annually in the 1770s and '80s by the Earl of Selbourne at Bowood in Wiltshire, and the two million planted at Holkham in Norfolk between 1782 and 1805.[24] Old-enclosed 'woodland' areas, in contrast, generally witnessed less new planting.

Tree planting was intimately connected with the rise of great estates because only those owning extensive properties could afford to put hundreds of acres out of agricultural production, foregoing immediate for medium- or long-term financial benefit. The new climate of political stability was also important, for only those who expected to pass on land to their children and grandchildren would plant over it.[25] The enclosure of heaths and moors was a further encouragement, for forestry made good economic use of the more marginal land. But landowners were also fired up by patriotism and by the writings of John Evelyn, whose book *Sylva, or a Discourse on Forest Trees* of 1664 was followed by a rash of similar texts, including Stephen Switzer's *Ichnographica Rustica* of 1718.[26] People believed that wood and timber supplies were running low, Batty Langley in 1728, for example, stating that 'our nation will be entirely exhausted of building timber before sixty years are ended'. Men like Phillip Miller (1731), James Wheeler (1747), Edmund Wade (1755) and William Hanbury (1758) were also concerned about the military implications of a timber shortage, and throughout the century the government worried about how to provide the vast quantities of timber required by the Royal Navy dockyards.[27] Yet landowners also planted simply to beautify their estates, and to demonstrate their extent, as well as to provide cover for game.[28]

Most of these new woods were *plantations*, consisting entirely of timber trees and without a coppiced understorey, a reflection in part of the declining value of underwood in many, although not all, parts of the country as industrialization proceeded. Deciduous species – particularly oak, sweet chestnut and beech – were mixed with a rather larger number of conifer 'nurses', usually Scots pine, spruce and larch. In the words of Nathaniel Kent, they comprised 'Great bodies of firs, intermixed with a lesser number of forest trees'[29] Because it was difficult to deal with weeds, and also because significant losses were anticipated from the depredations of rabbits and other animals, the trees were usually planted more closely than would be the case today, often at a density of nearly two per square metre. They were then progressively thinned, starting with the conifers: a process which began when the plantation was 10 years old, sometimes earlier.[30] Plantations thus became, over time, less coniferous and more deciduous in character, and also less densely timbered. In most cases, the final timber crop was itself only thinned, so that the plantation lived on in the landscape. In some contexts, however, plantations of pure conifer – larch and Scots pine – were planted, entirely for commercial purposes. Already there were critics of the effect these had upon the landscape, although less to the establishment of plantations on moors and heaths than to their impact on more domesticated terrain. As Wordsworth put it, describing such plantations in the Lake District:

To those who plant for profit, and are thrusting every tree out of the way to make way for their favourite, the Larch, I would utter . . . a regret, that they should have selected these lovely vales for their vegetable manufactory, when there is so much barren and irreclaimable land in the neighbouring moors, and in other parts of these islands.[31]

It is often suggested that post-medieval woods, whatever their precise character, were and are of minimal importance in terms of nature conservation. But judgements are as ever made difficult by the necessity of distinguishing between the immediate state of the areas in question, and their condition as they reached and passed maturity. Because plantations were often managed for aesthetics as much as for their monetary value, the trees within them were frequently retained for longer than would have been the case in traditionally managed woods – thus providing in abundance the kinds of micro-habitat associated with only mature or over-mature specimens. Many woods planted in the eighteenth and nineteenth centuries are now important local nature reserves, such as Old Park Plantation in Church Fenton, Yorkshire or Rock Plantation near Markfield in Nottinghamshire.

When first planted the smaller woods and belts probably benefited the more common farmland birds, and almost certainly further encouraged – together with the cultivation of root crops – the spread of the pigeon. But in addition, in Yalden's words, a number of woodland mammals 'were saved in time by the provision of new habitat'.[32] The red squirrel had become relatively rare by the seventeenth century. It hardly figures in the payments made by churchwardens for the eradication of vermin.[33] Its numbers recovered markedly in the eighteenth century, however, and almost certainly as a direct consequence of afforestation. Deer also benefited, although they remained fairly rare in the wild, and the return of the red deer to Dorset at the start of the nineteenth century was the result of deliberate re-introduction from Scotland.[34]

In certain circumstances, these new woods acquired many of the characteristics of ancient woodland. Coppices were still sometimes planted,[35] and might be colonized, with surprising speed, by many of the key 'indicator species' (dogs mercury, wood anemone, primrose and the rest), at least where they had been planted beside ancient hedges or close to existing woods. Such 'pseudo-ancient woods' can be found in many old-enclosed districts, and many are included in Natural England's *Ancient Woodland Inventory*. Nor was the management of existing areas of ancient woodland entirely neglected by landowners in this period, although it is noticeable that coppice rotations often increased in length, from around 9 or 10 years in the seventeenth century, to 13 or 14 years by the late nineteenth. This development probably reflects an increase in the density of standard trees, as the price of timber – and of oak bark, used for tanning leather – rose relative to that of underwood products. The growth rate of the coppice was thus reduced by canopy shade, as the tithe files of the 1830s sometimes indicate.[36] At Congham in Norfolk, for example, the coppice was said to be 'much injured by the timber',[37] while at Fulmodestone in the same county it would have been 'much better if timber was thinner'.[38]

We should also note that the 'great replanting' tended to extend woodland and woodland-edge environments into areas from which these had been absent for several centuries, even millennia: champion districts, or areas of heath, down and moor. It served, like the spread of hedges, to homogenize the lowland landscape. It also changed the distribution of some native trees: beech was now planted far to the north of its natural range, while the Scots pine, which had apparently died out in lowland England in the Roman period, and only sparingly planted in gardens in the seventeenth century, was widely established in parks and on estates in the eighteenth, and began to act like an indigenous plant once again, spreading of its own accord. By 1844, William Howitt could describe how the 'sandy heaths of Surrey are covered in many places with miles of Scots fir'.[39]

Hunting and shooting

The upsurge in planting was in part fuelled by the development of organized game shooting, and in a wider sense it was through an obsession with field sports that great estates made their greatest impact on the environment. During the eighteenth century shooting became more organized and formalized, the consequence of a number of factors.[40] At the start of the century, as we have seen, guns were large and unwieldy by modern standards. Birds were generally shot at or near the ground, by small groups of friends accompanied by setters and spaniels. Shooting was a casual pastime, and it was generally accepted that legally qualified sportsmen could shoot without asking over a neighbour's land. By 1760, however, the average length of guns had dropped to 3' 6", and by 1790 to 2' 6", allowing birds to be shot in larger numbers, and in the air.[41] Shooting steadily became more competitive, and shoots involved larger numbers of participants, culminating in the emergence of the *battue* in the early nineteenth century, in which large numbers of birds were driven towards the waiting guns. The scale of aerial slaughter was then further increased. In the 1840s and '50s French gun-makers developed breach-loading guns, which broke in two for loading and which used integral cartridges, fired by a hammer which struck a central pin, a system which was further elaborated through the 1860s and '70s by British gunsmiths. In the nineteenth century, shooting became one of the great pivots around which the social life of the 'polite' was organized, providing one of the spaces where marriages were negotiated and political and commercial deals clinched.

Greater numbers of birds were now required, and systematic rearing and preservation were rendered easier by enclosure and the consolidation of ownership – there was little point in carefully rearing game if it simply wandered off on to a neighbour's land. John Byng, visiting Blenheim in 1787, noted 'In various parts of the park . . . clusters of faggots around a coop, where are hatched and reared such quantities of pheasants that I almost trod upon them in the grass'.[42] And it was the pheasant, rather than the partridge, which became the main quarry in lowland England. It occupied relatively small territories, and could thus be raised in large numbers; it was ideally suited to the new style of shooting. '*Phasianus colchinus* shot up over the tree-tops like a rocket, its long tail flaunting, its cocketting cry an incitement to the sportsmen below'.[43] But the pheasant is a woodland bird, and thus major campaigns of planting were required to provide it with a suitable habitat. It was, moreover, a bird of the woodland edge, seldom straying more than twenty metres from the boundary with open ground, thus ensuring that many of the new plantations took the form of clumps or long, narrow belts.[44] When first planted the dense stands of young trees provided excellent cover but as they matured the bare ground beneath needed to be underplanted, sometimes with indigenous box but often with aliens like snowberry and Oregon grape from north America, Portugal laurel from the Mediterranean, or rhododendron *ponticum* from south-west Asia, 'the crowning plant for game cover'.[45]

In upland areas, and at a slightly later date, it was the shooting and management of grouse which had the greatest impact, especially in the east of the country – on the North York Moors and on the eastern flanks of the Pennines – where the most extensive areas of heather moorland, the principal habitat of the grouse, could be found. What was initially a casual sport was again transformed by the spread of enclosure and developments in firearms, as well as by the growing enthusiasm for the picturesque, and an associated appreciation of upland scenery among the social elite.[46] The steady improvement in upland roads and the elaboration of the rail network also served to make the remote moors more accessible. Here, too, the sport developed in such a way that the birds were driven towards the guns, concealed behind the new enclosure walls cutting up the moors, or in specially constructed stone butts. Shooting in this manner was well established by the 1830s and ubiquitous by the 1870s.[47]

As in the lowlands, larger numbers of birds were required.[48] Grouse will eat insects when young, and will sporadically consume bilberry and other moorland plants, but its principal food is heather. Small areas of moorland had sporadically been burned for centuries in order to encourage the growth of succulent young shoots for the sheep flocks. This practice was adopted in a more systematic form in the 1850s, spreading rapidly through the 1860s.[49] Long strips or 'swales' of vegetation were burned in rotation so that there were always areas in different stages of regrowth in reasonable proximity. The ecology of the moors was altered in other ways. Drains were often dug into the wetter areas, in order to encourage the growth of heather at the expense of purple moor-grass, cotton grass and bog-moss, something which deprived birds such as snipe and redshank of suitable nesting areas.[50]

Estates vied with each other to maximize the amount of game which was shot, the magazine called *The Field*, which first appeared in 1853, regularly publishing the numbers bagged by individuals and parties. But large concentrations of plump game birds were a magnet for poachers. The Black Act of 1723 was followed by important pieces of anti-poaching legislation in 1755, 1770, 1773, culminating in the Night Poaching Act of 1817. This laid down a penalty of 7 years imprisonment to any person caught with equipment which might be used for poaching in 'any forest, chase, park, wood, plantation, close or other open or enclosed ground'.[51] Unnatural concentrations of game birds were also, more importantly in the present context, a target for non-human predators, and as early as 1792 John Byng described how hawks, nesting in quarries, were being destroyed because of the threat they posed to game.[52] Gamekeepers waged a long and savage war on a variety of birds: the crow, the jay, rook and various forms of gull, which would take eggs and young game birds; and the peregrine falcon, the sparrowhawk, the kestrel, the osprey, the hen harrier, buzzards and red kite, together with various kinds of owl, which predated on adults.[53] The decline of most of these species in the course of the nineteenth century, while in part the result of habitat change, was mainly a consequence of improvements in firearms technology and an increase in the intensity of game preservation.[54] No less than 17,000 gamekeepers were recorded in Britain in the census of 1871.[55] Naturalists saw them as the principal enemies of wildlife, one in 1876 describing how they 'seize every opportunity of destroying almost every wild bird, beast and reptile that is not game'.[56] The red kite, once one of our commonest birds of prey, was extinct in England by the end of the century. The hen harrier, still moderately common at the start of the nineteenth century, had gone by its end.[57] The buzzard fared little better. It was extinct in Kent as early as 1810, and in Norfolk by 1820; by 1865 it was said to be 'by no means common and nearly exterminated in the eastern and midland counties'.[58] By the end of the century it was confined to Devon, Cornwall, and the far north-west of England.[59]

Gamekeepers also worked hard to control stoats, weasels, rats and foxes, but it was their success against the pine marten, polecat and wildcat which had the most serious consequences. The latter was still relatively common in the north of England, and in the Welsh Marches, in 1800 but was last recorded at Eslington in Northumberland in 1853.[60] In 1800 the pine marten was present in every English county except Wiltshire. By 1850 it had disappeared from much of Midland and southern England, and by the early twentieth century survived only in the Lake District and possibly the Cheviots.[61] The polecat was found in every county until 1850, in spite of many centuries of hostility towards it. By the early twentieth century, it survived only in parts of Cumberland and Yorkshire (Figure 24).[62]

The chronology of this latter decline may reflect the arrival of the breach-loading gun in 1851. Indeed, to some extent declines in wildlife in this period were related as much to the character and wider availability of firearms,

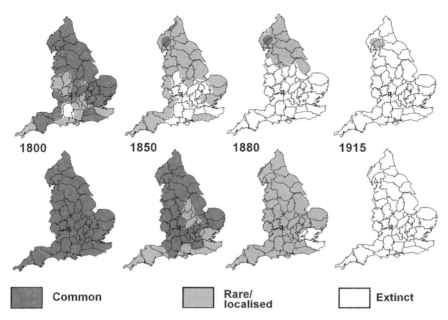

1800   1850   1880   1915

■ Common   ■ Rare/localised   □ Extinct

FIGURE 24 *The progressive elimination of the pine marten* (top) *and polecat* (below) *from England in the course of the nineteenth and early twentieth centuries. The effective disappearance of both species was largely, although not entirely, the consequence of persecution by gamekeepers (after Langley and Yalden 1977).*

as they were to game preservation *per se*. Recreational shooting included both the targeting of rare species so that they could be stuffed and displayed, and the casual slaughter of birds for idle amusement. In 1835 Charles Waterton described how, on the Yorkshire canals, 'not a water-man steers his boat along them but who has a gun ready to procure the Kingfisher', adding: 'If I may judge by the disappearance of the Kite, the raven, and the Buzzard from this part of the country I should say that the day is at no great distance when the Kingfisher will be seen no more in this neighbourhood, where once it was so plentiful'.[63]

In areas where game shooting was important systematic attempts were made to eradicate foxes. But elsewhere they were carefully preserved as a quarry. Until the end of the seventeenth century, fox hunting was largely a matter of pest control. Members of the aristocracy and gentry did hunt foxes recreationally, but usually by surrounding the animal within the earth and setting dogs upon it. The classic form of the 'sport', involving a long chase across country, is usually said to have developed in the Midlands, and especially in Northamptonshire, Leicestershire, and Rutland, counties which always held pride of place in the geography of hunting.[64] Organized fox-hunting required, it is said, a countryside divided up into large blocks of property rather than one characterized by a multiplicity of intermingled peasant farms; and one dominated by grass rather than by arable. The former allowed hunters to pursue the fox without the objections of proprietors; the latter ensured that its scent held up well, as well as allowing the horses to ride fast, without damaging standing crops.[65] The enclosure and grassing-down of the Midland 'shires' in the course of the eighteenth century produced (in the words of the writer Surtees) a landscape comprising 'grass, grass, grass, nothing but grass for miles and miles', ideally suited to hunting.[66] The emergence of the most notable hunts, like the Quorn or Pytcheley, thus went hand-in-hand with the spread of enclosure.[67]

This plausible story has, however, recently been questioned by Jon Finch and Jane Bevan.[68] The earliest organized hunts in England actually began, in the late seventeenth century, in unenclosed chalkland areas, such as the Wolds of Yorkshire, and they were well established in the Midlands before 1750. There, huntsmen shunned areas already enclosed, preferring to hunt across the surviving open fields and changed the location of their activities as enclosure proceeded. They avoided, wherever possible, jumping hedges and other obstacles, preferring a clean run across open ground, following the ribbons of unploughed ground beside slades, and the various 'green ends' and cow commons; or riding across the wide expanses of the fallow fields.[69] The Midlands rose to prominence as the character of the sport itself developed, reflecting changes in the landscape. The ploughing up of wolds, downs and heaths in light soil areas reduced the number of foxes to be found there and, together with the virtual eradication of fallows, made it harder to ride uninterrupted for long distances. In the Midlands, in contrast, the area of pasture increased with enclosure. By the second quarter of the nineteenth century, hunters were beginning to take pride in jumping the new hedges.[70]

Hunting made its own particular contribution to the environment. Enclosure removed many of the areas of rough ground where foxes could find shelter, so that landowners were obliged to establish coverts – small areas of gorse and other scrub, often planted with a few ornamental trees – where foxes could breed in safety, and where huntsmen could expect to find their quarry. These developed, through natural succession, into the small woods in field corners which are often found in the Midlands, and sporadically elsewhere.[71] Some hunts even created artificial earths, networks of brick tunnels, to encourage the fox to breed. Fox hunting was less damaging to wildlife than game shooting, for the fox had no predators which keepers needed to persecute. The establishment of coverts provided some, admittedly fairly marginal, additions to local habitats; and while many thousands of individual foxes met with an untimely and brutal end, everything possible was done to encourage the fox as a species. Indeed, it has been argued that, without the rise of organized hunting, the fox might well have disappeared altogether from large areas of England, such was the scale of persecution by farming communities and gamekeepers.[72]

Parks and gardens

In the course of the eighteenth and nineteenth centuries, as estates grew larger, and as smaller 'villa' properties proliferated and suburbs expanded, gardens and ornamental grounds came to occupy a larger and larger area of the country. In the early decades of the eighteenth century, the gardens of the social elite were still laid out in a geometric style but, under the influence of designers like Charles Bridgeman, the more fashionable examples became simpler, with less emphasis on parterres and more on smooth lawns, clipped hedges, gravel paths, and areas of ornamental woodland. Enclosing walls began to be removed – especially where a house possessed a deer park – and replaced by a sunken fence or 'ha ha', so that uninterrupted views could be enjoyed out from the garden across wider, and often wilder, prospects.[73] By the 1730s, William Kent was designing pleasure grounds which were entirely irregular in appearance, with trees scattered as individual specimens, or gathered into clumps.[74] These tendencies were taken further after c.1750. Under the influence of Lancelot 'Capability' Brown, Richard Woods and Nathaniel Richmond, it became fashionable to clear away all geometric gardens and walled courts from the vicinity of mansions, relocate kitchen gardens to some less visible position, and to remove formal features in the wider landscape, especially avenues. Ornamental pleasure grounds, characterized by winding paths and specimen (and often exotic) trees and shrubs, continued to exist but they were now placed to one side of the house. The park – an expanse of grazed turf irregularly scattered with trees – was now the principal setting for the fashionable mansion. Some of these 'landscape parks' were created by modifying earlier deer parks but most were new creations, made at the expense of the working countryside. Sometimes they included a lake of irregular or serpentine form; most featured clumps of trees; and they were often surrounded in whole of part by a woodland belt which served to block out close views of the working countryside.[75]

In part the enthusiasm for these casually irregular landscapes reflected the new enthusiasm for 'nature' which emerged among the social elite as England became more urbanized, industrialized and intensively cultivated.[76] But the fact that successive designers in the landscape tradition found fault with the allegedly artificial, *unnatural* character of their predecessor's work should remind us that nature is a problematic and shifting concept. These elegant landscapes did not closely resemble any of the surviving semi-natural landscapes in England except, perhaps, a kind of tidied-up version of the traditional deer park. In part they fulfilled a number of social needs. Surrounded by woodland belts, and with entrances guarded by lodges, the park was a landscape of exclusion, symbolising the increasing segregation of landowners from local communities.[77] Settlements were occasionally removed when parks were created, and roads and footpaths were often closed or diverted.[78] Parks also served to articulate social relations within the upper levels of society, defining the boundaries of the 'polite', marking off the owners of large estates and the occupants of 'villas' on the fringes of town both from members of local farming communities and from less wealthy, more decidedly middle-class neighbours, not least because the creation of a park demanded a commodity which they lacked – land in reasonable abundance. Above all, the removal of orchards, nut grounds, fish ponds, dovecotes, and farm yards from the vicinity of the mansion, something which always accompanied the destruction of walled geometric gardens, expressed a lack of involvement in the active production of luxury food: indeed, the sharp decline in interest in displaying forms 'intermediate exploitation' beside a mansion was one of the most striking aspects of the 'landscape' style.[79] Even deer were increasingly excluded from parks and replaced by sheep and cattle. In part this was because they played havoc with ornamental planting and thus made unsuitable denizens of these manicured and designed landscapes. But more importantly they, like fish, rabbits and pigeons, fell somewhere between the new enthusiasms for agricultural 'improvement', and for the shooting and hunting of animals which were more clearly 'wild'. Fish ponds, rabbit warrens and the like thus came to occupy an uneasy position in the minds of landowners, and appeared archaic and unfashionable.[80] At Chatsworth, as we have seen (above, p. 64), the main view from the mansion, into the eighteenth century, had remained across the great canal complex, still used as a fish farm, and out to the rabbit warren on the far side of the river Derwent. As late as 1756–57, there were 335 breeding couples there.[81] But when Capability Brown was commissioned to modernize the landscape in 1758, the warren was the first feature to be targeted. A note in the accounts records that 'The Warren was destroyed 1758, sold all the rabbits'.[82]

Especially in counties where smaller 'villas' were thick on the ground, parks collectively occupied very large tracts of land. In Hertfordshire, to the north of London, they already accounted for around 6 per cent of the surface area by 1766, but this had increased to some 10 per cent by the 1880s.[83] Today, surviving parklands often form islands of relatively unimproved pasture within what are otherwise intensively farmed landscapes. This contrast would have been less marked in the eighteenth and nineteenth centuries but in the arable east especially they would have provided some refuge for mammals and birds displaced from local pastures by the shift to arable husbandry, and from the neighbouring commons by enclosure. Some of the older parks and pleasure grounds are now particularly rich floristically. The Great Lawn at Chatsworth, probably laid out by William Kent in the 1730s but in an area already partly lawned by 1699, is a good example.[84] No less than 56 species of angiosperm have been recorded here, including many not normally thought of as inhabiting lawns, such as tormentil (*Potentilla erecta*), heath milkwort (*Polygala serpyllifolia*) and yellow mountain pansy (*Viola lutea*).[85]

Many parks were provided with lakes, an important boon to wildlife, especially wildfowl. Many today function as County Wildlife Sites or Sites of Special Scientific Interest, such as that at Eridge Park on the Kent/Sussex border. Parks also usually contained much old timber. Earlier hedgerow trees were almost always retained when parks were laid out, most of them pollards which ceased to be cropped as soon as they became features of these ornamental landscapes.[86] This practice provided an instant parkland appearance, while ancient specimens around a mansion hinted, often spuriously, at a family's longevity in a particular location. An affection for old trees was, however, something more widely shared at the time. Contemporaries describe a countryside filled with ancient, named trees, a source of pride to local people. James Grigor typically described in the 1830s how the oak called 'King of Thorpe' in Norfolk had 'become to the villagers an object of veneration and awe: their children know it, and run eagerly and proudly to show it to us'.[87] The Sherwood Forest oaks, the Boscobel Oak in Shropshire (where Charles II had allegedly found refuge), the great oak at Winfarthing in south Norfolk, were all firmly on the tourist trail. But however widely shared an affection for old trees might have been the sheer scale of the demand for wood and timber ensured that practical considerations generally took precedence over aesthetic and romantic ones. Standards were generally felled before they were a century old; pollards would be cut up for firewood once their productivity declined in senescence. It was thus usually only the wealthy who could afford to preserve ancient trees from the woodman's axe, propping up particular specimens with wooden poles, or binding their splitting trunks with iron. Eighteenth-century estate maps often show examples close to country houses, such as the 'Queen Oak' in Brocket Park in Hertfordshire, depicted (with a seat around it) on a map of 1798.[88] At nearby Panshanger in 1757 a visitor to the home of Spencer Cowper described how 'The finest oak in all this country is in his woods – 5 yards & a half round, & not the least decayed – he has made a grand Walk thro the coppice to it'.[89] The strong association of the oldest trees, so important as we have seen for biodiversity (above, p. 24), and the parks and gardens of the wealthy, is still apparent today. In Norfolk, for example, it has been calculated that over half the oaks existing today with girths of six metres or more are found in such locations.[90]

As well as retaining trees from the earlier agricultural landscape, Brown and his contemporaries also planted vast numbers of new ones, in belts and clumps, and as free-standing specimens. Most were indigenous hardwoods, mainly oaks and elms, with some ash and beech and the occasional lime and sweet chestnut. But conifers, especially cedar of Lebanon, Scots pine and larch, were more prominent than we usually think: because of their shorter lifespan, these have not usually survived to the present, ensuring the dominance of their longer-lived indigenous companions.

Parks continued to be the main setting for great mansions and smaller villas alike into the nineteenth century, but gardens then began to return to prominence, grew increasingly formal and geometric in design, and were once again placed below the main facades of the mansion. Under mid-century designers like William Andrews Nesfield formal parterres of box became popular once more. Yet fashions had not quite come full circle: such gardens were placed, not in walled enclosures, but on low balustraded terraces affording open views across the park.[91] Their parterres, moreover, were filled with bedding plants – geraniums, pelargoniums, lobelias, calceolarias and similar tender exotics, raised in glasshouses or other sheltered locations and planted out in flamboyant and colourful displays in the summer months. There were changes, too, in the design of parks. A more diverse planting pallet was employed, with larger numbers of horse chestnut, lime, and copper beech and with increasing numbers of exotics like monkey puzzle, Lombardy poplar, Turkey oak and Wellingtonia.[92]

Although Victorian parks and gardens thus boasted large numbers of introduced aliens, we should not underestimate the importance of these in the eighteenth century, not so much in the wider parkland as in the pleasure grounds beside country houses, and in the gardens of fashionable villas and large suburban houses. Indeed, the eighteenth century saw a 'positive deluge of new plants' from America and Asia.[93] This was a period in which commercial nurseries flourished. In 1700 few had existed outside the environs of London. By 1800, they were widespread in the provinces, providing hedging for the new enclosures, trees for the new plantations – and a wide range of novel ornamentals for gardens.[94] No less than 445 species of tree and shrub are said to have been introduced in the course of the eighteenth century, including Weymouth pine (1705), Indian bean tree (1722), weeping willow (1730), pitch pine (1743), ginkgo (1750), tree of heaven (1751), red maple (1755) and Lombardy poplar (1758).[95] Further introductions followed in the nineteenth century, as gardens became more elaborate and diverse and arboretums became popular, including tree fern (1801), western yellow pine (1826), Douglas fir (1826), grand fir (1830), noble fir (1831), sitka spruce (1831), lodgepole pine (1831), Monterey pine (1833), Wellingtonia (1853), Lawson cypress (1854) and Japonica (1869). In addition, there was a vast range of new herbaceous plants, including ceanothus, pyrethrum, yarrow, michaelmas daisy, annual and perennial phlox, the belladonna lily, the arum lily, gypsophilla, as well as the verbenas, calceolarias, petunias, and pelargoniums destined for parterres, all of which joined the accumulated ranks of exotic flowers introduced in previous centuries.[96] We have insufficient evidence to evaluate the environmental impact of eighteenth- and nineteenth-century pleasure grounds and gardens, so filled with exotic plants. Some of the introduced species – like Michaelmas daisy and Phlox – produced large amounts of nectar, and would thus have benefited invertebrates. But many probably provided limited sustenance, while the manicured character of prosperous grounds may have ensured restricted opportunities for indigenous flora, or fauna, to establish themselves. This said, as we shall see, the gardens of the later nineteenth and twentieth centuries unquestionably provided a wealth of niches, so we should perhaps be cautious here.

Although the cultivation of new species was pioneered in the grounds of the wealthy, some were soon taken up by farmers and even cottagers. The Lombardy poplar (*Populus nigra* Italica) features in many of Constable's paintings of the countryside around the Suffolk/Essex border, growing in hedges, beside rivers and close to farm houses. It was introduced from northern Italy only in 1758 and it is a surprise to see it looking so much at home in 'Constable Country'. In 1808 William Wood, a painter of landscapes and miniatures by profession but a dabbler in landscape design, prepared proposals for improving the park at Shrubland Hall near Coddenham, not far away. These included extensive planting of Lombardy poplars, a tree whose reputation had suffered, he suggested, because it had been widely planted beside the homes of 'the vulgar inhabitants'.[97]

Most introductions, even if – like the Lombardy poplar – widely planted in the countryside, did not become naturalized there. But a number were more successful, although possibly only after several decades or even centuries. The Turkey oak, introduced from Anatolia in 1735, was first recorded in the wild at the start of the twentieth century but its expansion since, especially on acid soils, makes it hard to believe it had not made itself at home in some places rather earlier. It is not a welcome addition to our flora, supporting few species of invertebrate and acting as host to the oak gall wasp, which infects native oaks.[98] Evergreen or holm oak, another native of southern Europe, introduced as early as c.1500, was widely established in the eighteenth century and first recorded in the wild in 1862, and has likewise become an aggressive coloniser in parts of southern England.[99] More serious is Rhododendron *ponticum*, which was planted not only in gardens and parks but also – as game cover – in estate woodland. It has since spread through woods and across heaths and moors, carpeting the ground and suppressing the growth of other plants. It has little value as a food plant to indigenous wildlife.[100]

A large number of herbaceous exotics introduced in this period likewise became naturalized, in some cases rapidly. Spring beauty (*Claytonia perfoliata*) was introduced in the second half of the eighteenth century, and by 1909 Amphlett and Rea were able to describe how it had 'spread rapidly over England since its first introduction not much more than a hundred years ago'.[101] Some naturalized species were relatively harmless, such as woolly or Grecian foxglove (*Digitalis lantana*), a native of Italy and the Balkans which was introduced in 1798, and is now widespread in woodland. But others were a serious threat to indigenous species. The hottentot fig, introduced in the seventeenth century and noted in the wild by the second half of the nineteenth, is a succulent with yellow flowers found especially on the coast of south-west England. It spreads vegetatively so that a single individual can colonize an area 50 metres across, completely displacing the native flora. Also harmful is the floating water fern (*Azolla filiculoides*), introduced in the first half of the nineteenth century to garden ponds and established in the wild by the 1850s.[102] It forms a dense mat of vegetation on the surface, shading out suspended algae and submerged plants, causing deoxygenation and leading to the death of fish and invertebrates. Two plants have caused particularly serious problems. Giant hogweed, a native of Central Asia, was planted as a curiosity in early nineteenth-century gardens and was being recorded in the wild at a number of locations by the 1880s. Himalayan balsam – 'policemen's helmet' – a tall annual herb with distinctive pink-purple flowers was introduced around 1830 and was first recorded in the wild in 1855, lining rivers in the West Country. Both plants are now widespread throughout England, their seeds carried by water, and often form great thickets beside rivers and streams which suppress the growth of other plants.

Nature studied and collected

In the first half of the eighteenth century interest in natural history increased among both the landowning elite and the expanding middle class, albeit focused on the collection, as much as on the study, of the natural world.[103] A steady stream of books and pamphlets catered for this market, such as the 24 published by Richard Bradley alone between 1714 and 1730. The period was, however, one in which studying nature was an activity carried out by people on their own, rather than as members of a group or organisation, and in which there was no agreement over systems of taxonomy – on how, precisely, the natural world should be ordered and classified.[104] This changed with the adoption, from the 1750s, of the simple binomial classificatory system developed by the Swedish scientist Linnaeus, which was lauded by Sir William Watson in an article in the *Gentlemen's Magazine* for 1754, and adopted by Benjamin Stillingfleet in his *Tracts* of 1759.[105] This development seems to have coincided with – and perhaps stimulated – a further increase of interest in natural history which was reflected in the establishment of the Society for Promoting Natural History in 1782 and of the Linnean Society in 1788, the year before the publication of Gilbert White's seminal work on *The Natural History and Antiquities of Selbourne*.[106]

These developments formed the foundations upon which a wider enthusiasm for natural history emerged in the early nineteenth century. The study of nature was considered an appropriately improving form of leisure for the growing ranks of manufacturers, merchants and professionals: several leading naturalists of the age, such as Dawson Turner, Edward Forster and William Brand, were bankers.[107] The falling cost of books as printing processes were modernized led to a veritable rash of publications, many of them guides to identification. Volumes on insects and birds were especially popular, the latter reflecting the wider interest in matters avian, for game shooting easily shaded off into the dispatch of rare or unusual birds which could be stuffed and displayed. Periodicals devoted to the subject also flourished, most notably John Claudius Loudon's *Magazine of Natural History*, established in 1828.

Local literary and philosophical societies had existed since the early eighteenth century, and these became more common as larger urban centres developed: Manchester gained one in 1781, Birmingham in 1800 and Leeds in 1819. In the 1820s and '30s, societies devoted entirely to natural history were also widely established, holding regular meetings and publishing transactions.[108] In addition to these essentially middle-class societies, however, groups largely or entirely involved in the study of botany appeared among the working-class populations of some industrial towns in the second half of the eighteenth century, especially in north-west England.[109] In 1811 an observer thought that there were 'very considerable' numbers of 'mechanical' botanists in the villages around Manchester.[110] Their meetings took place in pubs – 'the very heart of popular culture'[111] – and those that crystallized into more formal associations often – like the Black Cow Botanical Society in Manchester – took their name from their original meeting place (conversely, some pubs in the Manchester area have names reflecting their association with these groups, such as the 'Botanical Tavern' in Ashton or the 'Railway and Naturalist' in Prestwich).[112] Unlike the middle-class societies, which met on a week-day evening, these groups normally assembled on Sundays, the only day of rest afforded to working people. Members would compare specimens collected in the field and pool their resources in order to acquire the latest books on natural history. Artisan interest in botany was closely related to an enthusiasm for horticulture and herbalism, and the development of these groups is a testament to the powers of the industrial working class – mainly men but also, to some extent, women – to organize and educate themselves.[113] But it is also a sign that industrial cities did not yet form vast and continuous conurbations from which much of the flora of the countryside had been squeezed. The fieldwork of such men was, perforce, limited to areas which could be reached by horse-drawn tram or on foot. The countryside still lay near at hand, interdigitated with housing, factories and mills.

There was an increasing interest in the natural sciences at the small number of English universities in the middle decades of the century, but amateurs continued to dominate the study of the natural world, and the Botanical Society of London, which lasted from 1836 to 1856, attempted to expand its membership into the provinces by establishing a system of Corresponding Members and Local Secretaries. This was part of a scheme, directed by the great naturalist C. Watson, to create a country-wide network of collectors who would exchange specimens, using a standard checklist to ensure a common system of nomenclature. Watson himself pioneered the scientific study of plant distributions, dividing the country for this purpose into eighteen provinces which were later subdivided to create 112 'vice-counties', a system which served to facilitate the integration of local knowledge into wider schemes of understanding.[114]

The 1850s and '60s were perhaps the peak decades for popular interest in natural history, and the great age of the 'field clubs'. These groups originated in Scotland but rapidly spread to England, the two earliest probably being the Tyneside Field Club and the Cotteswold, in the Cotswolds, both founded in 1846. Rather than assembling in the evening, at some regular venue, such bodies met in the field, at locations which changed each month. Many soon began to hold evening meetings as well, a mixture of activities which appealed to a wide range of members: some, like the Cotteswold, also held special 'ladies meetings' at locations where the terrain was considered to be not too challenging.[115] Most took an interest in geology, archaeology and local history, as well as in botany and zoology. By 1873 there were around 170 local scientific societies, of various kinds, in Britain as a whole, of which 104 described themselves as field clubs.[116] Popular enthusiasm in the middle decades of the century was also reflected in the success of such books as John's *Flowers of the Field* and *British Birds in their Haunts*; Morris's *British Birds*; and Wood's *Common Objects of the Country*, which sold 100,000 copies in a single week.[117]

Bird-watching experienced particularly strong growth in part because of the wider availability of telescopes, and the increasing use of nesting-boxes and hides. Cheaper optical equipment also benefited the study of insects, lichen, and fungi, for the price of microscopes fell fivefold in the course of the 1830s. It should be noted, however, that the emphasis was still, and perhaps increasingly, on collecting. From the 1840s, entomologists began to use 'treacle', a variety of sugar-based mixtures, to attract insects, and especially moths; from the 1860s, box-traps were widely employed. New ways of killing insects, in a manner that both preserved them intact and spared the feelings of the squeamish, were developed, with chloroform giving way to Prussic acid, and finally from the 1850s to potassium cyanide. The Wardian Case – an almost-sealed glass contained invented in 1831 by Nathaniel Bagshaw Ward – allowed a range of plants, especially ferns, to flourish even if left unwatered, or kept indoors.[118]

As we have seen, people of all classes – contrary to what has sometimes been suggested or implied – had probably always been interested in the wildlife around them. In the eighteenth and nineteenth centuries, these relationships began to take new forms, in part because the social groups involved were less directly involved with the natural world than their predecessors had been, or their more rural neighbours continued to be. Removed from any intimacy with agricultural production, they could now regard nature not as threat and competitor, but as exclusively a source of interest and wonder. Plants were seen as wild flowers rather than as weeds; insects, birds and mammals were things to be observed in their own right, not because they threatened crops and livestock. The natural world was to be observed, but also categorized, and in a manner – using the standardized Latin forms of the Linnaean system, rather than a plethora of conflicting local and regional terms – which both facilitated comparison and discussion, and at the same time marked out the naming group as distinct, not so much from the working classes, as from the working agrarian population. Yet nature was also *collected*, for in the new industrial world acquisition as much as production were key social priorities. Fragments of the natural world became possessions, just as the study of nature required the acquisition of the right kinds of equipment. Knowledge of plants and birds might itself, in effect, be traded, in the form of publications but also as informal exchange; it became a form of social capital.

Nature did not necessary benefit from all the interest shown in it. The Wardian case was especially suitable for the preservation of ferns, which were collected with such enthusiasm that some areas became denuded of the rarer species, to the consternation of many naturalists. Attractive but infrequent species like forked spleenwort (*Asplenium septentrionale*) and royal fern (*Osmunda regalis*) were particularly badly affected.[119] Byfield quotes one disappointed description of a fern-hunting trip to Devon: 'all the available tresses of maidenhair fern have been shorn away'.[120] Orchids and even some rare bryophytes and lichens were reduced through indiscriminate collecting.[121] The progressive extension and elaboration of the rail network brought large numbers of collectors to the coast, some sections of which were likewise denuded, or so contemporaries believed, of molluscs and seaweeds. Among the artisan botanists, sometimes trading rare plants for a profit to wealthy collectors, it was not unknown for an entire stock of plants to be dug up in order to maintain a monopoly. In 1812 George Caley, a Middleton farrier, described how he searched in vain for specimens of the green-winged orchid (*Orchis morio*) at a particular spot, later learning that it 'had used to grow in great plenty where I had been looking for it and that the day before a person had gathered all the flowering plants he could meet with to prevent people from getting up the roots'.[122] The most poignant legacy of the Victorian fascination with natural history, however, are the collections of stuffed birds which can often still be found quietly mouldering away in the more remote recesses of country houses, accompanied by cases of birds' eggs. The bearded tit was almost brought to extinction by collecting; species like the Dartford warbler, already comparatively rare, were threatened, either because individuals were shot to be stuffed, or because their eggs were collected, or both.[123]

Whether all this marks an 'improvement' in attitudes towards nature is a moot point. The frenetic and violent attempts at pest control discussed in the last chapter, however vicious and misguided, were at least the work of people under constant threat from nature, attempting to protect their livelihoods and their families. There were, however, important shifts in popular attitudes to some animals. Cruel sports already had their critics in the sixteenth and seventeenth centuries. The city of Chester banned bear-baiting as early as 1596; around the same time Sir John Davies castigated this activity, together with cock-fighting, as 'filthy sports'; while Samuel Pepys at the end of the seventeenth century thought that they provided 'a very rude and nasty pleasure'.[124] Such attitudes became more widespread as industrialization proceeded, however, and culminated in the establishment, in 1824, of the Society for the Protection of Animals, later (from 1840) the *Royal* Society. Two years earlier, in 1822, the Act to Prevent Cruel Treatment of Cattle had been passed, and the new society lobbied hard to extend its terms to other creatures. In 1835, the Cruelty to Animals Act did indeed extend protection to dogs and sheep, prohibited bear-baiting and cock fighting, and in various other ways sought to promote the more humane treatment of domestic animals. But neither this piece of legislation, nor the subsequent Cruelty to Animals Act of 1849, was concerned with the preservation of wildlife. Those animals with which humans had a close working association were regarded in a different way to those which existed in the world of nature. But attitudes were changing, and for reasons which should by now be clear. As Hudson, writing about London, observed in the 1890s: 'It is a fact, although perhaps not a quite familiar one, that those who reside in the metropolis are more interested in and have a kindlier feeling for their wild birds than is the case in rural districts'.[125]

Conclusion

The environment of England was directly affected, in innumerable ways, by the agricultural and industrial revolutions. But these great transformations also had important indirect impacts, of a social and intellectual character, which likewise shaped the fortunes of wildlife. Parks and gardens covered ever larger areas of ground, forming portals through which a flood of new organisms were brought to these shores. The consolidation of large landed estates led to an upsurge in tree planting, with important long-term ecological effects; but, together with improvements in firearms technology, also ushered in new forms of recreational hunting which were associated with catastrophic declines in a number of birds and mammal species. At the same time, a population increasingly divorced from agricultural production engaged with nature in new ways, observing, recording and classifying plants and animals but also collecting them, sometimes to the point of local extinction.

CHAPTER EIGHT

Wildlife in depression, c.1870–1940

Depression and its consequences

Most discussions of England's environment in the later nineteenth century, and the first half of the twentieth, are dominated by the fate of agriculture. From the mid-1870s, farming began to slide into a long period of depression, principally caused by the expansion of the American railway network into the prairies of the mid-west, so that European markets were flooded with cheap grain. No longer kept artificially high by the operation of the Corn Law, repealed in 1846, wheat prices were halved between 1873 and 1893, while those for barley and oats fell by a third. Following a brief period of stabilization, a further intense depression occurred after 1896, this time affecting not only arable farmers but also livestock producers, as cheap meat began to be imported on refrigerated ships from the New World and Australia.[1] In an increasingly globalized world, British agriculture could not compete. Fortunes recovered during World War I but there was then a further slump, with only a slight recovery in the 1930s. Only in the period following the outbreak of war in 1939 did British agriculture return to long-term profitability, ushering in a period of intensive farming which has continued, more or less, to this day.

Many readers will be aware of the various effects which the agricultural depression supposedly had upon the countryside. Marginal land brought into cultivation during the agricultural revolution could now no longer be profitably farmed: areas of heavy, intractable clay soils, poor heathland and moors were abandoned to dereliction. Even the more general fabric of the farming landscape could no longer be adequately maintained. Henry Williamson in the 1930s described 'the dereliction, the mud, the weeds, the dilapidated buildings, swarms of rats, broken tiles, rotting floors . . . swampy meadows, cracked bridges, flat gates and overgrown hedges'.[2] Depression, moreover, led to a steep decline in agricultural rents which had disastrous effects on large landowners. The rental income from the Blickling estate in Norfolk, for example, fell from £11,685 in 1877 to £9,893 in 1892: a major recalculation of rents in 1894 resulted in a further reduction to £6,018.[3] Landowners were also assailed by Death Duties, introduced in 1894 and raised to 15 per cent by Lloyd George and subsequently, in 1919, to 40 per cent on estates valued at more than £200,000.[4] The dominance of the aristocracy and gentry in the affairs of the countryside was eroded by the Local Government Acts of 1888 and 1894, which vested power in elected County, District and Parish Councils. The age of the country house as the centre of the local universe was over, and many large estates were placed on the market, broken up and sold to tenants.[5]

While economic and social historians have traditionally represented the period as one of rural decline, historical ecologists and environmental historians have taken a different view, generally suggesting that wildlife flourished as the fortunes of farming waned. John Sheail, for example, has characterized the fate of the rural landscape in the twentieth century as 'a study of two halves'.

> Whilst farming was generally depressed, the countryside of the first half of the century was typically diverse, beautiful and rich in wildlife. Farming boomed in the second half of the century, as those concerned with the conservation of amenity and wildlife . . . came close to despair.[6]

Shrubb has suggested that the widespread decline in the intensity of farming benefited wildlife, especially a 'sharp reduction' in hedge management, with 'extensive increases . . . in the height and volume of hedges [which] would have affected the size of farmland bird populations considerably'. Rackham has similarly argued that:

> The period 1750-1870 was, on the whole, an age of agricultural prosperity in which hedgerow timber almost certainly decreased. The period 1870-1951 was, on the whole, an age of agricultural adversity, in which there was less money to spend on either maintaining or destroying hedges. Neglect gave innumerable saplings an opportunity to grow into trees.[7]

Indeed, he compared the numbers of trees shown on the First Edition Ordnance Survey 6" maps of the 1880s, with the 1951 Forestry Commission's estimates of the density of farmland timber, arguing that the number of hedgerow trees in England may have increased in this period from around 23 million to some 60 million.[8]

While wildlife flourished in the countryside, however, it was now seriously assailed by the expansion of towns and industry. The extent to which countryside gave way to roads, factories and housing escalated rapidly after c.1860. The population of England continued to rise rapidly, increasing from around 19 million to over 34 million by the outbreak of the First World War and reaching around 40 million by 1950.[9] But in addition, people became less densely packed into towns and cities. This was not primarily the consequence of the influence of social reformers, who railed against the squalor of overcrowded urban areas, but rather of technological developments, which allowed people to live at a distance from where they worked, and which permitted industry to disperse more widely, away from spatially restricted sources of energy. The British rail network expanded from around 6,800 miles in 1851 to 23,000 miles by 1914; but by this stage, cars and in particular buses had arrived on the scene.[10] In 1920, 200,000 cars were registered in Britain; by 1930 this figure had grown to nearly a million.[11] Of equal importance was the development of mains electricity. This was initially – from the later nineteenth century – produced and disseminated on a local basis, but in 1926 the Central Electricity Board was established, and by 1933 a series of regional grids with auxiliary interconnections for emergency use was in place. This fuelled what Hudson has described as a 'second industrial revolution', with an expansion of light engineering and manufacturing in southern England and the Midlands, accompanied by a decline in traditional heavy industries in the north and west.[12] Housing and industry, for a range of reasons, thus expanded further and further, gobbling up the countryside and its wildlife as it did so.

In fact, all the views baldly summarized in the foregoing paragraphs, while containing some truth, are misleading in a number of respects. This was not a 'golden age' for wildlife in the countryside, nor were the effects of mass urbanization as drastic or as unremittingly negative as many have suggested. In addition, there were other, more subtle social and economic changes – the development of large-scale state planning and the final demise of traditional management practices, especially on commons and other marginal land – which were to have equally profound impacts on the natural environment.

Benign neglect?

It is important at the outset to emphasize that the period between the 1870s and the outbreak of World War II was not one of unrelieved gloom in farming, and that the scale of depression was to some extent exaggerated by a farming industry now dependent on government intervention, and by right-wing writers like Henry Williamson or Adrian Bell, for whom the state of the countryside was used as a metaphor for the supposed moral decline of the nation more generally.[13] In reality, the fortunes of many livestock producers held up well as prices for cereals, and thus supplementary feed, fell dramatically, while even those of arable farmers varied over time, and were helped in many eastern areas by the cultivation, from the 1920s, of a new crop, sugar beet. The main consequence of depression was that farmers laid land to pasture, for livestock prices did not fall as far as those for wheat and barley, and – with improved access to distant urban markets – those for dairy produce remained buoyant. In 1880 there were round 14 million acres (5.7 million hectares) of arable land in England and Wales: by 1939 this had fallen to under nine million, almost entirely concentrated in the eastern counties (Figure 25).[14] Better transport and increasing levels of urbanization also encouraged other forms of diversification, such as the production of poultry, fruit and vegetables, and in some districts there was an expansion in the number of smallholdings, in part the consequence of direct government legislation. In some counties the county councils were, by the 1920s, the largest landowners, with the largest numbers of agricultural tenants.[15] There was some abandonment of marginal land, as we shall see, but most of England continued to be farmed, often at high levels of intensity.

It is true that the amount of money spent on artificial fertilizers, land drainage, and the other 'improvements' of the 'high farming' period declined, and this may have had a positive effect on wildlife. As field drains gradually became blocked, areas of damp grassland developed in places, to the benefit of a range of wild plants, and of breeding waders, snipe and redshank.[16] But as in earlier periods, a decline in the cultivation of cereal crops in areas formerly characterized by mixed farming may have caused reductions in the numbers of granivorous birds.[17] Moreover, the suggestion that hedges were allowed to grow tall and uncontrolled, or that fields filled with weeds, needs to be treated with particular caution. Photographs taken in the early twentieth century usually suggest a rather manicured and tidy countryside (Figure 26). Hedges were no longer exploited as a source of fuel and were less likely to be managed by regular coppicing or laying, not least because, in livestock areas, they were increasingly supplemented by fences of barbed wire, first used in England in the 1870s. In arable areas, especially, hedges appear to have been trimmed back more rigorously than ever, because they shaded crops and provided shelter for vermin, particularly rabbits. But even in livestock districts they were often kept in strict order: it was said in 1900 that in Cheshire 'old and tangled hedgerows, which afforded secure nesting places for warblers and other birds, [have] been grubbed up and replaced by mathematically straight thorn hedges or wire fences'.[18] Tennyson described in the 1930s how:

> In west Suffolk there are many long stretches with literally no hedges at all, or at the best hedges that are kept to, and often below, their proper size. And as the fields are large – they are very large in some places – and the country is flat, there is often nothing to break the view.[19]

The amalgamation of fields seems in many areas to have continued at a steady pace: in parts of eastern England the kind of prairie-like landscape which we usually associate with post-War agricultural intensification was already beginning to emerge. Butcher in the 1930s commented that on the Suffolk claylands:

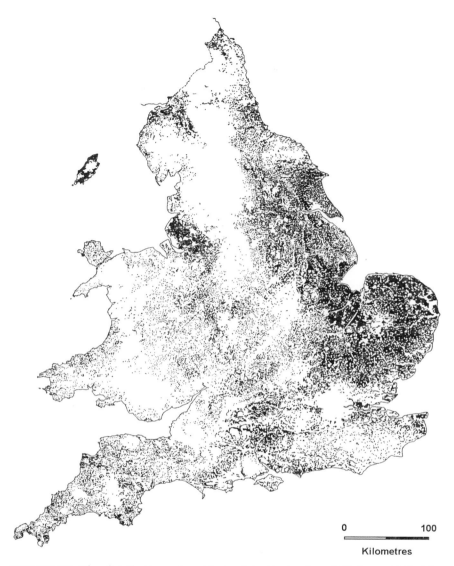

0   100

Kilometres

FIGURE 25 *The distribution of arable land in England and Wales, c.1940. The long agricultural depression had served to concentrate arable farming in the eastern counties, and especially in Norfolk, Suffolk, Cambridgeshire and Lincolnshire.*

Hedges around the fields, because of the shade they throw, are considered detrimental to good arable cultivation and so are kept as low as possible or even rooted out. Consequently one characteristic of the district is the hedgeless or almost hedgeless fields surrounded by deep ditches.[20]

FIGURE 26 *Harvesting at Marjoram's Farm, South Walsham, Norfolk in the early twentieth century. In spite of the popular image of the 'great depression', photographs of the arable areas of England in this period usually suggest a well-maintained, tidy countryside. Note the low-cut, sparsely-timbered hedges in the background.*

Such changes were encouraged by the adoption of tractors in place of horses, something which began in earnest in the inter-war years. Mosby described in the 1930s how, in north east Norfolk, there was 'a tendency in some areas to enlarge the fields by removing the intervening hedge. Where this has been done the farmers, particularly those who use a tractor plough, have reduced their labour costs'.[21]

The idea that the number of hedgerow trees increased in this period because of a neglect of maintenance is likewise probably incorrect. In some districts, a comparison of the Ordnance Survey 1:10,560 maps, surveyed in the 1880s and 90s, with the RAF vertical air photographs of 1946/7 actually suggests a significant *decrease* in hedgerow timber, of 50 per cent or more, although the comparison is not entirely straightforward, as the Ordnance Survey shows only trees of substantial size and omits examples where tightly packed, while the RAF photographs pose many practical problems of interpretation.[22] There are certainly good reasons why trees should have been lost in this period. Landowners had traditionally valued their property for the status it conferred, and the sport it provided, not simply for the income it supplied. Estate hedges were often densely timbered because trees (always retained in hand by owners) enhanced the appearance of a landed seat, as well as being a secure, long-term investment. Tenants held other views, for trees shaded out crops and robbed the soil of nutrients. Landlords, faced with increasing difficulties in keeping old tenants or attracting new ones in these difficult times, were more sensitive than they had formerly been to complaints on this subject. Where landowners fell into financial difficulties, moreover, large-scale timber sales were one obvious way of realizing assets. Rider Haggard noted large-scale felling of hedgerow oaks in 1902, commenting: 'I think that 'ere long this timber will be scarce in England'.[23] Thirty years later Lilias Rider Haggard described how 'the wholesale cutting of timber all over the country is a sad sight, but often the owner's last desperate bid to enable him to cling to the family acres. . .'.[24] And where estates were finally broken up and portions sold to former tenants, the latter were usually keen to thin the 'landlord's timber' not only to enhance yields but also to recoup some of the money expended on purchase.

Dereliction and abandonment

While dereliction of agricultural land did occur, its scale and character are often exaggerated. The complete abandonment of arable to weeds and scrub was particularly unusual, mainly concentrated in the 1880s and '90s and mostly in areas of former heathland, although some districts of poor clays were also affected. The weeds which developed on such land, including groundsel and ragwort, had considerable value for seed-eating birds like goldfinches.[25] But in most cases abandonment was shortlived: untilled land was brought back into cultivation or converted to pasture. Only in a few districts did extensive tracts of ploughland become permanently derelict, cultivation being no longer viable given the inputs of fertilizer, lime and the rest which were required. The East Anglian Breckland, in particular, became a byword for abandonment. Clare Sewell Read described in 1905 how 'Thousands of acres . . . are now derelict' in the area.[26] There was some reversal of this state of affairs during World War I. But Mosby in 1938 emphasized how 'many acres have gone out of cultivation following the phenomenal decline in prices' between 1919 and the early 1930s.[27]

More significant than the abandonment of arable was the gradual decline in the quality of many enclosed pastures, particularly in upland areas, or (once again) in places previously reclaimed from heathland. In part this was caused by the gradual neglect of liming and drainage. But it also reflected a marked decline in the numbers of sheep being kept, a consequence of the scale of foreign imports. While cattle numbers remained buoyant in England and Wales during the depression years, actually showing an increase between 1880 and 1939 of around 40 per cent, the numbers of sheep fell from 19.5 million to 13.4 million in 1920, a decline of over 30 per cent, albeit recovering to around 18 million by the 1930s.[28] Much land was thus grazed less intensively, the area recorded in government statistics as 'rough grazing' – moorland, heathland and the like – doubling from around 2.8 to 5.6 million acres (1.1–2.2 million hectares) between 1891 (the first year for which records included this category of land) and 1939.[29] Dudley Stamp, writing in the 1940s, described the typical condition of 'the upper fields bordering a moorland mass':

> Invasion by bracken (*Pteris aquiline*), often starting from the corners or margins of a field, and gradually spreading, is a very common phenomenon, for bracken requires constant cutting to keep it under. Invasion by gorse (*Ulex*) is another form of deterioration and so is the development of brambles.[30]

Such changes in the quality of improved and enclosed grazing shade off, almost imperceptibly, into a decline in the condition of those areas of heath and moor which had somehow survived enclosure and 'improvement' during the previous centuries. A report on the heaths at Iken in east Suffolk, for example, drawn up before they were purchased by the Forestry Commission in 1920, described them as exhibiting 'very strong growths of heather, bracken etc with gorse and thorn bushes and a number of pine groups in scattered form'.[31] By the 1930s, many surviving heaths and commons in the south and east of England were scrubbing over with whitethorn, blackthorn, furze and birch. A similar fate was experienced by some of the chalk downs in southern England, often on the steeper slopes, where the pastures were steadily colonized by juniper, gorse, spindle, hawthorn and dogwood.

In many cases, this development had additional causes. Most areas of rough grazing were either parcels of surviving common land or were 'poors' allotments' created, in the manner discussed in Chapter 3, to provide the poor with firing and – more rarely – with a place to pasture their livestock. In the later nineteenth and early twentieth century, however, fewer and fewer poor people kept livestock, while local farmers made less use of commons for grazing as the volume of motor traffic increased, for most examples were crossed by public roads. More importantly, commons and poors' allotments ceased to be cut for fuel or fodder. This appears to have happened gradually through the middle and later decades of the nineteenth century, and into the early twentieth. Clarke in 1918 noted a number of places in Norfolk where traditional forms of cutting and mowing persisted, but in general they had ceased.[32] Bird, describing the use of East Ruston 'Common' (really a poors' allotment) in the same county in 1909, noted that the cutting of flags, peat and furze for firing had more or less come to an end, and while fodder was still harvested the use of the common for grazing had much declined.[33] Some fuel allotments, as already noted, were never directly exploited by the poor, but rented out from the beginning – often for shooting – and the income employed for the purchase of coals. But the number so managed appears to have increased steadily with the passing decades. In Norfolk, for example, 55 per cent of allotment land was already, by 1833, used in the latter way; by 1845, 60 per cent; by 1883, 81 per cent; and by 1896, 92 per cent.[34] Even the poorest in society were, by the start of the twentieth century, turning their back on local fuels. Bird, describing East Ruston 'Common' in 1909, noted that the cutting of flags, peat and furze for firing had ceased 'since the old larger brick ovens and open chimneys have entirely disappeared', replaced, presumably, by grates and ranges designed for coal.[35] Surviving commons and most fuel allotments gradually became areas of scrub and woodland, and were used for fly tipping, dumping, fires and gypsy camps.

One striking feature of the period, shared by moorland and heath and also, as we have noted, enclosed fields on the margins of such land, was the inexorable spread of bracken. If allowed to grow to maturity the plant is unpalatable to livestock but if regularly harvested in the traditional manner, for bedding or firing, the young fronds can be consumed by sheep and cattle, which also keep the plant in check by treading. With declining numbers of stock, and a cessation of cutting, bracken spread unchecked across extensive areas of marginal, acidic land. Clarke in 1908 described how in East Anglia it was: 'certainly the dominant plant of the "breck" district, and on several heaths has usurped the position which heather occupied some 20 years ago. Bracken lacks its former economic importance'.[36] Gorse, no longer harvested for fuel or fencing, also expanded. Bird reported how at East Ruston 'The best parts of the common for grazing purposes are now being much encroached upon by the spreading of furze'.[37]

On chalk downland rabbits, continuing to increase in numbers in this period – in part because of the increase in the area of derelict land – often kept in check the growth of scrub and rank vegetation. Alien invaders they might have been, but to some extent they thus compensated for the decline in livestock numbers in areas of marginal grazing. In areas of heath, moreover, their burrowing activities provided opportunities for the ruderal plants formerly dependent on the disturbances resulting from periodic cultivation and the digging of heather turfs for fuel.[38] But in other ways they were less beneficial. They did little to arrest the spread of bracken, partly because of their small size but also because they were averse to consuming it. Contemporaries often connected the increasing significance of both, Michael Home for example memorably describing the hamlets and villages of the East Anglian Breckland as 'oases . . . fighting a losing battle against the insidious onslaughts of both rabbits and bracken'.[39]

Dereliction of these kinds was not, for the most part, environmentally beneficial. Vast numbers of rare heathland plants were lost, out-competed by coarser vegetation. Clarke described in 1918 how, on Barnham Common near Thetford, in Norfolk, 'the original steppe flora has been greatly reduced by the encroachments of furze'.[40] The spread of scrub also caused problems for the ground-nesting birds of heath and down, which require open tracts for 'feeding areas, to detect predators and allow chicks easy movement'.[41] Birds like the stone curlew, which had suffered dramatic declines during the previous period of agricultural intensification, did not now exhibit rapid recoveries.[42] A few bird species characteristic of heaths and downs probably benefited from the rougher conditions and the spread of scrub, such as the woodlark, but only within limits: once dereliction and regeneration reached a certain stage their numbers too will have been adversely affected.

The decline in traditional forms of management, which had everywhere struggled on, by a kind of rural inertia, through the middle and later decades of the nineteenth century, is apparent in many contexts. Often such practices came to an abrupt and final end with the advent of World War I, due to the labour shortages which arose as men went off in their thousands to die in the trenches. The coppicing of woodland often ceased at this point, never to be resumed, with major impacts on floristic diversity, as rare plants and butterflies were lost to the deepening shade. In surviving wetlands the management of fens for reed, sedge, and marsh hay was likewise abandoned. Turner in 1922 described how the impact of the War, and the decline in the market for chaff in London, was dramatically changing the appearance of the Norfolk Broads. Areas of fen and meadow, once mown for hay or litter or grazed by cattle, had 'reverted and their rough herbage is stronger and coarser than ever'.[43] Decline continued over the following decades, and T. Boardman described in 1939 how:

> Now, since acres upon acres of this material remain uncut and the vegetation gets into such a terrible tangle, the marshes have to be burned. Alders, birch and sallows are taking possession . . . When the marshes were mown regularly all the young trees were kept under. . .[44]

By the 1930s, many commercial reed beds, both here and in other wetland areas, were also being abandoned, as the local demand for thatching materials declined, and they too regenerated to scrub, and then woodland. All this caused problems for a wide range of wetland plants, and for a number of wetland birds, such as the reed warbler, lapwing and yellow wagtail, although overall the numbers of teal and mallard held up well in this period, probably because of the more stringent imposition of a close season on shooting.[45]

Other forms of traditional land management declined as a more direct consequence of the depressed state of particular sections of the farming economy. By 1940 the management of water meadows had 'largely broken down', even in their Wessex heartlands, Stamp in 1950 describing how, as a result, 'some parts of the valleys of the Test or the Wiltshire Avon present . . . a scene of desolation which is tragic'.[46] The system was closely tied to the practice of sheep-corn husbandry, and especially to the production of lambs, and although it could be adopted to serve the needs of dairy farmers up to a point, its main *raison d'etre* had now disappeared. In addition, however, irrigation clashed with the interests of recreational fishing, and with those of game shooting. The owners of fishing rights 'may not approve the interference caused by the weirs . . . a sportsman out for shooting may prefer to see a reed swamp than a tract of well tended meadow'.[47]

Great estates: Game preservation and exotic fauna

The demise of the landed estate, such an important influence on England's ecology in the eighteenth and nineteenth centuries, is often hastened in popular accounts. It is true that many landed families fell into financial difficulties from the 1880s. Janice de Saumarez described in 1895 how the income from the family's Suffolk estates (Shrubland, Livermere and Broke Hall) had fallen from between £10,000 and £12,000 *per annum* to virtually nothing. Tenants had been giving in their notice, and 'although we have arrived at the point of having no income, everything indicates a further fall of an indefinite and incalculable amount'.[48] But few estates were actually broken up in the period before the Great War, in part because most landed families had investments outside the agricultural sector, and were not entirely dependent on the fortunes of farming. Following the war there were more sales: the *Times* famously commented in 1922 that a quarter of England had changed hands during the previous 4 years. Yet in many cases, hard-pressed families sold off outlying farms but retained, at least for a while, the core of their properties.[49] Alternatively, estates passed intact to new owners, who had made their fortunes in industry or commerce – for well into the twentieth century the kudos attached to the ownership of landed property remained strong. Indeed, a number of entirely new country houses were actually erected in the first quarter of the twentieth century, and gardens and parks were frequently revamped and replanted.[50] It was only with the arrival of a more general economic depression in the 1930s that the supply of potential purchasers dried up, and estates began to fragment on some scale, although it was not until after World War II (during which many country houses had been occupied, and badly damaged, by the military) that sales and demolitions came thick and vast. Grandiose statements of wealth seemed increasingly anachronistic and pointless in the new, post-War world. Yet even then substantial numbers of large estates survived, and in many districts they remain an active force in the countryside to this day.

In some ways, the influence of landed estates on the environment reached a peak around 1900. The fashionable example set by the Prince of Wales at Sandringham in Norfolk, coupled with a more general enthusiasm for healthy outdoor activities and the need for landed estates to diversify their incomes, led to a further expansion in organized game shooting. Wealthy businessmen were now increasingly involved, paying for the privilege of joining a shoot, or even renting farms or entire estates during the shooting season. The numbers of game shot continued to rise (Figure 27). At Holkham in Norfolk the annual 'bag' increased from 3,252 partridges and 1,443 pheasants in 1853–4 to 4,599 partridges and 4,149 pheasants in 1900–01; at Stowlangtoft in Suffolk average bags of around 2,700 in the 1850s rose to an astonishing 13,296 in 1897–8.[51] The greatest expansion in shooting

FIGURE 27 *Game shooting continued to be a major influence of the rural environment of England well into the twentieth century: loading a game cart at Studley Royal, Yorkshire, in 1901.*

was in the uplands, where continued improvements in transport – with the advent of the motor car and further expansion of the rail network – made access easier. In Simmons' words, 'What landowners needed was a sport which appealed to the new rich, did not interfere with existing patterns of land use to any degree, and made money'.[52] The further expansion and systematization of heather burning produced ever larger numbers of birds; the new breech-loading guns ensured that 'it was difficult for even inexperienced financiers to miss and good shots might pile up carcases at a very high rate'. One Yorkshire shooting moor yielded 2,843 birds on a single day in August 1913.[53]

At least until the 1920s, there was continuing pressure on keepers to raise ever greater numbers of grouse, partridge, hare and other game. Armed not only with efficient breech-loading shotguns, but now with an array of poisons, they achieved this aim with considerable success. In 1911 there were no less than 23,000 individuals recorded in the census as gamekeepers: one, on average, for every 5.6 square kilometres of land, and significantly more than this in the prime sporting areas of East Anglia and southern England.[54] Ravens, crows, magpies, jays, hawks, harriers, buzzards and owls continued to be slaughtered on a vast scale. In spite of the spread of abandoned land badger numbers failed to register any recovery, while foxes were rare, or even eradicated altogether, where shooting was particularly important.[55]

As rabbit numbers continued to rise they were increasingly treated as game to be shot, while otter hunting, which has been practised on a casual basis for centuries, became more popular and intensive. By the 1920s, there were 23 organized otter hunts in the country: in 1933 no less than 434 otters met an untimely end. This said, it has been argued that – as to some extent with foxes – hunting served to maintain a species which was otherwise widely persecuted, and hunts often restricted their activities to merely capturing the unfortunate beasts, when numbers locally fell low.[56]

In the eighteenth and early nineteenth centuries, as we have seen, landowners had established exotic plants in their parks and pleasure grounds, and on occasions more widely on their estates. From the later nineteenth century, they seem to have taken an increasing interest in exotic fauna. At Tring in Hertfordshire Lionel Walter Rothschild, who succeeded to the immense family fortune (derived from banking) in 1915, and who was a keen naturalist, famously filled the park with zebras, emus, kangaroos, wallabies, and ostriches (Figure 28).[57] None seem to have escaped but the edible dormouse (*Glig glis*) – released into the park in 1902 – did manage to get out and, although it has not since spread far, is now well entrenched in the Chiltern Hills.[58] Other introductions have been more successful. The grey squirrel (*Sciurus carolinensis*) was released into the park at Henbury in Cheshire in 1876, and subsequently on a number of estates, most notably Woburn Abbey in Bedfordshire, apparently for no other reason than that it looked attractive and exotic.[59] There may have been earlier releases, in Kent in 1850 and at Dunham, also in Cheshire, in 1860. Large landowners took the lead in all this but they were not entirely responsible: four squirrels from Woburn were released in Kew Gardens, and no less than 91 in Regents Park.[60] The animal spread steadily through the countryside at a rate of around a mile a year and by 1930 was established across much of England.[61] A temporary reduction in numbers in the early 1930s, caused by disease,

FIGURE 28 *Kangaroos in the park at Tring, Hertfordshire, in c.1900. The late nineteenth and early twentieth centuries saw an increasing interest in keeping exotic fauna on the part of the landed elite. Many species introduced into parks subsequently escaped into the wild, with disastrous consequences.*

was followed by further dispersal and by 1945 it was probably present in every county except Norfolk, Suffolk, Cornwall and Cumberland.[62]

The spread of the grey squirrel was bad news for the indigenous red (*Sciurus vulgaris*). The grey was a larger and more aggressive animal, and spent more time on the ground, where many of the principal foods consumed by both species are most abundant.[63] It also lives longer and at higher densities than the red and successfully steals its food.[64] The red only has the advantage in pine forests. Here less food is available but, being a smaller animal, it requires less, and is also better able to secure what there is, as it can reach pine cones growing on fine branches. Increasingly out-competed in deciduous woodland, it thus retreated to districts with extensive conifer plantations. The grey may also have brought with it a virus, *parapoxvirus* (with similar symptoms to myxomatosis found in rabbits), to which it was more immune than the red. The advent of the grey may not, however, have been the only factor in the decline of the native squirrel, the numbers of which appear to have fluctuated significantly over the centuries, and which suffered a dramatic collapse between 1900 and 1920, before the grey had made any serious inroads. Habitat change – a decline in the density of hedgerow trees, reducing the squirrel's ability to spread through the countryside – and the expansion of urban and suburban areas – grey squirrels are better suited to life in gardens than reds – may also have contributed. But it is clear that the arrival of the grey did have a direct negative effect. In 1945 a 'survey of the distribution of two species . . . showed that wherever grey squirrels had been present for fifteen years or more, red squirrels had either vanished completely or survived only in small scattered groups'.[65] Today, the red has effectively retreated to the Isle of Wight, Cumbria, Northumberland and North Yorkshire. Grey squirrels had, and have, other problematic effects on the countryside, for they damage trees (especially sycamore and beech) by removing the bark in order to reach the sweet, sap-filled *Phloem* tissue beneath, sometime killing trees directly, more often weakening their resistance to disease and fungal attack.

Other significant introductions of alien fauna were made in this period. A number of new species of deer were released, partly out of interest, partly for sport. Various kinds of Sika deer (*Cervus nipon*) – Manchurian, Chinese, Formosan, and Japanese – were introduced at a number of places in the late nineteenth and early twentieth centuries, of which the last managed to establish itself in the wild and is now present in significant concentrations in Kent, in Dorset and Hampshire, and on the Lancashire/Yorkshire border.[66] Chinese water deer (*Hydropotes inermis*) were likewise introduced into, and escaped from, private parks, although here the main culprit may in fact be Whipsnade Zoo in Bedfordshire, from where there were several escapes in 1929. Preferring a habitat on the edge of water, water deer are now established to a limited extent in the Fens and Broads of East Anglia, and along the Suffolk coast.[67] Bizarrely, England now hosts a significant proportion of the world population of the species, which in its homeland is now endangered.[68] The muntjac deer (*Muntiacus reevesi*) has been the most successful of these arrivals. It was introduced into Woburn Park in Bedfordshire in 1894 and from there, it appears, the 12th Duke of Bedford deliberately released small groups into the surrounding countryside. They had not colonized very far even by the 1940s, at which point there were further releases, again by major landowners, at Elveden in Suffolk, Bicester in Oxfordshire and Corby in Northamptonshire. Only in the last decades of the century did the muntjac spread more widely, part of a more general increase in the numbers of all species of deer in England (below, p. 155). It is now widespread across much of southern and central England, where it has even been encountered in overgrown suburban gardens.[69] Muntjac more than most deer can cause serious problems in ancient woodland, consuming with relish characteristic plants like primrose, bluebell and common spotted orchid.[70] They may also compete with the native roe for food.[71]

Landscapes of diversification

As it became uneconomic to farm large areas for cereals or meat, new forms of land use were developed with, as I noted earlier, a significant expansion of dairying, small holding and market gardening. This development also reflected, of course, the increasingly urbanized character of England in this period, the decline in the proportion of the population with access to their own, or local, sources of eggs, poultry and vegetables. Commercial orchards also experienced significant expansion, both in new areas like the Fens, south-west Middlesex and southern Buckinghamshire, and in districts in which they had long been important, such as Kent, Herefordshire, Worcestershire and Gloucestershire.[72] But a more significant form of diversification in environmental terms was the development of fur farms. The Chilean coypu (*Myopotanus coypu*) began to be kept in East Anglia in the 1920s. An article in the *Transactions of the Norfolk and Norwich Naturalists Society* for 1931 emphasized, ominously, the importance of keeping the creatures securely fenced in, 'since the damage they might do to trees, dams, canals, river banks and so forth might be very serious'.[73] By the mid-1940s, they had indeed escaped and were widely established in the wild, particularly in Broadland. Besides breeding quickly, an individual adult coypu consumes about 25 per cent of its body weight daily. The coypu had some beneficial effects, most notably in arresting the steady encroachment of scrub and wet woodland across the open fens, but nevertheless 'in places their depredations are so intense that they are now considered a serious pest'.[74] Large areas were denuded of water lilies, bulrushes, reed-mace, and cowbane, and 'hundreds of acres of saw-sedge were laid low.'[75] A campaign of eradiation was launched in 1962: the last coypu was killed in 1987.

More serious in its long-term consequences, although with a negligible impact within the period covered by this book, was the farming of the

American mink (*Mustela vison*), which began in 1929. Predictably, some individuals had escaped within a few years, although breeding populations – in the valley of the River Teign in Devon – were not recorded until 1956.[76] As many readers will be aware, mink have subsequently (in part as a consequence of further releases) become a serious pest in many districts. It is the only one of our introduced species which is carnivorous, and it has made a significant impact in particular on the population of water voles. The American muskrat (*Ondatra zibethicus*) – a third exotic animal established on fur farms in the inter-War period – was less successful. There were over 80 Muskrat farms in the country by 1930, and substantial feral colonies were soon established in the Severn valley, and smaller ones in Surrey and Sussex. But a systematic programme of eradication, largely motivated by the damage the animals wrought to river banks, ensured that they were extinct by 1935.[77]

The most environmentally significant form of diversification – one which also reflected new social and political structures, especially the rise of direct state intervention in the economy – was forestry. The agricultural revolution and high farming periods had taken a terrible toll on ancient woodland, and new plantations had not made up for it. By 1913 there were only around 670,000 hectares of woodland in England, including both areas of ancient, semi-natural woodland, and plantations established in the course of the post-medieval period – no more than c.5.2 per cent of the country's land area.[78] The extent to which the nation was dependent on imported timber supplies, especially to provide pit props for coal mines, was made starkly apparent by the wartime blockade, and in 1916 the Prime Minister, H. H. Asquith, appointed the Forestry Sub-Committee of the Ministry of Reconstruction to consider the state of the country's wood and timber reserves.[79] This proposed that, over the following 80 years, no less than 1,770,000 acres (c.72,000 hectares) of land should be planted with trees, one and a half million acres by direct state purchase and planting, the rest through private enterprise or joint public/private schemes.[80] The Forestry Commission was duly established, and by 1950 302,000 acres (c.122,000 hectares) of land had been planted in England, by which time their first plantings were still less than 30 years old.[81] While concern for strategic timber reserves, especially of softwoods, was the main reason for the establishment of the Commission, as John Sheail has pointed out right from the start the government had other interests, especially the relief of unemployment in rural areas.[82]

The policies of the Commission were fundamentally influenced by continental forestry methods, by the need for fast-growing trees to rapidly replenish timber stocks and provide pit props, and by the kinds of terrain targeted for planting – almost exclusively upland moors and lowland heaths, or derelict fields reclaimed in the previous centuries from such terrain. It therefore concentrated on the planting of conifers, rather than of deciduous hardwoods. Sitka spruce, Norway spruce, Japanese larch and lodgepole pine were the main species used in upland locations; in the lowlands there was a greater emphasis on Scots pine, later on Corsican pine.[83] In fact, the initial plantings in some areas also included a significant proportion of indigenous hardwoods, principally oak and beech. In 1935 1,186 acres (480 hectares) of conifers were planted in Breckland, but as many as 428 acres (150 hectares) of hardwood trees. But it was difficult to establish hardwoods on heaths and moors and they grew more slowly than conifers; their use was soon abandoned and many existing plantings failed.[84] They remained significant in some areas, however, as in Breckland, where they were planted in strips beside the principal roads and railways. Here they still serve to provide an illusion of a forest more mixed in character than it actually is. In part these plantings were established to reduce the risk of fires spreading from the sparks emanating from trains or steam-driven road vehicles. Although indigenous woodland, in Oliver Rackham's memorable phrase, 'burns like wet asbestos',[85] young conifer plantations are highly combustible, and the new forests experienced a series of massive fires in the 1920s and early 30s. But the deciduous trees were also intended to reduce public opposition to the Commission's activities. Most of the districts targeted for planting were open landscapes, valued by ramblers and others. The new plantations, uniform and largely composed of alien species, appeared unpleasant and visually intrusive. In the 1930s the Commission's plans to plant 300 hectares in Upper Eskdale in the Lake District led to a prolonged campaign of opposition which culminated in a successful public subscription to raise the £2 per acre compensation required for not planting the land, much of which subsequently passed to the National Trust. The dispute also led to a voluntary agreement negotiated between the Commission and the Council for the Protection of Rural England – of which more later – which restricted the establishment of plantations within a central block of c.300 square miles of the Lakes.[86]

The sheer scale of the plantings, which completely transformed vast swathes of open countryside, was a major reason for opposition. Julian Tennyson described in 1939 how:

> The Commission has worked its way steadily through the centre of Breckland, buying and leasing estates, removing boundary after boundary, until now there is scarcely a couple of miles of ground left unplanted between Lakenheath Warren and Elveden in Suffolk and the road from Methwold to West Wretham in Norfolk. It has swept everything before it: the heaths and brecks in its paths have disappeared for ever. Small wonder that those who loved the old spirit of Breckland should complain that they can now scarcely even recognize their own country.[87]

There were also concerns about the impact of afforestation on biodiversity, although this in fact was complex, as it changed significantly over time. In heathland districts the stone curlew nested with some success in young plantations, and lapwings on the rides between them, although not for long. The former deserted the forests within 3 or 4 years of planting, the latter after around 7 years. A range of other birds, less rare but nevertheless characteristic of the heaths, likewise decreased, including skylark, meadow pipit, stonechat and whinchat, and although the ringed plover took to nesting on areas of nearby arable for a while it, too, soon largely deserted afforested areas.[88] There was in turn an expansion in the numbers of the more common farmland birds. In moorland districts the situation was similar: birds typical of open habitats, such as the greenshank, declined markedly, grouse and golden plover lost their nesting sites in the heather, while raptors like the buzzard were adversely affected by the contraction in their hunting grounds.[89] In the early stages of coniferization meadow pipits, whinchats and reed buntings flourished, while as trees increased in size redpolls, siskins and crossbills did well: all, indeed, have expanded their breeding ranges as a consequence of afforestation.[90] This in turn appears to have encouraged birds such as the merlin which feed on them, as well as on the various small mammals which gradually colonized the plantations.

Large-scale afforestation also had a major impact on vegetation, perhaps especially in upland areas. The dense conifers shaded out the plants beneath, especially in the early stages of growth, and their needles blanketed the ground, further increasing levels of soil acidity. In heathland areas heather, gorse and other plants often survived in the rides, but many species were lost. In Breckland, the largest afforested area in the lowlands, the rare local flora was badly affected: spiked and fingered speedwell (*Veronica spicata* and *V. triphyllus*) and field wormwood (*Artemisia campestris*) became rare, largely although not entirely as a consequence of afforestation, although some of the plants associated with ruderal conditions returned when areas were eventually clear-felled.[91] Characteristic heathland lichens were also badly affected: 'conifers have a very poor lichen flora'.[92] But while many of the distinctive moths, beetles and butterflies of the heathlands declined markedly, a surprising proportion of open-ground carabids were able to survive on trackways and rides, spreading more widely as the forest matured and the canopy opened, and when areas were clear-felled.[93] Moreover, certain species of beetle characteristic of coniferous woodland, unknown in southern Britain before the plantings, now appeared, some colonizing from Scotland, such as *Phloeostiba lapponica*, but others from Continental Europe, including *Plegaderus vulneratus*.[94]

The picture, although perhaps largely negative, is thus mixed and complex, and this is even more true if we take a longer view, into the later twentieth century, when the first plantings reached maturity and the Commission itself began to pursue more ecologically sensitive policies.[95] It has thus been suggested that the hen harrier, which had become extinct as we have seen in mainland Britain by the end of the nineteenth century, owes its successful return during the second half of the twentieth century to the new conifer plantations; afforestation may also be responsible for significant increases in the populations of green woodpeckers.[96] The massive expansion in the numbers of all species of deer, native and introduced, in England since the 1950s is also, in part, a consequence of the new plantations. By the end of the nineteenth century, few deer were to be found in the wild, except in parts of Devon and Cornwall: all were essentially animals kept in parks. Wild populations were probably already increasing in the early twentieth century but afforestation provided large tracts of cover where deer could proliferate, although other factors, including the relatively undisturbed character of the rural landscape as the mechanization of farming proceeded apace, have certainly contributed to the current population explosion.[97] People sometimes wonder why the recovery in deer numbers is not heralded as an environmental 'good news' story. But deer are now present in woodland at higher much densities than could be sustained naturally, reaping the rich harvest afforded by the surrounding fields, and thus do untold damage to woodland plants and trees, in some areas making it almost impossible to reinstate coppicing in ancient woods.[98]

Protecting nature

The interest in natural history which, as we have seen, burgeoned in the early and middle years of the nineteenth century continued into its later decades. Darwin's revolutionary ideas caused much disagreement among the ranks of amateurs, and the study of the natural world became more professionalized, with the establishment of laboratory-based biology at the country's universities. But popular interest remained strong. New national societies, like the British Ornithological Union, were founded; most counties now acquired their own Naturalists Societies; a string of county-based studies, of flora and ornithology, were produced, such as J. E. Harting's *Birds of Middlesex* in 1866 or Alexander Clark Kennedy's *Birds of Berkshire and Buckinghamshire* of 1868.[99] 'Nature studies' was part of the curriculum established by the 1870 Education Act; while the spread of bicycles from the 1890s, and subsequently of cars and buses, allowed greater access to the countryside for botanists and ornithologists.[100] The early volumes of the *Victoria County Histories*, which appeared between 1899 and 1908, all featured sections on *natural* history, alongside such things as descriptions of a county's archaeology and extracts from Domesday Book.[101] While rigorous amateur science continued, however, there was also an expansion of a softer, more whimsical style of writing, exemplified by the works of W. H. Hudson, such as *Nature in Downland* or *A Shepherd's Life*.[102] Bird spotting became more popular than ever and in general terms the period saw an increasing emphasis on observing wildlife and – among a dedicated minority – more carefully plotting its distributions and recording its behaviour. Conversely, there was a gradual decline in collecting, especially where this involved the killing of mammals or birds. In Allen's words, the

1880s saw 'the first, unmistakable signs . . . of a widely shared interest in watching birds without any attempt to shoot them'.[103]

We should not exaggerate the speed with which this latter attitude took hold. Well into the twentieth century, many keen naturalists were also sportsmen, and many of the rare birds reported in the journals of county societies were specimens that had been shot. Nevertheless, the new attitudes fused with wider concerns about cruelty to domestic animals, especially as there was now widespread awareness that many wild species were experiencing significant declines. The East Riding Association for the Protection of Sea-Birds was established in 1868 in Bridlington, arguably the first conservation movement in the world, and the Sea Birds Protection Act was passed in 1869. This was followed by the Wild Bird Protection Act of 1872; the Wild Fowl Preservation Act of 1876;[104] and by the much vaunted Wild Bird Protection Act of 1880, which established a national close season for a number of birds, and made it illegal to take their eggs.[105] Its effects were limited, however, because it was left to local authorities to decide which of the listed birds should be afforded protection, while no protection at all was given to adults outside the close season. Moreover, as Marchant and Watkins noted in 1897, 'Many rare birds, which are in danger of being exterminated, have been left out, for example, the kite, the osprey, the buzzard, and the hen harrier, and there might well have been added birds such as the kestrel, the golden eagle, the rose-coloured pastor, the heron and the crossbill', mostly birds of prey, of course, and thus considered a threat to game.[106] In fact, while the Act did not give national protection to these species, in a number of counties many were afforded a degree of local protection, through the enactment of specific Statutory Instruments, in part because of continued protests against their wanton destruction.[107]

Continued concern over the fate of the nation's birds, and in particular over their slaughter to provide plumage for women's hats, led to the foundation of the Society for the Protection of Birds, later the RSPB, in 1889. Its vigorous campaign against egg-collecting and indiscriminate shooting helped lead to further legislation: the 1896 Wild Birds Protection Act, which gave county councils the right to apply for orders to protect particular areas or species; and the Act of 1902, which allowed any birds or eggs which had been taken illegally to be confiscated. These were followed by Acts of 1904 and 1908, which forbade the use of pole traps; and by the Protection of Birds Act of 1925, which banned the use of lime to catch birds.[108]

The RSPB was one of several conservation movements which developed in the later nineteenth and early twentieth centuries.[109] These, although overlapping in their aims and membership, were of diverse character, their supporters putting varying degrees of emphasis on the preservation of rural landscapes, open spaces for recreation, ancient buildings and wildlife. The earliest was the Commons Preservation Society, founded in 1865 by John Stuart Mill, Lord Eversley, Sir Robert Hunter and Octavia Hill, the housing reformer. Although surviving areas of common land were often of prime conservation importance, the main interest of the society was in their preservation as areas for healthy recreation. Its founders were motivated by a similar concern for the moral and physical degeneration of the working class as proponents of new urban parks. A well-connected and energetic lobbying group, with keen legal expertise, the CPS was largely responsible for preserving Hampstead Heath, Epping Forest and other London commons from being built over, by persuading the Metropolitan Board of Works and subsequently the GLC to purchase them.[110] More important in the long run was the National Trust, founded in 1895 by Octavia Hill, Sir Robert Hunter, and Canon Hardwicke Rawnsley, a clergyman from the Lake District, with the aim of preserving 'for the benefit of the Nation . . . lands and tenements (including buildings) of beauty or historic interest' by outright acquisition.[111] Not surprisingly, the idea of preserving blocks of land where wildlife, especially its rarer forms, could flourish became increasingly popular among naturalists, especially ornithologists. And while wildlife conservation was not its main concern the first property acquired by the National Trust was in fact Wicken Fen in Cambridgeshire, one of the last fragments of undrained Fenland, a gift from Charles Rothschild (brother of Lionel Walter). In 1912 the 1,335 acres of salt marsh at Blakeney Point in Norfolk was purchased by public subscription and handed over to the National Trust, followed by the 1,821 acres of Scolt Head in 1923.[112] By this time that organization had acquired a number of other places because of their wildlife importance, such as Watermeads in Surrey in 1913.

Meanwhile, Rothschild himself was responsible for the establishment, in 1912, of the Society for the Promotion of Nature Reserves, which soon produced a list of sites which it believed should be preserved for the nation.[113] Rothschild himself bought Woodwalton Fen in Huntingdonshire and gave it to the Society as their first reserve, and soon afterwards the first of the County Wildlife Trusts, for Norfolk, was established in 1926 in order to save the coastal marshes at Cley from being drained for agriculture. Further reserves were established by the Trust over the following decades: at Martham in 1928; Alderfen Broad in 1930; Wretham Heath in 1938; and Weeting in 1942.[114] But it was not until 1946 that the Yorkshire Wildlife Trust was formed, initially to manage a reserve at Askam Moor, acquired by Sir Francis Terry and Arnold Rowntree to save it from development; this was followed by the establishment of the Lincolnshire Wildlife Trust in 1948.[115]

Wildlife reserves were initially viewed in essentially scientific terms, as open air laboratories and important habitats to be protected from development and disturbance – including disturbance by the general public. Many naturalists regarded the increasing numbers of trippers and holidaymakers now able to make their way far into the countryside as a major threat to wildlife. Gay in 1944 described how improvements in transport and especially the advent of the small car had led to:

> The ever-increasing popularity of Norfolk as a holiday resort. Hitherto summer visitors were mainly confined to the Broads and the coastal

towns, but now every village became accessible, and the beaches and quiet sea-shore, up to this time known to the comparatively few people interested in the bird-life there, were invaded by holiday-makers'.[116]

The fact that many of the earliest nature reserves were important coastal breeding sites is significant. There was much contemporary criticism of 'assemblages of caravans and converted buses which have littered and spoilt many a charming stretch of coast line'.[117] In the words of the Council for the Protection of Rural England in 1936, the period following the end of World War I had witnessed 'a national movement seawards'.[118]

The CPRE, formed in 1926, had no intention of acquiring tracts of land for conservation, but instead acted as a pressure group, protecting the countryside from urban expansion and from the more general threats posed by modernity and motor cars. Clough Williams-Ellis, Patrick Abercrombie and other leading members were appalled by the unplanned, scruffy sprawl of the inter-war years – the suburbs, road signs, adverts, holiday shacks, and petrol stations which formed, in the title of Williams-Ellis's famous book, 'The Octopus' that was strangling rural England.[119] But as Matlass has argued, the founders of the CPRE were not simply backward-looking reactionaries, nostalgically hanging on to a disappearing rural world.[120] They had an essentially modernist agenda which prioritised the importance of state planning against the *laissez-faire* attitudes of the Victorian past – asserting, in effect, the public over the private interest. The aims of the society, as stated in 1926, were to 'preserve all things of true value and beauty', but also to ensure 'the scientific and orderly development of all local resources'.[121] Many of the society's leading figures, like Abercrombie, were members of the emerging profession of town planners, and closely involved in the development of planning controls described in the next chapter.

As ideas of state intervention and large-scale spatial planning became more and more acceptable in the inter-War years, eventually triumphing during World War II, the concept that particular areas should be earmarked for nature conservation – as well as zoned for housing, industry or agricultural use – also came to seem more reasonable. So too did the idea that wider areas of scenic beauty should be subject to particularly tight planning controls. The CPRE argued for the creation of National Parks almost from its inception and persuaded the government to accept the idea in principal in 1931. Nothing was done in practice, however, largely because of financial constraints, but pressure continued, particularly from John Dower whose pamphlet *The Case for National Parks in Great Britain* was published in 1938.[122] The Society for the Promotion of Nature Reserves also continued to lobby actively, organizing an influential conference on 'Nature Preservation in Post-War Reconstruction' in 1941. The recovery of agriculture and the intensification of farming which came with the outbreak of War in 1939 caused widespread alarm among naturalists. As one observer put it in 1942: 'At the present time we see a great drive being made to bring into cultivation many more [marginal] lands, some of which are probably part of original England, and, if the war should continue for long, I imagine that a great drainage scheme will be instituted which will eventually dry up many of the existing sanctuaries for wild life'.[123] In the same year the government's Nature Reserves Investigation Committee was formed and in 1949 the National Parks and Access to the Countryside Act, as well as establishing the first National Parks, also set up the modern system of Sites of Special Scientific Interest (SSSI) – designated areas protected, because of their importance in wildlife conservation, from intensive agriculture or development.

Conclusion

The period between c.1870 and 1939 was not, in any simple and unproblematic manner, a 'golden age' for English wildlife, as many contemporaries were aware. The activities of gamekeepers, the establishment of state forests, the widespread decline in traditional management practices, and the continuation of intensive agriculture in arable districts, all damaged long-established habitats and led to continuing declines in a number of species of flora and fauna. In Cambridgeshire, for example, Preston has noted how rates of plant extinctions actually *rose* in the first 30 years of the twentieth century.[124] Yet at the same time, a variety of organizations devoted to the preservation of the countryside now came into existence. As state intervention in economic and social matters became more usual and acceptable, demands grew for coherent policies of land-use planning, and for legislation to protect important landscapes, habitats and species. Most conservationists saw the continued expansion of towns, the improvement of roads and the spread of suburbs as among the most important threats to the natural world. But just as some types of essentially artificial habitat in the countryside were being destroyed or altered out of all recognition by social and economic change, novel ones were emerging in urban and industrial areas.

CHAPTER NINE

New urban environments, c.1860–1950

Industry and pollution

Although the effects of industrial pollution may have been localized and limited in the period before c.1860, they became more severe and extensive thereafter as the scale of industrial production continued to grow. Changes in the methods of sewage disposal during the second half of the nineteenth century led to a gradual decline in the amount of effluent flowing directly into watercourses, but levels of industrial pollution remained high. In 1900 it was said of the Mersey that 'running as it does for the greater part between artificial banks and gathering fresh impurities with every mile, it is doubtful whether the river contains any fish below Stockport'.[1] Research carried out in the 1970s, when many northern rivers were still extensively polluted, shows that they carried an impoverished fauna dominated by the louse *Asellus aquaticus*, accompanied by small numbers of freshwater shrimps, the larvae of caddis flies and mayflies, and a fish population largely restricted to gudgeon (*Gobio gobio*) and roach (*Rutilus rutilus*).[2] It was in this period, moreover, that the effects of airborne pollution on flora and fauna became serious. Lichens and mosses were seriously affected: most lichens are killed by levels of atmospheric sulphur dioxide exceeding 150 micrograms per cubic metre. In urban areas, a variety of foliose lichens declined, and were subsequently replaced by the green alga *Desmococcus olivaceus*, first noted in western Europe in 1860, which is now almost universally found on trees in towns.[3] But higher forms of vegetation were also increasingly affected. One observer in 1882 bemoaned how, in south-east Lancashire, 'fruitful vales where vegetation flourished, roses grew in abundance, and the most delicate flowers thrived, have been changed by the deleterious compounds of coal-smoke into barren deserts'.[4] One Mrs Haweis was moved in 1886 to pen a book entitled *Rus in urbe: or flowers that thrive in London gardens and smoky towns*.[5] In northern towns and cities, trees and shrubs planted in public parks were frequently killed, or made ill and disfigured, by aerial pollution and needed to be regularly replenished by the civic authorities. By the earlier twentieth century smog damage to market garden crops, such as tomatoes, was one of the factors encouraging the migration of nurseries northwards, away from London, along the Lea valley; smog could even have a serious impact on grass, 'causing a slimy scum and creating acid conditions that destroy the useful bacteria in the soil'.[6]

The decline of lichens in industrial areas had a knock-on effect on certain kinds of fauna. It was noticed in the late 1840s how a number of species of moth in northern industrial towns and in London – principally the peppered moth (*Pachys betularia*) but also the waved umber (*Hemerophila abruptaria*), mottled beauty (*Boarmia repandata*) and grey dagger (*Acronycta*) – were beginning to exhibit significant changes in colour. Dark or black variants or 'melanic' forms, always present in low numbers, now showed a marked increase. Before industrialization such individuals were highly visible to predators against the mottled background of lichen-covered trees. But as lichens were killed off and tree trunks became blackened with soot, these forms flourished and by 1895 98 per cent of peppered moths in the Manchester area were of this type, the normal form now being the more vulnerable. This explanation for the change, often quoted as a powerful contemporary example of natural selection in action, was first advanced by J. W. Tutt in the 1890s and tested empirically by Kettlewell and Ford in the 1950s.[7] Although the validity of their work has since been challenged,[8] the theory has largely been confirmed by subsequent studies and – more powerfully – by the fact that, with the decline in aerial pollution since 1950, trees have become less sooted, the proportion of 'normal' moth forms has risen sharply and melanic forms have again become rare.[9] It is probable that pollution had a more general negative effect on insects in this period. It has thus been suggested that the marked recovery in the numbers of swifts and house martins in central London following the passing of the Clean Air Act in 1946 may be due in large part to the resultant improvement in the number of the insects which are their prime food source.[10] Some believed that accelerating levels of smoke pollution – both domestic and industrial in character – had a more generally deleterious effect on bird life.[11] When John Plant began to record the number of birds in Manchester's Peel Park in the 1850s, numbers were still healthy, with a total of 71 species, of which 34 were breeding. By the 1870s there were only 19, of which eight were breeding; in 1882 he could find only five species in the park, and only sparrow and starling were nesting there.[12]

All the varied industrial landscapes discussed in Chapter 5 continued to be created in the late nineteenth and early twentieth centuries – spoil heaps of great variety, quarries and the like – and on an even greater scale. Most still escaped the fate which has befallen so many in recent decades – reclaimed and 'greened' as a monotonous expanse of turf – instead developing in the organic manner, already described, towards woodland. But of greater significance for wildlife was the emergence for the first time of extensive, complex and continuous urban environments.

The extent and character of urban growth

The area of England devoted to housing and industry grew steadily between c.1860 and 1950. It was in this period that the great conurbations, based on Manchester, Newcastle, Birmingham and London, first really developed (Figure 29). In part, as I have already noted, this was a consequence of continued demographic growth, the country's population more than doubling between these two dates. But it was also due to improvements in transport systems. A higher density of railways, the appearance of buses and the spread of car ownership meant that people did not need to live close to where they worked. Housing thus spread more widely, and more thinly, across the landscape, especially in the inter-war years: this was the great age of the suburb.[13] We should not of course exaggerate the extent of all this building. Even in 1950 houses and gardens still accounted for less than eight per

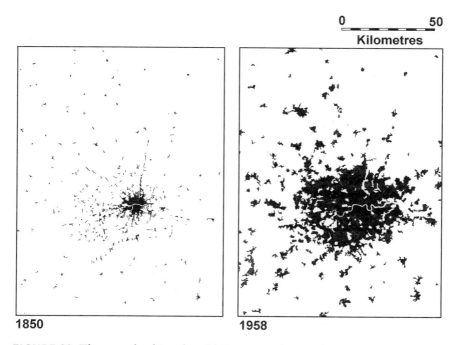

1850   1958

FIGURE 29 *The growth of London, 1850–1958 (after Sinclair 1964).*

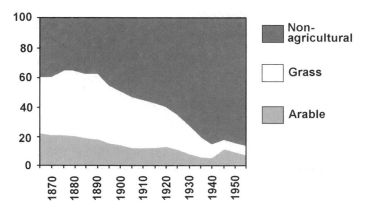

FIGURE 30 *Changing land use in Middlesex, 1865–1955 (after Preston 2000).*

cent of the total land area[14] This said, where large conurbations developed houses and industry often sprawled over an extensive tracts of ground. In Middlesex by 1950 over 80 per cent of the land area was occupied by houses, gardens, and other 'agriculturally unproductive land', most of it industrial in character (Figure 30).[15] The decline in farmland in the county since the middle of the nineteenth century had been phenomenal.

The character of town and city centres also changed in the later nineteenth and early twentieth centuries. Buildings became larger and their architecture more ornate, and larger areas of the ground surface were paved. Moreover, growing concern about the state of public hygiene, motivated in part by a series of bad outbreaks of typhoid and Asiatic cholera in the 1830s and 40s, led to the passing of the Public Health Act of 1848, which placed the supply of water, sewerage, drainage, cleansing and paving under the control of local bodies called 'Health Boards' which, together with existing municipal authorities, employed both national legislation and local bylaws to improve living conditions.[16] In 1855, the Metropolitan Board of works was established in London to provide a city-wide system of sewers.[17] Other large cities soon followed suit, although it was only in the 1870s and 80s that most major towns gained reasonable systems of sewage disposal, and even later that they obtained systematic refuse collection services.

Those with a background in the humanities might easily assume that the inexorable spread of bricks and mortar, concrete and asphalt, and the increasing scale and density of building in urban centres, were inimical to wildlife. But although existing habitats were often destroyed by urban growth important new ones were created. Towns and cities, as we shall see, displayed considerable variety, especially in terms of the density of houses and buildings, but their distinctive environmental character was shaped by three main features.[18] First, they contained many disturbed environments, the consequence of traffic, footfall, cycles of development and redevelopment, and the intense and regular cultivation of gardens and parks. Plants characteristic of advanced successional stages – such as species associated with ancient woodland – are thus generally absent. But others flourish, often in unusual combinations. The ability to tolerate disturbance is the key selective factor in urban contexts, ensuring that plant species with limited ranges in the countryside, being out-competed by rivals in most soil or moisture conditions, can thrive in a much wider range of circumstances, leading in turn to the development of plant communities of a kind never encountered in rural areas. Second, disturbed conditions provided good opportunities for introduced species, large numbers of which came from two sources: gardens, which accounted for increasing areas of ground; and industry, which sourced many of its raw materials from around the world. Aliens already present, such as Oxford ragwort (*Senechio squalidus*), also flourished. Urban areas were thus increasingly distinguished from rural districts by having floras comprising a mixture of indigenous and alien plants.[19] Indeed, the extent to which aliens have come to characterize the urban flora is often underestimated. Most dandelions found today in towns and cities, for example, are introduced species, *Taraxacum atacum* and *Taraxacum exacutum*, rather than the native *Taraxacum officinale* agg. Lastly, urban and suburban environments are characterized by considerable variety within a small compass: in Gilbert's words, they comprise a 'varied and small-scale habitat mosaic imposed by man'.[20] Within a single street, close juxtaposition of paved areas and gardens, and within the latter of lawns, hedges, flower beds and shrubberies, provided more diversity than could be found within an equivalent area of farmland (it should be emphasized that much of this had been true of the towns and cities of earlier periods: urban environments are considered in detail in this chapter principally because they now came to occupy a much greater area than ever before). These three factors together ensured that towns, while having less total vegetation cover than the countryside they replaced, usually boasted a higher number of plant species. This was also true of invertebrate populations; but the situation with higher fauna, unable to cope with high levels of disturbance and lack of cover, was more variable, and reflected the spatial organization of towns and cities.

City centre wildlife

As cities grew larger through the later nineteenth and early twentieth centuries, the density of buildings and the proportion of the ground surface paved or otherwise surfaced in their central districts both steadily increased, something that Hudson described, in the case of London in the 1890s, as the 'deadly filling-up process'.[21] Fitter, likewise discussing central London but some 50 years later, noted how 'the ground is completely covered with buildings, roads and railway lines and vegetation is almost non-existent. Yet even in this desert, quite a number of animals, especially birds, have managed to adapt themselves to the modern environment'.[22] The term 'desert' is, however, slightly misleading, for some gardens, roadside trees, and pockets of derelict land were usually present even at the heart of the greatest conurbations. Hadden's study of 1978 recorded no less than 157 plant species within the four square kilometres of London's W1, not only on islands of greenery but also elsewhere, in cracks in paved surfaces for example.[23] Indeed, distinctive communities develop in such contexts, in conditions of severe trampling but of fertile, if compact, soil, featuring such plants as annual meadow grass (*Poa annua*), procumbent pearlwort (*Sagina procumbens*), greater plantain (*Plantago major*) and dandelion (*Taraxacum* sp.).[24] Before 1950, floral diversity was often encouraged in city centres by of the presence of factories (now often relocated to the margins of built-up areas) processing raw materials imported from abroad. The refuse from woollen mills – the 'grey shoddy' combed from the wool – was thus full of seeds embedded in fleeces brought from Australia, Africa and South America, many of which – like the Australian piri piri (*Acaena novaezelandica*) – germinated successfully on neighbouring waste land.[25] Substantial numbers of foreign invertebrates were also to be found in such locations, and in general terms invertebrate faunas could be surprisingly rich, Parmenter recording over 200 species of fly on a bomb site in Cripplegate in 1953.[26] Mammal populations in contrast were low, due in large measure to a paucity of undisturbed sites: only rats and mice really flourished in the city centre. But many birds adapted well to built-up conditions. The tall public, commercial and industrial buildings erected in increasing numbers in the second half of the nineteenth century were in architectural styles (especially gothic, dominant from the 1860s) which featured an abundance of arches, ledges and recesses, making them ideal places for feral pigeons. These, as already noted, were widespread in urban areas, especially London, from an early date but their numbers now increased steadily. They were joined by starlings, swifts, house sparrows and – in the first half of the twentieth century, in London – by the black redstart and the kestrel. All 'have forsaken their rock faces and adapted to breeding on tall buildings'.[27] Other species flew regularly into the central areas of cities from the margins, attracted by such things as the grain dropped outside mills near docks. The house sparrow was the most numerous bird in inner cities by the late nineteenth century. Hudson in the 1890s claimed it was the only bird found in significant numbers in central London.[28] It was a general feeder and flexible in its choice of nesting site, as well as being tolerant of disturbance. Numbers may have peaked around 1900, for sparrows fed in particular on the dung of horses and the sweepings from their nosebags[29]: but like all city birds, they also benefited from the scraps intentionally proffered by the human inhabitants. All this said, the number of birds in city centres was to some extent kept in check by domestic and feral cats, Hudson in 1898 estimating that there were as many as three-quarters of a million in London alone.[30]

A number of particularly distinctive urban environments were emerging by the middle decades of the twentieth century. Stamp in 1950 referred to the 'changing location of industry which was taking place in the inter-War years' and described how 'there was in many of the older industrial centres an increasing degree of decay, as the older factories became obsolescent and eventually closed down, and were not replaced by new'.[31] Such areas of derelict land were further increased by bombing during World War II and by the clearance of slum dwellings after 1950. They were and are complex environments.[32] Demolition of buildings produces a substrate of brick rubble, usually rich in lime because of the abundance of fine mortar. This is initially colonized by species with windborn seeds, such as Oxford ragwort, groundsel, and buddleia (*Buddleja davidii*), but fairly minor differences in the character of the rubble, in terms of structure and alkalinity, ensure marked variations in the initial communities of plants. After a few years, the vegetation becomes dominated by tall perennial herbs with leafy stems, many of which are exotics and garden escapees. Rosebay willow herb is perhaps the most common but it is accompanied by michaelmas daisy, golden rod, garden lupin, tansy and Shasta daisy. Native plants are also present, including a range of thistles (creeping and spear especially), common mallow, buttercups and mugwort, wood margin plants like hedge woundwort and bracken, and species of neutral grassland such as yarrow or cat's-ear.[33]

After eight or so years these various communities develop into rough grasslands, as plants like false oat-grass, Yorkshire fog and red fescue obtain a hold, although still with stands of taller herbs, such as yarrow or michaelmas daisy: at this stage, thickets of Japanese knotweed also sometimes form.[34] Eventually they develop as scrub and then as woodland, although the distance of city centres from seed sources sometimes makes this a slow process. Ash, sycamore, broom, laburnum, hawthorn, rowan, elder and apple, together with willows, birch, cotoneasters and garden privet are usually prominent. 'Such woods are unlike any other self-sown examples in the country'.[35]

What makes these urban wastegrounds particularly interesting was, and is, their variety. Not only have different substrates generated variations on these broad successional themes, even on different parts of the same site, but the availability of seed sources creates radical differences in the character of communities. Indeed, different cities developed their own distinctive waste ground flora, the result of idiosyncrasies of geology, soils, climate, and history. Climate ensured, for example, that buddleia remained rare in cities in the north of England and that reed and Himalayan balsam came to dominate waste ground in the west, where there were and are also denser and more extensive stands of willow herb and Japanese knotweed than in drier eastern cities. The limestone cliffs around Bristol support large quantities of traveller's joy and its seeds are readily blown by the wind into the city, ensuring that the species became a major component of its wasteground flora. Oliver Gilbert has described in some detail the distinctive urban floras of Birmingham, Swindon, Teesside, Bristol, Hull, Leeds, Manchester,

Norwich and Sheffield.[36] The latter, for example, is characterized by colourful garden escapees, especially feverfew, goats rue and michaelmas daisy, tansy and golden rod, which in places formed distinctive flowery 'meadows'. The river Don flows through the centre of the city, and here – together with great thickets of Himalayan balsam – Gilbert recorded a number of large fig trees. These had evidently grown from seeds which had passed into the river in treated sewage, but what was curious was that they only occurred in the east of the city – the district associated with heavy industry – and that none appeared to be less than c.70 years old. Gilbert deduced that the establishment of the figs:

> Coincided with the height of the steel industry. At that time river water was used for cooling purposes and the Don ran at a constant 20 degrees centigrade: it was this special microclimate that enabled the trees to establish in such large numbers. Following the decline of the steel industry, river temperatures have returned to normal but mature trees are able to survive.[37]

The character of suburbia

These kinds of built-up or derelict landscapes accounted for only a small part of towns and cities by the 1950s. Much larger areas were occupied by suburbs, primarily residential in character, in which most houses were provided with gardens of some kind and within which there was more open space generally. These districts provided a greater range of habitats for wildlife: indeed, as Davis showed in 1978, in terms of arthropods the best predictor of diversity was the proportion of land in an urban area occupied by gardens and parks.[38] In the period before c.1920 urban and suburban growth tended to be closely associated with railway lines and stations, and to a lesser extent with the principal roads, so that built-up areas took the form of broad ribbons spreading out from major towns, leaving pockets of open countryside between. Moreover, where land was developed rather simple grids of roads were laid out and plots usually sold to a multiplicity of individuals or companies, who often developed them over a period of years or even decades. In part this was because difficulties in obtaining mortgages ensured that people at all social levels tended to rent their homes. Developers thus often leased out the houses they had erected rather than selling them, ensuring a slow return on their investment and limiting the amount of money available for further building. Although large-scale and rapid development sometimes occurred as often as not the transition from countryside to suburb was thus gradual.

It is important to emphasize that until the middle decades of the twentieth century, the development of suburbs was not 'planned', in the sense that

Health Boards – replaced in 1894 by the District Councils – or the new County Councils, established in 1888, decided on a strategic basis which areas could or could not be built over. Their involvement in the oversight of development was initially limited to the enforcement of bylaws concerning such things as the width of building plots. In 1909 The Housing and Town Planning Act established that District Councils could prepare planning schemes for any land in the course of development or likely to be developed, in order to ensure proper sanitary conditions and to prevent harm to owners of neighbouring properties.[39] But it was only in 1919 that the Housing and Town Planning Act made such schemes compulsory, and even then only for places where the population was above 20,000. In 1932 the Town and Country Planning Act extended planning schemes to rural land but local authorities were not obliged to draw them up, and were anyway obliged to compensate owners for any financial losses incurred by a refusal to grant development permission.[40] Attempts were also made to control low-density sprawl through the Restriction of Ribbon Development Act of 1935, which made all new building within 220 feet of classified roads subject to the control of the Local Authorities, although again with limited effects. Only with the passing of the 1947 Town and Country Planning Act were local authorities able to zone areas for development and allocate particular tracts as 'green belt' or otherwise retained as open space.

Late-nineteenth- and early twentieth-century suburbs took a variety of forms but – simplifying somewhat – we might envisage a spectrum, at one end of which were streets composed of rows of terraced houses – the homes of the lower middle or working classes, generally located towards town and city centres; and at the other, the more spacious roads of larger detached or semi-detached houses.[41] In general terms, the larger the house, the larger the garden, the greater the number of trees and shrubs, and the better the opportunities for wildlife to adapt to the new conditions: affluent areas also usually possessed more parks and other open spaces. This distinction is a little misleading, however, because by the start of the twentieth century the idea that urban landscapes should be laid out so that they included spaces for both recreation and nature was beginning to become established, especially through the writings of Ebenezer Howard. In his book *Tomorrow: a Peaceful Path to Real Reform* – published in 1898 but republished as *Garden Cities of Tomorrow* in 1902 – Howard not only urged an intensification of the existing tendency for homes to spread more widely and thinly across the landscape, so that there was 'a migratory movement of population from our overcrowded centres to sparsely-settled rural districts', but also that towns should have numerous green spaces in the form of private gardens and public parks, and be planned in such a way that 'all the fresh delights of the country – field, hedgerow, and woodland – not prim parks and gardens merely – would be within a few minutes walk or ride'.[42] Howard's ideas were put into practice most effectively in the development of Letchworth Garden City, which began to be laid out in north Hertfordshire in 1902.

Here, even the smallest houses were provided with gardens, and existing landscape features were preserved wherever possible: indeed, it is said that the city was built without felling a single tree.[43] As a result of these ideas, the extent of green infrastructure came, in some areas and some cases, to be less closely tied to the social status of an area's inhabitants.

In the inter-war period, the pace of suburban development accelerated: indeed, it has been estimated that around a third of the country's present housing stock was erected in the 20 years between 1919 and 1939.[44] Increases in car ownership, expansion in bus services, and improvements in the road network allowed a greater spread of housing, while the development of faster trains, some of them electric, made commuting over considerable distances a possibility for many. An expansion in the number of middle class jobs and the easier availability of mortgages increased levels of home ownership significantly. This, coupled with the expansion in light engineering and related activities, ensured rapid suburbanization in many parts of the West Midlands and the south especially.[45] Much of this took the form of streets of classic 'semis', with gardens larger than those accompanying earlier artisan terraces although still smaller than those associated with the larger detached homes, which also continued to be built, often now in more rural locations close to major rail lines.[46] Little controlled by planners, houses also sprawled across the countryside more generally, lining major roads as 'ribbon development' in order to reduce the costs of sewering and electricity supply. In addition, the inter-war period saw an increase in the numbers of council houses. Legislation to encourage the erection of council houses had been passed as early as 1890, with the Housing of the Working Class Act allowing Urban and Rural District Councils to apply for central government funding to erect houses. But few made use of this opportunity and it was only in 1919 that the Addison Act made it obligatory for councils to build houses, and under the 'Homes fit for Heroes' policy local authority expenditure on housing was subsidized. Further Acts, in 1923 and 1924, resulted in a government subsidy being paid on every house built, whether by local authorities or by private landowners.[47] All this added further to the area of low-density housing.

Garden wildlife

Private gardens had existed in England for centuries, as we have seen, but in ecological terms their importance now increased considerably simply because they came to occupy so large a proportion of the country's land surface. Together with parks and playing fields, they accounted for nearly a third of the area of British towns and cities by the 1950s, a total of around 5,000 square kilometres of land.[48] Domestic gardens were in some ways as unnatural as the streets and houses which surrounded them, stocked as they were with plants often ill-suited to local conditions and subject to regular disturbance through trimming, mowing and weeding.[49] In the twentieth century, as never before, they served as reservoirs from which alien species invaded the wider landscape, especially the urban landscape. Yet gardens were, or could be, also incredibly rich in native fauna and flora. Their benefits in this respect depended on their design, on the kinds of plant established within them, on the extent of cover provided by shrubs and trees, and on the diversity of habitats they provided within a circumscribed area.

In the late nineteenth century, there were major changes in the character of garden design among the wealthy and fashionable. Highly formal and geometric layouts involving the profligate use of bedding-out plants fell from favour.[50] Designers like William Robinson and Gertrude Jekyll instead advocated the planting of hardy perennial flowers, some of which were versions of indigenous species but others introduced, in wide herbaceous borders and beds. Such 'Arts and Crafts' gardens still had structured elements, often for example featuring compartments defined by yew or privet hedging and displays of roses arranged in geometric beds. But they also contained areas of less formal planting which at the largest residences, on the fringes of town, included woodland gardens: even in the smaller gardens shrubberies were a major feature. Robinson in particular advocated the creation of 'wild' areas where mixtures of native and introduced species would be planted in a casual, informal manner. At his own home, Gravetye manor is Sussex, he planted drifts of *scilla*, cyclamen and narcissus between the stools of hazel in the coppiced woods. Such designs were suited, not so much to the rolling acres of the established country house, but to the kind of large house in the countryside or on the edge of it, with extensive but not unmanageable grounds, of the kind now desired by many successful businessmen.[51]

Robinson's predilection for planting hardy exotics in the peripheral parts of gardens, on the edge of towns, had the predictable effect of encouraging their dispersal into the countryside, often many decades or centuries after their initial introduction.[52] White comfrey (*Symphytum orientale*), for example, one of Robinson's favourites, is a native of southern Russia which was first introduced as a garden plant as early as 1752, but which does not seem to have spread far before the later nineteenth century: it is now widely established in the countryside. Japanese knotweed, introduced at the start of the nineteenth century, likewise only really spread in the wild at this time.[53] It is now common on river banks throughout England, a serious threat to indigenous marginal vegetation. Canadian golden rod, a taller version of the native plant (reaching a height of two metres), was first planted in gardens in 1648, but it fell from favour because of its invasive tendencies. Robinson thought it ideal for the 'wild garden', particularly if planted with the American michaelmas daisy. Both are now widespread, not only in urban wastelands but – in the case of the former especially – in the countryside, again forming dense stands along watercourses.[54] Buddleia *Buddleja davidii* was another significant introduction of the period, brought from China in the 1890s. It spread rapidly throughout the country, in part (like Oxford ragwort before it) along the newly expanded rail network.[55] It was soon widely established in coastal districts, and on dry sandy soils in the countryside, but mainly in urban areas. Although an alien invader, capable of displacing indigenous plants, its attractiveness to butterflies has ensured that it is not regarded by naturalists with quite the horror reserved for plants like the rhododendron.

Elements of the Arts and Crafts style were widely adopted in the late nineteenth century and – in increasingly distorted forms – in small suburban gardens right through the first half of the twentieth. Crazy paving, for example, is a dim echo of the elegant paths of stone designed by Edwin Lutyens; the privet hedges separating innumerable front gardens from the public road are derived from the hedged compartments in Jekyll's designs. Smaller suburban gardens typically featured central lawns flanked by paths and borders of hardy perennials, and while many gardeners continued to practise some bedding-out, hardy perennials formed the principal planting.[56] Pergolas, rockeries, shrubberies and ponds were common features, again with origins in the designs of Jekyll and her contemporaries.

Some aspects of twentieth-century suburban gardens were inimical to wildlife. There was little if any continuity between the pastures and meadows of the former fields, and the lawns of suburbia, for the turf was usually removed when houses were erected, and when sold for use elsewhere was generally cleansed of wild flowers.[57] Indeed, then as so often today 'weeds' of any kind in lawns were regarded as a sign of gardening failure, and in general, although contemporary gardening books extolled the 'beauties of nature', the prevailing aesthetic was one of neat tidiness. Gardeners often waged a strenuous, almost paranoid war on pests of all kinds. 'At the first sign of the oncoming of the devastating host the gardener must be ready to attack and exterminate it. For if once the invading army be allowed to capture the citadel all will be lost'.[58] This war was fought with an array of chemicals which have since either been banned, or are normally available in weakened form in proprietary products. DDT, carbolic acid, formaldehyde, nicotine and copper sulphate were all used with gay abandon to eradicate weeds and insects. 'Mice and rats can also be poisoned, one of the most effective substances for this purpose being phosphate paste'.[59] On the other hand, publications such as Daglish's *The Book of Garden Animals* of 1928 show that many of the denizens of suburban England were fascinated by garden wildlife, especially garden birds.[60] Bird baths and bird tables were standard garden features from at least the late nineteenth century. Moreover, certain stylistic aspects of suburban gardens were especially conducive to wildlife. Most of the hardy perennials crammed into the borders and beds produced substantial quantities of nectar, pollen and seeds which were eagerly consumed by insects, especially butterflies and moths. Indeed, many of the species which are today listed as useful plants in 'wildlife gardens' were recommended by late–nineteenth- and early twentieth-century garden writers, such as hollyhock, sunflower, anemone, Shasta daisy, nicotiana, Michaelmas daisy or Phlox.[61]

It is also important to emphasize the numerous wild plants which survived the frenetic attentions of the gardener. Domestic gardens had for centuries been developing a distinctive weed flora, and Tutin in the 1950s and 1960s recorded 95 species over a period of – 25 years in a 0.5 hectare example in Leicester.[62] These were in part the weeds of arable fields; in part the kinds of plants, associated with regular disturbance of the ground, and which had characterized the unmade roads and general disorder of pre-industrial cities and towns; but they also included species like creeping cinquefoil or shepherd's purse, otherwise found in the different environments of grasslands and hedgebanks. The reduced competition between adventitious weeds resulting from regular weeding creates communities whose members share only an ability to survive attempts at eradication: here, more than anywhere else in towns and cities, plants grew in circumstances – of soil type, drainage, shade – in which, in the countryside, they would have been out competed by rivals, and in consequence plants like selfheal (*Prunella vulgaris*), characteristic of grazed damp grassland, could be found growing beside woodland species like wood avens (*Geum urbanum*), in assemblages which were 'unnatural', but no more so than those associated with grazed downland or meadows.[63] Alien and indigenous plants also happily coexisted: in regularly mown lawns grasses and low-growing plants like white clover (*Trifolium repens*) were accompanied by alien invaders such as creeping speedwell (*Veronica filiformis*), which was introduced into flower beds in the early nineteenth century but, for reasons which remain unclear, suddenly developed in the inter-war years as a 'beautiful but rampant' lawn weed.[64] Some garden habitats, however, more directly mimicked those found in the wider landscape. Garden walls boasted assemblages similar to those found on cliffs and rock faces, although as the Latin name of ivy-leaved toadflax (*Cymbalaria muralis*) and the English name of wallflower (*Cheiranthus cheir*) suggest, many had long made these artificial habitats their principal homes.[65] Risbeth in 1948 recorded 186 species of vascular plant and 32 bryophytes growing on walls in the town of Cambridge; Payne noted 150 on urban walls in south-east Essex.[66]

Gardens were, not surprisingly, home to a wide range of invertebrates. Between 1926 and 1973, over 700 different species of insect were recorded in a single suburban garden in Blackheath, London.[67] Robbins, describing the wealth of Lepidoptera in one example near Victoria Park in London in the 1880s, observed that 'Evidently there is a garden fauna just as there is a fauna of cultivated land'.[68] Moreover, as the new gardens matured their hedges, shrubberies and trees – especially in the larger examples – provided cover and nesting sites for a wide range of birds, typically the starling, green finch, chaffinch, house-sparrow, great and blue tit, mistle thrush, song thrush, blackbird, robin, hedge-sparrow, and wren. Most were the commoner farmland birds, especially those which prefer some woodland, scrub or hedgerows: true open-country birds like the lapwing or the skylark, and even those that prefer moderately open conditions such as the tree pipit and the stock dove, were not well adapted to this environment.[69] In the larger gardens, and especially those lying towards the margins of towns, a greater range of birds could be found, including linnet, bullfinch, pied wagtail, great spotted woodpecker and even tawny owl.[70] This reflects the fact that – as recent studies have shown – birds adapt to gardens most readily in circumstances where they can also exploit other kinds of habitat.[71] Daglish, writing in 1928, also described how frogs and toads regularly visited sub-urban ponds, and how 'the Crested Newt is also frequently found in gardens, beneath large stones and old walls', as was the smooth newt. The slow worm was, he suggested, now 'usually found in far great numbers near houses than in the open country'.[72] In gardens lying on the fringes of town, moreover, close to the countryside, grass snakes and a variety of lizards could then be found. Rats and mice were ubiquitous in the suburbs, as they had long been in the towns, and hedgehogs, moles and shrews soon established themselves as residents. Foxes were sporadically reported from urban gardens in the 1930s and '40s but in such low numbers that they were simply regarded as remnants of the wild populations living in the surviving fragments of countryside, especially commons and heaths; or were 'almost certainly escapees from captivity'.[73] The age of the urban fox was still to come.

The story is not entirely a positive one, of course. Gardens, as should by now be clear, were the main portal through which naturalized aliens continued to arrive in this country, and much damage was done to *sphagnum* bogs in the west of England to supply the gardener's need for peat.[74] But overall, the spread of gardens in the course of the nineteenth and twentieth centuries was probably good for wildlife, something most graphically illustrated by the study, admittedly begun in the 1970s, by Jennifer Owen of a small suburban example in Leicester. Over a 30-year period, she recorded no less than 2,673 species of flora and fauna, including butterflies, moths, beetles, hoverflies, mammals and birds: including 54 per cent of Britain's ladybird species, 23 per cent of its bees, 19 per cent of its sawflies, 48 per cent of its harvestmen and 15 per cent of its centipedes.[75] This was not a garden specially designed for wildlife: 'The vegetation tends to be denser and more luxuriant than in many gardens, but it is nevertheless neat, attractive and productive, and does not differ markedly from neighbouring gardens'.[76] It is probable that this range of species would have been less in gardens in the period before 1950 – many had not sufficiently matured to provide shelter enough for some of Owen's species, and insecticide use, as noted, was generally at a higher level. But the differences were probably marginal.

Survival of the countryside

Biological diversity in urbanizing areas was also maintained by the survival of fragments of the old rural landscape. Even today, some areas of farmland – albeit usually used for grazing ponies – can be found within 15 kilometres of the centre of London. Half a century or so ago real, working farms could be found even further into the capital. Dairy farms still existed at Dulwich and Highgate, within five miles of Charing Cross, into the inter-war period: Coldharbour Farm in Mottingham, between Catford and Chislehurst, was still operating in 1950.[77] Pockets of farmland survived better in the period up to the 1950s because market gardens and small dairies, in particular, were more common than they are today. Moreover, the 1947 Town and Country Planning Act not only limited the extent of unplanned sprawl in green belts but also encouraged the infilling of remaining pockets of open ground in those areas that *were* zoned for development.

Even when fields were sold off and built over, elements of the old landscape could demonstrate a remarkable degree of resilience, especially in the lower-density suburbs. Development tended to occur in small blocks, as individual fields were sold off to builders, and hedges often survived on their boundaries, albeit degenerating over time and fragmenting as individual house owners replanted them, or replaced them with fences.[78] Even where hedges disappeared altogether hedgerow trees often remained. The more ancient specimens might continue to provide, for a while, homes for tawny or barn owls. Such survivals were not simply the fortuitous side effect of patterns of development. In some cases, as for example in Wembley in the 1930s, the Town Planning Permits issued by the Urban District Council stipulated the retention of established trees as development proceeded.[79] Moreover, those wishing to purchase homes in the suburbs wanted to live in an environment that was still at least partly rural in character. Fired up by the example of Letchworth, developers increasingly retained hedges and trees. Sales particulars for one new estate in south Hertfordshire, on what was effectively becoming the northern edge of London, emphasized in 1913 that: 'It is desired to preserve the rural characteristics of the locality as much as possible, and with that object in view the natural hedges and as many of the trees will be retained as is consistent with convenient development'.[80]

Pockets of woodland have demonstrated a surprising ability to survive. Within the borough of Haringey, between 6 and 8 kilometres from the centre of London, there are no less than five areas of ancient woodland – Highgate Wood, Queens Wood, Coldfall Wood, Bluebell Wood and North Wood – which still boast a wide range of woodland plants and associated fauna. In Highgate Wood alone over 900 species of invertebrate, 338 moths, 353 fungi, seven types of bat and 70 bird species have been recorded, the latter including golden oriole, pied flycatcher, barn owl and long-eared owl. Nor was it only ancient woodland which survived to provide havens for wildlife in this way. Knighton Spring, a few kilometres from the centre of Leicester, is a small oak and ash plantation established in 1840, which is now a local nature reserve. Not all elements of the old landscape survived equally well, however. Streams were frequently culverted and ponds usually fared badly. In Bushey in suburbanizing south Hertfordshire an example on Little Bushey Lane, 'formerly used as a watering place for cattle', was ordered by the council in 1910 to be filled in as a 'public nuisance'.[81] The urge to tidy away the more unsightly elements of the old rural landscape also affected many areas of former common land which, having escaped enclosure, were now engulfed in suburbs. Indeed, their survival in such contexts was often the consequence of pressure from middle-class residents, backed up by the lobbying power of the Commons Preservation Society. Commons in suburbanizing areas were beginning a new career, as a recreational resource. Although increasingly overgrown and neglected as traditional management practices declined, they remained important for wildlife, and many became a battle-ground between those wishing to turn them into areas resembling public parks, and those who desired a more 'rustic' appearance. Fortunately, many of the great commons surrounding London, such as Wimbledon Common or Hampstead Heath, retained much of their rural character although as they became surrounded by housing their wildlife underwent significant change. During the first half of the twentieth century rook, skylark, stonechat, reed bunting, pheasant, sand martin, nightingale, redstart, wood warbler and a number of others were lost as breeding species on Hampstead Heath. But at the same time, birds formerly rare increased in numbers, such as bullfinch, jay, green and greater spotted woodpecker, wood pigeon and moorhen.[82] The heath continued to be home to numerous butterflies, with six different species being recorded there in 1944, but it was noted that 'the flora of parts of the Heath to which the public has access has suffered somewhat from their attentions', although in railed-off areas plants like lesser spearwort and marsh marigold (on pond margins) or red campion and guelder rose (in wooded areas) continued to flourish.[83]

Parks and open spaces

The survival of elements of the rural landscape thus shades off without clear division into the creation of new kinds of open space. Public parks went through a number of stylistic phases in the nineteenth and early twentieth centuries. The first, of early or mid-nineteenth-century date, were usually created from scratch, generally as part of upper-class suburban developments. Some, however, originated as the grounds of private mansions which were acquired by civic authorities or others and devoted to public recreation, while a few (especially in London) had still older origins, as royal deer parks or former commons. In their design, early parks broadly resembled the gardens laid out around country houses and were intended as improving educational spaces, and places for peaceful promenade.[84] They usually included, often within a very small area, a diversity of features: open water, shrubberies, elaborate displays of flowers, lawns with free-standing trees, and rockeries. Although much of the planting featured exotic species, large numbers of indigenous plants either colonized from what was then nearby countryside, or survived from earlier pastures or wood-pastures on the site. Warren in the 1870s recorded no less than 181 species of flowering plant and fern within Kensington Gardens and Hyde Park.[85] But parks, like other urban environments, were dynamic, their flora changing with different management regimes, new planting and adventitious arrivals. By the1950s further surveys in these two parks recorded many significant changes, with a decline in several of the species dominant in the late nineteenth century, such as Sun spurge (*Euphorbia helioscopia*) and lesser celandine (*Ranunculus ficaria*).[86]

Older parks like this, with a varied range of habitats and numerous trees, attracted a wide range of birds. In the central London parks in the 1920s and '30s, for example, starlings, house sparrow, wood pigeon, mallard, blackbird, great and blue tit, robin, carrion crow, jackdaw, greenfinch, chaffinch, spotted fly-catcher, tawny owl, mute swan, moorhen, coot, mistle- and song-thrush, hedge-sparrow, cuckoo, wren and tufted duck, and even great spotted woodpecker, were all recorded as nesting species while non-breeding visitors, especially in winter, included the ubiquitous gulls, brambling, grey wagtail, treecreeper, fieldfare, kingfisher, lesser spotted woodpecker, sparrowhawk, heron, and great crested grebe. In November 1925, no less than 3,981 individual birds from 25 species – 14.5 to the acre – were recorded in Kensington Gardens.[87] Many were doubtless attracted there by the fact that, as Hudson noted in the case of Hyde Park in 1898, they were regularly fed by visitors and encouraged by the park authorities as 'ornaments'.[88] In city centres, where there were few large gardens, parks often provided the only habitat for hedgehogs, and in the course of the twentieth century, they became home to increasing numbers of grey squirrels, some as we have seen deliberately released there. Numerous butterflies also frequented such places, attracted by the nectar of plants like aubretia and buddleia.

Parks became more numerous towards the end of the nineteenth century, partly as a consequence of local government reforms and increasing civic pride, partly as a result of the Public Health Act of 1875. But at the same time their design changed, in ways generally less beneficial to wildlife: 'the emphasis on active recreation in parks increased steadily throughout the last decades of the nineteenth, and into the twentieth century, edging horticulture and promenading into supporting roles'.[89] Existing parks were simplified to provide more space for organized sports – tennis, football, bowls and cricket – and new parks were generally designed with the needs of sport rather than genteel recreation in mind. While they often still included some areas of ornamental garden, their layout was dominated by extensive areas of open grass, occupied by football and cricket pitches, where 'trampling, rolling and mowing . . . destroys all the taller plants, leaving to a large extent pure grassland'.[90] Trees provided limited cover, but these extensive islands of green were frequented by birds which preferred open spaces, such as starlings and gulls, and on occasion lapwings, all attracted by the abundant harvest of earthworms.

There were other kinds of green spaces within urban and suburban areas. Cemeteries increased steadily in numbers through the nineteenth century, reflecting urban growth, municipal reform and Victorian piety. Here again a broad distinction can be made between the elaborately planted private examples created on the edges of the larger towns and cities in the early and middle decades of the nineteenth century, many influenced by the design of contemporary parks and gardens and more specifically by the writings of the landscape gardener John Claudius Loudon; and the more open and generally blander designs of the later nineteenth and twentieth centuries.[91] It is the former which, following a period of neglect in the course of the twentieth century, often evolved (like Abney Park or Highgate in London) into wildlife havens.[92] Covering a larger area were golf courses, which experienced a boom in the late nineteenth and early twentieth centuries, often being laid out at the same time as adjacent areas were being developed for housing. While their role in maintaining biodiversity on coastal dunes or upland moors may be debated, in suburban situations golf courses have always, on balance, been a benefit. Many retained large numbers of trees, and in some cases fragments of hedgerow and even blocks of woodland, from the earlier landscape. Where they were established at the expense of heathland, heather and other characteristic plants usually survived (although often accompanied, on the greens themselves, by species brought in with the maritime turf employed for this purpose such as sea milkwort (*Glaux maritime*) and sea plantain (*Plantago maritime*)).[93] Some golf courses developed from landscape parks, and preserved much of the parkland planting (itself often, as we have seen, originating as hedgerow trees). While chemical weedkillers were being widely employed by the inter-war period on greens and fairways, the long grass, roughs and scrub areas – which might account for as much as 70 per cent of the total course area – were less intensively managed.[94] Recent studies have demonstrated that golf courses carry more bird and insect species than adjoining areas of agricultural pasture[95]: and while this contrast will have been less marked in the period before 1950, when agricultural pastures were less subject to re-seeding and chemical 'improvement', they may often have sustained as many plants and animals as the farmland they replaced.

Urban edgelands

From the mid-nineteenth century, distinctive 'edgelands' began to develop on the margins of the larger conurbations, although they were also interdigitated with them in complex ways, often extending deep into their interiors along river floodplains. Here such things as power stations, rubbish dumps and sewage works were located, away from city centres and residential areas. These provided further novel habitats, many rivalling or even surpassing those now available in the countryside.

Instead of earth closets and 'night soil men', and the direct discharge of effluent into streams and rivers, by the last decades of the nineteenth century major cities had sophisticated sewage systems. Waste was taken via a network of sewers to 'sewage farms' where it was filtered through a series of shallow pools. These, rich in worms and insects, formed habitats similar to estuaries and mudflats, providing ideal feeding grounds for waders like the black-tailed godwit, curlew, golden plover, dunlin and sandpiper, while the surrounding land, if endowed with sufficient cover, afforded breeding places for water-loving species like yellow wagtail, reed-bunting, sedge warbler, and moorhen.[96] Such cover was often provided by rich growths of fat hen, docks, thistles and classic plants of the sewage sludge like tomatoes, the seeds of which easily survived the long journey through the sewage pipes. Vast numbers of the more common birds – gulls, starlings, finches – also came daily to feed. In the inter-war years, the sewage farms became meccas for bird watchers and were renowned for their rare birds: even the avocet was sporadically sighted at London examples.[97]

Rubbish disposal also became more organized and centralized, with most cities being ringed by dumps and tips, utilizing old brick-pits and quarries or – in the case of London – low-lying, derelict marshland. Disposal methods became more rigorous and standardized. From the early years of the twentieth century the preferred method, gradually adopted by municipal authorities, was for refuse to be deposited in shallow layers which were then sealed with soil or other inert materials, before a further layer was added. The surface soil was well-worked and warmed by the decay of the rubbish below, which provided a rich supply of nutrients; but constant disturbance ensured that only transient plants, fast-growing annuals, could survive. In Mabey's words, a dump is like 'a huge compost heap, and is mightily congenial to plant growth. The snag is the bulldozers and the ominous looming of the next smothering layer of garbage'.[98] But there were usually some less disturbed areas towards the margins of the tip where slower-growing plants could survive.

Many of the characteristic plants of the rubbish dump were natives, the usual flowering plants of waste places and newly turned garden soil – shepherd's purse, petty spurge, groundsel, fat hen, stinking mayweed.[99] But dumps were also characterized by a remarkable range of aliens including garden escapees like honesty, gypsophila, delphinium, night-scented stock, hollyhock, buddleia, and sweet William; species generating from kitchen waste, such as potatoes and tomatoes; and plants originating from the sweepings from bird cages, such as common sunflower and canary grass.[100] Because many people in urban areas kept chickens, numerous cereals could also be found growing there. By the 1920s, naturalists were noting the rich and complex flora of urban tips. Melville and Smith described 170 alien plants growing on that at Dagenham near London, the giant hogweed and the dock *Rumex patientia* forming 'a veritable forest of vegetation over eight feet high that must be seen to be believed'.[101]

Rubbish dumps also boasted large invertebrate populations, including a variety of indigenous wasps and bees – yellow-legged mining bee, white-zoned mining bee – but also numerous introduced species, especially the house cricket (*Acheta domestica*) from north Africa and south-west Asia, and various cockroaches.[102] A profusion of insects, abundant worms and the decomposing rubbish itself attracted slow worms, the common lizard, and various kinds of toad, frog and newt – even Natterjack toads have been found breeding on dumps in Bedfordshire and Surrey.[103] But refuse tips were, above all, associated with large numbers of birds.[104] Few actually bred there, due to the high levels of disturbance and paucity of shelter, but they regularly came to feed there. Wheatear, whinchat, skylark, tree pipit, corn bunting and reed bunting were frequent visitors, while ravens, rooks, jackdaws, carrion crows and hooded crows were numerous. Vast numbers of gulls were and are attracted to tips, including the black headed, herring, common and black-backed.[105] Indeed, the presence of tips and sewage farms, and to a lesser extent the proliferation of the new kinds of urban parks, seem to have radically changed the habits of gulls. Until the late nineteenth century, most were almost exclusively maritime in their habits – in 1866 it was said that only the black-headed gull was ever seen in London, and then only *en route* elsewhere.[106] But in the first half of the twentieth century they spent increasing amounts of their time, in winter at least, on inland sites.

Expanding urban populations also required large amounts of water, and the numbers of reservoirs increased steadily through the second half of the nineteenth century and into the twentieth. In the north-west of England especially many were located well outside urban areas, on high moorlands. By 1860 the chain of reservoirs in Longendale to the east of Manchester covered in all some 346 hectares.[107] In Simmons' words, 'when the neighbouring uplands had all been carved into territories by local authorities, then the tentacular reach for resources stretched further', so that from 1891 Liverpool was served with water from the great lake Vyrnwy in Montgomeryshire, while at the start of the twentieth century the village of Thirlmere in Cumbria was destroyed when a great reservoir was constructed to provide for distant Manchester.[108] The environmental impact of upland reservoirs was on balance probably negative but in lowland areas, where they tended to be located on the margins of cities, they were more beneficial. Those constructed to serve London in the Lea and Thames valleys had, by the 1940s, 'made London one of the best centres for the study of aquatic birds in the whole British Isles'.[109] But, while also containing the fish, algae and other freshwater organisms which provided the food for such wildfowl, their sides were bare concrete, so that they lacked marginal vegetation and reedbeds, and the birds and invertebrates that went with them. More important in this respect, as the twentieth century proceeded, were gravel pits.

The development of concrete, and its extensive use in the inter-War years for buildings and transport infrastructure, created a massive demand for sand and gravel. Improvements in pumping technology, using pumps driven by diesel, meant that the removal of aggregates from valley floors was now feasible, leading to the creation of large areas of open water which could not easily be reclaimed, or used for dumping refuse. Great strings of lakes thus appeared in the main river valleys around London, especially beside the Colne between Uxbridge and Rickmansworth, the Lea from Ware to Hackney and also around Darenth in Kent.[110] Other notable concentrations developed elsewhere, especially in the east Midlands, along the valleys of the Trent in Derbyshire and Nottinghamshire. These workings were further expanded in the post-War years, and new ones added, so that by the end of the twentieth century there were around 15,000 hectares of flooded gravel pits in the United Kingdom, mostly in England.

The extraction of gravel unquestionably led to localized plant extinctions. But the resulting pits were a boon for wildlife, especially as they were not kept neat and tidy like urban reservoirs or the lakes in country house parks. Not only were they soon fringed by areas of reedswamp, marginal vegetation and willow scrub, but adjacent spoil heaps also provided a wide range of additional habitats.[111] Flooded pits attracted, in particular, flocks of wintering wildfowl, including pochard and tufted duck; today around 60 per cent of breeding little ringed plovers and over a third of breeding great crested grebes depend on flooded pits.[112] Indeed, the recovery in numbers of both species in the course of the twentieth century is almost entirely due to their proliferation. Flooded pits also provided conditions in which rare species of dragonfly, such as the keeled skimmer (*Orthetrum coerulensis*), could flourish. The number now used as reserves and even designated as SSSIs throughout England, and especially lowland England, is astonishing. Among many noteworthy examples is the Attenborough reserve near in Nottinghamshire, close to the border with Derbyshire, created by gravel extraction from 1929 until 1967; Felmersham Pits in Bedfordshire; and Old Slade in Buckinghamshire, which 'although surrounded by human activity and despoiled countryside, supports 200 plants and 100 bird species (45 breed there)'.[113]

Alongside gravel pits, reservoirs and rubbish dumps, the 'edgelands' were also often the locations of coal-fired power stations, many of which were, by the 1940s, using pulverized coal as their main fuel. The combustion of this material produces a residue of 'fly ash' or pulverized fuel ash which is principally composed of glassy spheres of alumnosilicates. This material is now often used as an engineering fill, or as a component in concrete, but in the past much was simply pumped into lagoons. Its extreme alkalinity and salinity, and high levels of boron, ensured that it underwent only a slow succession, resembling in some ways that which occurs on sand dunes or infertile calcareous silts. Salt-tolerant wind-blown species, such as coltsfoot (*Tussilago farfara*) or varieties of hawkweed, were gradually displaced by legumes like ribbed melilot (*Melilotus officinalis*) and colourful perennials like yellow-wort (*Blackstonia perfoliata*) and yellow rattle (*Rhinanthus minor*), sometimes accompanied by southern marsh orchid (*Dactylorhiza majalis*) or common spotted orchid (*Dactylorhiza fuchsii*), the process culminating in the development of birch/willow woodland. Some fly ash contains hollow spheres which float on the surface of the lagoon as 'islands' which are gradually colonized by reed, reed-mace and floating sweet grass.[114]

Weirdly and wonderfully, nature survived in the most uncongenial of places, and made them its own.

Conclusion

None of this is to deny that the steady expansion of urban and industrial areas in the period between c.1860 and 1950 caused acute problems for much indigenous wildlife. Slow-colonizing plants and those associated with traditionally managed agricultural habitats more generally – flowers of grazed grassland, meadow and coppiced woods – suffered marked declines in urbanizing areas. In the century between 1869 and 1969 no less than 78 native and naturalized species became extinct within the county of Middlesex, mainly as a consequence of the growth of London.[115] Some species of bird, unable to adapt to the new conditions, also disappeared, at least as regular breeders. In the century and a half following 1833, the number of species breeding in the area around Brent reservoir in Middlesex thus declined from 70 to 43, the losses mainly being of the rarer and more specialist species.[116] On the other hand, for good or ill the actual *numbers* of species increased in urbanizing districts due to the successful establishment of a wave of new aliens, especially garden escapees. The 76 plant species lost from Middlesex were more than matched by the 100 new species which successfully established themselves here over the same period.[117]

The idea that towns and suburbs were environmentally sterile areas, which displaced a wildlife-rich countryside, is thus at best an oversimplification. They comprised a wide variety of habitats different from, but in some respects no less rich in wildlife than, those of the rural landscape. Already, in 1898, Hudson was noting how in many suburban areas 'the bird population is actually greater . . . than in the country proper', albeit featuring fewer species.[118] Two years later Coward and Oldham described how:

> Along the northern border of the [Cheshire] Plain the country is rapidly losing much of its charm owing to the extension of the southern suburbs of Manchester, and here the requirements of a residential district, rather than the proximity of factories, are yearly curtailing the haunts of many birds. It must, however, be borne in mind that the plantations, shrubberies, and extensive gardens, as well as the ground devoted to the cultivation of market produce in these suburban districts, have undoubtedly contributed, directly and indirectly, to the increase of others.[119]

In the post-War period, as the practice of farming was transformed by a new agricultural revolution, the niches provided by urban wastelands, suburban gardens and the rest came in many districts to provide more space for plants and animals than was afforded by the surrounding countryside, beyond the city limits.

CHAPTER TEN

Conclusion: Nature, history and conservation

As many readers will be aware, the period covered by this book ends at a crucial point in time, when another great transformation of the countryside, more drastic than anything wrought by the 'agricultural revolution', was beginning. World War II brought the long agricultural depression to an abrupt end: the arable acreage in England and Wales rose by around five million acres (c.2 million hectares) between 1939 and 1945 and the fabric of the 'traditional' landscape was assaulted as never before.[1] One writer, observing changes in the Essex countryside, described how:

> The plough has been put into the pasture. Hedges have been cut down to the ground and ditches opened up everywhere. Fields which the villagers swore never had been any good, and never would be, have been coaxed into fertility. Spruce copse and oak wood alike have been felled; and even village commons have been ploughed and planted.[2]

Naturalists and conservationists, while bemoaning these changes, were not in general unduly alarmed. Many believed that the return to agricultural prosperity would prove short-lived, vanishing with the peace. Others, more optimistically, thought that the widespread acceptance of state planning – which had been steadily developing through the early twentieth century, and was greatly encouraged by the experiences of War – would be brought to bear on environmental as well as on economic matters. In reality, continued food shortages ensured that the national government, and latterly the European Economic Community, introduced a range of subsidies to further increase production. This, moreover, came at a time when a barrage of new technological developments was becoming available to farmers. Tractors increased rapidly in numbers; combine harvesters were introduced from America. Both worked most effectively in large fields: hedge removal thus proceeded apace, especially in arable districts.[3] 'Ninety-odd acres of wheat in a block – a fine sight'.[4] Between 1946 and 1970 around 4,500 miles of hedge were destroyed each year in England and Wales, with the greatest losses occurring in the eastern counties,[5] and especially in areas of long-enclosed 'ancient countryside' where small, irregularly-shaped fields posed particular problems for machinery.[6] Countless farmland trees were felled, something compounded from the late 1960s by the impact of Dutch elm disease. Fields were more effectively drained, many remaining areas of heathland were reclaimed, ponds filled in, coastal marshlands ploughed, streams and rivers canalized, and numerous areas of ancient woodland grubbed out and converted to arable.[7] Pesticides and herbicides became widely available and the use of chemical fertilisers massively increased, while sowing gradually became concentrated in the autumn months, leading to a decline in the area of winter stubbles.[8]

To remain competitive in this new world, farms continued to grow in size and were increasingly obliged to specialize either in arable or in livestock production. The focus of arable farmers on growing crops, moreover, could now be absolute. The adoption of tractors and the availability of cheap fertilisers ensured that they no longer needed to maintain livestock for manure or for traction: across eastern England especially the numbers of sheep and cattle fell drastically, leading to the ploughing of ancient pastures and meadows, and giving further encouragement to the rationalization of field patterns. Numerous other aspects of the new farming adversely affected wildlife: large scale re-seeding and improvement of pastures; the decline of tillage crops in pastoral areas; and subsidy-fuelled increases in stocking densities in the uplands, which led to further declines in the extent and condition of heather moor and an expansion of acidic grassland, and often bracken.[9] Other manifestations of the post-War love of modernity took their toll. Many of the ancient woods which had survived the drive to create more agricultural land were replanted, with the encouragement of subsidies from the Forestry Commission, with conifers. In 1953, myxomatosis was introduced to control the huge population of rabbits, and with considerable success, although with problematic knock-on effects in surviving areas of common land, heath and down, where the strenuous efforts of these introduced aliens had to some extent retarded, as we have seen, regeneration to woodland.

It is easy to criticize the intensive farming, and other new forms of land use, which emerged in the 1950s, 60s and 70s. But we should also remember (for many ecologists do not) the deprivations of the wartime years, the continued threat of hunger during the peace, and the political attitudes which these engendered right across Europe. And while the role of the state in all this, particularly in the form of government subsidies for land drainage, hedge removal and other forms of 'modernization', is easily criticized, it is also important to remember the beneficial aspects of increased state intervention, especially in terms of new forms of spatial planning. The 1947 Town and Country Planning Act made this compulsory over the whole country; it also, building on earlier initiatives by the London County Council, made provision for 'green belts' around major urban centres.[10] It is difficult to exaggerate the importance of all this for the English landscape. The 1920s and 30s had seen a steady expansion of suburbia, and without the new planning frameworks, the return of peace would certainly have seen the disappearance of further extensive tracts of countryside under various forms of low-density sprawl. The National Parks and Access to the Countryside Act of 1949, moreover, allowed for the designation and management of National Parks, Areas of Outstanding Natural Beauty, and National Nature Reserves, thus preserving some key areas of conservation significance from the wider environmental crisis.[11]

All this said, there is no denying that the second half of the twentieth century, and especially the period up to c.1980, was an appalling time for wildlife. The numbers of mammals, birds and invertebrates present in the countryside fell steeply; habitats rich in native flora were lost at an awesome rate. Many invertebrates were killed off by the application of pesticides, while birds and mammals suffered as the amounts of both shelter, and food, available in the wild declined dramatically. Even the new modes of spatial planning, and the enthusiasm for nature reserves, SSSIs and National Parks, had their downsides. The designation of certain areas as 'special' carried with it the implication that undesignated ones were not, while tighter controls on the spread of suburban sprawl increased the density of housing and factories within areas zoned for development, posing an increasing threat to the gardens and derelict industrial land, suburban farms and smallholdings, where a higher and higher proportion of the nation's wildlife was now to be found. By the start of the twenty-first century, the majority of developments were on 'brown field' rather than on 'green field' sites.[12] Moreover, the new ideas of spatial planning did not always serve to preserve the countryside, for they also led to the appearance of government-sponsored New Towns in the area around London and – in attempts to fuel economic growth – elsewhere. Indeed, as the population continued to increase the total area of built-up land in England grew by around 27 per cent between 1951 and 2000, so that it now covered around a tenth of the total land area.[13]

It is true, of course, that the last decades of the century saw the institution of further measure to reverse the onslaught on wildlife. The 1981 Wildlife and Countryside Act provided additional protection for SSSIs and more generally for a range of native species, while the 1997 Hedgerows Regulations made it harder to remove hedges. The 1980s saw the establishment of the county Farming and Wildlife Advisory Groups, and the 1990s the development of Biodiversity Action Plans.[14] Of particular importance were the various agro-environment schemes which were developed from the 1980s, and the associated proactive role of English Nature, subsequently Natural

England, in helping farmers and landowners to increase the wildlife value of their properties. Numerous new nature reserves have been created by county councils, wildlife trusts and others; the quality of rivers improved, and atmospheric pollution steadily declined. Nevertheless, six species of flowering plant have become completely extinct in England since 1973, while the number of farmland birds has declined catastrophically since the 1970s.[15] Some old and familiar threats continued: in spite of the 1954 Wild Birds Protection Act, raptors like the hen harrier continued to face persecution on some shooting estates.

It is not the purpose of this book to explore the impact of these slightly more welcome developments which have taken place since the early 1980s. Nor is it my remit to revisit the earlier phase of post-war intensification, so aptly described by Rackham as 'the years that the locust hath eaten'.[16] Others have written with more skill and knowledge on this depressing subject. My intention has rather been to provide some historical perspective on the real character of what are sometimes viewed as the timeless and natural landscapes which existed in England before these profound changes took place. In reality, as should by now be apparent, in all periods since the advent of farming the countryside has comprised a collection of essentially artificial environments, the extent and character of which have been constantly changing in response to variations in population pressure, developments in technology, and the emergence of new forms of social and economic organization.

In 1650, the development of specialized farming regions, the widespread enclosure of open fields, yet the survival of vast tracts of intensively managed woodland, heathland, wetland and other 'waste', ensured that England possessed a particularly rich and varied wildlife, although much of it already comprised introduced species. But the eighteenth and early nineteenth century witnessed a profound environmental transformation, the consequence of rapid population growth and a transition to a fossil fuel economy. Vast areas of non-arable habitats were destroyed and the countryside became more homogenous, especially in lowland England. Specialist species, such as open-country birds, lost out: and while farmland fauna in general may have benefited from some agricultural changes, especially the new crops and rotations, the reduction in the numbers of farmland trees, the removal or replanting of hedges and the changes in their management were detrimental to even the commoner species. Industrialization and urbanization may have had limited, and arguably even beneficial effects on our flora and fauna, at least before the middle decades of the nineteenth century, creating a range of new habitats. But other developments in this period, especially the rise of organized game shooting, improvements in firearms, and a rash of new plant introductions were less positive.

The later nineteenth and first half of the twentieth centuries saw massive urban expansion and a long period of agricultural depression. Surviving areas of common land – especially the remaining areas of heath and fen – became increasingly derelict, with a marked loss in botanical interest. Woodland, too, was increasingly neglected. At the same time, the need for large landowners to make up for falling rental incomes ensured a further expansion of game shooting, and a further onslaught on perceived predators of game birds, which continued on some scale into the inter-war years. Where large estates were broken up, moreover, land fell into the hands of new owners who, through necessity or cultural preference, viewed the land in more purely agricultural terms, ensuring further losses of trees and hedges. In the spreading suburbs, however, in areas of urban dereliction, and in the new 'edgelands', novel habitats, often as rich as anything now to be found in the countryside, were emerging, albeit characterized by increasing numbers of alien plants and invertebrates.

Relatively few of the 100,000 or so species present in Britain as a whole became extinct at a *national* level as a consequence of the changes described in this book, or even as a result of the more dramatic developments of the period after 1950: perhaps 21 species of flowering plant, around 16 mosses and liverworts, 13 lichens and a single species of the larger fungi.[17] The extinctions in England of the pine marten and polecat, and of birds of prey like the hen harrier and red kite, have been reversed by recolonization or reintroduction from Wales and Scotland during the later twentieth century.[18] But regional and local extinctions have been numerous, especially in the suburbanized and intensively cultivated south and east of the country.[19] Since 1750, one species of flowering plant has been lost on average every 1.7 years from Middlesex, and every 2 years from Cambridgeshire.[20] The country's native flora, and much of its fauna, has become more and more spatially restricted and many species face an uncertain future even in national terms. Forty per cent of our butterflies, for example, are currently under threat.[21] Over the period covered by this book losses have, on the whole, been heaviest among 'specialist' species, those with the more exacting requirements, and especially those plants and animals most closely associated with the kinds of essentially artificial habitat (heaths, downs, woods, wetlands) created by medieval and early post-medieval farming, but destroyed wholesale in the course of the eighteenth, nineteenth and twentieth centuries. The traditional 'wastes' have been progressively reduced and fragmented, limiting the opportunities for these specialized organisms to move from one remaining 'island' to the next.[22] Less adversely affected have been the generalists, the flora and fauna associated with farmland, and which have often been able to adapt to urban, or at least suburban, conditions. As Fox has noted in the case of butterflies, 'As is probably the case for many taxa, the massive decline and extinction of specialist species are being masked by the colonisation of generalists'.[23]

Biodiversity, if correctly defined not as the total number of species in any area but as the maintenance of healthy populations of a particular district's characteristic species, is thus closely associated with the fate of what biologists often describe – perhaps incorrectly – as 'semi-natural' habitats. It is arguably here, in particular, that an historical perspective on English wildlife is most useful. Current understandings of what many of these key habitats should be like are largely based on observations and descriptions made when natural history first became culturally important, in the early and especially the middle decades of the nineteenth century. But by that time the various forms of management that had brought them into existence were already in decline. In particular, it is easy to underestimate the extent to which moors, heaths and other common land were exploited for fuel, as much as for grazing, in the period before industrialization; and how far the cessation of regular cutting and digging changed their ecology. Further declines in the intensity of exploitation came of course in the later nineteenth and twentieth centuries, as these areas became less regularly grazed, leading to further changes in their character: and their often current derelict or semi-derelict condition makes it particularly hard to reconstruct their earlier nature, or natures.

Historical research can certainly help to elucidate the circumstances which shaped such habitats at the varying stages of their development, and especially the contribution made by human activity. But the relationships between society and economy on the one hand, and the environment on the other, are usually complex and subtle. They have sometimes been simplified in the past by ecologists who, while accustomed to seeing infinite complexity in natural systems, fail on occasions to assume the same of human ones. It might appear obvious, to take but one instance, that a decline in farming fortunes in the first half of the twentieth century, and thus in the intensity with which the countryside was exploited, should have been a boon to wildlife: but, as we have seen, and for some very complicated reasons, the inverse was probably the case. Yet while the links between the form and extent of habitats, and social and economic developments, are indeed often infinitely complex, they are always there. Man, not God, made the countryside, and to manage valued habitats into the future, we need a more sophisticated understanding of their human as much as their natural history.

The habitats created by industry and urbanization can also, as we have seen, have conservation importance. This has long been true: the gravel pits which have become important wildlife reserves in the course of the twentieth century have their medieval counterparts in the flooded peat excavations of the Norfolk Broads. Nature does not reside only, or even now in some districts mainly, in the countryside. Most ecologists are fully aware of this, but the wider public still tend, in an unproblematic manner, to equate nature and the rural. Kelcey has noted how, at the same time as agricultural intensification wrought increasing havoc on the traditional countryside, industrial development 'contributed much to the continued existence of rare and unusual species . . . prevented some of the common species from becoming rare, and led to diversification of habitats. . .'.[24] And it is hard to argue with such a view. Of course, this is not to adopt an entirely relativist position: not all artificial habitats are equivalent, in interest or diversity, to each other, not least because some can be created almost instantly while others (such as ancient woodland) take a long time to develop, and are not easily formed from scratch. Nevertheless, as Davis has also pointed out, the environmental impact of industrial development and other forms of modern land use change is clearly not universally negative: it depends on circumstances and on essentially subjective judgements.

> If an area of average farm land is developed into a housing estate, the fauna and flora will certainly be different but it would be unwise to assume that it would eventually be any less rich or interesting . . . If the same area were exploited for gravel, the ecotones of the resulting flooded pit might well produce an absolute enrichment and diversification of fauna and flora. However, an exceptional area of farmland, one of the few remaining fritillary *Fritillaria meleagris* L. meadows for example, is unlikely to be replaced by any habitat of comparable individuality and scientific interest.[25]

Yet as we have seen, there are grounds for doubting whether the snakes-head fritillary is, in fact, anything more than a garden escapee (above, pp. 11–12): and the problems of relativism, raised but not solved by an historical perspective, are especially acute when we consider introduced or – to use that loaded term – 'alien' species. There is no doubt that a mass of invasive organisms are now causing serious problems to English wildlife, from Himalayan balsam to muntjac deer, and this is a major worry to conservationists. But what makes this issue particularly complex is a failure on the part of some to distinguish between aliens *per se*, which may simply reduce marginally the frequencies of ecologically equivalent native species, or fill what are effectively vacant niches; and those aggressive invaders which are a real threat to indigenous wildlife.[26] It is further complicated by the way that some of those working in the humanities like to draw crass analogies between the determination of ecologists to prevent the wholesale naturalization of new species from abroad, and the ravings of the far right against human immigrants and refugees:[27] a situation which is itself not much helped by the unfortunate language sometimes employed by ecologists themselves. Yalden rightly criticized the 'sentimental' suggestion from 'some quarters' that introduced species like the grey squirrel had a 'right' to live here, continuing:

> The native species certainly have the right to be here, more right than we have, but the exotic introductions have no right to be here, and no right to eliminate our native species. The whole point of biodiversity is that different parts of the World have different faunas and floras.[28]

Yet many people like grey squirrels – they may be the only wild mammals they regularly encounter – and introduced species like the rabbit are deeply embedded in our environment as much as in our culture. Their eradication, even if possible, would hardly be desirable. More importantly, as Yalden's own excellent work demonstrates so clearly, it is very hard to define what actually constitutes our 'native fauna'. Many important indigenous species have been wiped out entirely, or now live in very restricted areas, while many of our most familiar animals were introduced from abroad, albeit often in the remote past. Probably around a third of our mammals represent introduced species.[29] We still acknowledge grey squirrel, muntjac, sika, Chinese water deer, and mink as aliens: 'coming over here and stealing our nuts'. But we somehow think differently about fallow deer, rabbit, brown hare, harvest mouse, house mouse, black rat and brown rat, to say nothing of the innumerable immigrant invertebrates living in our homes and arable fields. As Rotherham and Lambert have noted, 'what is acceptable and what is alien vary with time'.[30] The little owl is now a valued part of our fauna, but when introduced from France in the 1930s it was considered a serious threat to native species.[31] Similar difficulties, and contradictions, surround our flora. In the British Isles as a whole today there are around 2,200 different species of indigenous flowering plant, but over 1,100 'reasonably well-established aliens'[32]: nearer 1,800, according to some estimates.[33] Some of these, moreover, provide sustenance for fauna otherwise under threat: buddleia and other naturalized garden plants provide excellent nectar sources; introduced trees do not necessarily support fewer invertebrates, birds and mammals than native ones.[34] Again, reactions to aliens are culturally conditioned, even irrational. Michaelmas daisy is an obvious immigrant, but what naturalist does not bemoan the loss of the immigrant poppy, almost sprayed out of existence in our neat, herbicide-sodden fields? The fact that alien plants are a more important component of urban than of rural environments may account for some of the hostility shown towards them: precisely because they do not live in the countryside they do not fit into our concept of what is 'natural'. The extent to which such species have established themselves beyond urban areas, and the scale of the resultant damage to indigenous wildlife, are debated.[35] But most of our rural environment has long been dominated by alien plants: fields of cereals and associated weeds, plantations of foreign conifers. The voices of those calling for indigenous purity of wildlife are drowned out by the sound of the closing stable door.

The danger with historical approaches is that they can lead to a kind of shifting and indecisive subjectivity, an uncertainty which might be appropriate to discussions carried out in ivory towers, but which is of little use in the real world, where decisions have to be taken about such matters as how to deal with 'invaders'. There are also dangers in driving, as the logic laid out in the course of this book seems to suggests we should, too substantial a wedge between the 'rural' and the 'natural'. Apart from anything else, if it became widely accepted that recent, urban and industrial environments can be as good for wildlife as traditional, ancient, rural ones – that nature resides in the town as much as in the countryside – it would be hard indeed to oppose the uncontrolled eruption of housing and industrial development across ordinary farmland on grounds of biodiversity. In spite of the popular impression that England is becoming very rapidly urbanized, according to some estimates more agricultural land has been planted up as woodland of varying kinds in the last 25 years, than has been built over.[36] But there is a serious shortage of homes in this country, and strong pressure from some political quarters to allow a resumption of the kind of low-density uncontrolled sprawl which was slowed by the planning reforms of the post-war years. On the other hand, the disarticulation of the 'rural' from the 'natural' might serve to emphasize the specifically cultural importance of traditional landscapes, bringing to the fore quite different reasons for their preservation. The countryside, apart from producing food, is simply different from the town, fulfilling a very real need for space and solitude, peace and quiet, away from the endless noise and activity of the '24/7' culture: it can provide that sense of apartness captured so well in the writings of Robert Macfarlane.[37] It contains innumerable traces of – constitutes vital evidence for the study of – our past, our history. And it is firmly embedded in all aspects of our culture: in our literature, in our art. People do not visit Dedham Vale primarily to see the flora and fauna, but because Constable painted the landscape there, Lombardy poplars and all. And on top of all this, of course, the countryside – parts of it at least – remains home to a range of plants and animals which will never, ever be able to establish themselves in towns and suburbs.

Whether in the town or in the country our flora and fauna exist and have long existed within an almost completely man-made world. In the 1990s a number of people – strongly influenced by Frans Vera's ideas, and at a time when it appeared that there was serious agricultural over-production in Europe – advocated that large areas should be 're-wilded', returned in effect to the dynamic, grazed savannas which supposedly existed in Mesolithic times. We should, it was argued – and still is by some – try to create extensive areas where 'natural processes get the chance to evolve', in place of the essentially cultural landscapes in which nature currently exists, its various forms shaped by human management.[38] Quite how any of this would ever work in practice has always been unclear – what animals would have done the work of auroch and how they would have been fenced in are never clearly explained. But more serious are the broader philosophical issues raised by such a policy. What exactly would we be creating, and how 'natural' would it be? A few ecologists pine for a time 'before humans messed up the ecosystem', but even if we could kill everybody off our 'original' landscape, whatever that may have been like, could never return. As Peterken has noted, the pre-Neolithic vegetation of England – in its condition of 'original-naturalness', 'before people became a significant ecological factor', was different from what it would be in a state of 'present-naturalness', defined as the 'state that would prevail now if people had not become a significant ecological actor', simply because of climatic changes and of other entirely natural influences and process which have operated over the intervening millennia. But more radically different still would be 'future-natural' environments, which Peterken defines as those 'which would eventually develop if people's influence were completely and permanently removed'. This is because so many new species have been introduced into the country since prehistoric times, while others have become extinct.[39] Large areas of a 'future-natural' forest – of the kind of woodland which would emerge if nature was somehow to be left to its own devices – would thus consist primarily of sycamore trees.

We must accept the essentially unnatural character of our natural heritage, and we must also celebrate what Richard Mabey has evocatively termed the 'unofficial countryside', of gravel pits, wasteland and sewage farms. But we must also strive to preserve what remains of our 'traditional' countryside, for cultural reasons as much as for biological ones. As I have emphasized, it has been the loss of particular environments – wetlands, downlands, heaths – and the declines in the specialists associated with these that has been the most striking development of the last few centuries, and such areas should indeed be afforded particular attention. Should we also actively recreate them, in places where they have been lost? The widespread replanting of species-rich hedges and woodland over the last few decades has certainly brought real benefits, both aesthetically and in terms of wildlife conservation; and more heaths, downs and wetlands are certainly required, simply to ensure healthy populations of birds like the stone curlew, as well as to sustain a wide range of endangered plants.[40] This said, when we create new heaths, for example, by clearing away conifer plantations or secondary woodland, grinding the stumps and stripping the topsoil, at great expense; and then attempt to maintain the result – an impoverished, artificial, species-poor habitat – by mimicking long-redundant economic and agrarian activities: then we are certainly doing something a little odd. Such a procedure might make more sense if informed by an historical perspective, for there is a very real danger here of a 'one size fits all' approach, and of basing our restoration policies on one type, and phase, of habitat development. In the case of heathland, we might thus consider restoring some of the wood-pasture heaths which were common in the past, rather than insisting on uprooting every existing tree; we might replicate some of the modes of exploitation other than grazing which once existed, such as the systematic and regular stripping of areas of heather and its roots. When we undertake such actions, however, we are of course effectively *farming* wildlife, as we now so often do on nature reserves and in other contexts, rather than watching wildlife adapt – as it has always done in the past – to changes wrought to the environment primarily for our own practical and economic benefit.

All these are crucial issues, because the environment of England – as all must be aware – faces more challenges, and more complex challenges, than perhaps ever before. Continuing increases in population, and radical reductions in household size, put more and more pressure on space. Our insatiable demand for energy threatens to cover the rural landscape with wind turbines and 'solar farms'. Above all, globalization, and perhaps climate change, bring not only more foreign plants and animals to these shores but also – more worrying by far – new pests and diseases, especially of trees. The most recent and serious is ash *chalara* but there are of course others, threatening a population of farmland trees with an age structure skewed by a century or more of economic under-exploitation. Managing change to protect and enhance our wildlife for future generations will involve some hard thinking, and the formulation of radical new policies: and for this we may need an historical perspective on England's wildlife, almost as much as a scientific one.

NOTES

Chapter 1

1 R. Williams, *Key Words: a vocabulary of culture and society* (London: Croom Helm, 1976), p. 184.

2 K. D. Bennett, 'Holocene pollen stratigraphy of central East Anglia, England and comparison of pollen zones across the British Isles', *New Phytologist* 109 (1988), 251. O. Rackham, *Woodlands* (London: Collins, 2006), pp. 82–90.

3 O. Rackham, *Ancient Woodland* (Colvend: Castlepoint Press, 2003), pp. 108–9. O. Rackham, *History of the Countryside* (London: Dent, 1986), p. 330.

4 F. Vera, *Grazing Ecology and Forest History* (Wallingford: CABI Publishing, 2002), p. 92.

5 Vera, *Grazing Ecology and Forest History*, p. 88.

6 Ibid., pp. 377–9.

7 K. Hodder, P. Buckland, K. Kirby and J. Bullock, 'Can the pre-Neolithic provide suitable models for re-wilding the landscape in Britain', *British Wildlife* 20, 5 (special supplement) (2009), 4–15.

8 Rackham, *Ancient Woodland*, pp. 502–3; Rackham, *Woodlands*, pp. 92–8.

9 F. E. Clements, *Plant Succession: an analysis of the development of vegetation* (Washington: Carnegie Institution, 1916).

10 A. G. Tansley, *The British Islands and their Vegetation*, vol. 1 (Cambridge: Cambridge University Press, 1949).

11 H. William and I. C. Nisbet-Drury, 'Succession', *Journal of the Arnold Arboretum* 54 (1973), 331–68. J. Connell and R. Slatyer, 'Mechanisms of succession in natural communities and their role in community stability and organisation', *The American Naturalist* 111 (1977), 119–1144.

12 D. Worcester, *The Wealth of Nature: environmental history and the ecological imagination* (Oxford: Oxford University Press, 1993), p. 165.

13 I. Simmons, *The Environmental Impact of Late Mesolithic Cultures* (Edinburgh: Edinburgh University Press, 1996).

14 D. W. Yalden, *The History of British Mammals* (London: Poyser, 1999), p. 95.

15 P. V. Watson, 'Man's impact on the chalklands: some new pollen evidence', in M. Bell and S. Limbrey (eds), *Archaeological Aspects of Woodland Ecology* (Oxford: British Archaeological Reports, International Series, vol. 146, 1982), pp. 75–92.

16 J. H. Tallis, 'Forest and moorland in the south Pennine uplands in the mid-Flandrian period III. The spread of moorland – local, regional and national', *Journal of Ecology* 79 (1991), 401–15.

17 P. Fowler, *The Farming of Prehistoric Britain* (Cambridge: Cambridge University Press, 1983). F. Pryor, *Farmers in Prehistoric Britain* (Stroud: Tempus, 1998).

18 P. Fowler, *Farming in the First Millennium AD* (Cambridge: Cambridge University Press, 2002), pp. 16–18. B. Roberts and S. Wrathmell, *Region and Place; a study of English rural settlement* (London: English Heritage, 2002), p. 43.

19 Yalden, *History of British Mammals*, p. 128.

20 P. Dark, *The Environment of Britain in the First Millennium AD* (London, 2000), pp. 81–129. V. Straker, A. Brown, R. Fyfe and J. Jones, 'Romano-British environmental background' in Webster (ed.) *The Archaeology of South West England* (Taunton, 2007), pp. 145–50; p. 149. T. Brown and G. Foard, 'The Saxon landscape: a Regional Perspective', in P. Everson and T. Williamson (eds), *The Archaeology of Landscape* (Manchester, 1998), pp. 67–94; p. 75.

21 S. Rippon, *Beyond the Medieval Village: the diversification of landscape character in southern Britain* (Oxford: Oxford University Press, 2008), pp. 121–2, 168–9.

22 H. E. Hallam, *The Agrarian History of England and Wales, Vol 2. 1042-1350* (Cambridge: Cambridge University Press, 1988), p. 512.

23 Roberts and Wrathmell, *Region and Place*, pp. 1–3. Rackham, *History of the Countryside*, pp. 1–5. T. Williamson, *Shaping Medieval Landscapes: settlement, society, environment* (Macclesfield: Windgather, 2003).

24 D. Hall, *Medieval Fields* (Aylesbury, 1982). D. Hall, *The Open Fields of Northamptonshire* (Northampton: Northamptonshire Record Society, 1995).

25 Rackham, *History of the Countryside*, pp. 4–5.

26 B. M. S. Campbell, 'Commonfields origins – the regional dimension', in T. Rowley (ed.), *The Origins of Open Field Agriculture* (London: Croom Helm, 1981), pp. 112–29. E. Martin and M. Satchell, *Wheare Most Inclosures Be. East Anglian Fields, History, Morphology and Management*, published as *East Anglian Archaeology* 124, (Ipswich, 2008). D. Roden, 'Field systems of the Chilterns and their Environs', in A. R. H. Baker and R. A. Butlin (eds), *Studies of Field Systems in the British Isles* (Cambridge: Cambridge University Press, 1973), pp. 325–76.

27 T. Williamson, *Environment, Society and Landscape in Early Medieval England: time and topography* (Woodbridge: Boydell, 2013).

28 Williamson, *Environment, Society and Landscape*, pp. 125–46.

29 E. Kerridge, *The Common Fields of England* (Manchester: Manchester University Press, 1992), pp. 25–30.

30 Kerridge, *The Common Fields*, pp. 77–9.

31 J. A. Yelling, *Common Field and Enclosure in England 1450-1850* (London: Macmillan, 1977). T. Williamson, 'Understanding enclosure', *Landscapes* 1, 1 (2000), 56–79. M. Reed, 'Pre-parliamentary enclosure in the East Midlands and its impact on the landscape', *Landscape History* 3 (1981), 60–8.

32 B. M. S. Campbell, *English Seigniorial Agriculture* (Cambridge: Cambridge University Press, 2000).

33 J. Thirsk, *England's Agricultural Regions and Agrarian History 1500-1750* (London: Macmillan, 1987). E. Kerridge, *The Agricultural Revolution* (London: Allen and Unwin, 1967).

34 M. Chase, 'Can history be green? A prognosis', *Rural History* 3 (1992), 243–54.

35 Yelling, *Common Field and Enclosure in England*. Williamson, 'Understanding Enclosure', pp. 68–9.

36 Yalden, *History of British Mammals*, pp. 111–12, 140.

37 Ibid., p. 119.

38 E. M. Nicholson, *Birds and Man* (London: Collins, 1951); R. K. Murton, *Man and Birds* (London: Collins, 1971).

39 H. Mourier and O. Winding, *Collins Guide to Wild Life in House and Home* (London: Collins, 1975), pp. 5–6.

40 Rackham, *History of the Countryside*, pp. 31–2.

41 P. E. Hulme, 'Biological invasions in Europe: drivers, pressures, states, impacts and response', in R. E. Hester and R. M. Harrison (eds), *Issues in Environmental Science and Technology*, vol. 25 (Cambridge: Royal Society of Chemistry, 2007), pp. 56–80. S. Thomas and T. Dines, 'Non-native invasive plants in Britain: a real, not imagined, problem', *British Wildlife* 21 (2010), 177–83.

42 D. A. Webb, 'What are the criteria for presuming native status?', *Watsonia* 15 (1985), 231–6. D. A. Pearmain, '"Far from any house" – assessing the status of doubtfully native species in the flora of the British Isles', *Watsonia* 26 (2007), 271–90.

43 M. Bishop, S. P. Davis and J. Grimshaw, *Snowdrops: A Monograph of Cultivated Galanthus* (Maidenhead: Griffin Press, 2002).

44 R. Mabey, *Flora Britannica* (London: Concise edn, Chatto and Windus, 1998), pp. 138–9.

45 B. Gillam, *The Wiltshire Flora* (London: Pisces Publications, 1993). P. Oswald, 'The fritillary in Britain: a historical perspective', *British Wildlife* 3 (1992), 200–10.

46 G. C. Druce, *The Flora of Oxfordshire* (London, 1886), p. 387.

47 R. Mabey, *Weeds: the story of outlaw plants* (London: Profile Books, 2010), pp. 197–8, 271–3. M. Campbell-Culver, *The Origin of Plants* (London: Headline Books, 2001), pp. 28–9, 38–9, 103, 117.

48 T. Pakenham, *Meetings with Remarkable Trees* (London: Weidenfeld and Nicolson: Weidenfeld and Nicolson, 1996), pp. 168–9.

49 J. Gerrard, *The Herball or Generall Historie of Plantes* (London, 1597), p. 1299.

50 T. Green, 'Is there a case for the Celtic maple or the Scots Plane?', *British Wildlife* 16 (2005), 184–8.

51 J. Evelyn, *Sylva* (London, 1662), p. 121.

52 Campbell-Culver, *Origin of Plants*, pp. 122–44.

53 Yaldem, *History of British Mammals*, p. 122.

54 D. J. Rackham, '*Rattus rattus*: the introduction of the black rat into Britain', *Antiquity* 53 (1979), 112–20. P. Armitage, B. West and K. Steedman, 'New evidence of the black rat in Roman London', *The London Archaeologist* 4 (1984), 375–83.

55 Yalden, *History of British Mammals*, p. 127.

56 N. Sykes, 'The dynamics of status symbols: wildfowl exploitation in England AD 410–1550', *Archaeological Journal* 161 (2004), pp. 82–105; S. Kent, *Farmers as Hunters: the implications of sedentism* (Cambridge: Cambridge University Press, 1989); Y. Hamilakis, 'The sacred geography of hunting: wild animals, social power and gender in early farming societies', in E. Kotjabopoulou, Y. Hamilakis, P. Halstead, C. Gamble, and V. Elefanti (eds), *Zooarchaeology in Greece: recent advances* (London: British School at Athens, 2003), pp. 239–47.

57 Yalden, *History of British Mammals*, p. 127–8.

58 T. Williamson, 'Fish, fur and feather: man and nature in the post-medieval landscape', in K. Barker and T. Darvill (eds), *Making English Landscapes* (Bournemouth: Bournemouth University School of Conservation Sciences Occasional Paper, 1997), pp. 92–117.

59 R. Liddiard (ed.), *The Medieval Deer Park: new perspectives* (Macclesfield: Windgather, 2007).

60 J. Birrell, 'Deer and deer farming in medieval England', *Agricultural History Review* 40 (1993), 112–26.

61 R. Liddiard, *Landscapes of Lordship: Norman Castles and the Countryside in Medieval Norfolk, 1066-1200* (Oxford: British Archaeological Reports, British Series, vol. 309, 2000).

62 T. Williamson, *Polite Landscapes: gardens and society in eighteenth-century England* (Stroud: Sutton, 1995), pp. 22–4. J. Fletcher, *Gardens of Earthly Delight: the history of deer parks* (Oxford: Windgather, 2011), pp. 162–5.

63 Rackham, *History of the Countryside*, pp. 129–39. P. A. Pettit, *The Royal Forests of Northamptonshire* (Northampton: Northamptonshire Record Society, 1968).

64 B. Noddle, 'The animal bones', in R. Shoesmith (ed.), *Hereford Excavations* (York: Council for British Archaeology, 1985), pp. 84–94; E. Higgs, W. Greenwood and A. Garrard, 'Faunal report', in P. Rahtz (ed.), *The Saxon and Medieval Palace at Cheddar: excavations 1960-82* (Oxford: British Archaeological Reports, British Series, vol. 65, 1979), pp. 353–62; N. Sykes and R. Carden, 'Were fallow deer spotted (OE*pohha/*pocca) in Anglo-Saxon England? Reviewing the evidence for *Dama dama dama* in early medieval Europe', *Medieval Archaeology* 55 (2011), 139–62. C. Hough, 'Deer in Sussex place-names', *Antiquaries Journal* 88 (2008), 43–7.

65 U. Albarella and S. J. Davis, 'Mammals and birds from Launceston Castle, Cornwall: decline in status and the rise of agriculture', *Circaea* 12 (1996), 1–156.

66 J. Bourdillon and J. Coy, 'Animal bone', in H. Graham and S. Davies (eds), *Excavations at Melbourne Street, Southampton, 1971-6* (York: Council for British Archaeology, 1980), pp. 79–121.

67 R. G. Haynes, 'Vermin traps and rabbit warrens on Dartmoor', *Post-Medieval Archaeology* 4 (1970), 147–64.

68 C. L. Orgill, 'The introduction of the rabbit into England', *Antiquity* 10 (1936), 462–3.

69 J. E. Harting, *The Rabbit* (London, 1898)), pp. 37, 57. T. Williamson, *Rabbits, Warrens and Archaeology* (Stroud: Tempus, 2007), pp. 160–1.

70 Williamson, *Rabbits, Warrens and Archaeology*, pp. 31–88. J. Sheial, *Rabbits and their History* (Newton Abbot: David and Charles, 1971).

71 C. Oman, *The Great Revolt of 1381* (Oxford: Clarendon Press, 1906), p. 65.

72 *Calendar of Inquisitions Post Mortem*, vol. 16, 235.

73 Rackham, *History of the Countryside*, pp. 50–1.

74 C. Currie, 'The early history of carp and its economic significance in England', *Agricultural History Review* 39 (1991), pp. 97–107.

75 C. Dyer, 'The consumption of fish in medieval England', in M. Aston (ed.), *Medieval Fish, Fisheries and Fish Ponds in England* (Oxford: British Archaeological Reports, British Series, vol. 182, 1988), pp. 27–35.

76 J. McCann, *The Dovecotes of Suffolk* (Ipswich, 1988). A. Grant, 'Animal resources', in G. Astill and A. Grant (eds), *The Countryside of Medieval England* (Oxford: Blackwell, 1988), pp. 149–87.

77 Norfolk Record Office Le Strange ND 22.34.

78 K. J. Walker, 'Using data from local floras to assess floristic change', *Watsonia* 24 (2003), 305–19, esp. 315. D. E. Allen, 'Sources of error in local lists', *Watsonia* 13 (1981), 215–20.

Chapter 2

1 J. U. Nef, *The Rise of the British Coal Industry* (London: Routledge, 1932), pp. 19–32. M. W. Flinn, *The History of the British Coal Industry Vol. 2, 1700-1830* (Oxford: Oxford University Press, 1984), p. 26.

2 R. G. Wilkinson, 'The English Industrial Revolution', in D. Worcester (ed.), *The Ends of the Earth: perspectives on modern environmental history* (1988), pp. 80–99. B. Thomas, 'Was There an energy crisis in Great Britain in the seventeenth century?', *Explorations in Economic History* 23 (1986), 124–52. P. Warde, *Energy Consumption in England and Wales 1560-2000* (2006), pp. 32–9; 67.

3 O. Rackham, *The History of the Countryside* (London: Dent, 1986), p. 88.

4 Forestry Commission, 'National Forest Inventory: woodland area statistics, England' (Edinburgh, 2011).

5 Including woodlands which have been largely replanted with conifers in recent centuries: http://archive.defra.gov.uk/environment/biodiversity/documents/indicator/200904f5.

6 G. F. Peterken, *Natural Woodland: ecology and conservation in northern temperate regions* (Cambridge: Cambridge University Press, 1996), p. 17.

7   Rackham, *History of the Countryside*, pp. 119–52.

8   O. Rackham, *Trees and Woodland in the British Landscape* (London: Dent, 1976), p. 121.

9   P. Dallas, 'Sustainable environments: common wood pastures in Norfolk', *Landscape History* 31 (2010), 23–36.

10 Hertfordshire Archives and Local Studies 10996 A/B.

11 Rackham, *History of the Countryside*, pp. 65–8.

12 O. Rackham, *Woodlands* (London: Collins, 2006), pp. 348–73.

13 P. H. Colebourne, 'Discovering ancient woods', *British Wildlife* 1 (1989), 61–75.

14 Colebourne, 'Discovering ancient woods', p. 70.

15 Ibid., p. 74.

16 M. Warren, 'European butterflies on the brink', *British Wildlife* 1 (1989), 185–96.

17 S. P. Carter, 'Habitat change and bird populations', *British Wildlife* 1 (1990), 324–34.

18 Ibid., p. 328.

19 P. Dolman, S. Hinsley, P. Bellamy and K. Watts, 'Woodland birds in patchy landscapes. The evidence base for strategic networks', *Ibis* 149 (2007), 146–60.

20 Colebourne, 'Ancient woodland', p. 70.

21 J. White, 'What is a veteran tree and where are they all?', *Quarterly Journal of Forestry* 91, 3 (1997), 222–6. J. White, 'Estimating the age of large and veteran trees in Britain', *Forestry Commission Information Note 250* (Alice Holt: Forestry Commission, 1999).

22 P. A. Briggs, 'Bats in trees', *Arboricultural Journal* 22 (1998), 25–35. K. J. Kirby and C. M. Drake (eds), *Dead Wood Matters* (Peterborough: English Nature, 1993). A. Orange, *Lichens on Trees* (Cardiff: National Museum of Wales, 1994). H. J. Read and M. Frater, *Woodland Habitats* (London: Routledge, 1999). H. J. Read, *Veteran Trees: a guide to good management* (Peterborough: English Nature, 2000).

23 K. Alexander, 'The invertebrates of Britain's wood pastures', *British Wildlife* 11(1999), 108–17.

24 D. A. Ratcliffe, 'Post-medieval and recent change in British vegetation: the culmination of human influence', *New Phytologist* 98 (1984), 73–100.

25 J. Parry, *Heathland* (London: National Trust, 2003); N. Webb, *Heathlands* (London: Collins, 1986).

26 Rackham, *History of the Countryside*, pp. 299–303; T. Williamson, *Sutton Hoo and its Landscape; the context of monuments* (Oxford: Windgather, 2008), pp. 81–5.

27 E. Kerridge, *The Agricultural Revolution* (London: Allen and Unwin, 1967), pp. 43–51.

28 M. Bailey, 'The rabbit and the medieval East Anglian economy', *Agricultural History Review* 36 (1988), 1–20. J. Sheail, *Rabbits and their History* (Newton Abbot: David and Charles, 1971), pp. 35–73. T. Williamson, *Rabbits, Warrens and Archaeology* (Stroud: Tempus, 2007), pp. 97–109.

29 J. Norden, *The Surveyor's Dialogue* (London, 1618), p. 234.

30 G. Edwards (ed.), *George Crabbe: selected poems* (1991), p. 5.

31 Norfolk Record Office, MC3/45. Blickling Hall, Map of 1729, no catalogue number.

32 A. Cox, *RCHME Survey of Bedfordshire. Brickmaking: a history and gazetteer* (Bedford: Bedfordshire County Council, 1979), p. 27.

33 Cox, *Brickmaking*, pp. 28–9.

34 T. Barrett-Lennard, 'Two hundred years of estate management at Horsford during the 17th and 18th centuries', *Norfolk Archaeology* 20 (1921), 20, 57–139.

35 Ratcliffe, 'Post-medieval and recent change in British vegetation', p. 73.

36 G. Barnes, P. Dallas, H. Thompson, N. Whyte and T. Williamson, 'Heathland and wood pasture in Norfolk: ecology and landscape history', *British Wildlife* 18 (2007), 395–403.

37 C. Tubbs, 'Grazing the lowland heaths', *British Wildlife* 2 (1990), 276–89.

38 W. G. Clarke, 'Some Breckland characteristics', *Transactions of the Norfolk and Norwich Naturalists Society* 8 (1908), 555–78.

39 Norden, *Surveyor's Dialogue*, p. 235.

40 M. R. Postgate, 'The field systems of Breckland', *Agricultural History Review* 10 (1962), 80–101.

41 R. J. Pakeman and A. G. Marshall, 'The seedbanks of the Breckland heaths and heath grasslands, eastern England, and their relationship to the vegetation and the effects of management', *Journal of Biogeography* 24, 3 (1987), 375–90. P. Dolman and W. Sutherland, 'The ecological changes of Breckland grass heath and the consequences of management', *Journal of Applied Ecology* 29, 2 (1992), 402–13.

42 P. J. Grubb, H. E. Green, and R. C. J. Merrifield, 'The ecology of chalk heath: its relevance to the calciole-calcifuge and soil acidification problems', *Journal of Ecology* 57 (1969), 175–212.

43 M. R. Postgate, 'The Open Fields of Cambridgeshire', unpublished PhD thesis, University of Cambridge, 1964.

44 C. Tubbs, 'Grazing the Lowland Heaths', *British Wildlife* 2 (1990), 276–89. Parry, *Heathland*.

45 A. Young, *Observations on the Present State of the Waste Lands of Great Britain* (London, 1773), p. 37.

46 R. G. Bunce and D. Fowler, *Heather in England and Wales* (London: HMSO, 1984). Rackham, *History of the Countryside*, pp. 305–6. L. Dudley Stamp, *The Land of Britain: its use and misuse* (London: Geographical Publications, 1950), pp. 145–56.

47 A. Fleming, *The Dartmoor Reaves* (London: Batsford, 1988).

48 Rackham, *History of the Countryside*, pp. 315–16.

49 D. Hey, 'Yorkshire and Lancashire', in J. Thirsk (ed.), *The Agrarian History of England and Wales*, vol. 5.1 (Cambridge: Cambridge University Press,

1984), pp. 59–88. D. Hey, 'Moorlands', in J. Thirsk (ed.), *The English Rural Landscape* (Oxford: Oxford University Press, 2000), pp. 188–209.

50 J. A. Hanley, *Progressive Farming*, 4 vols (London: Caxton Publishing, 1949), II, pp. 33–4.

51 I. R. Rotherham, *Peat and Peat Cutting* (Princes Risborough: Shire, 2011). I. G. Simmons, *The Moorlands of England and Wales: an Environmental History 8000 BC – AD 2000* (Edinburgh: Edinburgh University Press, 2003), p. 233.

52 Bunce and Fowler, *Heather in England and Wales*; Rackham, *History of the Countryside*, pp. 320–1.

53 D. A. Ratcliffe, 'Upland birds and their conservation', *British Wildlife* 2 (1990), 1–12.

54 J. J. Hopkins, 'British meadows and pastures', *British Wildlife* 1 (1990), 202–13.

55 Hopkins, 'British meadows and pastures', p. 203.

56 Ibid., p. 205.

57 Ibid., pp. 206–7.

58 Kerridge, *Agricultural Revolution*, pp. 42–56.

59 D. A. Ratcliffe, *A Nature Conservation Review, Vol. 2, Site Accounts* (Cambridge: Cambridge University Press and the Nature Conservancy Council, 1977), pp. 141–6.

60 J. Andrews, 'British estuaries: an internationally important habitat for birds', *British Wildlife* 1 (1989), 76–88.

61 Lord F. Hervey (ed.), *Suffolk in the Seventeenth Century: the breviary of Suffolk by Robert Reyce* (London: J. Murray, 1902), p. 35.

62 J. Allen, V. Potter and M. Poulter, *The Building of Orford Castle: a translation from the Pipe Rolls 1163-78* (Orford, 2002).

63 A. Reeves and T. Williamson, 'Marshes', in J. Thirsk (ed.), *Rural England: an illustrated history of the landscape* (Oxford: Oxford University Press, 2000), pp. 150–66.

64 C. P. Petch, 'Reclaimed lands of west Norfolk', *Transactions of the Norfolk and Norwich Naturalists Society* 16, 2 (1947), 106–9.

65 C. Beardall and D. Casey, *Suffolk's Changing Countryside* (Ipswich: Suffolk Wildlife Trust, 1995), pp. 54–5.

66 Beardall and Casey, *Suffolk's Changing Countryside*, p. 54.

67 D. A. Ratcliffe, 'Post-medieval and recent change in British vegetation', p. 79.

68 C. Taylor, 'Fenlands', in J. Thirsk (ed.), *Rural England: an illustrated history of the landscape* (Oxford: Oxford University Press, 2000), pp. 167–87. H. C. Darby, *The Medieval Fenland* (Cambridge: Cambridge University Press, 1940).

69 T. Williamson, *The Norfolk Broads: a landscape history* (Manchester: Manchester University Press, 1997), pp. 84–7, 98–104.

70 W. Dugdale, *The History of Inbanking and Drayning of Diverse Fens and Marshes . . .* (London, 1662), p. ix.

71 J. Russell Smith (ed.), *The Complete Works of Michael Drayton*, vol. 3 (London, 1876), p. 32.

72 Perhaps this doesn't matter, if the only concern is the farming of wildlife: see A. Bowley, 'The Great Fen – a waterland for the future', *British Wildlife* 18 (2007), 415–23.

73 T. A. Rowell, 'Management of peatlands for conservation', *British Wildlife* 1 (1989), 146–56.

74 C. Newbold, 'Historical changes in the nature conservation interest of the fens of Cambridgeshire', in H. Cook and T. Williamson (eds), *Water Management in the English Landscape: field, marsh and meadow* (Edinburgh: Edinburgh University Press, 1999), pp. 210–26.

75 Taylor, 'Fenlands'. C. C. Taylor, 'Post-medieval drainage of marsh and Fen', in H. Cook and T. Williamson (eds), *Water Management in the English Landscape: field, marsh and meadow* (Edinburgh: Edinburgh University Press, 1999), pp. 141–56.

76 H. C. Darby, *The Draining of the Fens*, 2nd edn (Cambridge: Cambridge University Press, 1966). N. James, 'The Transformation of the fens', in T. Kirby and S. Oosthuizen (eds), *An Atlas of Cambridgeshire and Huntingdonshire History* (Cambridge: Anglia Polytechnic University, 2000), p. 7.

77 A. Winchester and A. Staughton, 'Stints and sustainability: managing stocking levels on commons land in England c.1600-2000', *Agricultural History Review* 58 (2010), 30–48.

78 Barrett-Lennard, 'Two hundred years of estate management', p. 70.

79 The National Archive, E134/43 & 44 Eliz/Mich7.

Chapter 3

1 O. Rackham, *The History of the Countryside* (London: Dent, 1986), p. 334–5.

2 E. Kerridge, *The Farmers of Old England* (London: Allen and Unwin, 1973), pp. 21–2.

3 A. Brian, 'Lammas meadows', *Landscape History* 15 (1983), 57–69. A. Brian, 'The allocation of strips in lammas meadows by the casting of lots', *Landscape History* 21 (1999), 43–58.

4 J. J. Hopkins, 'British meadows and pastures', *British Wildlife* 1 (1990), 202–13. P. Marren, 'Harvests of beauty: the conservation of hay meadows', *British Wildlife* 6 (1995), 235–43.

5 J. H. Bettey, 'The development of water meadows in Dorset', *Agricultural History Review* 25 (1977), 37–43. J. H. Bettey, 'Water meadows in the southern counties of England', in H. Cook and T. Williamson (eds), *Water Management in the English Landscape* (Edinburgh: Edinburgh University Press, 1999), pp. 179–95. E. Kerridge, 'The floating of the Wiltshire water meadows', *Wiltshire Archaeological Magazine* 55 (1953), 105–18. E. Kerridge, 'The sheepfold in Wiltshire and the floating of the water meadows', *The Economic History Review* 6 (1954), 282–9. R. L. Cutting and I. P. F. Cummings,

'Water meadows: their form, ecology and plant ecology', in H. F. Cook, H. F. and T. Williamson (eds), *Water Management*, pp. 157–79.

6 H. Cook, K. Stearne and T. Williamson, 'The origins of water meadows in England', *Agricultural History Review* 51 (2003), 155–62.

7 Cutting and Cummings, 'Water meadows', pp. 159–60.

8 H. Cook and T. Williamson, 'Introducing water meadows', in H. Cook and T. Williamson (eds), *Water Meadows: history, ecology and conservation* (Oxford: Windgather, 2007), pp. 1–7.

9 T. Davis, *General View of the Agriculture of the County of Wiltshire* (London, 1794), p. 34.

10 H. P. Moon and F. H. W. Green, 'Water meadows in Southern England', in L. Dudley Stamp (ed.), *The Land of Britain, The Report of the Land Utilisation Survey of Britain* Pt. 89 (London: Geographical Publications, 1940), Appendix 2, pp. 373–90.

11 Bettey, 'Water meadows in the southern counties', pp. 184–5.

12 S. Wade Martins and T. Williamson, 'Floated water-meadows in Norfolk: a misplaced innovation', *Agricultural History Review* 42 (1994), pp. 20–37. T. Williamson, 'Floating in context; meadows in the long term', in H. Cook and T. Williamson (eds), *Water Meadows: history, ecology and conservation* (Oxford: Windgather, 2007), pp. 35–51.

13 R. L. Cutting, 'Drowning by numbers: the functioning of bedwork water meadows', in H. Cook and T. Williamson (eds), *Water Meadows*, pp. 70–81. I. Cummings, 'The effects of floating on plant Communities', in H. Cook and T. Williamson (eds), *Water Meadows: history, ecology and conservation* (Oxford: Windgather, 2007), pp. 82–93.

14 J. S. Rodwell (ed.), *British Plant Communities, Volume 3: Grassland and Montane Communities* (Cambridge: Cambridge University Press, 1993).

15 J. Sheail, 'The formation and maintenance of water-meadows in Hampshire, England', *Biological Conservation* 3 (1971), 101–6.

16 W. Marshall, *The Rural Economy of the Southern Counties* (London, 1798).

17 M. Shrubb, *Birds, Scythes and Combines: a history of birds and agricultural change* (Cambridge: Cambridge University Press, 2003), p. 208.

18 P. J. Wilson, 'Britain's arable weeds', *British Wildlife* 3 (1991), 149–61. Sir E. Salisbury, *Weeds and Aliens* (London: Collins, 1961), pp. 144–96.

19 Rackham, *History of the Countryside*, 164–79. B. K. Roberts and S. Wrathmell, *An Atlas of Rural Settlement in England* (London: English Heritage, 2000). B. Roberts and S. Wrathmell, *Region and Place; a study of English rural settlement* (London: English Heritage, 2002). T. Williamson, *Shaping Medieval Landscapes: settlement, society, environment* (Macclesfield: Windgather, 2003), pp. 91–118. Rackham, *History of the Countryside*, pp. 4–6.

20 R. Lovegrove, *Silent Fields: the long decline of a nation's wildlife* (Oxford: Oxford University Press, 2007), p. 40.

21 Ibid., p. 259.

22 Slater described the open-fields in the chalkland parishes of Clothall and Bygrave in north Hertfordshire when they still lay unenclosed: G. Slater,

The English Peasantry and the Enclosure of Common Fields (London: Constable, 1907), pp. 41–5.

23 The poor received compensation for the loss of such resources in a number of Midland enclosures, such as Clipston, Aldwincle, Harlestone, Wappenham, Wadenhoe, and Wollaston in Northamptonshire.

24 D. Hall, *The Open Fields of Northamptonshire* (Northampton: Northamptonshire Record Society, 1995), p. 264.

25 Northamptonshire Record Office Map 3133.

26 British Library Add. Mss. 78141 A. Northampton Record Office uncatalogued enclosure map of Wollaston; Northampton Record Office Map 4447.

27 S. G. Upex, 'The uses and functions of ponds within early landscapes in the east Midlands', *Agricultural History Review* 52 (2004), 125–40.

28 Northampton Record Office map 1555.

29 A. G. Louverre, 'The atlas of rural settlement GIS', *Landscapes* 11 (2010), 21–44. T. Williamson, *Environment, society and landscape in early medieval England: time and topography* (Woodbridge: Boydell, 2013), pp. 140–5.

30 A. E. Brown and C. C. Taylor, 'The origins of dispersed settlement: some results from Bedfordshire', *Landscape History* 11 (1989), 61–82.

31 T. Williamson, R. Liddiard and T. Partida, *Champion. The making and unmaking of the English Midland landscape* (Liverpool: Liverpool University Press, 2013), pp. 140–1; D. Hall, 'Enclosure in Northamptonshire', *Northamptonshire Past and Present* 9 (1997), 351–68.

32 Quoted in D. Hall, *Open Fields of Northamptonshire*, p. 22.

33 Williamson et al., *Champion*, pp. 133–43.

34 W. Johnson, 'Hedges: a review of some early literature', *Local Historian* 13 (1978), 195–204.

35 W. R. Mead, *Pehr Kalm: a Finnish visitor to the Chilterns in 1748* (Aston Clinton: Privately published, 2003), p. 116; Johnson, 'Hedges: a review of some early literature'.

36 W. Marshall, *The Rural Economy of Norfolk* (London, 1787), p. 96.

37 A. Young, *General View of the Agriculture of Hertfordshire* (1804), p. 49.

38 E. Pollard, M. D. Hooper and N. W. Moore, *Hedges* (London: Collins, 1974), pp. 79–85.

39 G. Barnes and T. Williamson, *Hedgerow History: ecology, history and landscape character* (Oxford: Windgather Press, 2006), pp. 73–80. A. Willmott, 'The woody species of hedges with special reference to age in Church Broughton, Derbyshire, *Journal of Ecology* 68 (1980), 269–86. J. Hall, 'Hedgerows in West Yorkshire: the Hooper method examined', *Yorkshire Archaeological Journal* 54 (1982), 103–9.

40 R. and N. Muir, *Hedgerows: their history and wildlife* (London: Michael Joseph, 1997), pp. 96–104. A. Brooks, *Hedging: a practical conservation handbook* (London: British Trust for Conservation Volunteers, 1975).

41 Barnes and Williamson, *Hedgerow History*, pp. 3–4. E. Martin and M. Satchell, *Wheare Most Inclosures Be: East Anglian Fields, History, Morphology and Management* (Ipswich, 2008), pp. 237–43.

42 Hertfordshire Archives and Local Studies D/ELw/E4.

43 D. K. Clements and R. J. Tofts, 'Hedges make the grade: a look at the wildlife value of hedges', *British Wildlife* 4 (1992), 87–95. Moore et al., *Hedges*, pp. 117–59.

44 R. T. Forman and J. Baudry, 'Hedgerow and hedgerow networks in landscape ecology', *Environmental management* 8 (1984), 495–510.

45 P. E. Bellamy, 'The influence of hedge structure, management and landscape context on the value of hedgerows to birds', *Journal of Environmental Management* 60 (2000), 33–49.

46 London School of Economics Coll Misc 38/3 f.8.

47 Norfolk Record Office NRS 12793 3F F8.

48 R. J. O'Connor and M. Shrubb, *Farming and Birds* (Cambridge: Cambridge University Press, 1986), p. 129.

49 D. Walker, *General View of the Agriculture of the County of Hertford* (London, 1795), p. 13. S. Wade Martins and T. Williamson, *Roots of Change: farming and the landscape in East Anglia, c.1700-1870* (Exeter: Exeter University Press, 1999), p. 25. Martin and Satchell, *Wheare Most Inclosures Be*, pp. 343–4.

50 Rackham, *History of the Countryside*, pp. 218–21.

51 J. Theobald, 'Changing landscapes, changing economies: holdings in Woodland High Suffolk 1600-1840', Unpublished MA dissertation, University of East Anglia 1993. West Suffolk Record Office, T1/1/6.

52 Together with 569 'spars' or immature specimens: Hertfordshire Archives and Local Studies D/EBb/E27.

53 Clements and Toft, 'Wildlife value of hedges', p. 89.

54 Norfolk Record Office NRS 11126.

55 Norfolk Record Office Beauchamp-Proctor 334; NRO NRS 11126.

56 Norfolk Record Office WIS 138, 166X3.

57 J. Norden, *The Surveyors' Dialogue* (London, 1618), p. 201.

58 Hertfordshire Archives and Local Studies DE/X905/P1: undated map of a farm at Flaunden, early eighteenth century.

59 B. Lennon, 'Estimating the age of groups of trees in historic landscapes', *Arboricultural Journal* 32 (2009), 167–88. H. J. Read, 'Pollards and pollarding in Europe', *British Wildlife* 19 (2008), 250–9.

60 Norfolk Record Office, WIS 138, 166X3.

61 Norfolk Record Office PD 703/45-6; West Suffolk Record Office, T1/1/6.

62 Hertfordshire Archives and Local Studies D/EBb/E27.

63 Hertfordshire Archives and Local Studies D/EAm/E3.

64 Hertfordshire Archives and Local Studies D/ECd/E14.

65 Shrubb, *Birds, Scythes and Combines*, p. 19.

66 H. Mourier and O. Winding, *Collins Guide to Wild Life in House and Home* (London: Collins, 1975), pp. 5–6.

67 I. Wyllie, 'The bird community of an English parish', *Bird Study* 23 (1976), 39–50.

68 P. C. Lack, *Birds on Lowland Farms* (London: HMSO, 1992).

69 Shrubb, *Birds, Scythes and Combines*, pp. 298–305.

70 W. Johnson (ed.), *Gilbert White's Journal* (London: Routledge, 1931), p. 147.

71 D. MacDonald and P. Barrett, *Collins Field Guide to Mammals of Britain and Northern Europe* (London: Collins, 1993), p. 273.

72 T. Bell, *The History of British Quadrupeds* (London, 1837), p. 67.

73 Worcestershire Record Office, Lechmere of Hanley Castle 705: 134/1531.

74 J. H. Wilson (ed.), *Wymondham Inventories* (Norwich: Centre of East Anglian Studies, 1983), p. 15.

75 A. H. Cocks, 'Vermin paid for by churchwardens in a Buckinghamshire parish', *Zoologist* Series 3, 16 (1852), 61–4. C. Oldham, 'Payments for vermin by some Hertfordshire churchwardens', *Transactions of the Hertfordshire. Natural History Society* 18 (1929), 79–112. R. Lovegrove, *Silent Fields: the long decline of a nation's wildlife* (Oxford: Oxford University Press, 2002).

76 Lovegrove, *Silent Fields*, pp. 79–100.

77 E. L. Jones, 'The bird pests of British agriculture in recent centuries', *Agricultural History Review* 20 (1972), 107–25.

78 Lovegrove, *Silent Fields*, pp. 93.

79 Ibid., pp. 257–9.

80 Ibid., pp. 251–4, 260–3.

81 Ibid., p. 95.

82 Ibid., p. 57.

83 Ibid., p. 199

84 Ibid., Appendix 1.

85 R. Isham (ed. and trans.), *The Journal of Thomas Isham of Lamport in the County of Northamptonshire* (Norwich, 1875).

Chapter 4

1 Thomas Cleer's map of Norwich, c.1696: Norwich Heritage Centre, Norwich.

2 J. Schofield, *London 1100-1600: the archaeology of a capital city* (Sheffield, 2011), p. 343.

3 M. Reed, 'The urban landscape 1540-1700', in P. Clarke (ed.), *The Cambridge Urban History of Britain*, vol. 2, 1540–1840 (Cambridge: Cambridge University Press, 2000), p. 306.

4 R. S. R. Fitter, *London's Natural History* (London: Collins, 1945), pp. 51–2, 86–7.

5 Ibid., p. 59.

6   D. J. Rackham, 'The introduction of the black rat into Britain', *Antiquity* 53 (1979), 112–20. O. Rackham, *History of the Countryside* (London: Dent, 1986), pp. 46–7.

7   W. Johnson (ed.), *Gilbert White's Journal* (London: Routledge, 1931), p. 146.

8   R. Mabey, *The Unofficial Countryside* (London: Pimlico, 1999), p. 29.

9   R. Mabey, *Weeds: the story of outlaw plants* (London: Profile Books, 2010).

10 B. N. K. Davis, 'Wildlife, urbanisation and industry', *Biological Conservation* 10 (1976), 249–91. J. Box, 'Conserving or greening? The challenge of post-industrial landscapes', *British Wildlife* 4 (1993), 273–79.

11 http://webarchive.nationalarchives.gov.uk/20110303145213/http:/ukbap.org. uk/library/UKBAPPriorityHabitatDescriptionsRevised20100730.pdf

12 T. Turner, *English Garden Design: history and styles since 1650* (Woodbridge: Antique Collector's Club, 1986). M. Hadfield, *A History of British Gardening* (London: Penguin, 1985), pp. 103–78. J. Dixon Hunt and E. de Jong (eds), *The Anglo-Dutch Garden in the Age of William and Mary*, published as *Journal of Garden History* 8, 2&3 (1988). T. Williamson, *Polite Landscapes: gardens and society in eighteenth-century England* (Stroud: Sutton, 1995), pp. 24–31.

13 T. Williamson, *The Archaeology of the Landscape Park: landscape design in Norfolk, England 1680-1840* (Oxford: British Archaeological Reports, British Series, vol. 268, 1998), pp. 33–4.

14 M. Campbell-Culver, *The Origins of Plants* (London: Headline Books, 2001), pp. 120–67.

15 O. Rackham, *Woodlands* (London: Collins, 2006), p. 363.

16 A natural cross between the natives *Tilia cordata* and *T. platyphyllos*, but seldom planted in the working countryside.

17 J. Freeman (ed.), *Thomas Fuller: the Worthies of England* (London, 1952), p. 523. East Suffolk Record Office 942.64 Som.

18 Williamson, *Polite Landscapes*, pp. 31–5.

19 T. Williamson, 'Fish, fur and feather: man and nature in the post-medieval landscape', in K. Barker and T. Darvill (eds), *Making English Landscapes* (Bournemouth: Bournemouth University School of Conservation Sciences Occasional Paper, 1997), pp. 92–117. M. Barley, 'Rural buildings in England', in J. Thirsk (ed.), *The Agrarian History of England and Wales. Volume 5.2: 1640-1750* (Cambridge: Cambridge University Press, 1985), pp. 590–685.

20 C. Currie, 'Fish ponds as garden features', *Garden History* 18, 1 (1990), 22–33.

21 G. Isham, *Rushton Triangular Lodge* (London: HMSO, 1970).

22 P. Everson, 'Quarrendon, Aylesbury Vale, Buckinghamshire'. Unpublished report for English Heritage (Swindon, 1999), p. 50.

23 Hertfordshire Archives and Local Studies XIII.30.

24 J. Barnatt and T. Williamson, *Chatsworth: a landscape history* (Macclesfield, 2005), pp. 32–4, 44. W. Senior, *Lees* and *Edensor* (1617), maps in bound volume of early seventeenth-century surveys, Chatsworth Archives, Chatsworth House, Derbyshire.

25 J. Thirsk, 'Agricultural innovations and their diffusion', in J. Thirsk (ed.), *The Agricultural History of England and Wales. Volume 5.2, 1640-1750* (Cambridge: Cambridge University Press, 1985), pp. 533–89.

26 R. North, *The Discourse of Fish and Fish Ponds* (London, 1723).

27 R. Payne Galwey, *The Book of Duck Decoys* (London, 1886). A. Heaton, *Duck Decoys* (Princes Risborough: Shire, 2001).

28 Payne Galwey, *Duck Decoys*, p. 2.

29 East Suffolk Record Office HA 93/3/48.

30 E. Dennison and V. Russett, 'Duck decoys: their function and management with reference to Nyland Decoy, Cheddar', *Somerset Archaeology and Natural History* 133 (1989), 141–54.

31 D. Defoe, *A Tour through the Whole Island of Great Britain*, vol. 1 (London, 1724), p. 120.

32 E. P. Thompson, *Whigs and Hunters: the origin of the Black Act* (London: Allen Lane, 1975), p. 105.

33 J. Bettey, 'Origins of the Wiltshire rabbit industry', *Antiquaries Journal* 84 (2004), 381–93. G. E. Mingay, 'The East Midlands', in J. Thirsk (ed.), *The Agrarian History of England and Wales*, vol. 5.1 (Cambridge: Cambridge University Press, 1984), pp. 89–128. A. Harris, 'The rabbit warrens of east Yorkshire in the eighteenth and nineteenth centuries', *Yorkshire Archaeological Journal* 42 (1967–70), 429–41. A. Harris and D. A. Spratt, 'The rabbit warrens of the Tabular Hills, North Yorkshire', *Yorkshire Archaeological Journal* 63 (1991), 177–98.

34 T. Williamson, *Rabbits, Warrens and Archaeology* (Stroud: Tempus, 2007), pp. 89–126.

35 Harris, 'Rabbit warrens of east Yorkshire', p. 436.

36 Thompson, *Whigs and Hunters*, p. 105.

37 K. Thomas, *Man and the Natural World: changing attitudes in England 1500-1800* (London: Allen Lane, 1983), p. 49.

38 J. Fletcher, *Gardens of Earthly Delight: the history of deer parks* (Oxford: Windgather, 2011), pp. 176–87.

39 Williamson, *Polite Landscapes*, p. 24.

40 Charles II, 1670 and 1671: An Act for the better preservation of the Game, and for secureing Warrens not inclosed, and the severall Fishings of this Realme. *Statutes of the Realm*, vol. 5, 1628–80 (London, 1819), pp. 745–6.

41 Thompson, *Whigs and Hunters*.

42 P. B. Munsche, *Gentlemen and Poachers: the English Game Laws 1671-1831* (Cambridge: Cambridge University Press, 1981).

43 M. Brander, *The Hunting Instinct: the development of field sports over the ages* (London: Oliver and Boyd, 1964), pp. 87–101.

44 Munsche, *Gentlemen and Poachers*, pp. 8–19.

45 Thomas, *Man and the Natural World*, p. 71.

46 R. Mabey, *Flora Britannica* (London: Concise edn, Chatto and Windus, 1998), pp. 14–27. G. Grigson, *The Englishman's Flora* (London: Paladin, 1975). Thomas, *Man and the Natural World*, pp. 81–7.

47 Ibid., p. 85.

48 Act 2, Scene 2, lines 55–60.

49 R. Lovegrove, *Silent Fields: the long decline of a nation's wildlife* (Oxford: Oxford University Press, 2007), p. 85.

50 Review by Michael McCarthy, *The Independent*, 23 March 2007.

51 L. Mascall, *A Book of Engines and Traps to take Polecats, Buzardes, Rattes, Mice and all other Kindes of Vermine and Beasts* whatever (London, 1590). Lovegrove, *Silent Fields*, pp. 79–94.

52 Lovegrove, *Silent Fields*, p. 93.

Chapter 5

1   B. R. Mitchell and P. Deane, *Abstract of British Historical Statistics* (Cambridge: Cambridge University Press, 1962), pp. 5–6.

2   B. A. Holderness, 'Prices, productivity and output', in G. E. Mingay (ed.), *The Agrarian History of England and Wales*, vol. 6 (Cambridge: Cambridge University Press, 1989), pp. 84–189. J. V. Beckett, *The Agricultural Revolution* (Oxford: Basil Blackwell, 1990), p. 9.

3   M. Overton, *Agricultural Revolution in England* (Cambridge: Cambridge University Press, 1996), pp. 121–8.

4   M. W. Flinn, *The History of the British Coal Industry Vol. 2, 1700-1830* (Oxford: Oxford University Press, 1984), p. 27.

5   M. Palmer and P. Neaverson, *Industry in the Landscape, 1700-1900* (London: Routledge, 1994), pp. 94–119.

6   E. Kerridge, *The Agricultural Revolution* (London: Allen and Unwin, 1967). E. Kerridge, 'The agricultural revolution reconsidered', *Agricultural History Review* 43 (1969), 463–76.

7   F. Mendels, 'Proto-industrialisation: the first phase of the industrialisation process', *Journal of Economic History* 32 (1972), 241–61. P. Hudson, 'Proto-industrialization', *Recent Findings of Research in Economic and Social History* 10 (1990), 1–4.

8   D. Defoe, *A Tour through the Whole Island of Great Britain*, vol. 3 (London, 1727), pp. 99–100.

9   N. Cossons, *The BP Book of Industrial Archaeology* (Newton Abbot: David and Charles, 1987), p. 32.

10 K. Pomeranz, *The Great Divergence: China, Europe, and the making of the modern world economy* (Princeton: Princeton University Press, 2001), p. 67.

11 M. Jacob, *The Cultural Meaning of the Scientific Revolution* (New York, 1988). Pomeranz, *The Great Divergence*, p. 68.

12 Flinn, *History of the British Coal Industry*, p. 114.

13 N. von Tunzelmann, *Steam Power and British Industrialisation to 1860* (Oxford: Clarendon Press, 1978), pp. 224, 289.

14 P. Belford, 'Sublime cascades: water and power in Coalbrookdale', *Industrial Archaeology Review* 29 (2007), 133–48.

15 B. P. Hindle, *Roads, Tracks and their Interpretation* (London: Batsford, 1993), pp. 64–6.

16 W. Albert, *The Turnpike Road System in England 1663–1840* (Cambridge: Cambridge University Press, 1972). P. Langford, *Polite and Commercial People: England, 1727-1783* (Oxford: Oxford University Press, 1989), pp. 391–408.

17 Cossons, *Industrial Archaeology*, p. 256.

18 E. A. W. Wrigley, *Continuity, Chance and Change: the character of the Industrial Revolution in England* (Cambridge: Cambridge University Press, 1988), pp. 54–5.

19 W. G. Hoskins, *The Making of the English Landscape* (London: Hodder and Stoughton, 1956), pp. 224–6. M. Palmer and P. Neaverson, *Industry in the Landscape, 1700-1900* (London: Routledge, 1994), pp. 1–17.

20 I. Simmons, *An Environmental History of Great Britain: from 10,000 years ago to the present* (Edinburgh: Edinburgh University Press, 2001), pp. 166–7, 172.

21 F. Engels, *The Condition of the Working Class in England in 1844*.

22 Simmons, *Environmental History of Great Britain*, p. 161. B. W. Clapp, *An Environmental History of Britain since the Industrial Revolution* (London: Longman, 1994), p. 70.

23 P. Brimblecombe, *The Big Smoke: a history of air pollution in London since medieval times* (London: Methuen, 1987).

24 S. Mosley, *The Chimney of the World: a history of smoke pollution in Victorian and Edwardian Manchester* (Cambridge: White Horse Press, 2001), pp. 21, 37.

25 I. Simmons, *Environmental History of Great Britain*, p. 151. V. M. Conway, 'Ringinglow bog, near Sheffield, Part 2. The present surface', *Journal of Ecology* 37 (1949), 148–70.

26 D. A. Ratcliffe, 'Post-medieval and recent change in British vegetation: the culmination of human influence', *New Phytologist* 98 (1984), 73–100.

27 B. W. Clapp, *An Environmental History of Britain since the Industrial Revolution* (London: Longman, 1994), p. 74.

28 T. A. Coward and C. Oldham, *The Birds of Cheshire* (Manchester: Sherrat and Hughes, 1900), p. 1.

29 Conway, 'Ringinglow bog', pp. 163, 166.

30 L. H. Grindon, *Manchester Walks and Wild Flowers* (Manchester, 1859), p. 142.

31 H. B. Rogers, 'The suburban growth of Victorian Manchester', *Journal of the Manchester Geographical Society* 58 (1961–62), 1–12.

32 Ibid., p. 7.

33 Ibid., p. 4.

34 Grindon, *Manchester Walks and Wild Flowers*, pp. 1, 49, 69.

35 D. J. Sinclair, 'The growth of London since 1800', in K. M. Clayton (ed.), *Guide to the London Excursion: 20th International Geography Congress* (London, 1964), pp. 13–18. K. M. K. Young and P. L. Garside, *Metropolitan London: politics and urban change 1837-1981* (London: Edward Arnold, 1982), pp. 4, 15.

36 Anon., *The Village London Atlas: the growth of Victorian London* (London: Alderman Press, 1986).

37 B. N. K. Davis, 'Wildlife, urbanisation and industry', *Biological Conservation* 10 (1976), 269–91.

38 J. W. Heslop Harrison and J. A. Richardson, 'The magnesian limestone area of Durham and its vegetation', *Transactions of the Northumberland Naturalists Union* 2 (1953), 1–28. See also A. Davies, 'Nature after minerals: a major role for quarries in nature conservation', *British Wildlife* 18 (2007), 305–12.

39 J. Box, 'Conserving or greening? The challenge of post-industrial landscapes', *British Wildlife* 4 (1993), 273–9.

40 E. F. Greenwood, 'Derelict industrial land as a habitat for rare plants in S. Lancs. (v.c.59) and W. Lancs. (v.c.60)', *Watsonia* 12 (1978), 33–40.

41 A. Maddock (ed.), *UK Biodiversity Action Plan: priority habitat descriptions* (Peterborough: English Nature, 2011).

42 J. Barnatt and R. Penny, *The Lead Legacy: the prospects for the Peak District's lead mining heritage* (Bakewell: Peak District National Park Authority, 2004).

43 english-nature.org.uk/citation/citation: accessed December 2012.

44 Cossons, *Industrial Archaeology*, p. 254.

45 J. G. Kelcey, 'Industrial development and wildlife conservation', *Environmental Conservation* 2, 2 (1973), 104. R. Mabey, *The Unofficial Countryside* (London, 1999), pp. 59–60.

46 A. Byfield, 'The Basingstoke Canal: Britain's richest waterway under threat', *British Wildlife* 2 (1990), 13–21.

47 Byfield, 'Basingstoke Canal', p. 13.

48 Byfield, 'Basingstoke Canal', p. 16.

49 I. Walton and C. Cotton, *The Complete Angler* (London, 1853), p. 131.

50 C. Dixon, *The Game Birds and Wild Fowl of the British Islands: being a handbook for the naturalist and sportsman* (London, 1895), p. 234.

51 Mabey, *Unofficial Countryside*, p. 62.

52 P. E. Hulme, 'Biological invasions in Europe: drivers, pressures, states, impacts and response', in R. E. Hester and R. M. Harrison (eds), *Issues in Environmental Science and Technology*, vol. 25 (Cambridge: Royal Society of Chemistry, 2007), pp. 56–80.

53 O. L. Gilbert, *The Ecology of Urban Habitats* (London: Chapman and Hall, 1989), p. 285.

54 Gilbert, *Ecology of Urban Habitats*, pp. 282–3.

55 T. T. Macan, 'Freshwater invertebrates', in D. L. Hawksworth (ed.), *The Changing Flora and Fauna of Britain* (London: Taylor and Francis, 1974), pp. 143–55.

56 C. E. Shaw, 'Canals', in J. P. Saidge (ed.), *Travis's Flora of South Lancashire* (Liverpool: Liverpool Botanical Society, 1963), pp. 71–3.

57 Cossons, *Industrial Archaeology*, pp. 277–8.

58 C. C. Druce, *The Flora of Oxfordshire* (London, 1886), pp. 241–2. D. H. Kent, 'Senechio squalidus L in the British Isles 1. Early records (to 1877)', *Proceedings of the Botanical Society of the British Isles* 2 (1958), 115–18. D. H. Kent, 'Senechio squalidus L in the British Isles 2. The spread from Oxford', *Proceedings of the Botanical Society of the British Isles* 3 (1960), 115–18.

59 R. Mabey, *Flora Britannica* (London: Concise edn, Chatto and Windus, 1998), p. 17.

60 Ibid., pp. 179–80.

61 E. Lees, *The Botany of Worcestershire* (Worcester, 1867), pp. xvii, 74.

62 Fitter, *London's Natural History*, p. 161.

63 J. G. Dony, 'Notes on the Bedfordshire railway flora', *Bedfordshire Naturalist* (1955), 12–16.

64 Gilbert, *Ecology of Urban Habitats*, pp. 129–30.

65 R. Jefferies, *Nature Near London* (London, 1913), p. 181.

66 Kelcey, 'Industrial development and wildlife conservation', p. 105.

67 G. Edelen (ed.), *The Description of England: the Classic Contemporary Account of Tudor Social Life, by William Harrison* (London: Folger Shakespeare Library, 1994), p. 281.

68 P. Kalm, *Kalm's Account of his Visit to England on his Way to America in 1748*, translated by J. Lucas (London, 1892), pp. 137–8.

69 A. Cox, *RCHME Survey of Bedfordshire. Brickmaking: a history and gazetteer* (Bedford: Bedfordshire County Council, 1979), p. 27.

70 Cox, *Brickmaking*, p. 44.

71 S. Birtles, '"A Green Space Beyond Self Interest": the Evolution of Common Land in Norfolk c.750-2003'. Unpublished PhD thesis, University of East Anglia, 2003.

72 Birtles, 'Green Space Beyond Self Interest', pp. 196, 307–9.

73 I. Whyte, *Transforming Fell and Valley: Landscape and Parliamentary Enclosure in North West England* (Lancaster: University of Lancaster, Centre for North West Regional Studies, 2003), p. 76.

74 Ibid.

75 J. Parry, *Heathland* (London: National Trust, 2003), p. 62.

Chapter 6

1 B. Campbell and M. Overton, 'A new perspective on medieval and early-modern agriculture: six centuries of Norfolk farming, 1250-1850', *Past and Present* 141 (1993), 38–105. M. Overton, 'The determinants of crop yields in

early modern England', in B. Campbell and M. Overton (eds), *Land, Labour and Livestock* (Manchester: Manchester University Press, 1991), pp. 284–332. P. O'Brien, 'Agriculture and the home market for English industry, 1660-1820', *English Historical Review* 100 (1985), 773–800.

2 J. V. Beckett, *The Agricultural Revolution* (Oxford: Basil Blackwell, 1990), pp. 11–18.

3 T. Williamson, *The Transformation of Rural England: farming and the landscape 1700-1870* (Exeter: Exeter University Press, 2002), pp. 20–2.

4 T. Williamson, 'Post-medieval field drainage', in H. Cook and T. Williamson (eds), *Water Management in the English Landscape: field, marsh and meadow* (Edinburgh: Edinburgh University Press, 1999), pp. 41–52.

5 Williamson, *Transformation of Rural England*, pp. 80–1.

6 Ibid., pp. 158–63.

7 G. Clarke, M. Huberaman and P. H. Lindert, 'A British food puzzle, 1770-1850', *Economic History Review* 48 (1995), 213–37.

8 J. Mokyr, *The Lever of Riches: technological creativity and economic progress* (Oxford: Oxford University Press, 1990), p. 111.

9 G. M. De Rougemont, *Collins Field Guide to the Crops of Britain and Europe* (London: Collins, 1989), p. 280.

10 Shrubb, *Birds, Scythes and* Combines, pp. 6–7.

11 F. M. L. Thompson, 'The second Agricultural Revolution', *Economic History Review* 21 (1968), 62–77.

12 S. Wade Martins, *Farms and Fields* (London: Batsford, 1995), pp. 101–2. J. D. Chambers and G. E. Mingay, *The Agricultural Revolution 1750-1880* (London: Batsford, 1966), p. 170. N. Goddard, *Harvests of Change: the Royal Agricultural Society of England 1838-1988* (London, 1988).

13 Thompson, 'The second agricultural revolution', pp. 74–5.

14 Ibid., pp. 73–4.

15 P. Roe, 'Norfolk Agriculture in 1850'. Unpublished M.Phil thesis, University of East Anglia, Norwich 1975, pp. 61–2.

16 A. D. M. Phillips, 'Arable land drainage in the nineteenth century', in H. Cook and T. Williamson (eds), *Water Management in the English Landscape: field, marsh and meadow* (Edinburgh: Edinburgh University Press, 1999), pp. 53–72.

17 N. Harvey, *The Industrial Archaeology of Farming in England and Wales* (London: Batsford, 1980), p. 81.

18 A. D. M. Phillips, *The Underdraining of Farmland in England During the Nineteenth Century* (Cambridge: Cambridge University Press, 1989).

19 J. Gregory, 'Mapping improvement: reshaping rural landscapes in the eighteenth century', *Landscapes* 6 (2005), 62–82.

20 A. Young, *The Farmer's Tour Through the East of England*, 4 vols (London, 1771), vol. 2, p. 1.

21 G. G. Druce, *The Flora of Oxfordshire* (London, 1868), p. 293.

22 Ibid., p. 2.

23 C. C. Babbington, *Flora of Cambridgeshire* (Cambridge, 1860), p. xv.

24 J. Caird, 'General View of British Agriculture', *Journal of the Royal Agricultural Society of England* Second Series 14 (1878), 124–5, 273–332.

25 M. Shrubb, *Birds, Scythes and Combines: a history of birds and agricultural change* (Cambridge: Cambridge University Press, 2003), p. 88.

26 Ibid., pp. 91–2.

27 J. Swayne, 'The bustard', *Wiltshire Archaeological Magazine* 2 (1885), 212.

28 H. Stevenson, *The Birds of Norfolk* (London, 1870), p. 17.

29 H. Stevenson, 'Ornithological notes', *Transactions of the Norfolk and Norwich Naturalists Society* 2 (1876), 306. J. G. Truck, 'Note on the great bustard in Suffolk', *Transactions of the Norfolk and Norwich Naturalists' Society* 5 (1891), 209–11.

30 T. W. Beastall, *The Agricultural Revolution in Lincolnshire* (Lincoln: History of Lincolnshire Committee, 1978), p. 144.

31 A. Harris, 'The rabbit warrens of east Yorkshire in the eighteenth and nineteenth centuries', *Yorkshire Archaeological Journal* 42 (1967–70), 429–41.

32 Ibid.

33 Druce, *Flora of Oxfordshire*, p. 246.

34 J. Bailey and G. Culley, *General View of the Agriculture of Northumberland and Westmoreland* (London, 1805), p. 238; A. Pringle, *General View of the Agriculture of Westmoreland* (London, 1805), p. 322. Williamson, *Transformation of Rural England*, pp. 120–1.

35 M. Havinden, 'Lime as a means of agricultural improvement: the Devon example', in C. W. Chalklin and M. A. Havinden (eds), *Rural Change and Urban Growth* (London: Longman, 1974), pp. 104–34. E. J. T. Collins, 'The Economy of Upland Britain 1750-1950', in R. B. Tranter (ed.), *The Future of Upland Britain* (Reading: Centre for Agricultural Strategy, 1978), vol. 2, pp. 586–651.

36 H. W. Gardner and H. V. Garner, *The Use of Lime in British Agriculture* (London: Farmer and Stockbreeder Publications, 1957). R. Williams, *Limekilns and Limeburning* (Princes Risborough: Shire, 1989), pp. 8–11.

37 D. Hey, 'Yorkshire and Lancashire', in J. Thirsk (ed.), *The Agrarian History of England and Wales*, vol. 2 (Cambridge: Cambridge University Press, 1984), pp. 59–88.

38 Williams, *Limekilns and Limeburning*, pp. 16–23.

39 A. Winchester, 'The farming landscape', in W. Rollinson (ed.), *The Lake District: landscape history* (Newton Abbot: David and Charles, 1989), pp. 76–101.

40 Ibid., pp. 94–5.

41 D. A. Ratcliffe, 'Upland birds and their conservation', *British Wildlife* 2 (1990), 1–12.

42 Ratcliffe, 'Upland birds', p. 6. D. A. Ratcliffe, 'Post-medieval and recent change in British vegetation: the culmination of human influence', *New Phytologist* 98 (1984), 80.

43 Shrubb, *Birds, Scythes and Combines*, pp. 105–6.

44 R. J. P. Kain, *An Atlas and Index of the Tithe-Files of Mid Nineteenth Century England and Wales* (Cambridge: Cambridge University Press, 1986), pp. 195, 205.

45 E. E. Briault, *The Land of Britain: Sussex* (Land Utilisation Survey Pts 13 and 14) (London: Geographical Publications, 1947), p. 490.

46 P. Armstrong, 'Changes in the Suffolk Sandlings: a study of the disintegration of an eco-system', *Geography* 58 (1973), pp. 1–8.

47 J. Chapman, 'The extent and nature of parliamentary enclosure', *Agricultural History Review* 35 (1987), 25–35. Chapman's estimates of the extent of parliamentary enclosure are arguably a little on the high side. On the other hand, this total excludes waste removed by other means, as well as numerous small pockets of unploughed ground lying within the open fields whose extent was not detailed in the enclosure acts.

48 C. D. Preston, 'Engulfed by suburbia or destroyed by the plough: the ecology of extinction in Middlesex and Cambridgeshire', *Watsonia* 23 (2000), 59–81.

49 D. Defoe, *A Tour Through the Whole Island of Great Britain*, vol. 1 (London, 1724), p. 119.

50 R. L. Hills, *Machines, Mills and Uncountable Costly Necessities* (Norwich: Goose and Son, 1967), pp. 60–72. H. C. Darby, *The Draining of the Fens* (Cambridge: Cambridge University Press, 1940). C. Taylor, 'Fenlands', in J. Thirsk (ed.), *Rural England: an illustrated history of the landscape* (Oxford: Oxford University Press, 2000), pp. 167–87.

51 Ibid., p. 75.

52 J. A. Clarke, 'On the Great Level of the Fens', *Journal of the Royal Agricultural Society of England* 8 (1848), 80–133.

53 Babbington, *Flora of Cambridgeshire*, pp. xv1–xvii.

54 H. M. Upcher, 'President's address', *Transactions of the Norfolk and Norwich Naturalists' Society* 3 (1884), 564–633.

55 H. Stevenson, 'Ornithological notes', *Transactions of the Norfolk and Norwich Naturalists Society* 4 (1887), 125–39.

56 M. Williams, *The Draining of the Somerset Levels* (Cambridge: Cambridge University Press, 1970), pp. 123–68.

57 Ibid., pp. 145–50.

58 A. Winchester, *England's Landscape: the North West* (London: Collins/English Heritage, 2006), pp. 100–4; C. Taylor, 'Post-medieval drainage of marsh and fen', in H. Cook and T. Williamson (eds), *Water Management in the English Landscape: field, marsh and meadow* (Edinburgh: Edinburgh University Press, 1999), pp. 141–56; D. Hall, C. E. Wells and E. Huckerby, *The Wetlands of Greater Manchester* (Lancaster: Lancaster University Archaeological Unit, 1995), pp. 126–7.

59 Shrubb, *Birds, Scythes and Combines*, pp. 128–9. Preston, 'Engulfed by suburbia or destroyed by the plough', p. 67.

60 E. Pollard, M. D. Hooper and N. W. Moore, *Hedges* (London: Collins, 1974), pp. 118–9.

61 G. Barnes and T. Williamson, *Hedgerow History: ecology, history and landscape character* (Oxford: Windgather Press, 2006), pp. 130–2.

62 J. H. Turner, 'On the necessity of reducing the size and number of hedges', *Journal of the Royal Agricultural Society of England* 6 (1845), 479–88; W. Cambridge, 'On the advantages of reducing the size and number of hedges', *Journal of the Royal Agricultural Society of England* 6 (1845), 333–42.

63 Rev St John Priest, *General View of the Agriculture of the County of Buckinghamshire* (London, 1813), p. 123.

64 J. Boys, *General View of the Agriculture of the County of Kent* (London, 1813), p. 61.

65 H. Holland, *General View of the Agriculture of Cheshire* (London, 1813), p. 121.

66 A. Young, *General View of the Agriculture of Hertfordshire* (London, 1804), p. 52.

67 R. E. Green, P. E. Osbourne and E. J. Steers, 'The distribution of passerine birds in hedgerows during the breeding season in relation to the characteristics of the hedgerow and adjacent farmland', *Journal of Applied Ecology* 31 (1994), 677–92.

68 C. C. Babbington, *Flora of Cambridgeshire* (Cambridge, 1860), p. xv.

69 J. Caird, *English Agriculture 1851-2* (London, 1852), p. 310.

70 B. Jennings, 'A longer view of the Wolds', in J. Thirsk (ed.), *Rural England: An illustrated history of the landscape* (Oxford: Oxford University Press, 2000), p. 71.

71 W. Cobbett, *Rural Rides* (London, 1853), p. 585.

72 Essex Record Office D/P 126/3/2.

73 S. Lambert (ed.), *House of Commons Sessional Papers of the Eighteenth Century: George III; Reports of the Commissioners of Land Revenue, 8–11, 1792* (Delaware: Scholarly Resources, 1977), pp. 708, 724, 748.

74 Ibid., p. 749.

75 Ibid., p. 776.

76 T. Ruggles, 'Picturesque farming', *Annals of Agriculture* 6 (1786), 175–84. W. Marshall, *Planting and Rural Ornament* (London, 1796), pp. 100–1.

77 A. F. J. Brown, *Prosperity and Poverty: rural Essex, 1700-1815* (Chelmsford: Essex Record Office, 1996), p. 34.

78 Shrubb, *Birds, Scythes and Combines*, pp. 51–9.

79 C. Stoate, 'The changing face of lowland farming and wildlife part 1: 1845–1945', *British Wildlife* 6 (1995), 341–50.

80 Shrubb, *Birds, Scythes and Combines*, pp. 167–9.

81 E. L. Jones, 'The bird pests of British agriculture in recent centuries', *Agricultural History Review* 20 (1972), 107–25.

82 Shrubb, *Birds, Scythes and Combines*, p. 51.

83 Ibid., pp. 51–2.

84 Ibid., p. 52.

85 Ibid., pp. 266–7.

86 Ibid., p. 93.

87 G. White, *The Natural History and Antiquities of Selbourne in the County of Southampton* (London, 1813), p. 113.

88 Jones, 'Bird pests', p. 121.

89 J. Sheail, *Rabbits and their History* (Newton Abbot: David and Charles, 1971), pp. 135–7.

90 M. E. Turner, *Volume 190: Home Office Acreage Returns HO67. List and Analysis*, 3 vols (London: List and Index Society, 1982), vol. 2, p. 53.

91 Turner, *Home Office Acreage Returns*, vol. 2, p. 151.

92 Ibid., p. 154.

93 P. M. Cannon and I. Reid, 'The influence of relic ridge-and-furrow on the soil water regime of an ancient meadow, Cumbria, England', *Global Ecology and Biogeography Letters* 3 (1993), 18–26.

94 S. G. Upex, 'The uses and functions of ponds within early landscapes in the east Midlands', *Agricultural History Review* 52 (2004), 125–40.

95 R. A. Robinson, J. D. Wilson and H. P. Crick, 'The importance of arable habitats for farmland birds in grassland landscapes', *Journal of Applied Ecology* 38 (2001), 1059–69.

96 T. A. Coward and C. Oldham, *The Birds of Cheshire* (Manchester: Sherrat and Hughes, 1900), p. 4.

97 Phillips, 'Arable land drainage in the nineteenth century', pp. 70–92.

98 A. D. M. Phillips, *The Staffordshire Reports of Andrew Thompson to the Inclosure Commissioners, 1858-68: landlord investment in Staffordshire agriculture in the mid nineteenth century* (Stafford: Staffordshire Record Society, 1996), p. 116.

99 G. Barnes, 'Woodland in Norfolk: a landscape history'. Unpublished PhD, School of History, University of East Anglia, 2003.

100 J. Bailey Denton, 'The effects of under drainage on our rivers and arterial channels', *Journal of the Royal Agricultural Society of England* 24 (1863), 573–89.

101 Shrubb, *Birds, Scythes and Combines*, p. 225.

102 E. Salisbury, *Weeds and Aliens* (London: Collins, 1961), pp. 118–9.

103 M. George, *The Land Use, Ecology and Conservation of Broadland* (Chichester: Packard Publishing, 1992), pp. 105–12.

104 Turner, 'On the necessity of reducing the size and number of hedges'. Cambridge, 'On the advantages of reducing the size and number of hedges'. J. Grant, 'A few remarks on the large hedges and small enclosures of Devonshire and adjoining counties', *Journal of the Royal Agricultural Society of England* 5 (1845), 420–9.

105 C. W. Hoskyns, *Talpa, or the Chronicles of a Clayland Farm* (London, 1865), pp. 46–8.

106 A. Jessop, *Arcady: for better, for worse* (London, 1887), p. 6.

107 N. Penford and I. Francis, 'Common land and nature conservation in England and Wales', *British Wildlife* 2 (1990), 65–76.

108 White's *Norfolk Directory* (1885), pp. 104–5.

Chapter 7

1 P. Langford, *A Polite and Commercial people: England 1727-1783* (Oxford: Oxford University Press, 1992), pp. 59–124. M. Girouard, *The English Town* (London: Yale University Press, 1989), pp. 186–9. H. J. Habbakuk, 'Economic functions of English landowners in the seventeenth and eighteenth centuries', *Explorations in Entrepreneurial History* 6 (1953), 92–102.

2 V. Knox, 'On the Pleasures of a Garden' (1779), quoted in J. Dixon Hunt and P. Willis (eds), *The Genius of the Place: the English landscape garden 1620-1820* (London: Paul Elek, 1975), p. 331. W. Cowper, *The Task: a poem in six books*, Book 1 (London, 1785), line 749.

3 W. Chambers, *A Dissertation on Oriental Gardening* (London, 1772), p. v.

4 C. Watkins and B. Cowell, *Uvedale Price (1747-1829): decoding the picturesque* (Woodbridge: Boydell, 2012). R. P. Knight, *The Landscape: a didactic poem* (London, 1794). U. Price, *An Essay on the Picturesque* (London, 1794). W. Gilpin, *Three Essays on Picturesque Beauty, on Picturesque Travel, and on Sketching Landscape* (London, 1792).

5 J. Phibbs, 'The picturesque moment', *Architectural Association Newsletter* 3 (1992), 3–4. T. Williamson, *Polite Landscapes: gardens and society in eighteenth-century England* (Stroud: Sutton, 1995), pp. 149–51.

6 Price, *Essay on the Picturesque*, vol. 1, p. 24.

7 M. Reed, 'The transformation of urban space 1700–1840', in P. Clarke (ed.), *The Cambridge Urban History of Britain*, vol. 2 (Cambridge: Cambridge University Press, 2000), pp. 615–40.

8 O. L. Gilbert, *The Ecology of Urban Habitats* (London: Chapman and Hall, 1989), p. 247.

9 S. Spooner, '"A prospect two field's distance": rural landscapes and urban mentalities in the eighteenth century', *Landscapes* 10 (2009), 101–22. Girouard, *English Town*. C. Miele, 'From aristocratic ideal to middle-class idyll: 1690–1840', in A. Saint (ed.), *London Suburbs* (London, 1990), pp. 31–56.

10 D. Defoe, *A Tour through the Whole Island of Great Britain*, vol. 1 (London, 1724), p. 3.

11 A. Young, *General View of the Agriculture of Hertfordshire* (London, 1804), p. 18.

12 H. Clemenson, *English Country Houses and Landed Estates* (London: Croom Helm, 1982). C. Rawding, 'Society and place in nineteenth-century north Lincolnshire', *Rural History: economy, society, culture* 3, 1 (1992), 59–85.

13 Clemenson, *English County Houses*, pp. 7–9.

14 T. Williamson, 'Archaeological perspectives on landed estates: research agendas', in J. Finch and K. Giles (eds), *Estate Landscapes: design, improvement and power in the post-medieval landscape* (Woodbridge: Boydell, 2007), pp. 1–18.

15 Norfolk Record Office MC3/592.

16 Norfolk Record Office NRS 14625.

17 Clemenson, *English County Houses*, pp. 15–18.

18 J. V. Beckett, *The Aristocracy in England 1660-1914* (Oxford: Basil Blackwell, 1986).

19 J. Finch, 'Pallas, Flora and Ceres: landscape priorities and improvement on the Castle Howard estate, 1699–1880', in J. Finch and K. Giles (eds), *Estate Landscapes: design, improvement and power in the post-medieval landscape* (Woodbridge: Boydell, 2007), pp. 19–38.

20 B. Short, 'The evolution of contrasting communities within rural England', in B. Short (ed.), *The English Rural Community: image and analysis* (Cambridge: Cambridge University Press, 1992), pp. 19–43. J. Thirsk, *England's Agricultural Regions and Agrarian History 1500-1700* (London: Macmillan, 1987). J. Thirsk, 'English rural communities: structures, regularities, and change in the sixteenth and seventeenth centuries', in B. Short (ed.), *The English Rural Community: image and analysis* (Cambridge: Cambridge University Press, 1992), pp. 44–61.

21 Thirsk, *England's Agricultural Regions*. Short, 'Evolution of contrasting communities'.

22 P. J. W. Langley and D. W. Yalden, 'The decline of the rarer carnivores in Great Britain during the nineteenth century', *Mammal* Review 7, 3&4 (1977), 95–116.

23 A. MacNair and T. Williamson, *William Faden and Norfolk's Eighteenth-Century Landscape* (Oxford: Windgather, 2010), pp. 119–25.

24 H. Prince, 'The changing rural landscape', in G. Mingay (ed.), *The Cambridge Agrarian History of England and Wales*, vol. 6 (Cambridge: Cambridge University Press, 1987), pp. 7–83.

25 S. Daniels, 'The political iconography of woodland in later eighteenth-century England', in D. Cosgrove and S. Daniels (eds), *The Iconography of Landscape* (Cambridge: Cambridge University Press, 1988).

26 S. Switzer, *Ichnographica Rustica* (London, 1718), p. 336.

27 P. Miller, *The Gardener's Dictionary* (London, 1731); J. Wheeler, *The Modern Druid* (London, 1747); E. Wade, *A Proposal for Improving and Adorning the Island of Great Britain; for the maintenance of our navy and shipping* (London, 1755); W. Hanbury, *An Essay on Planting* (London, 1758).

28 P. B. Munsche, *Gentlemen and Poachers: the English game laws 1671-1831* (Cambridge: Cambridge University Press, 1981), pp. 8–27.

29 N. Kent, *General View of the Agriculture of the County of Norfolk* (London, 1796), p. 87.

30 T. Williamson, *The Archaeology of the Landscape Park* (Oxford: British Archaeological Reports, British Series, vol. 268, 1988), pp. 184–5.

31 W. Wordsworth, *Guide to the Lakes of Westmoreland and Cumberland* (London, 1810), p. 83.

32 Yalden, *History of British Mammals*, p. 172.

33 Lovegrove, *Silent Fields*, pp. 95–6.

34 Yalden, *History of British Mammals*, p. 172.

35 E. J. T. Collins, 'The coppice and underwood trades', in G. E. Mingay (ed.), *The Agrarian History of England and Wales Vol. 6, 1750–1850* (Cambridge: Cambridge University Press, 1989), pp. 484–501.

36 G. Barnes, 'Woodlands in Norfolk: a landscape history'. Unpublished PhD thesis, University of East Anglia, Norwich 2003, pp. 214–5, 226–8, 294–307.

37 The National Archive IR 18/5861. Tithe file, Congham, Norfolk.

38 The National Archive IR 18/5937. Tithe file, Fulmodeston, Norfolk.

39 W. Howitt, *The Rural Life in England* (London, 1844), p. 83.

40 P. B. Munsche, *Gentlemen and Poachers: the English Game Laws, 1671-1831* (Cambridge: Cambridge University Press, 1981).

41 M. Hastings, *English Sporting Guns and Accessories* (London: Ward Lock, 1969). C. Chevenix Trench, *A History of Marksmanship* (London: Longman, 1972).

42 C. B. Andrews (ed.), *The Torrington Diaries* (London: Eyre and Spottiswoode, 1934), vol. 1, p. 395.

43 H. Hopkins, *The Long Affray* (London: Secker and Warburg, 1985), p. 68.

44 P. Delabere Blaine, *An Encyclopaedia of Rural Sports: or a complete account of . . . Hunting, Shooting, Racing &c* (London, 1838), p. 854. D. Hill and P. Robertson, *The Pheasant: ecology, management and conservation* (Oxford: BSP Professional, 1988), pp. 38–45.

45 A. Forsyth, 'Game preservation and fences', *Journal of the Horticultural Society* 1 (1946), 201.

46 A. Done and R. Muir, 'The landscape history of grouse shooting in the Yorkshire Dales', *Rural History* 12, 2 (2001), 195–210.

47 B. P. Martin, *The Glorious Grouse: a natural and unnatural history* (Newton Abbot: David and Charles, 1990), p. 25. Done and Muir, 'Landscape history of grouse shooting', p. 203.

48 I. G. Simmons, *The Moorlands of England and Wales: an environmental history 8000–2000* (Edinburgh: Edinburgh University Press, 2003), pp. 139–40.

49 A. Raistrick, *The Face of North West Yorkshire* (Lancaster: Dalesman, 1949), p. 75.

50 Simmons, *Moorlands*, p. 39.

51 Munsche, *Gentlemen and Poachers*, pp. 76–105.

52 C. Bruyn-Andrews, *The Torrington Diaries*, vol. 3 (London: Eyre and Spottiswoode, 1936), p. 85.

53 B. Vesey-Fitzgerald, *British Game* (London: Collins, 1953), pp. 199–205.

54 Lovegrove, *Silent Spring*, pp. 43–6, 125–6; 129–30, 133–4, 137–40, 147, 149, 160–1167.

55 S. Tapper, *Game Heritage: an ecological review, from shooting and gamekeeping records* (Fordingbridge: Game Conservancy, 1992).

56 F. Norgate, 'Notes on the nesting habits of certain birds', *Transactions of the Norfolk and Norwich Naturalists' Society* 2 (1876), 195–206.

57 Lovegrove, *Silent Spring*, pp. 118–27.

58 A. G. More, 'On the distribution of birds in Great Britain during the nesting season', *Ibis* 1 (1865).

59 Lovegrove, *Silent Spring*, pp. 234–40.

60 Langley and Yalden, 'Decline of the rarer carnivores', pp. 108–12.

61 Ibid., pp. 105–8.

62 Ibid., pp. 98–104.

63 D. E. Allen, *The Naturalist in Britain: a social history* (London: Allen Lane, 1976), p. 143.

64 R. Carr, *English Fox Hunting: a history* (London: Weidenfeld and Nicolson, 1976), p. 68.

65 Ibid., p. 69. J. Patten, 'Fox coverts for the squirearchy', *Country Life* 23 (September 1971), 726–40.

66 E. D. Cumming (ed.), *R. S. Surtees, Town and Country Papers* (London, 1929), p. 90.

67 C. A. Markham, 'Early foxhounds', in R. Serjeantson (ed.), *Victoria County History of Northamptonshire*, vol. 2 (London: Constable, 1906), pp. 355–73.

68 J. Bevan, 'Agricultural change and the development of foxhunting in the eighteenth century', *Agricultural History Review* 58 (2010), 49–25. J. Finch, '"Grass, grass, grass": fox-hunting and the creation of the modern landscape', *Landscapes* 5, 2, 41–52.

69 Bevan, 'Agricultural change and the development of foxhunting', pp. 61, 72.

70 Ibid., pp. 73–4.

71 Carr, *English Fox Hunting*, pp. 113–4.

72 Yalden, *History of British Mammals*, p. 174.

73 P. Willis, *Charles Bridgeman and the English Landscape garden*, revised edn (London: Elysium, 2002).

74 J. Dixon Hunt, *William Kent: landscape gardener. An assessment and catalogue of his designs* (London: Zwemmer, 1987).

75 D. Stroud, *Capability Brown* (London: Country Life, 1965). R. Turner, *Capability Brown and the Eighteenth-Century English Landscape* (London: Weidenfeld and Nicolson, 1985). D. Jacques, *Georgian Gardens: the reign of Nature* (London: Thames and Hudson, 1983). T. Williamson, *Polite Landscapes: gardens and society in eighteenth-century England* (Stroud: Sutton, 1995). T. Williamson, *The Archaeology of the Landscape Park: garden design in Norfolk, England, 1680–1840* (Oxford: British Archaeological Reports, British Series, vol. 268, 1998).

76 J. C. Loudon, *The Suburban Gardener and Villa Companion* (London, 1838), p. 162. K. Thomas, *Man and the Natural World* (London: Allen Lane, 1983), pp. 260–9.

77   T. Williamson, *Polite Landscapes*, pp. 100–9.

78   Langford, *Polite and Commercial People*, p. 440; Richard Muir, *The Lost Villages of Britain* (London: Michael Joseph, 1982), pp. 202–21. J. Broad, 'Understanding village desertions in the seventeenth and eighteenth centuries', in C. Dyer and R. Jones (eds), *Deserted Villages Revisited* (Hatfield: University of Hertfordshire Press, 2010), pp. 121–39. T. Williamson, 'At pleasure's lordly call: the archaeology of emparked settlements', in C. Dyer and R. Jones (eds), *Deserted Villages Revisited* (Hatfield: University of Hertfordshire Press, 2010), pp. 162–81.

79   Williamson, *Polite Landscapes*, pp. 100–18.

80   T. Williamson, 'Fish, fur and feather: man and nature in the post-medieval landscape', in K. Barker and T. Darvill (eds), *Making English Landscapes* (Bournemouth: Bournemouth University School of Conservation Sciences Occasional Paper, 1997), pp. 92–117.

81   Chatsworth House archives, Derbyshire AS/1061.

82   Chatsworth House archives, Derbyshire, AS/1062 and 1063.

83   Estimates based on Drury and Andrews *Map of the County of Hertfordshire* (London, 1766) and the First Edition Ordnance Survey 6"maps.

84   J. Barnatt and T. Williamson, *Chatsworth: a landscape history* (Macclesfield: Windgather Press, 2005), pp. 50–73, 95–100.

85   O. L. Gilbert, 'The ancient lawns of Chatsworth, Derbyshire', *Journal of the Royal Horticultural Society* 108 (1983), 471–4.

86   O. Rackham, 'Pre-existing trees and woods in country-house parks', *Landscapes* 5, 2 (2004), 1–15; Williamson, *Polite Landscapes*, pp. 94–6.

87   J. Grigor, *The Eastern Arboretum, or a Register of Remarkable Trees, Seats, Gardens &c in the County of Norfolk* (London, 1841), p. 158.

88   Hertfordshire Archives and Local Studies, Hertford: DE/P/P15.

89   Hertfordshire Archives and Local Studies, Hertford: 9M73/958.

90   G. Barnes and T. Williamson, *Ancient Trees in the Landscape: Norfolk's arboreal heritage* (Oxford, 2011), pp. 136–7.

91   B. Elliott, *Victorian Gardens* (London: Batsford, 1986).

92   M. Campbell-Culver, *The Origins of Plants* (London: Headline Books, 2001).

93   Campbell-Culver, *The Origins of Plants*, p. 149.

94   J. Harvey, *Early Nurserymen* (Chichester: Phillimore, 1975).

95   I. G. Simmons, *An Environmental History of Great Britain, from 10,000 years ago to the present* (Edinburgh: Edinburgh University Press, 2001), p. 142. Campbell-Culver, *The Origins of Plants*, pp. 148–81.

96   Campbell-Culver, *The Origins of Plants*.

97   East Suffolk Record Office, Ipswich: Shrubland Hall archives, currently uncatalogued: notes for improving the park, c.1808, by William Wood. See also T. Williamson, 'Shrubland before Barry: a house and its landscape 1660–1880', in Christopher Harper-Bill, Carole Rawcliffe and Richard Wilson (eds), *East Anglia's History: studies in honour of Norman Scarfe* (Woodbridge: Boydell, 2002), pp. 189–212.

98 A. Mitchell, *Trees of Britain and Northern Europe* (Second edn, London, 1974), p. 235. K. Alexander, J. Butler and T. Green, 'The value of different tree and shrub species to wildlife', *British Wildlife* 17 (2006), 19–28.

99 Mitchell, *Trees*, p. 257.

100 J. R. Cross, 'Biological flora of the British Isles: *Rhododendron ponticum* L', *Journal of Biology* 63 (1975), 345–64.

101 J. Amphlett and C. Rea, *The Botany of Worcestershire* (Birmingham: Cornish Brothers, 1909), p. 154.

102 A. Hussner, 'NOBANIS – Invasive Alien Species Fact Sheet – *Azolla filiculoides*'. *Online Database of the North European and Baltic Network on Invasive Alien Species* (2006). Heinrich Heine University, Düsseldorf. http://www.nobanis.org/files/factsheets/Azolla_filiculoides.pdf. Retrieved 19 November 2012.

103 Allen, *The Naturalist in Britain*, pp. 26–51.

104 Ibid., pp. 45–51.

105 B. Stillingfleet, *Tracts Relating to Natural History, Husbandry and Physick* (London, 1759).

106 G. White, *The Natural History and Antiquities of Selbourne* (London, 1813).

107 Allen, *Naturalist in Britain*, pp. 73–83. P. Marren, 'Darwin's war-horse: beetle-collecting in nineteenth-century England', *British Wildlife* 19 (2008), 153–9.

108 Allen, *Naturalist in Britain*, pp. 158–78.

109 A. Secord, 'Science in the Pub: artisan botanists in early nineteenth-century Lancashire', *History of Science* 32 (1994), 269–315. J. Percy, 'Scientists in humble life: the artisan naturalists of south Lancashire', *Manchester Region History Review* 5 (1991), 3–10. J. Cash, *Where There's a Will There's a Way: an account of the labours of naturalists in humble life* (London, 1873).

110 Ibid., p. 279.

111 Ibid., p. 272.

112 Percy, 'Scientists in humble life'.

113 Secord, 'Science in the pub', p. 282. E. P. Thompson, *The Making of the English Working Class* (London: Gollancz, 1980), 322.

114 Allen, *Naturalist in Britain*, pp. 111–16.

115 Ibid, pp. 158–75.

116 Ibid., p. 170.

117 Rev C. A. Johns, *Flowers of the Field* (London, 1851). Rev C. A. Johns, *British Birds in their Haunts* (London, 1862). F. O. Morris, *A History of British Birds* (London, 1863). Rev J. G. Wood, *The Common Objects of the Country* (London, 1858). J. F. M. Clarke, *Bugs and the Victorians* (New Haven: Yale University Press, 2009), p. 9.

118 D. E. Allen, *The Victorian Fern Craze: a history of Pteridomania* (London: Hutchinson, 1969).

119 Allen, *Fern Craze*.

120 A. Byfield, 'Victorian pteridomania – Britain's fern craze', *British Wildlife* 17 (2006), 411–19.

121 D. A. Ratcliffe, 'Post-medieval and recent change in British vegetation: the culmination of human influence', *New Phytologist* 98 (1984), 73–100.

122 Secord, 'Science in the Pub', p. 288.

123 M. Shrubb, *Birds, Scythes and Combines: a history of birds and agricultural changes* (Cambridge: Cambridge University Press, 2003), pp. 319–20. B. Mearns and R. Mearns, *The Bird Collectors* (London: Academic Press, 1998).

124 R. Morris, *Chester in the Plantagenet and Tudor Reigns* (Chester, 1893), pp. 333–4. R. Latham and W. Matthews (eds), *The Diary of Samuel Pepys*, vol. 7 (London: G.Bell and Son, 1970), p. 246.

125 W. H. Hudson, *Birds of London* (London, 1898), p. 31.

Chapter 8

1 R. Perren, *Agriculture in Depression 1870-1940* (Cambridge: Cambridge University Press, 1995). P. J. Perry, *British Farming in the Great Depression: an historical geography* (Newton Abbot: David and Charles, 1974).

2 H. Williamson, *The Story of a Norfolk Farm* (London: Faber, 1940), p. 206.

3 Norfolk Record Office MC3.

4 F. M. L. Thompson, *English Landed Society in the Nineteenth Century* (London: Routledge and Kegan Paul, 1963), pp. 325, 330.

5 H. Clemenson, *English Country Houses and Landed Estates* (London: Croom Helm, 1982).

6 J. Sheail, *An Environmental History of Twentieth-Century Britain* (London: Palgrave, 2002), p. 110.

7 M. Shrubb, *Birds, Scythes and Combines: a history of birds and agricultural change* (Cambridge: Cambridge University Press, 2003), p. 120; O. Rackham, *The History of the Countryside* (London: Dent, 1986), p. 223.

8 Rackham, *History of the Countryside*, p. 223.

9 B. R. Mitchell and P. Deane, *Abstract of British Historical Statistics* (Cambridge: Cambridge University Press, 1971), pp. 8–10.

10 N. Cossons, *The BP Book of Industrial Archaeology* (Newton Abbot: David and Charles, 1987), p. 278.

11 A. J. P. Taylor, *English History 1914-1945* (Oxford: Clarendon Press, 1965), p. 302.

12 K. Hudson, *The Archaeology of the Consumer Society* (London: Heinemann, 1981).

13 A. Bell, 'The family farm', in H. J. Massingham (ed.), *England and the Farmer* (London: Batsford, 1941). Williamson, *Story of a Norfolk Farm*. R. J. Moore-Collyer, 'Aspects of the urban-rural divide in inter-War Britain', *Rural History* 10 (1999), 103–24. R. J. Moore-Collyer, 'Back to basics: Rolf Gardiner, H. J.Massingham and "A kinship in husbandry"', *Rural History* 12 (2002),

85–108. S. Wade Martins and T. Williamson, *The Countryside of East Anglia: changing landscapes, 1870-1950* (Woodbridge: Boydell, 2008), pp. 51–2.

14   L. Dudley Stamp, *The Land of Britain: its use and misuse* (London: Geographical Publications, 1950), p. 481.

15   Q. Bone, 'Legislation to revive small farming in England, 1887–1914', *Agricultural History Review* 49 (1975), 653–61. C. W. Rowell, 'County council smallholdings 1908–58', *Agriculture* 50 (1959), 109–14. Wade Martins and Williamson, *Countryside of East Anglia*, pp. 58–60.

16   Shrubb, *Birds, Scythes and Combines*, p. 227.

17   R. A. Robinson, J. D. Wilson and H. P. Crick, 'The importance of arable habitats for farmland birds in grassland landscapes', *Journal of Applied Ecology* 38 (2001), 1059–69.

18   T. A. Coward and C. Oldham, *The Birds of Cheshire* (Manchester: Sherrat and Hughes, 1900), p. 6.

19   J. Tennyson, *Suffolk Scene: a book of description and adventure* (London, 1939), p. 41.

20   R. W. Butcher, *The Land of Britain: Suffolk* (London: Geographical Publications, 1941), p. 357.

21   J. E. G. Mosby, *The Land of Britain: Norfolk* (London: Geographical Publications, 1938), pp. 203–4.

22   Wade Martins and Williamson, *Countryside of East Anglia*, pp. 124–6.

23   H. R. Haggard, *Rural England,* 2 vols (London: Longman, Green and Co., 1902), vol. 2, p. 506.

24   L. R. Haggard and H. Williamson, *Norfolk Life* (London, 1943), p. 97.

25   I. Simmons, *An Environmental History of Great Britain from 10,000 Years Ago to the Present* (Edinburgh: Edinburgh University Press, 2001), p. 181.

26   *Eastern Daily Press*, 24 June 1905, 8.

27   Mosby, *Norfolk*, p. 181.

28   Dudley Stamp, *The Land of Britain*, p. 481.

29   Ibid.

30   Ibid., p. 156.

31   Forestry Commission Archives, Santon Downham, uncatalogued.

32   W. G. Clarke, 'The natural history of Norfolk commons', *Transactions of the Norfolk and Norwich Naturalists Society* 10 (1918), 294–318.

33   M. C. H. Bird, 'The rural economy, sport, and natural history of East Ruston Common', *Transactions of the Norfolk and Norwich Naturalists Society* 8, 5 (1909), 631–70.

34   S. Birtles, '"A Green Space beyond Self Interest": the evolution of common land in Norfolk'. Unpublished PhD thesis, University of East Anglia, 2003, p. 205.

35   Bird, 'East Ruston Common', p. 638.

36   W. G. Clarke, 'Some Breckland characteristics', *Transactions of the Norfolk and Norwich Naturalists' Society* 8 (1908), 555–78.

37 Bird, 'East Ruston Common', p. 645.

38 P. Dolman and W. Sutherland, 'The ecological changes of Breckland grass heaths and the consequences of management', *Journal of Applied Ecology* 29 (1992), pp. 402–13.

39 M. Home, *Autumn Fields* (London: Methuen, 1944), p. 15.

40 Clarke, 'Natural history of Norfolk commons', p. 308.

41 Shrubb, *Birds, Scythes and Combines*, p. 225.

42 Ibid.

43 E. L. Turner, 'The status of birds in Broadland', *Transactions of the Norfolk and Norwich Naturalists' Society* 11 (1922), 228–40.

44 E. T. Boardman, 'The development of a Broadland estate at How Hill Ludham, Norfolk', *Transactions of the Norfolk and Norwich Naturalists' Society* 15 (1939), 14.

45 B. B. Riviere, *A History of the Birds of Norfolk* (London, 1930). Shrubb, *Birds, Scythes and Combines*, pp. 147–8.

46 Stamp, *Land of Britain*, p. 85.

47 Ibid.

48 East Suffolk Record Office HA 61:436/1260.

49 E. Bujak, *England's Rural Realms: landownership and the agricultural revolution* (London: Tauris Academic, 2007). Wade Martins and Williamson, *Countryside of East Anglia*, pp. 73–80.

50 J. Brown, *Gardens of a Golden Afternoon* (London: Allen Lane, 1982). Wade Martins and Williamson, *Countryside of East Anglia*, pp. 87–91.

51 West Suffolk Record Office HD 934.

52 Simmons, *Environmental History of Britain*, p. 158.

53 I. G. Simmons, *The Moorlands of England and Wales: an environmental history 8,000 BC – AD 2000* (Edinburgh: Edinburgh University Press, 2003), pp. 139–40.

54 S. Tapper, *Game Heritage* (Fordingbridge: Game Conservancy, 1992).

55 Haggard and Williamson, *Norfolk Life*, p. 128.

56 D. J. Jefferies, 'The changing otter population of Britain 1700–1989', *Biological Journal of the Linnaean Society* 38 (1989), 61–89.

57 Hertfordshire Gardens Trust and T. Williamson, *The Parks and Gardens of West Hertfordshire* (Letchworth: Hertfordshire Gardens Trust, 2000), pp. 97–8.

58 P. and M. Morris, 'A long-term study of the edible dormouse in Britain', *British Wildlife* 22 (2010), 153–61. D. W. Yalden, *The History of British Mammals* (London, 1999), pp. 194–5.

59 M. Shorten, *Squirrels* (London, 1954), p. 79.

60 Ibid.

61 A. D. Middleton, *The Grey Squirrel* (London: Sidgwick & Jackson, 1931).

62 Shorten, *Squirrels*, p. 87.

63   K. Laider, *Squirrels in Britain* (Newton Abbot: David and Charles, 1980),
     p. 48.

64   R. E. Kenward, K. Hodder, R. Rose, C. Walls, T. Parish, J. Holm, P.
     Morris, S. Walls and F. Doyle, 'Comparative demography of red squirrels
     (Sciurus vulgaris) and grey squirrels *(Sciurus carolinensis)* in deciduous
     and conifer woodland', *Journal of Zoology* 244 (1998), 7–21. J. M. Bryce
     et al., 'Competition between Eurasian Red and Introduced Eastern Grey
     Squirrels: the energetic significance of body-mass differences', *Proceedings
     of the Biological Sciences* 268, 1477 (2001), 1731–36. L. A. Wauters et al.,
     'Interspecific competition in tree squirrels: do introduced grey squirrels
     (Sciurus carolinensis) deplete tree seeds hoarded by red squirrels (*S. vulgaris*)?',
     Behavioural Ecology and Sociobiology 51 (2002), 360–7.

65   Shorten, *Squirrels*, p. 178.

66   P. R. Ratcliffe, 'Distribution and current status of Sika deer, *Cervus nippon*, in
     Great Britain', *Mammal Review* 17 (1987), 39–58.

67   A. Cooke and L. Farrell, *Chinese Water Deer* (Fordingbridge: British Deer
     Society, 1987).

68   I. D. Rotherham and R. A. Lambert, 'Good science, good history and
     pragmatism: managing the way ahead', in I. D. Rotherham and R. A. Lambert
     (eds), *Invasive and Introduced Plants and Animals: human perceptions,
     attitudes and approaches to management* (London: Earthscan, 2011),
     pp. 355–66.

69   N. Chapman, S. Harris. and A. Stanford, '"Reeves" muntjac *Muntiacus reevesi* in
     Britain: their history, spread, habitat selection and the role of human intervention
     in accelerating their dispersal', *Mammal Review* 24 (1994), 113–60.

70   A. S. Cooke and K. H. Lakhani, 'Damage to coppice regrowth by muntjac
     deer *Muntiacus reevesi* and protection with electric fencing', *Biological
     Conservation* 75 (1996), 231–8.

71   P. Dolman and W. Waeber, 'Ecosystem and competition impacts of introduced
     deer', *Wildlife Research* 35, 3 (2008), 202–14.

72   Stamp, *Land of Britain*, pp. 108–24.

73   P. E. T. Cavill-Worsley, 'A fur farm in Norfolk', *Transactions of the Norfolk
     and Norwich Naturalists Society* 13 (1931), 104–15.

74   J. M. Lambert, 'The chief Norfolk habitats', in British Association for
     the Advancement of Science, *Norwich and its Region* (Norwich 1961),
     pp. 51–8.

75   E. A. Ellis, 'Some effects of selective feeding by the coypu (*Myocasto coypus*)
     on the vegetation of Broadland', *Transactions of the Norfolk and Norwich
     Naturalists' Society* 20 (1963), 32–5.

76   Yalden, *History of British Mammals*, pp. 190–2. J. Birks, 'Feral mink and
     nature conservation', *British Wildlife* 1 (1989), 313–23.

77   Gosling and Baker, 'The eradication of muskrats and coypus from Britain',
     Biological Journal 38, 1 (1989), 39–51.

78   Stamp, *Land of Britain*, p. 173.

79 G. Ryle, *Forest Service: the first forty-five years of the Forestry Commission in Great Britain* (Newton Abbot: David and Charles, 1969), pp. 25–39.

80 Ryle, *Forest Service*, pp. 25–39.

81 Ibid., pp. 298–9.

82 J. Sheail, *An Environmental History of Twentieth-Century Britain* (London: Palgrave, 2002), pp. 84–90.

83 Ryle, *Forest Service*.

84 Forestry Commission Archive, Santon Downham, Suffolk: *Thetford Forest, Working Plan*, 1960, Chapter 10; Forestry Commission, *Annual Reports* 1927–40.

85 O. Rackham, *Woodlands* (London: Collins, 2006), p. 56.

86 A. Crosby and A. Winchester, 'A sort of national property?', in A.Winchester (ed.), *England's Landscape: the North West*, pp. 236–7; I. G. Simmons, *The Moorlands of England and Wales* (Edinburgh: Edinburgh University Press, 2003), pp. 156–7.

87 Tennyson, *Suffolk Scene*, p. 76.

88 W. A. Cadman, 'Bird life at Thetford', *Journal of the Forestry Commission* 6 (1936), 24–6.

89 D. A. Ratcliffe, 'Upland birds and their conservation', *British Wildlife* 2 (1990), 1–12. Shrubb, *Birds, Scythes and Combines*, p. 30.

90 S. P. Carter, 'Habitat change and bird populations', *British Wildlife* 1 (1990), 324–34.

91 A. Byfield, 'Heathland, plantations and the Forestry Commission: a botanical perspective', *British Wildlfe* 20 (2009), 267–72.

92 C. Hitch and P. Lambley, 'The lichens of Breckland and the effects of afforestation', in P. Ratcliffe and J. Claridge (eds), *Thetford Forest Park: the ecology of a pine* forest (Edinburgh: Forestry Commission, 1996), pp. 58–66.

93 Y-C. Lin, R. James and P. Dolman, 'Conservation of heathland ground beetles (Coleoptra, Carabidae): the value of lowland coniferous plantations', *Biology and Conservation* 16, 5 (2007), 1337–58.

94 R. C. Welch and P. Hammond, 'Breckland coleoptera', in P. Ratcliffe and J. Claridge (eds), *Thetford Forest Park: the ecology of a pine* forest (Edinburgh: Forestry Commission, 1996), pp. 92–102.

95 J. Tsouvalis, *A Critical Geography of Britain's State Forests* (Oxford: Oxford University Press, 2000), pp. 179–99.

96 Carter, 'Habitat change and bird populations'. G. W. Temperley and E. Blezard, 'The status of the green woodpecker in northern England', *British Birds* 44 (1951), 24–6.

97 Simms, *Environmental History*, pp. 252–3. Rackham, *History of the Countryside*, pp. 49–50. Rackham, *Woodlands*, pp. 537–42, N. Chapman and R. Whitta, 'The history of the deer of Thetford Forest', in P. Ratcliffe and J. Claridge (eds), *Thetford Forest Park: the ecology of a pine forest* (Alice Holt, 1996), pp. 141–9.

98 P. Dolman, R. Fuller, R. Gill, D. Hooton and R. Tabor, 'Escalating ecological impact of deer in lowland woodland', *British Wildlife* 21 (2010), 242–54.

99 J. E. Harting, *Birds of Middlesex* (London, 1866); Alexander Clark Kennedy, *Birds of Berkshire and Buckinghamshire* (London, 1868).

100 D. E. Allen, *The Naturalist in Britain* (London: Allen Lane, 1976), pp. 187–243.

101 J. Beckett and C. Watkins, 'Natural history and local history in late Victorian and Edwardian England: the contribution of the Victoria County History', *Rural History* 22 (2011), 59–88.

102 W. H. Hudson, *Nature in Downland* (London, 1900). W. H. Hudson, *A Shepherd's Life: impressions of the South Wiltshire Downs* (London, 1910).

103 Allen, *Naturalist in Britain*, p. 231.

104 J. McCormick, *Reclaiming Paradise: the global environmental movement* (London: John Wiley, 1992), p. 4.

105 J. R. V. Marchant and W. Watkins, *Wild Birds Protection Acts 1880-1896* (London, 1897).

106 Ibid., p. 43.

107 D. A. Stroud, 'The status and legislative protection of birds of prey and their habitats in Europe', in D. B. A. Thompson (ed.), *Birds of Prey in a Changing Environment* (Edinburgh, 2003), pp. 51–83.

108 D. Evans, *A History of Nature Conservation in Britain* (London: Routledge, 1992), pp. 34–5; 47–8.

109 McCormick, *Reclaiming Paradise*, pp. 1–24.

110 B. Cowell, 'The commons preservation society and the campaign for Berkhamsted common, 1866–70', *Rural History* 13, 2 (2002), 145–62.

111 M. Waterson, *The National Trust: the first hundred years* (London, 1994). G. Murphy, *Founders of the National Trust* (London: Christopher Helm, 1987).

112 Evans, *History of Nature Conservation in Britain*, pp. 46–7;

113 Ibid., p. 45.

114 C. E. Gay, 'The Norfolk Naturalists Trust', *Transactions of the Norfolk and Norwich Naturalists' Society* 16 (1944), 3–13.

115 Evans, *History of Nature Conservation*, pp. 52–3.

116 Ibid., p. 4.

117 Lord Justice Scott, *Report on the Committee on Land Utilisation in Rural Areas*, Command Paper 6378 (London: HMSO, 1942), p. 25. See also J. Sheial, 'The impact of recreation on the coast: the Lindsey County Council (Sandhills) Act, 1932', *Landscape Planning* 4 (1977), 53–72. J. Sheail, *An Environmental History of Twentieth-Century Britain* (London: Palgrave, 2002), pp. 36–41.

118 Ibid., p. 131.

119 C. Williams-Ellis, *England and the Octopus* (London: G.Bles, 1928).

120 D. Matless, *Landscape and Englishness* (London: Reaktion, 1998).

121 Sheail, *Environmental History*, p. 106.

122 Ibid., p. 117.

123 E. C. Keith, 'The policy of the society', *Transactions of the Norfolk and Norwich Naturalists Society* 15 (1942), 311–18.

124 C. D. Preston, 'Engulfed by suburbia or destroyed by the plough: the ecology of extinction in Middlesex and Cambridgeshire', *Watsonia* 23 (2000), 59–81.

Chapter 9

1 T. A. Coward and C. Oldham, *The Birds of Cheshire* (Manchester: Sherrat and Hughes, 1900), p. 1.

2 Department of Environment, *River Pollution Survey 1970* (London, 1972).

3 J. R. Laundon, *Lichens* (Princes Risborough: Shire, 1984), p. 19.

4 S. Mosley, *The Chimney of the World: a history of smoke pollution in Victorian and Edwardian Manchester* (Cambridge: White Horse Press, 2001), p. 42.

5 Mrs Haweis, *Rus in urbe: or flowers that thrive in London gardens and smoky towns* (London, 1885).

6 R. S. R. Fitter, *London's Natural History* (London: Collins, 1945), pp. 181–2.

7 J. W. Tutt, 'Melanism and melanochroism in British Lepidoptera', *Entomologist's Record 1*: pp. 5–7, 49–56, 84–90, 121–5, 169–72, 228–34, 293–300, 317–25. E. B. Ford, *Ecological Genetics* (London, 1964). H. B. D. Kettlewell, 'Selection experiments on industrial melanism in the Lepidoptera', *Heredity* 9 (1955), 323–42. H. B. D. Kettlewell, 'Further selection experiments on industrial melanism in the Lepidoptera', *Heredity* 10 (1956), 287–301.

8 T. D. Sargent, C. D. Millar, D. M. Lambert, 'The "classical" explanation of industrial melanism. Assessing the evidence', *Evolutionary Biology* 30 (1998), 299–322. J. A. Coyne, 'Not black and white. Review of Majerus, Melanism: evolution in action', *Nature* 396 (1998), 35–6.

9 L. M. Cook, 'Changing views on melanic moths', *Biological Journal of the Linnean Society* 69 (2000), 431–41.

10 S. Cramp and J. Gooders, 'The return of the house martin', *London Bird Report* 31 (1967), pp. 93–8.

11 F. S. Mitchell, *Birds of Lancashire* (London, 1885), p. ix.

12 Ibid., pp. ix–x.

13 T. Rowley, *The English Landscape in the Twentieth Century* (London, 2006), pp. 195–216. A. Jackson, *Semi-Detached London: suburban development, life and transport, 1900-1939* (London: Allen and Unwin, 1973).

14 L. Dudley Stamp, *The Land of Britain: its use and misuse* (London: Geographical Publications, 1950), p. 196. This is an upper figure, arrived at by adding to the 4.6 per cent of land surface occupied by 'houses and gardens' the 3.3 per cent described as land 'agriculturally unproductive'.

15 C. D. Preston, 'Engulfed by suburbia or destroyed by the plough: the ecology of extinction in Middlesex and Cambridgeshire', *Watsonia* 23 (2000), p. 72.

16 M. Daunton (ed.), *The Cambridge Urban History of Britain, Volume 3, 1840-1950* (Cambridge: Cambridge University Press, 2000). Rowley, *English Landscape*, pp. 121–63.

17 N. Cossons, *The BP Book of Industrial Archaeology* (Newton Abbot: David and Charles, 1987), pp. 218–20.

18 O. L. Gilbert, *The Ecology of Urban Habitats* (London: Chapman and Hall, 1989), pp. 9–17.

19 K. J. Walker, 'The last thirty five years: recent changes in the flora of the British Isles', *Watsonia* 26 (2007), 291–302. D. Pearmain and K.Walker, 'Alien plants in Britain: a real or imagined problem?', *British Wildlife* 21 (2009), 22–7.

20 Ibid., p. 15.

21 W. H. Hudson, *Birds of London* (London, 1898), p. 193.

22 Fitter, *London's Natural History*, p. 116.

23 R. M. Hadden, 'Wild flowers of London W1', *London Naturalist* 57 (1978), 26–33.

24 Gilbert, *Ecology of Urban Environments*, p. 177.

25 Ibid., p. 112.

26 L. Parmenter, 'City bombed sites survey: the flies of the Cripplegate bombed site', *London Naturalist* 33 (1955), 89–100.

27 Gilbert, *Ecology of Urban Environments*, p. 3.

28 Hudson, *Birds of London*, p. 105.

29 Fitter, *London's Natural History*, p. 119. J. D. Summers-Smith, *The House Sparrow* (London, 1963).

30 Hudson, *Birds of London*, p. 294.

31 Dudley Stamp, *The Land of Britain*, p. 427.

32 O. L. Gilbert, *The Flowering of the Cities: the natural flora of urban commons* (Peterborough: English Nature, 1992).

33 Gilbert, *Flowering of the Cities*, p. 8.

34 Ibid., pp. 9–10.

35 Ibid., p. 12.

36 Ibid., pp. 21–5.

37 O. L. Gilbert, 'The ecology of an urban river', *British Wildlife* 3 (1992), 129–36.

38 B. N. K. Davis, 'The ground arthropods of London gardens', *London Naturalist* 58 (1978), 15–24.

39 A. E. Telling and R. Duxbury, *Planning Law and Procedure* (Oxford: Oxford University Press, 2005), p. 3. E. G. Bentley, *A Practical Guide in the Preparation of Town Planning Schemes* (London: George Phillip, 1911).

40 Telling and Duxbury, *Planning Law*, pp. 3–6.

41 H. Barrett and J. Phillips, *Suburban Style: the British home, 1840-1960* (London: Little, Brown and Co., 1987).

42 E. Howard, *Garden Cities of Tomorrow* (London: Sonnenschein, 1902), p. 112.

43 M. Miller, *English Garden Cities: An Introduction* (London: English Heritage, 2010), pp. 18–22.

44 Rowley, *English Landscape in the Twentieth Century*, pp. 203–5.

45 K. Hudson, *The Archaeology of the Consumer Society: the Second Industrial Revolution in Britain* (London: Heinemann, 1983).

46 A. Jackson, *Semi-Detached London: Suburban Development, Life and Transport 1900–1939* (London: Allen and Unwin, 1973); I. Bentley, I. Davis and P. Oliver, *Dunroamin: the suburban semi and its enemies* (London: Barrie and Jenkins, 1981); Barrett and J. Phillips, *Suburban Style*, pp. 125–35.

47 W. Pedley, *Labour on the Land* (London: King and Staples, 1941), pp. 91–3.

48 R. H. Best and J. T. Coppock, *The Changing Use of Land in Britain* (London: Faber, 1962).

49 Gilbert, *Ecology of Urban Habitats*, p. 247. R. M. Smith, K. Thompson and K. J. Gaston, 'Urban domestic gardens: composition and richness of the vascular plant flora, and implications for native biodiversity', *Biological Conservation* 129 (2006), 312–22.

50 R. Bisgrove, *The Gardens of Gertrude Jekyll* (London: Frances Lincoln, 1992). D. Ottewill, *The Edwardian Garden* (London: Yale University Press, 1989). W. Robinson, *The English Flower Garden* (London, 1883). G. Jekyll, *Wood and Garden* (London, 1899).

51 The Hertfordshire Gardens Trust and T. Williamson, *The Parks and Gardens of West Hertfordshire* (Letchworth: Hertfordshire Gardens Trust, 2000), pp. 91–5.

52 R. Mabey, *Weeds: the story of outlaw plants* (London: Profile Books, 2010), p. 169. I. D. Rotherham, 'History and perception in animal and plant invasions: the case of acclimatization and wild gardeners', in I. D. Rotherham and R. A. Lambert (eds), *Invasive and Introduced Plants and Animals: human perceptions, attitudes and approaches to management* (London: Earthscan, 2011), pp. 233–48.

53 Ibid., pp. 166–70.

54 Ibid.

55 R. Mabey, *Flora Britannica* (London: Concise edn, Chatto and Windus, 1998), pp. 170–1.

56 Barrett and Phillips, *Suburban Style*, pp. 184–8

57 F. H. Farthing, *Saturday in my Garden* (London, 1911), p. 21.

58 Ibid., p. 284.

59 A. G. L. Hellyer, *Practical Gardening for Amateurs* (London: Collingridge, 1935), p. 164.

60 E. Fitch Daglish, *The Book of Garden Animals* (London, 1928).

61 Harding, *Saturday in my Garden*, pp. 27–75. C. Baines, *How to Make a Wildlife Garden* (London: Frances Lincoln, 1985), pp. 112–32.

62 T. G. Tutsin, 'Weeds of a Leicester garden', *Watsonia* 9 (1973), 263–7.

63 Gilbert, *Ecology of Urban Environments*, pp. 247–8.

64   E. B. Bangerter and D. H. Kent, 'Veronica filiformis in the British Isles', Proceedings of the Botanical Society of the British Isles 2 (1957), 197–217.

65   Gilbert, Ecology of Urban Environments, pp. 251–2.

66   S. Risbeth, 'The flora of Cambridge walls', Journal of Ecology 36 (1948), 136–48. R. M. Payne, 'The flora of wall in south-eastern Essex', Watsonia 12 (1978), 41–6.

67   A. A. Allen, 'The coleopteran of a suburban garden', Entomologists' Record and Journal of Variation 63 (1951), 61–4, 187–90, 256–9; 64 (1952), 61–6, 92–3; 65 (1953), 225–31; 68 (1954), 215–22.

68   R. W. Robbins, 'Lepidoptera of a London garden fifty years ago', London Naturalist (1939), 40–1.

69   Fitch Daglish, Book of Garden Animals, pp. 8–54. Fitter, London's Natural History, pp. 134–5.

70   Ibid., p. 136.

71   M. Toms, 'Are gardens good for birds or birdwatchers', British Wildlife 19 (2007), 77–83.

72   Daglish, Garden Animals, p. 81.

73   Ibid., p. 195.

74   D. A. Ratcliffe, 'Post-medieval and recent change in British vegetation: the culmination of human influence', New Phytologist 98 (1984), 73–100.

75   J. Owen, Wildlife of a Garden: a thirty year study (Peterborough: Royal Horticultural Society, 2010).

76   Ibid., p. 16.

77   Fitter, London's Natural History, p. 188.

78   L. R. Williams and J. McLaughlin, 'Tracing old hedgerows in suburban areas', Local Historian, May 1988, 65–8.

79   Ibid., p. 66.

80   Bushey Museum, Bushey, Hertfordshire: sale catalogue for 'Bushey Village estate', 1912.

81   Hertfordshire Archives and Local Studies, Off Acc 717: Bushey Urban District Council minutes, 23 March 1901.

82   Fitter, London's Natural History, p. 144.

83   Ibid., p. 146.

84   B. Elliott, Victorian Gardens (London: Batsford, 1986). H. Conway, People's Parks: the design and development of Victorian parks in Britain (Cambridge, 1991).

85   J. B. L. Warren, 'The flora of Hyde Park and Kensington Gardens', Journal of Botany 9 (1871), 227–38.

86   D. H. Kent, 'Notes on the flora of Kensington Gardens and Hyde Park', Watsonia 1 (1950), 296–300. D. E. Allen, 'The flora of Hyde Park and Kensington Gardens, 1958–62', Proceedings of the Botanical Society of the British Isles 6 (1965), 1–20.

87 Fitter, *London's Natural History*, pp. 140–5.

88 Hudson, *Birds in London*, pp. 15–17.

89 H. Jordan, 'Public parks, 1885–1914', *Garden History* 22 (1994), 85–113.

90 Fitter, *London's Natural History*, p. 205.

91 J. C. Loudon, *On the Laying Out, Planting and Managing of Cemeteries* (London, 1843). S. Curl, *The Victorian Celebration of Death* (Stroud: Sutton Publishing, 2004).

92 Gilbert, Ecology of Urban Habitats, pp. 218–38. S. Curl (ed.), *Kensal Green Cemetery. The origins and development of the general cemetery of All Souls, Kensal Green, London, 1824-2001* (Chichester: Phillimore, 2001).

93 Fitter, *London's Natural History*, p. 205.

94 English Nature, *On Course Conservation: managing golf's natural heritage* (Peterborough: Nature Conservation Council, 1989). M. R. Terman, 'Natural links: naturalistic golf courses as wildlife habitat', *Landscape and Urban Planning* 38 (1997), pp. 183–97. A. C. Gange, D. E. Lindsay, and J. M. Schofield, 'The ecology of golf courses', *Biologist* 50 (2003), 63–8. R. Mabey, *The Unofficial Countryside* (London: Pimlico, 1999), pp. 114–16.

95 R. A. Tanner and A. C. Gange 'Effects of golf courses on local biodiversity', *Landscape and Urban Planning* 71 (2005), 137–46.

96 B. S. Milne, 'A report on the bird population of Bedington sewage farm', *London Bird Report* 20 (1955), 39–54. A. W. Boyd, 'Sewage farms as bird habitats', *British Birds* 50 (1957), 253–63.

97 Fitter, *London's Natural History*, pp. 174–5.

98 Mabey, *Unofficial Countryside*, p. 140.

99 A. Darlington, *The Ecology of Refuse Tips* (London: Heinemann, 1969), p. 28.

100 Ibid., 31–7. Mabey, *Unofficial Countryside*, pp. 139–47.

101 R. Melville and R. Smith, 'Adventive flora of the Metropolitan Area, 1: recent adventives on London Rubbish', *Report of the Botanical Exchange Club* (1927), 444–54.

102 Darlington, *Refuse Tips*, p. 88.

103 Ibid., p. 70.

104 A. Gibbs, 'The bird population of rubbish dumps', *London Bird Report* 26 (1961), pp. 104–10.

105 Ibid., pp. 90–8.

106 Fitter, *London's Natural History*, pp. 176–7.

107 I. Simmons, *The Moorlands of England and Wales: an environmental history 8000BC – AD 2000* (Edinburgh: Edinburgh University Press, 2003), p. 131.

108 I. Simmons, *An Environmental History of Great Britain: from 10,000 Years Ago to the Present* (Edinburgh: Edinburgh University Press, 2001), p. 161.

109 Fitter, *London's Natural History*, p. 165.

110 Ibid., pp. 148–51.

111 J. Andrews, 'Principles of restoration of gravel pits for wildlife', *British Wildlife* 2 (1990), 80–8. Mabey, *Unofficial Countryside*, pp. 46–57. J. Andrews and D. Kinsman, *Gravel Pit Restoration for Wildlife* (Sandy: RSPB, 1990).

112 K. P. Keywood and W. D. Melluish, 'A report on the bird populations of four gravel pits in the London area, 1948–51', *London Bird Report* 17 (1953), 43–72.

113 J. G. Kelcey, 'Industrial development and wildlife conservation', *Environmental Conservation* 2, 2 (1973), 99–108.

114 P. Shaw, 'Orchid woods and floating islands – the ecology of fly ash', *British Wildlife* 5 (1994), 149–57.

115 D. H. Kent, *The Historical Flora of Middlesex* (London: Ray Society, 1975).

116 L. A. Batten, 'Breeding bird species in relation to increasing urbanisation', *Bird Study* 19 (1972), 157–66.

117 Kent, *Historical Flora of Middlesex*.

118 Hudson, *Birds in London*, p. 155.

119 T. A. Coward and C. Oldham, *The Birds of Cheshire* (Manchester: Sherrat and Hughes, 1900), p. 4.

chapter 10

1 B. Short, C. Watkins and J. Martin (eds), *The Front Line of Freedom: British farming in the Second World War* Agricultural History Review Supplement Series 4 (2007), 5.

2 C. H. Warren, *This Land is Yours* (London: Eyre and Spottiswoode, 1943), p. ix.

3 E. Pollard, M. D. Hooper and N. W. Moore, *Hedges* (London: Collins, 1974), pp. 59–68. G. Barnes and T. Williamson, *Hedgerow History: ecology, conservation and landscape character* (Macclesfield, 2006), pp. 21–3.

4 H. Upcher, 'Norfolk farming', *Norfolk and Norwich Naturalists' Society* 16 (1946), 97–105.

5 W. H. Dowdeswell, *Hedgerows and Verges* (London: Allen and Unwin, 1987), p. 118. R. Muir and N. Muir, *Hedgerows: their history and wildlife* (London: Michael Joseph, 1997), pp. 225–6.

6 W. Baird and J. Tarrant, *Hedgerow Destruction in Norfolk 1946-70* (Norwich: Centre of East Anglian Studies, 1970).

7 M. Shoard, *The Theft of the Countryside* (London: Temple Smith, 1980).

8 R. A. Robinson and W. J. Sutherland, 'Post-war changes in arable farming and biodiversity in Great Britain', *Journal of Applied Ecology* 39 (2002), 157–76. M. Shrubb, *Birds, Scythes and Combines: a history of birds and agricultural change* (Cambridge: Cambridge University Press, 2003), pp. 170–99.

9 P. Anderson and D. Yalden, 'Increased sheep numbers and the loss of heather in the peak district, England', *Biological Conservation* 20 (1981), 195–213.

D. A. Ratcliffe, 'Post-medieval and recent change in British vegetation: the culmination of human influence', *New Phytologist* 98 (1984), 73–100.

10 T. Rowley, *The English Landscape in the Twentieth Century* (London: Hambledon Continuum, 2006), pp. 112–14.

11 D. Evans, *A History of Nature Conservation in Britain* (London: Routledge, 1992).

12 T. Dixon, 'Urban land and property ownership patterns in the UK: trends and forces for change', *Land Use Policy* 26 (2009).

13 There are slight differences in current estimates due to the difficulty of defining 'urban land'. P. Bibby, 'Land use change in Britain', *Land Use Policy* (2009). B. N. K. Davis, 'Wildlife, ubanisation and industry', *Biological Conservation* 10 (1976), pp. 249–91.

14 The Earl of Cranbrook, 'Fifty years of statutory nature conservation in Great Britain', in D. L. Hawsworth (ed.), *The Changing Wildlife of Great Britain and Ireland* (London: Systematics Association, 2001), pp. 1–23.

15 T. Rich, 'Flowering plants', in D. Hawksworth (ed.), *The Changing Wildlife of Great Britain and Ireland* (London: Taylor and Francis, 2001), p. 32. R. Fox, 'Butterflies and moths', in D. Hawksworth (ed.), *The Changing Wildlife of Great Britain and Ireland* (London: Taylor and Francis, 2001), pp. 300–27.

16 O. Rackham, *Woodlands* (London: Collins, 2006), p. 69.

17 See the various contributions in D. Hawksworth (ed.), *The Changing Wildlife of Great Britian and Ireland* (London: Taylor and Francis, 2001).

18 J. Birks, 'The polecat in Britain – continuing recovery', *British Wildlife* 20 (2009), 237–44. R. Lovegrove, *Silent Fields: the long decline of a nation's wildlife* (Oxford: Oxford University Press, 2007), pp. 268–77.

19 K. J. Walker, 'The last thirty five years: recent changes in the flora of the British Isles', *Watsonia* 26 (2007), 291–302.

20 C. D. Preston, 'Engulfed by suburbia or destroyed by the plough: the ecology of extinction in Middlesex and Cambridgeshire', *Watsonia* 23 (2000), 61.

21 Fox, 'Butterflies and moths', p. 300.

22 Preston, 'Engulfed by suburbia or destroyed by the plough', pp. 76–7. Fox, 'Butterflies and moths', p. 322.

23 Fox, 'Butterflies and moths', p. 300.

24 J. G. Kelcey, 'Industrial development and wildlife conservation', *Environmental Conservation* 2, 2 (1973), 99–108.

25 Davis, 'Wildlife, Urbanisation and industry', pp. 282–4.

26 I. D. Rotherham and R. A. Lambert, 'Good science, good history and pragmatism: managing the way ahead', in I. D. Rotherham and R. A. Lambert (eds), *Invasive and Introduced Plants and Animals: human perceptions, attitudes and approaches to management* (London: Earthscan, 2011), pp. 355–66. Rotherham and R. A. Lambert, 'Good science, good history'.

27 C. Smout, 'How the concept of alien species emerged and developed in 20th-century Britain', in I. D. Rotherham and R. A. Lambert (eds), *Invasive*

and Introduced Plants and Animals: human perceptions, attitudes and approaches to management (London: Earthscan, 2011), pp. 55–66.

28 D. W. Yalden, *The History of British Mammals* (London: Poyser, 1999), p. 204.

29 Corbet and Yalden give figures of 41 indigenous and 19 introduced: G. B. Corbet and D. W. Yalden, 'Mammals', in D. Hawksworth (ed.), *The Changing Wildlife of Great Britain and Ireland* (London: Taylor and Francis, 2001), pp. 399–409. Amongst our freshwater fish there are now 13 established aliens, compared with 42 indigenous species.

30 Rotherham and R. A. Lambert, 'Good science, good history'.

31 I. D. Rotherham and R. A. Lambert, 'Balancing species history, human culture and scientific insight: introduction and overview', in I. D. Rotherham and R. A. Lambert (eds), *Invasive and Introduced Plants and Animals: human perceptions, attitudes and approaches to management* (London: Earthscan, 2011), pp. 3–18.

32 Rich, 'Flowering plants', p. 28.

33 M. Hill, R. Baker, G. Broad, P. J. Chandler, G. H. Copp, A. Ellis, D. Jones, C. Hoyland, I. Laing, M. Longshaw, N. Moore, D. Parrot, D. Pearamain, C. Preston, R. Smith and R. Waters, *Audit of Non-Native Species in England* (English Nature Report 662, Peterborough, 2005).

34 K. Alexander, J. Butler and T. Green, 'The value of different tree and shrub species to wildlife', *British Wildlife* 17 (2006), 19–28.

35 D. Pearamain and K. Walker, 'Alien plants in Britain: a real or imagined problem?', *British Wildlife* 21 (2009), 22–7. S. Thomas and T. Dines, 'Non-native invasive plants in Britain: a real, not imagined, problem', *British Wildlife* 21 (2010), 177–83.

36 Bibby, 'Land use change in Britain'.

37 R. Macfarlane, *The Wild Places* (London: Granta, 2008).

38 As proposed by Vera himself: F. Vera, 'Large scale nature development: the Oostvaardersplassen', *British Wildlife* 20 (2009), 28–36.

39 G. F. Peterken, *Natural Woodland: ecology and conservation in northern temperate regions* (Cambridge: Cambridge University Press, 1996), p. 13.

40 A. Byfield, 'Heathland, plantations and the Forestry Commission: a botanical perspective', *British Wildlfe* 20 (2009), 267–72. Ansden, M. Allison, P. Bradley, M. Coates, M. Kemp and N. Phillips, 'Increasing the resilience of our lowland heaths and acid grassland', *British Wildlife* 22 (2010), 101–9. D. Driver, *When to Convert Woods and Forests to Open Habitat in England* (Edinburgh: Forestry Commission, 2010).

BIBLIOGRAPHY

Albarella, U. and Davis, S. J., 'Mammals and birds from Launceston Castle, Cornwall: decline in status and the rise of agriculture', *Circaea* 12 (1996), 1–156.

Albert, W., *The Turnpike Road System in England 1663–1840* (Cambridge: Cambridge University Press, 1972).

Alexander, K., 'The invertebrates of Britain's wood pastures', *British Wildlife* 11 (1999), 108–17.

Alexander, K., Butler, J. and Green, T., 'The value of different tree and shrub species to wildlife', *British Wildlife* 17 (2006), 19–28.

Allen, A. A., 'The coleopteran of a suburban garden', *Entomologists' Record and Journal of Variation* 63 (1951), 61–4, 187–90, 256–9; 64 (1952), 61–6, 92–3; 65 (1953), 225–31; 68 (1954), 215–22.

Allen, D. E., 'The flora of Hyde Park and Kensington Gardens, 1958-62', *Proceedings of the Botanical Society of the British Isles* 6 (1965), 1–20.

—, *The Victorian Fern Craze: a history of Pteridomania* (London: Hutchinson, 1969).

—, *The Naturalist in Britain: a social history* (London: Allen Lane, 1976).

—, 'Sources of error in local lists', *Watsonia* 13 (1981), 215–20.

Allen, J., Potter, V. and Poulter, M., *The Building of Orford Castle: a translation from the pipe rolls 1163-78* (Orford: Orford Museum, 2002).

Amphlett, J. and Rea, C., *The Botany of Worcestershire* (Birmingham: Cornish Brothers, 1909).

Anderson, P. and Yalden, D., 'Increased sheep numbers and the loss of heather in the Peak District, England', *Biological Conservation* 20 (1981), 195–213.

Andrews C. B. (ed.), *The Torrington Diaries, Vol. 1* (London: Eyre and Spottiswoode, 1934).

Andrews, J., 'British estuaries: an internationally important habitat for birds', *British Wildlife* 1 (1989), 76–88.

—, 'Principles of restoration of gravel pits for wildlife', *British Wildlife* 2 (1990), 80–8.

Andrews, J. and Kinsman, D., *Gravel Pit Restoration for Wildlife* (Sandy: RSPB, 1990).

Anon., *The Village London Atlas: the growth of Victorian London* (London: Alderman Press, 1986).

Ansden, M., Allison, M., Bradley, P., Coates, M., Kemp, M. and Phillips, N., 'Increasing the resilience of our lowland heaths and acid grassland', *British Wildlife* 22 (2010), 101–9.

Armitage, P., West, B. and Steedman, K., 'New evidence of the black rat in Roman London', *The London Archaeologist* 4 (1984), 375–83.

Armstrong, P., 'Changes in the Suffolk Sandlings: a study of the disintegration of an eco-system', *Geography* 58 (1973), 1–8.

Babbington, C. C., *Flora of Cambridgeshire* (Cambridge, 1860).

Bailey, M., 'The rabbit and the medieval East Anglian economy', *Agricultural History Review* 36 (1988), 1–20.

Bailey, J. and Culley, G., *General View of the Agriculture of Northumberland and Westmoreland* (London, 1805).

Bailey Denton, J., 'The effects of under drainage on our rivers and arterial channels', *Journal of the Royal Agricultural Society of England* 24 (1863), 573–89.

Baines, C., *How to Make a Wildlife Garden* (London: Frances Lincoln, 1985).

Baird, W. and Tarrant, J., *Hedgerow Destruction in Norfolk 1946-70* (Norwich: Centre of East Anglian Studies, 1970).

Bangerter, E. B. and Kent, D. H., '*Veronica filiformis* in the British Isles', *Proceedings of the Botanical Society of the British Isles* 2 (1957), 197–217.

Barley, M., 'Rural buildings in England', in J. Thirsk (ed.), *The Agrarian History of England and Wales. Volume 5.2: 1640–1750* (Cambridge: Cambridge University Press, 1985), pp. 590–685.

Barnatt, J. and Penny, R., *The Lead Legacy: the prospects for the Peak District's lead mining heritage* (Bakewell: Peak District National Park Authority, 2004).

Barnatt, J. and Williamson, T., *Chatsworth: a landscape history* (Macclesfield: Windgather Press, 2005),

Barnes, G., 'Woodland in Norfolk: a landscape history'. Unpublished PhD, School of History, University of East Anglia, 2003.

Barnes, G. and Williamson, T., *Hedgerow History: ecology, history and landscape character* (Oxford: Windgather Press, 2006).

—, *Ancient Trees in the Landscape: Norfolk's arboreal heritage* (Oxford, 2011).

Barnes, G., Dallas, P., Thompson, H., Whyte, N. and Williamson, T., 'Heathland and wood pasture in Norfolk: ecology and landscape history', *British Wildlife* 18 (2007), 395–403.

Barrett, H. and Phillips, J., *Suburban Style: the British home, 1840–1960* (London: Little, Brown and Co., 1987).

Barrett-Lennard, T., 'Two hundred years of estate management at Horsford during the 17th and 18th centuries', *Norfolk Archaeology* 20 (1921), 57–139.

Batten, L. A., 'Breeding bird species in relation to increasing urbanisation', *Bird Study* 19 (1972), 157–66.

Beardall, C. and Casey, D., *Suffolk's Changing Countryside* (Ipswich: Suffolk Wildlife Trust, 1995).

Beastall, T. W., *The Agricultural Revolution in Lincolnshire* (Lincoln: History of Lincolnshire Committee, 1978).

Beckett, J. and Watkins, C., 'Natural history and local history in late Victorian and Edwardian England: the contribution of the Victoria County History', *Rural History* 22 (2011), 59–88.

Beckett, J. V., *The Aristocracy in England 1660–1914* (Oxford: Basil Blackwell, 1986).

—, *The Agricultural Revolution* (Oxford: Basil Blackwell, 1990).

Belford, P., 'Sublime cascades: water and power in Coalbrookdale', *Industrial Archaeology Review* 29 (2007), 133–48.

Bell, A., 'The family farm', in H. J. Massingham (ed.), *England and the Farmer* (London: Batsford, 1941).

Bell, T., *The History of British Quadrupeds* (London, 1837).

Bellamy, P. E., 'The influence of hedge structure, management and landscape context on the value of hedgerows to birds', *Journal of Environmental Management* 60 (2000), 33–49.

Bennett, K. D., 'Holocene pollen stratigraphy of central East Anglia, England and comparison of pollen zones across the British Isles', *New Phytologist* 109 (1988), 237–53.

Bentley, E. G., *A Practical Guide in the Preparation of Town Planning Schemes* (London: George Phillip, 1911).

Bentley, I., Davis, I. and Oliver, P., *Dunroamin: the suburban semi and its enemies* (London: Barrie and Jenkins, 1981).

Best, R. H. and Coppock, J. T., *The Changing Use of Land in Britain* (London: Faber, 1962).

Bettey, J. H., 'The development of water meadows in Dorset', *Agricultural History Review* 25 (1977), 37–43.

—, 'Water meadows in the southern counties of England', in H. Cook and T. Williamson (eds), *Water Management in the English Landscape: field, marsh and meadow* (Edinburgh: Edinburgh University Press, 1999), pp. 179–95.

—, 'Origins of the Wiltshire rabbit industry', *Antiquaries Journal* 84 (2004), 381–93.

Bevan, J., 'Agricultural change and the development of foxhunting in the eighteenth century', *Agricultural History Review* 58 (2010), 49–25.

Bird, M. C. H., 'The rural economy, sport, and natural history of East Ruston Common' *Transactions of the Norfolk and Norwich Naturalists Society* 8, 5 (1909), 631–70.

Birks, J., 'Feral mink and nature conservation', *British Wildlife* 1 (1989), 313–23.

—, 'The polecat in Britain – continuing recovery', *British Wildlife* 20 (2009), 237–44.

Birrell, J., 'Deer and deer farming in medieval England', *Agricultural History Review* 40 (1993), 112–26.

Birtles, S., '"A Green Space Beyond Self Interest": the Evolution of Common Land in Norfolk c.750-2003'. Unpublished PhD thesis, University of East Anglia, 2003.

Bisgrove, R., *The Gardens of Gertrude Jekyll* (London: Frances Lincoln, 1992).

Bishop, M., Davis, S. P. and Grimshaw, J., *Snowdrops: a monograph of cultivated Galanthus* (London: Griffin Press, Maidenhead, 2002).

Boardman, E. T., 'The development of a Broadland estate at How Hill Ludham, Norfolk', *Transactions of the Norfolk and Norwich Naturalists' Society* 15 (1939), 14.

Bone, Q., 'Legislation to revive small farming in England, 1887–1914', *Agricultural History Review* 49 (1975), 653–61.

Bourdillon, J. and Coy, J., 'Animal bone', in H. Graham and S. Davies (eds), *Excavations at Melbourne Street, Southampton, 1971-6* (York: Council for British Archaeology, 1980), pp. 79–121.

Bowley, A., 'The Great Fen – a waterland for the future', *British Wildlife* 18 (2007), 415–23.

Box, J., 'Conserving or greening? The challenge of post-industrial landscapes', *British Wildlife* 4 (1993), 273–9.

Boyd, A. W., 'Sewage farms as bird habitats', *British Birds* 50 (1957), 253–63.

Boys, J., *General View of the Agriculture of the County of Kent* (London, 1813).

Brander, M., *The Hunting Instinct: the development of field sports over the ages* (London: Oliver and Boyd, 1964).

Brian, A., 'Lammas meadows', *Landscape History* 15 (1983), 57–69.

—, 'The allocation of strips in lammas meadows by the casting of lots', *Landscape History* 21 (1999), 43–58.

Briault, E. E., *The Land of Britain: Sussex* (Land Utilisation Survey Pts 13 and 14) (London: Geographical Publications, 1942).

Briggs, P. A., 'Bats in trees', *Arboricultural Journal* 22 (1998), 25–35.

Brimblecombe, P., *The Big Smoke: a history of air pollution in London since medieval times* (London: Methuen, 1987).

Broad,, J. 'Understanding village desertions in the seventeenth and eighteenth centuries', in C. Dyer and R. Jones (eds), *Deserted Villages Revisited* (Hatfield: University of Hertfordshire Press, 2010), pp. 121–39.

Brooks, A., *Hedging: a practical conservation handbook* (London: British Trust for Conservation Volunteers, 1975).

Brown, J., *Gardens of a Golden Afternoon* (London: Allen Lane, 1982).

Brown, A. F. J., *Prosperity and Poverty: rural Essex, 1700–1815* (Chelmsford: Essex Record Office, 1996).

Brown, T. and Foard, G., 'The Saxon landscape: a regional perspective', in P. Everson and T. Williamson (eds), *The Archaeology of Landscape* (Manchester: Manchester University Press, 1998), pp. 67–94.

Brown, A. E. and Taylor, C. C., 'The origins of dispersed settlement: some results from Bedfordshire', *Landscape History* 11 (1989), 61–82.

Bruyn-Andrews, C., *The Torrington Diaries*, vol. 3 (London: Eyre and Spottiswoode, 1936).

Bryce, J. M., Speakman, J. R., Johnson, P. J. and Macdonald, D. W., 'Competition between Eurasian Red and introduced eastern Grey Squirrels: the energetic significance of body-mass differences', *Proceedings of the Biological Sciences* 268 (2001), 1731–36.

Bujak, E., *England's Rural Realms: landownership and the agricultural revolution* (London: Tauris Academic, 2007).

Bunce, R. G. and Fowler, D., *Heather in England and Wales* (London: HMSO, 1984).

Butcher, R. W., *The Land of Britain: Suffolk* (London: Geographical Publications, 1941).

Byfield, A., 'The Basingstoke Canal: Britain's richest waterway under threat', *British Wildlife* 2 (1990), 13–21.

—, 'Victorian pteridomania – Britain's fern craze', *British Wildlife* 17 (2006), 411–18.

—, 'Heathland, plantations and the Forestry Commission: a botanical perspective, *British Wildlfe* 20 (2009), 267–72.

Cadman, W. A., 'Bird life at Thetford', *Journal of the Forestry Commission* 6 (1936), 24–6.

Caird, J., *English Agriculture 1851-2* (London, 1852).

—, 'General view of British agriculture', *Journal of the Royal Agricultural Society of England*, Second Series 14 (1878), 273–332.

Cambridge, W., 'On the advantages of reducing the size and number of hedges', *Journal of the Royal Agricultural Society of England* 6 (1845), 333–42.

Campbell, B. M. S., 'Commonfield origins – the regional dimension', in T. Rowley (ed.), *The Origins of Open Field Agriculture* (London: Croom Helm, 1981), pp. 112–29.

—, *English Seigniorial Agriculture* (Cambridge: Cambridge University Press, 2000).

Campbell, B. and Overton, M., 'A new perspective on medieval and early-modern agriculture: six centuries of Norfolk farming, 1250-1850', *Past and Present* 141 (1993), 38–105.

Campbell-Culver, M., *The Origin of Plants* (London: Headline Books, 2001).

Cannon, P. M. and Reid, I., 'The influence of relic ridge-and-furrow on the soil water regime of an ancient meadow, Cumbria, England', *Global Ecology and Biogeography Letters* 3 (1993), 18–26.

Carr, R., *English Fox Hunting: a history* (London: Weidenfeld and Nicolson, 1976).

Carter, S. P., 'Habitat change and bird populations', *British Wildlife* 1 (1990), 324–34.

Cash, J., *Where There's a Will There's a Way: an account of the labours of naturalists in humble life* (London, 1873).

Cavill-Worsley, P. E. T., 'A fur farm in Norfolk', *Transactions of the Norfolk and Norwich Naturalists Society* 13 (1931), 104–15.

Chambers, W., *A Dissertation on Oriental Gardening* (London, 1772).

Chambers, J. D. and Mingay, G. E., *The Agricultural Revolution 1750–1880* (London: Batsford, 1966).

Chapman, J., 'The extent and nature of parliamentary enclosure', *Agricultural History Review* 35 (1987), 25–35.

Chapman, N. and Whitta, R., 'The history of the deer of Thetford Forest', in P. Ratcliffe and J. Claridge (eds), *Thetford Forest Park: the ecology of a pine forest* (Alice Holt, 1996), pp. 141–9.

Chapman, N., Harris, S. and Stanford, A., 'Reeves' muntjac *Muntiacus reevesi* in Britain: their history, spread, habitat selection and the role of human intervention in accelerating their dispersal', *Mammal Review* 24 (1994), 113–60.

Chase, M., 'Can history be green? A prognosis', *Rural History* 3 (1992), 243–54.

Chevenix Trench, C., *A History of Marksmanship* (London: Longman, 1972).

Clapp, B. W., *An Environmental History of Britain since the Industrial Revolution* (London: Longman, 1994).

Clarke, J. A., 'On the Great Level of the Fens', *Journal of the Royal Agricultural Society of England* 8 (1848), 80–133.

Clarke, W. G., 'Some Breckland characteristics', *Transactions of the Norfolk and Norwich Naturalists Society* 8 (1908), 555–78.

—, 'The natural history of Norfolk commons', *Transactions of the Norfolk and Norwich Naturalists Society* 10 (1918), 294–318.

Clarke, J. F. M., *Bugs and the Victorians* (New Haven: Yale University Press, 2009).

Clarke, G., Huberaman, M. and Lindert, P. H., 'A British food puzzle, 1770–1850', *Economic History Review* 48 (1995), 213–37.

Clark Kennedy, A., *Birds of Berkshire and Buckinghamshire* (London, 1868).

Clemenson, H., *English Country Houses and Landed Estates* (London: Croom Helm, 1982).

Clements, F. E., *Plant Succession: an analysis of the development of vegetation* (Washington: Carnegie Institution, 1916).

Clements, D. K. and Tofts, R. J., 'Hedges make the grade: a look at the wildlife value of hedges', *British Wildlife* 4 (1992), 87–95.

Cobbett, W., *Rural Rides* (London, 1853).

Cocks, A. H., 'Vermin paid for by churchwardens in a Buckinghamshire parish', *Zoologist* Series 3, 16 (1852), 61–4.

Colebourne, P. H., 'Discovering ancient woods', *British Wildlife* 1 (1989), 61–75.

Collins, E. J. T., 'The economy of upland Britain 1750-1950', in R. B. Tranter (ed.), *The Future of Upland Britain*, vol. 2 (Reading: Centre for Agricultural Strategy, 1978), pp. 586–651.

—, 'The coppice and underwood trades', in G. E. Mingay (ed.), *The Agrarian History of England and Wales Vol. 6, 1750–1850* (Cambridge: Cambridge University Press, 1989), pp. 484–501.

Connell, J. and Slatyer, R., 'Mechanisms of succession in natural communities and their role in community stability and organisation', *The American Naturalist* 111 (1977), 119–1144.

Conway, V. M., 'Ringinglow bog, near Sheffield, Part 2. The present surface', *Journal of Ecology* 37 (1949), 148–70.

Cooke, A. and Farrell, L., *Chinese Water Deer* (Fordingbridge: British Deer Society, 1987).

Cooke, A. S. and Lakhani, K. H., 'Damage to coppice regrowth by muntjac deer *Muntiacus reevesi* and protection with electric fencing', *Biological Conservation* 75 (1996), 231–8.

Cook, L. M., 'Changing views on melanic moths', *Biological Journal of the Linnean Society* 69 (2000), 431–41.

Cook, H. and Williamson, T., 'Introducing water meadows', in H. Cook and T. Williamson (eds), *Water Meadows: history, ecology and conservation* (Oxford: Windgather, 2007), pp. 1–7.

Cook, H., Stearne, K. and Williamson, T., 'The origins of water meadows in England', *Agricultural History Review* 51 (2003), 155–62.

Conway, H., *People's Parks: the design and development of Victorian parks in Britain* (Cambridge: Cambridge University Press, 1991).

Cossons, N., *The BP Book of Industrial Archaeology* (Newton Abbot: David and Charles, 1987).

Coward, T. A. and Oldham, C., *The Birds of Cheshire* (Manchester: Sherrat and Hughes, 1900).

Cowell, B., 'The Commons Preservation Society and the campaign for Berkhamsted common, 1866-70', *Rural History* 13, 2 (2002), 145–62.

Cowper, W., *The Task: a poem in six books*, Book 1 (London, 1785).

Coyne, J. A., 'Not black and white. Review of Majerus, Melanism: evolution in action', *Nature* 396 (1998), 35–6.

Cox, A., *RCHME Survey of Bedfordshire. Brickmaking: a history and gazetteer* (Bedford: Bedfordshire County Council, 1979).

Cramp, S. and Gooders, J., 'The return of the house martin', *London Bird Report* 31 (1967), 93–8.

The Earl of Cranbrook, 'Fifty years of statutory nature conservation in Great Britain', in D. L. Hawksworth (ed.), *The Changing Wildlife of Great Britain and Ireland* (London: Systematics Associations, 2001), pp. 1–23.

Crosby, A. andWinchester, A., 'A sort of national property?', in A. Winchester (ed.), *England's Landscape: the North West* (London: Collins/English Heritage, 2006), pp. 236–7.

Cross, J. R., 'Biological flora of the British Isles: *Rhododendron ponticum* L', *Journal of Biology* 63 (1975), 345–64.

Cumming, E. D. (ed.), *R. S. Surtees,Town and Country Papers* (London: Blackwood, 1929).

Cummings, I., 'The effects of floating on plant communities', in H. Cook and T. Williamson (eds), *Water Meadows: history, ecology and conservation* (Oxford: Windgather, 2007), pp. 82–93.

Curl, J. S. (ed.), *Kensal Green Cemetery. The origins and development of the general cemetery of All Souls, Kensal Green, London, 1824–2001* (Chichester: Phillimore, 2001).

—, *The Victorian Celebration of Death* (Stroud: Sutton Publishing, 2004).

Currie, C., 'Fish ponds as garden features', *Garden History* 18.1 (1990), 22–33.

—, 'The early history of carp and its economic significance in England', *Agricultural History Review* 39 (1991), 97–107.

Cutting, R. L., 'Drowning by numbers: the functioning of bedwork water meadows', in H. Cook and T. Williamson (eds), *Water Meadows: history, ecology and conservation* (Oxford: Windgather, 2007), pp. 70–81.

Cutting, R. L. and Cummings, I. P. F., 'Water meadows: their form, ecology and plant ecology', in H. F. Cook and T. Williamson (eds), *Water Management in the English Landscape: field, marsh and meadow* (Edinburgh: Edinburgh University Press, 1999), pp. 157–79.

Dallas, P., 'Sustainable environments: common wood pastures in Norfolk', *Landscape History* 31 (2010), 23–36.

Daniels, S., 'The political iconography of woodland in later eighteenth-century England', in D. Cosgrove and S. Daniels (eds), *The Iconography of Landscape* (Cambridge: Cambridge University Press, 1988), pp. 51–72.

Darby, H. C., *The Medieval Fenland* (Cambridge: Cambridge University Press, 1940).

—, *The Draining of the Fens*, 2nd edn (Cambridge: Cambridge University Press, 1966).

Darlington, A., *The Ecology of Refuse Tips* (London: Heinemann, 1969).

Daunton, M. (ed.), *The Cambridge Urban History of Britain, Volume 3, 1840–1950*, (Cambridge: Cambridge University Press, 2000).

Davies, A., 'Nature after minerals: a major role for quarries in nature conservation', *British Wildlife* 18 (2007), 305–12.

Davis, T., *General View of the Agriculture of the County of Wiltshire* (London, 1794), p. 34.

Davis, B. N. K., 'Wildlife, urbanisation and industry', *Biological Conservation* 10 (1976), 249–91.

—, 'The ground arthropods of London gardens', *London Naturalist* 58 (1978), 15–24.

Dark, P., *The Environment of Britain in the First Millennium AD* (London: Duckworth, 2000).

Defoe, D., *A Tour through the Whole Island of Great Britain* (London, 1724).

Delabere Blaine, P., *An Encyclopaedia of Rural Sports: or a complete account of . . . hunting, shooting, racing &c* (London, 1838).

Dennison, E. and Russett, V., 'Duck decoys: their function and management with reference to Nyland Decoy, Cheddar', *Somerset Archaeology and Natural History* 133 (1989), 141–54.

Dixon, C., *The Game Birds and Wild fowl of the British Islands: being a handbook for the naturalist and sportsman* (London, 1895).

Dixon, T., 'Urban land and property ownership patterns in the UK: trends and forces for change', *Land Use Policy* 26 (2009), S43–53.

Dixon Hunt, J., *William Kent: landscape gardener. An assessment and catalogue of his designs* (London: Zwemmer, 1987).

Dixon Hunt, J. and de Jong, E. (eds), *The Anglo-Dutch Garden in the Age of William and Mary*, published as *Journal of Garden History* 8, 2&3 (1988).

Dixon Hunt, J. and Willis, P. (eds), *The Genius of the Place: the English landscape garden 1620–1820* (London: Paul Elek, 1975).

Dolman, P., Fuller, R., Gill, R., Hooton, D. and Tabor, R., 'Escalating ecological impact of deer in lowland woodland', *British Wildlife* 21 (2010), 242–54.

Dolman, P., Hinsley, S., Bellamy, P. and Watts, K., 'Woodland birds in patchy landscapes. The evidence base for strategic networks', *Ibis* 149 (2007), 146–60.

Dolman, P. and Sutherland, W., 'The ecological changes of Breckland grass heath and the consequences of management', *Journal of Applied Ecology* 29, 2 (1992), 402–13.

Dolman, P. and Waeber, W., 'Ecosystem and competition impacts of introduced deer', *Wildlife Research* 35, 3 (2008), 202–14.

Done, A. and Muir, R., 'The landscape history of grouse shooting in the Yorkshire Dales', *Rural History* 12, 2 (2001), 195–210.

Dony, J. G., 'Notes on the Bedfordshire railway flora, *Bedfordshire Naturalist* 9 (1955), 12–16.

Dowdeswell, W. H., *Hedgerows and Verges* (London: Allen and Unwin, 1987).

Driver, D., 'When to convert woods and forests to open habitat in England'. Forestry Commission Advice Note (Edinburgh: Forestry Commission, 2010).

Druce, G. C., *The Flora of Oxfordshire* (London, 1886).

Dudley Stamp, L., *The Land of Britain: its use and misuse* (London: Geographical Publications, 1950).

Dugdale, W., *The History of Inbanking and Drayning of Diverse Fens and Marshes* . . . (London, 1662).

Dyer, C., 'The consumption of fish in medieval England', in M. Aston (ed.), *Medieval Fish, Fisheries and Fish Ponds in England* (Oxford: British Archaeological Reports, British Series, vol. 182, 1988), pp. 27–35.

Edelen, G. (ed.), *The Description of England: the classic contemporary account of Tudor social life, by William Harrison* (London: Folger Shakespeare Library, 1994).

Edwards, G. (ed.), *George Crabbe. Selected Poems* (London: Penguin, 1991).

Elliott, B., *Victorian Gardens* (London: Batsford, 1986).

Ellis, E. A., 'Some effects of selective feeding by the coypu (*Myocasto coypus*) on the vegetation of Broadland', *Transactions of the Norfolk and Norwich Naturalists' Society,* 20 (1963), 32–5.

Engels, F., *The Condition of the Working Class in England in 1844,* (London: Penguin edn, 1987).

Evans, D., *A History of Nature Conservation in Britain* (London: Routledge, 1992).

Evelyn, J., *Sylva* (London, 1664).

Everson, P., 'Quarrendon, Aylesbury Vale, Buckinghamshire'. Unpublished report for English Heritage (Swindon, 1999).

Everson, P. and Williamson, T., 'Gardens and designed landscapes', in P. Everson and T. Williamson (eds), *The Archaeology of Landscape: studies presented to Christopher Taylor* (Manchester: Manchester University Press, 1998), pp. 139–65.

Farthing, F. H., *Saturday in my Garden* (London: Grant Richards, 1911).

Finch, J., 'Pallas, Flora and Ceres: landscape priorities and improvement on the Castle Howard estate, 1699-1880', in J. Finch and K. Giles (eds), *Estate landscapes: design, improvement and power in the post-medieval landscape* (Woodbridge: Boydell, 2007), pp. 19–38.

—, "Grass, grass, grass': fox-hunting and the creation of the modern landscape', *Landscapes* 5 (2004), 41–52.

Fitch Daglish, E., *The Book of Garden Animals* (London, 1928).

Fitter, R. S. R., *London's Natural History* (London: Collins, 1945).

Fleming, A., *The Dartmoor Reaves* (London: Batsford, 1988).

Fletcher, J., *Gardens of Earthly Delight: the history of deer parks* (Oxford: Windgather, 2011).

Flinn, M. W., *The History of the British Coal Industry Vol. 2, 1700–1830* (Oxford: Oxford University Press, 1984).

Ford, E. B., *Ecological Genetics* (London: Methuen, 1964).

Forman, R. T. and Baudry, J., 'Hedgerow and hedgerow networks in landscape ecology', *Environmental management* 8 (1984), 495–510.

Forsyth, A., 'Game preservation and fences', *Journal of the Horticultural Society* 1 (1946), 201.

Fowler, P. J., *The Farming of Prehistoric Britain* (Cambridge: Cambridge University Press, 1983).

—, *Farming in the First Millennium AD* (Cambridge: Cambridge University Press, 2002).

Fox, R., 'Butterflies and moths', in D. Hawksworth (ed.), *The Changing Wildlife of Great Britain and Ireland* (London: Taylor and Francis, 2001), 300–27.

Freeman, J. (ed.), *Thomas Fuller: the Worthies of England* (London: Allen and Unwin, 1952).

Gange, A. C., Lindsay, D. E. and Schofield, J. M., 'The ecology of golf courses', *Biologist* 50 (2003), 63–8.

Gardner, H. W. and Garner, H. V., *The Use of Lime in British Agriculture* (London: Farmer and Stockbreeder Publications, 1957).

Gay, C. E., 'The Norfolk Naturalists Trust', *Transactions of the Norfolk and Norwich Naturalists' Society* 16 (1944), 3–13.

George, M., *The Land Use, Ecology and Conservation of Broadland* (Chichester: Packard Publishing, 1992).

Gerrard, J., *The Herball or Generall Historie of Plantes* (London, 1597).

Gibbs, A., 'The bird population of rubbish dumps', *London Bird Report* 26 (1961), 104–10.

Gilbert, O. L., *The Flowering of the Cities: the natural flora of 'urban commons'* (Peterborough: English Nature, 1982).

—, 'The ancient lawns of Chatsworth, Derbyshire', *Journal of the Royal Horticultural Society* 108 (1983), 471–4.

—, *The Ecology of Urban Habitats* (London: Chapman and Hall, 1989).

—, 'The ecology of an urban river', *British Wildlife* 3 (1992), 129–36.

Gillam, B., *The Wiltshire Flora* (London: Pisces Publications, 1993).

Gilpin, W., *Three Essays on Picturesque Beauty, on Picturesque Travel, and on Sketching Landscape* (London, 1792).

Girouard, M., *The English Town* (Yale University Press, London, 1989).

Goddard, N., *Harvests of Change: the Royal Agricultural Society of England 1838–1988*, (London, 1988).

Gosling, L. M. and Baker, S. J., 'The eradication of muskrats and coypus from Britain', *Biological Journal* 38, 1 (1989), 39–51.

Grant, A., 'Animal resources', in G. Astill and A. Grant (eds), *The Countryside of Medieval England* (Oxford: Blackwell, 1988), pp. 149–87.

Grant, J., 'A few remarks on the large hedges and small enclosures of Devonshire and adjoining counties', *Journal of the Royal Agricultural Society of England* 5 (1845), 420–9.

Green, R. E., Osbourne, P. E. and Steers, E. J., 'The distribution of passerine birds in hedgerows during the breeding season in relation to the characteristics of the hedgerow and adjacent farmland', *Journal of Applied Ecology* 31 (1994), 677–92.

Green, T., 'Is there a case for the Celtic maple or the Scots Plane?', *British Wildlife* 16 (2005), 184–8.

Gregory, J., 'Mapping improvement: reshaping rural landscapes in the eighteenth century', *Landscapes* 6 (2005), 62–82.

Grigor, J., *The Eastern Arboretum, or a Register of Remarkable Trees, Seats, Gardens &c in the County of Norfolk* (London, 1841).

Grigson, G., *The Englishman's Flora* (London: Paladin, 1975).

Grindon, L. H., *Manchester Walks and Wild Flowers* (Manchester, 1859).

Grubb, P. J., Green, H. E. and Merrifield, R. C. J., 'The ecology of chalk heath: its relevance to the calciole-calcifuge and soil acidification problems', *Journal of Ecology* 57 (1969), 175–212.

Habbakuk, H. J., 'Economic functions of English landowners in the seventeenth and eighteenth centuries', *Explorations in Entrepreneurial History* 6 (1953), 92–102.

Hadden, R. M., 'Wild flowers of London W1', *London Naturalist* 57 (1978), 26–33.

Hadfield, M., *A History of British Gardening* (London: Penguin, 1985).

Haggard, H. R., *Rural England*, 2 vols (London: Longman, Green and Co., 1902).

Haggard, L. R. and Williamson, H., *Norfolk Life* (London: Faber, 1943).

Hall, D., *Medieval Fields* (Princes Risborough: Shire, 1982).

—, *The Open Fields of Northamptonshire* (Northampton: Northamptonshire Record Society, 1995).

—, 'Enclosure in Northamptonshire', *Northamptonshire Past and Present* 9 (1997), 351–68.

Hall, D., Wells, C. E. and Huckerby, E., *The Wetlands of Greater Manchester* (Lancaster: Lancaster University Archaeological Unit, 1995), 126–7.

Hall, J., 'Hedgerows in West Yorkshire: the Hooper method examined', *Yorkshire Archaeological Journal* 54 (1982), 103–9.

Hallam, H. E., *The Agrarian History of England and Wales, Vol. 2, 1042–1350* (Cambridge: Cambridge University Press, 1988).

Hamilakis, Y., 'The sacred geography of hunting: wild animals, social power and gender in early farming societies', in E. Kotjabopoulou, Y. Hamilakis,

P. Halstead, C. Gamble, and V. Elefanti (eds), *Zooarchaeology in Greece: recent advances* (London: British School at Athens, 2003), pp. 239–47.

Hanbury, W., *An Essay on Planting* (London, 1758).

Hanley, J. A., *Progressive Farming*, 4 vols (London: Caxton Publishing, 1949).

Harris, A., 'The rabbit warrens of east Yorkshire in the eighteenth and nineteenth centuries', *Yorkshire Archaeological Journal* 42 (1967–70), 429–41.

Harris, A. and Spratt, D. A., 'The rabbit warrens of the Tabular Hills, North Yorkshire', *Yorkshire Archaeological Journal* 63 (1991), 177–98.

Harting, J. E., *Birds of Middlesex* (London, 1866).

—, *The Rabbit* (London, 1898).

Harvey, J., *Early Nurserymen* (Chichester: Phillimore, 1975).

Harvey, N., *The Industrial Archaeology of Farming in England and Wales* (London: Batsford, 1980).

Hastings, M., *English Sporting Guns and Accessories* (London: Ward Lock, 1969).

Havinden, M., 'Lime as a means of agricultural improvement: the Devon example', in C. W. Chalklin and M. A. Havinden (eds), *Rural Change and Urban Growth* (London: Longman, 1974), pp. 104–34.

Haynes, R. G., 'Vermin traps and rabbit warrens on Dartmoor', *Post-Medieval Archaeology* 4 (1970), 147–64.

Heaton, A., *Duck Decoys* (Princes Risborough: Shire, 2001).

Hellyer, A. G. L., *Practical Gardening for Amateurs* (London: Collingridge, 1935).

Hertfordshire Gardens Trust and Williamson, T., *The Parks and Gardens of West Hertfordshire* (Letchworth: Hertfordshire Gardens Trust, 2000).

Hervey, Lord F. (ed.), *Suffolk in the Seventeenth Century: the breviary of Suffolk by Robert Reyce* (London: J. Murray, 1902).

Heslop Harrison, J. W. and Richardson, J. A., 'The magnesian limestone area of Durham and its vegetation', *Transactions of the Northumberland Naturalists Union* 2 (1953), 1–28.

Hey, D., 'Yorkshire and Lancashire', in J. Thirsk (ed.), *The Agrarian History of England and Wales*, vol. 5.1 (Cambridge: Cambridge University Press, 1984), pp. 59–88.

—, 'Moorlands', in J. Thirsk (ed.), *The English Rural Landscape* (Oxford: Oxford University Press, 2000), pp. 188–209.

Higgs, E., Greenwood, W. and Garrard, A., 'Faunal report', in P. Rahtz (ed.), *The Saxon and Medieval Palace at Cheddar: excavations 1960-82* (Oxford: British Archaeological Reports, British Series, vol. 65, 1979), pp. 353–62.

Hill, D. and Robertson, P., *The Pheasant: ecology, management and conservation* (Oxford: BSP Professional, 1988).

Hill, M., Baker, R., Broad, G., Chandler, P. J., Copp, G. H., Ellis, A., Jones, D., Hoyland, C., Laing, I., Longshaw, M., Moore, N., Parrot, D., Pearamain, D., Preston, C., Smith, R. and Waters, R., *Audit of Non-Native Species in England* (Peterborough: English Nature, 2005).

Hopkins, H., *The Long Affray* (London: Secker and Warburg, 1985).

Hills, R. L., *Machines, Mills and Uncountable Costly Necessities* (Norwich: Goose and Son, 1967).

Hindle, B. P., *Roads, Tracks and their Interpretation* (London: Batsford, 1993).

Hitch, C. and Lambley, P., 'The lichens of Breckland and the effects of afforestation', in P. Ratcliffe and J. Claridge (eds), *Thetford Forest Park: the ecology of a pine forest* (Edinburgh: Forestry Commission, 1996), pp. 58–66.

Hodder, K., Buckland, P., Kirby, K. and Bullock, J., 'Can the pre-Neolithic provide suitable models for re-wilding the landscape in Britain', *British Wildlife* 20, 5 (special supplement) (2009), 4–15.

Holderness, B. A., 'Prices, productivity and output', in G. E. Mingay (ed.), *The Agrarian History of England and Wales,* vol. 6 (Cambridge: Cambridge University Press, 1989), pp. 84–189.

Holland, H., *General View of the Agriculture of Cheshire* (London, 1813).

Home, M., *Autumn Fields* (London: Methuen, 1944).

Hopkins, J. J., 'British meadows and pastures', *British Wildlife* 1 (1990), 202–13.

Hoskins, W. G., *The Making of the English Landscape* (London: Hodder and Stoughton, 1956).

Hoskyns, C. W., *Talpa, or the Chronicles of a Clayland Farm* (London, 1865).

Hough, C., 'Deer in Sussex place-names', *Antiquaries Journal* 88 (2008), 43–7.

Howard, E., *Garden Cities of Tomorrow* (London: Sonnenschein, 1902).

Howitt, W., *The Rural Life in England* (London, 1844).

Hudson, P., 'Proto-industrialization', *Recent Findings of Research in Economic and Social History* 10 (1990), 1–4.

Hudson, K., *The Archaeology of the Consumer Society* (London: Heinemann, 1981).

Hudson, W. H., *Birds of London* (London: Methuen, 1898).

—, *Nature in Downland* (London: Dent, 1900).

—, *A Shepherd's Life: impressions of the South Wiltshire Downs* (London, 1910).

Hulme, P. E., 'Biological invasions in Europe: drivers, pressures, states, impacts and response', in R. E. Hester and R. M. Harrison (eds), *Issues in Environmental Science and Technology* 25 (Cambridge: Royal Society of Chemistry, 2007), pp. 56–80.

Isham, G., *Rushton Triangular Lodge* (London: HMSO, 1970).

Isham, R. (ed. and trans.), *The Journal of Thomas Isham of Lamport in the County of Northamptonshire* (Norwich, 1875).

Jackson, A., *Semi-Detached London: suburban development, life and transport, 1900–1939* (London: Allen and Unwin, 1973).

Jacob, M., *The Cultural Meaning of the Scientific Revolution* (New York, 1988).

Jacques, D., *Georgian Gardens: the reign of Nature* (London: Thames and Hudson, 1983).

James, N., 'The transformation of the Fens', in T. Kirby and S. Oosthuizen (eds), *An Atlas of Cambridgeshire and Huntingdonshire History* (Cambridge: Anglia Polytechnic University, 2000), p. 7.

Jefferies, D. J., 'The changing otter population of Britain 1700-1989', *Biological Journal of the Linnaean Society* 38 (1989), 61–89.

Jefferies, R., *Nature Near London* (London, 1913).

Jekyll, G., *Wood and Garden* (London: Longman, Green and Co., 1899).

Jennings, B., 'A longer view of the Wolds', in J. Thirsk (ed.), *Rural England: an illustrated history of the landscape* (Oxford: Oxford University Press, 2000), pp. 62–77.

Jessop, A., *Arcady: for better, for worse* (London, 1887).

Rev Johns, C. A., *Flowers of the Field* (London, 1851).

—, *British Birds in their Haunts* (London, 1862).

Johnson, W., 'Hedges: a review of some early literature', *Local Historian* 13 (1978), 195–204.

—(ed.), *Gilbert White's Journal* (London: Routledge, 1931).

Jones, E. L., 'The bird pests of British agriculture in recent centuries', *Agricultural History Review* 20 (1972), 107–25.

Jordan, H., 'Public parks, 1885-1914', *Garden History* 22 (1994), 85–113.

Kain, R. J. P., *An Atlas and Index of the Tithe-Files of Mid Nineteenth Century England and Wales* (Cambridge: Cambridge University Press, 1986).

Kalm, P., *Kalm's Account of his Visit to England on his Way to America in 1748*, translated by J. Lucas (London, 1892).

Keith, E. C., 'The policy of the society', *Transactions of the Norfolk and Norwich Naturalists Society* 15 (1942), 311–18.

Kelcey, J. G., 'Industrial development and wildlife conservation', *Environmental Conservation* 2, 2 (1973), 99–108.

Kent, D. H., 'Notes on the flora of Kensington Gardens and Hyde Park', *Watsonia* 1 (1950), 296–300.

—, '*Senechio squalidus* L in the British Isles 1. Early records (to 1877)', *Proceedings of the Botanical Society of the British Isles* 2 (1958), 115–18.

—, '*Senechio squalidus* L in the British Isles 2. The spread from Oxford', *Proceedings of the Botanical Society of the British Isles* 3 (1960), 115–18.

—, *The Historical Flora of Middlesex* (London: Ray Society, 1975).

Kent, N., *General View of the Agriculture of the County of Norfolk* (London, 1796).

Kent, S., *Farmers as Hunters: the implications of sedentism* (Cambridge: Cambridge University Press, 1989).

Kenward, R. E., Hodder, K., Rose, R., Walls, C., Parish, T., Holm, J., Morris, P., Walls, S. and Doyle, F., 'Comparative demography of red squirrels (*Sciurus vulgaris*) and grey squirrels (*Sciurus carolinensis*) in deciduous and conifer woodland', *Journal of Zoology*, 244 (1998), 7–21.

Kerridge, E., 'The floating of the Wiltshire water meadows', *Wiltshire Archaeological Magazine* 55 (1953), 105–18.

—, 'The sheepfold in Wiltshire and the floating of the water meadows', *The Economic History Review* 6 (1954), 282–9.

—, *The Agricultural Revolution* (London: Allen and Unwin, 1967

—, 'The agricultural revolution reconsidered', *Agricultural History Review* 43 (1969), 463–76.

—, *The Farmers of Old England* (London: Allen and Unwin, 1973).

—, *The Common Fields of England* (Manchester, 1992).

Kettlewell, H. B. D., 'Selection experiments on industrial melanism in the Lepidoptera', *Heredity* 9 (1955), 323–42.

—, 'Further selection experiments on industrial melanism in the Lepidoptera', *Heredity* 10 (1956), 287–301.

Keywood, K. P. and Melluish, W. D., 'A report on the bird populations of four gravel pits in the London area, 1948-51', *London Bird Report* 17 (1953), 43–72.

Kirby, K. J. and Drake, C. M. (eds), *Dead Wood Matters* (Peterborough: English Nature, 1993).

Knight, R. P., *The Landscape: a didactic poem* (London, 1794).

Lack, C., *Birds on Lowland Farms* (London: HMSO, 1992).

Laider, K., *Squirrels in Britain* (Newton Abbot: David and Charles, 1980).

Lambert, J. M., 'The chief Norfolk habitats', in British Association for the Advancement of Science, *Norwich and its Region* (Norwich, 1961), 51–8.

Lambert, S. (ed.), *House of Commons Sessional Papers of the Eighteenth Century: George III; Reports of the Commissioners of Land Revenue, 8-11, 1792* (Delaware: Scholarly Resources, 1977).

Langford, P., *Polite and Commercial People: England, 1727–1783* (Oxford: Oxford University Press, 1989).

Langley, P. J. W. and Yalden, D. W., 'The decline of the rarer carnivores in Great Britain during the nineteenth century', *Mammal* Review 7, 3&4 (1977), 95–116.

Latham, R. and Matthews, W. (eds), *The Diary of Samuel Pepys*, vol. 7 (London: G. Bell and Son, 1970).

Laundon, J. R., *Lichens* (Princes Risborough: Shire, 1984).

Lees, E., *The Botany of Worcestershire* (Worcester, 1867).

Lennon, B., 'Estimating the age of groups of trees in historic landscapes', *Arboricultural Journal* 32 (2009), 167–88.

Liddiard, R., *Landscapes of Lordship: Norman castles and the countryside in medieval Norfolk, 1066–1200* (Oxford: British Archaeological Reports, British Series, vol. 309, 2000).

—, (ed.), *The Medieval Deer Park: new perspectives* (Macclesfield: Windgather, 2007).

Lin, Y-C., James, R. and Dolman, P., 'Conservation of heathland ground beetles (Coleoptra, Carabidae): the value of lowland coniferous plantations', *Biology and Conservation* 16, 5 (2007), 1337–58.

Loudon, J. C., *The Suburban Gardener and Villa Companion* (London, 1838).

—, *On the Laying Out, Planting and Managing of Cemeteries* (London, 1843).

Louverre, A. G., 'The atlas of rural settlement GIS', *Landscapes* 11 (2010), 21–44.

Lovegrove, R., *Silent Fields: the long decline of a nation's wildlife* (Oxford: Oxford University Press, 2002).

Mabey, R., *Flora Britannica* (London: Concise edn, Chatto and Windus, 1998).

—, *The Unofficial Countryside* (London: Pimlico, 1999).

—, *Weeds: the story of outlaw plants* (London: Profile Books, 2010).

Macan, T. T., 'Freshwater invertebrates', in D. L. Hawksworth (eds), *The Changing Flora and Fauna of Britain* (London: Taylor and Francis, 1974), pp. 143–55.

MacDonald, D. and Barrett, P., *Collins Field Guide to Mammals of Britain and Northern Europe* (London: Collins, 1993).

MacFarlane, R., *The Wild Places* (London: Granta, 2008).

MacNair, A. and Williamson, T., *William Faden and Norfolk's Eighteenth-Century Landscape* (Oxford: Windgather, 2010).

Maddock, A. (ed.), *UK Biodiversity Action Plan; priority habitat descriptions* (Peterborough: English Nature, 2011).

Markham, C. A., 'Early foxhounds', in R. Serjeantson (ed.), *Victoria County History of Northamptonshire*, vol. 2 (London: Constable, 1906), pp. 355–73.

Marchant, J. R. V. and Watkins, W., *Wild Birds Protection Acts 1880–1896* (London, 1897).

Marren, P., 'Harvests of beauty: the conservation of hay meadows', *British Wildlife* 6 (1995), 235–43.

—, 'Darwin's war-horse: beetle-collecting in nineteenth-century England', *British Wildlife* 19 (2008), 153–9.

Marshall, W., *The Rural Economy of Norfolk* (London, 1787).

—, *Planting and Rural Ornament* (London, 1796).

—, *The Rural Economy of the Southern Counties* (London, 1798).

Martin, B. P., *The Glorious Grouse: a natural and unnatural history* (Newton Abbot: David and Charles, 1990).

Martin, E. and Satchell, M., *Wheare Most Inclosures Be. East Anglian fields, history, morphology and management*, published as *East Anglian Archaeology* 124 (Ipswich, 2008).

Mascall, L., *A Book of Engines and Traps to take Polecats, Buzardes, Rattes, Mice and all other Kindes of Vermine and Beasts* whatever (London, 1590).

Matless, D., *Landscape and Englishness* (London: Reaktion 1998).

McCann, J., *The Dovecotes of Suffolk* (Ipswich, 1988).

McCarthy, M., Review of Lovegrove, *Silent Fields*, *The Independent*, 23 March 2007.

McCormick, J., *Reclaiming Paradise: the global environmental movement* (London: John Wiley, 1992).

Mead, W. R., *Pehr Kalm: a Finnish visitor to the Chilterns in 1748* (Aston Clinton: Privately published, 2003).

Mearns, B. and Mearns, R., *The Bird Collectors* (London: Academic Press, 1998).

Melville, R. and Smith, R. 'Adventive flora of the Metropolitan Area, 1: recent adventives on London rubbish', *Report of the Botanical Exchange Club* 8 (1927), 444–54.

Mendels, F., 'Proto-industrialisation: the first phase of the industrialisation process', *Journal of Economic History* 32 (1972), 241–61.

Middleton, A. D., *The Grey Squirrel* (London: Sidgwick & Jackson, 1931).

Miele, C., 'From aristocratic ideal to middle-class idyll: 1690-1840', in A. Saint (ed.), *London Suburbs* (London, 1990), pp. 31–56.

Miller, P., *The Gardener's Dictionary* (London, 1731).

Miller, M., *English Garden Cities: an introduction* (London: English Heritage, 2010), pp. 18–22.

Milne, B. S., 'A report on the bird population of Bedington sewage farm', *London Bird Report* 20 (1955), 39–54.

Mingay, G. E., 'The East Midlands', in J. Thirsk (ed.), *The Agrarian History of England and Wales, Vol. V.1* (Cambridge: Cambridge University Press, 1984), pp. 89–128.

Mitchell, A., *Trees of Britain and Northern Europe,* second edn (London: Collins, 1974).

Mitchell, B. R. and Deane, P., *Abstract of British Historical Statistics* (Cambridge: Cambridge University Press, 1962).

Mitchell, F. S., *Birds of Lancashire* (London, 1885).

Mokyr, J., *The Lever of Riches: technological creativity and economic progress* (Oxford: Oxford University Press, 1990).

Moon, H. P. and Green, F. H. W., 'Water meadows in southern England', in L. Dudley Stamp (ed.), *The Land of Britain, The Report of the Land Utilisation Survey of Britain* Pt. 89 (London: Geographical Publications, 1940).

Moore-Collyer, R. J., 'Aspects of the urban-rural divide in inter-War Britain', *Rural History* 10 (1999), 103–24.

—, 'Back to basics: Rolf Gardiner, H. J. Massingham and "A kinship in husbandry"', *Rural History* 12 (2002), 85–108.

More, A. G., 'On the distribution of birds in Great Britain during the nesting season', *Ibis* 1 (1865), 1–27, 119–42, 425–8.

Morris, F. O., *A History of British Birds* (London, 1863).

Morris, P. and Morris, M., 'A long-term study of the edible dormouse in Britain', *British Wildlife* 22 (2010), 153–61.

Morris, R., *Chester in the Plantagenet and Tudor Reigns* (Chester, 1893).

Mosby, J. E. G., *The Land of Britain: Norfolk* (London: Geographical Publications, 1938).

Mosley, S., *The Chimney of the World: a history of smoke pollution in Victorian and Edwardian Manchester* (Cambridge: White Horse Press, 2001)

Mourier, H. and Winding, O., *Collins Guide to Wild Life in House and Home* (London: Collins, 1975).

Muir, R., *The Lost Villages of Britain* (London: Michael Joseph, 1982).

Muir, R. and Muir, N., *Hedgerows: their history and wildlife* (London: Michael Joseph, 1997).

Munsche, P. B., *Gentlemen and Poachers: the English game laws 1671–1831* (Cambridge: Cambridge University Press 1981).

Murphy, G., *Founders of the National Trust* (London: Christopher Helm, 1987).

Murton, R. K., *Man and Birds* (London: Collins, 1971).

Nature Conservation Council, *On Course Conservation: managing golf's natural heritage* (Peterborough: Nature Conservation Council, 1989).

Nef, J. U., *The Rise of the British Coal Industry* (London: Routledge, 1932).

Newbold, C., 'Historical changes in the nature conservation interest of the fens of Cambridgeshire', in H. Cook and T. Williamson (eds), *Water Management in the English Landscape: field, marsh and meadow* (Edinburgh: Edinburgh University Press, 1999), pp. 210–26.

Nicholson, E. M., *Birds and Man* (London: Collins, 1951).

Noddle, B., 'The animal bones', in R. Shoesmith (ed.), *Hereford Excavations* (York: Council for British Archaeology, 1985), 84–94.

Norden, J., *The Surveyor's Dialogue* (London, 1618).

Norgate, F., 'Notes on the nesting habits of certain birds', *Transactions of the Norfolk and Norwich Naturalists' Society* 2 (1876), 195–206.

North, R., *The Discourse of Fish and Fish Ponds* (London, 1723).

O'Brien, P., 'Agriculture and the home market for English industry, 1660-1820', *English Historical Review* 100 (1985), 773–800.

O'Connor, R. J. and Shrubb, M., *Farming and Birds* (Cambridge: Cambridge University Press, 1986).

Oldham, C., 'Payments for vermin by some Hertfordshire churchwardens', *Transactions of the Hertfordshire. Natural History Society* 18 (1929), 79–112

Oman, C., *The Great Revolt of 1381* (Oxford: Clarendon Press, 1906).

Orange, A., *Lichens on Trees* (Cardiff: National Museum of Wales, 1994).

Orgill, C. L., 'The introduction of the rabbit into England', *Antiquity* 10 (1936), 462–3.

Oswald, P., 'The fritillary in Britain: a historical perspective', *British Wildlife* 3 (1992), 200–10.

Ottewill, D., *The Edwardian Garden* (London: Yale University Press, 1989).

Overton, M., 'The determinants of crop yields in early modern England', in B. Campbell and M. Overton (eds), *Land, Labour and Livestock* (Manchester: Manchester University Press, 1991), pp. 284–332.

—, *The Agricultural Revolution in England* (Cambridge: Cambridge University Press, 1996).

Owen, J., *Wildlife of a Garden: a thirty year study* (Royal Horticultural Society, Peterborough, 2010).

Pakeman, R. J. and Marshall, A. G., 'The seedbanks of the Breckland heaths and heath grasslands, eastern England, and their relationship to the vegetation and the effects of management', *Journal of Biogeography* 24, 3 (1987), 375–90.

Pakenham, T., *Meetings with Remarkable Trees* (London: Weidenfeld and Nicolson, 1996).

Palmer, M. and Neaverson, P., *Industry in the Landscape, 1700–1900* (London: Routledge, 1994).

Palmer R. (ed.), *Everyman's Book of English Country Songs* (London: Dent, 1979).

Parmenter, L., 'City bombed sites survey: the flies of the Cripplegate bombed site', *London Naturalist* 33 (1955), 89–100.

Parry, J., *Heathland* (London: National Trust, 2003).

Patten, J., 'Fox coverts for the squirearchy', *Country Life* 23 September 1971, 726–40.

Payne, R. M., 'The flora of walls in south-eastern Essex', *Watsonia* 12 (1978), 41–6.

Payne Galwey, R., *The Book of Duck Decoys* (London, 1886).

Pearmain, D., '"Far from any house" – assessing the status of doubtfully native species in the flora of the British Isles', *Watsonia* 26 (2007), 271–90.

Pearmain, D. and Walker, K., 'Alien plants in Britain: a real or imagined problem?', *British Wildlife* 21 (2009), 22–7.

Pedley, W., *Labour on the Land* (London: King and Staples, 1941).

Penford, N. and Francis, I., 'Common land and nature conservation in England and Wales', *British Wildlife* 2 (1990), 65–76.

Percy, J., 'Scientists in humble life: the artisan naturalists of south Lancashire', *Manchester Region History Review* 5 (1991), 3–10.

Perren, R., *Agriculture in Depression 1870–1940* (Cambridge: Cambridge University Press, 1995).

Perry, P. J., *British Farming in the Great Depression: an historical geography* (Newton Abbot: David and Charles, 1974).

Petch, C. P., 'Reclaimed lands of west Norfolk', *Transactions of the Norfolk and Norwich Naturalists Society* 16 (1947), 106–9.

Peterken, G. F., *Natural Woodland: ecology and conservation in northern temperate regions* (Cambridge: Cambridge University Press, 1996).

Pettit, P. A., *The Royal Forests of Northamptonshire* (Northampton: Northamptonshire Record Society, 1968).

Phibbs, J., 'The picturesque moment', *Architectural Association Newsletter* 3 (1992), 3–4.

Phillips, A. D. M., 'Arable land drainage in the nineteenth century', in H. Cook and T. Williamson (eds), *Water Management in the English Landscape: field, marsh and meadow* (Edinburgh: Edinburgh University Press, 1999), pp. 53–72.

—, *The Underdraining of Farmland in England During the Nineteenth Century* (Cambridge: Edinburgh University Press, 1989).

—, *The Staffordshire Reports of Andrew Thompson to the Inclosure Commissioners, 1858-68: landlord investment in Staffordshire agriculture in the mid nineteenth century* (Stafford: Staffordshire Record Society, 1996).

Pollard, E., Hooper, M. D. and Moore, N. W., *Hedges* (London: Collins, 1974).

Pomeranz, K., *The Great Divergence: China, Europe, and the making of the modern world economy* (Princeton: Princeton University Press, 2001).

Postgate, M. R., 'The field systems of Breckland', *Agricultural History Review* 10 (1962), 80–101.

—, 'The Open Fields of Cambridgeshire', unpublished PhD thesis, University of Cambridge, 1964.

Preston, C. D., 'Engulfed by suburbia or destroyed by the plough: the ecology of extinction in Middlesex and Cambridgeshire', *Watsonia* 23 (2000), 59–81.

Price, U., *An Essay on the Picturesque* (London, 1794).

Prince, H., 'The changing rural landscape', in G. Mingay (ed.), *The Cambridge Agrarian History of England and Wales*, vol. 6 (Cambridge: Cambridge University Press, 1987), 7–83.

Pringle, A., *General View of the Agriculture of Westmoreland* (London, 1805).

Pryor, F., *Farmers in Prehistoric Britain* (Stroud: Tempus, 1998).

Rackham, D. J., '*Rattus rattus*: the introduction of the black rat into Britain', *Antiquity* 53 (1979), 112–20.

Rackham, O., *Trees and Woodland in the British Landscape* (London: Dent, 1976).

—, *The History of the Countryside* (London: Dent, 1986).

—, *Ancient Woodland* (Colvend: Castlepoint Press, 2003).

—, 'Pre-existing trees and woods in country-house parks', *Landscapes* 5, 2 (2004), 1–15.

—, *Woodlands* (London: Collins, 2006).

Raistrick, A., *The Face of North West Yorkshire* (Lancaster: Dalesman, 1949).

Ratcliffe, D. A., *A Nature Conservation Review, Vol. 2, Site Accounts* (Cambridge: Cambridge University Press and the Nature Conservancy Council, 1977).

—, 'Post-medieval and recent change in British vegetation: the culmination of human influence', *New Phytologist* 98 (1984), 73–100.

—, 'Upland birds and their conservation', *British Wildlife* 2 (1990), 1–12.

Ratcliffe, P. R., 'Distribution and current status of Sika deer, *Cervus nippon*, in Great Britain', *Mammal Review* 17 (1987), 39–58.

Rawding, C., 'Society and place in nineteenth-century north Lincolnshire', *Rural History: economy, society, culture* 3, 1 (1992), 59–85.

Read, H. J., *Veteran Trees: a guide to good management* (Peterborough: English Nature, 2000).

—, 'Pollards and pollarding in Europe', *British Wildlife* 19 (2008), 250–9.

Read, H. J. and Frater, M., *Woodland Habitats* (London: Routledge, 1999).

Reed, M., 'Pre-parliamentary enclosure in the East Midlands and its impact on the landscape', *Landscape History* 3 (1981), 60–8.

—, 'The urban landscape 1540-1700', in P. Clarke (ed.), *The Cambridge Urban History of Britain*, vol. 2, 1540–1840 (Cambridge: Cambridge University Press, 2000).

—, 'The transformation of urban space 1700-1840', in P. Clarke (ed.), *The Cambridge Urban History of Britain*, vol. 2 (Cambridge: Cambridge University Press, 2000), pp. 615–40.

Reeves, A. and Williamson, T., 'Marshes', in J. Thirsk (ed.), *Rural England: an illustrated history of the landscape* (Oxford: Cambridge University Press, 2000), pp. 150–66.

Rich, T., 'Flowering plants', in D. Hawksworth (ed.), *The Changing Wildlife of Great Britain and Ireland* (London: Taylor and Francis, 2001), pp. 23–49.

Rippon, S., *Beyond the Medieval Village: the diversification of landscape character in southern Britain* (Oxford: Oxford University Press, 2008).

Risbeth, S., 'The flora of Cambridge walls', *Journal of Ecology* 36 (1948), 136–48.

Robbins, R. W., 'Lepidoptera of a London garden fifty years ago', *London Naturalist* (1939), 40–1.

Roberts, B. K. and Wrathmell, S., *An Atlas of Rural Settlement in England* (London: English Heritage, 2000).

Roberts, B. and Wrathmell, S., *Region and Place; a study of English rural settlement* (London: English Heritage, 2002).

Robinson, R. A. and Sutherland, W. J., 'Post-war changes in arable farming and biodiversity in Great Britain', *Journal of Applied Ecology* 39 (2002), 157–76.

Robinson, W., *The English Flower Garden* (London, 1883).

—, *The Wild Garden* (London, 1870).

Robinson, R. A., Wilson, J. D. and Crick, H. P., 'The importance of arable habitats for farmland birds in grassland landscapes', *Journal of Applied Ecology* 38 (2001), 1059–69.

Roden, D., 'Field systems of the Chilterns and their environs', in A. R. H. Baker and R. A. Butlin (eds), *Studies of Field Systems in the British Isles* (Cambridge: Cambridge University Press, 1973), pp. 325–76.

Rodwell, J. S. (ed.), *British Plant Communities, Volume 3: Grassland and Montane Communities* (Cambridge: Cambridge University Press, 1993).

Roe, P., 'Norfolk Agriculture in 1850'. Unpublished M.Phil thesis, University of East Anglia, Norwich 1975.

Rogers, H. B., 'The suburban growth of Victorian Manchester', *Journal of the Manchester Geographical Society* 58 (1961–2), 1–12.

Rotherham, I. R., *Peat and Peat Cutting* (Shire: Princes Risborough, 2011a).

Rotherham, I. D., 'History and perception in animal and plant invasions: the case of acclimatization and wild gardeners', in I. D. Rotherham and R. A. Lambert (eds), *Invasive and Introduced Plants and Animals: human perceptions, attitudes and approaches to management* (London: Earthscan, 2011b), pp. 233–48.

Rotherham, I. D. and Lambert, R. A., 'Balancing species history, human culture and scientific insight: introduction and overview', in I. D. Rotherham and R. A. Lambert (eds), *Invasive and Introduced Plants and Animals: human perceptions, attitudes and approaches to management* (London: Earthscan, 2011a), pp. 3–18.

—, 'Good science, good history and pragmatism: managing the way ahead', in I. D. Rotherham and R. A. Lambert (eds), *Invasive and Introduced Plants and Animals: human perceptions, attitudes and approaches to management* (London: Earthscan, 2011b), pp. 355–66.

De Rougemont, G. M., *Collins Field Guide to the Crops of Britain and Europe* (London: Collins, 1989).

Rowell, C. W., 'County council smallholdings 1908-58', *Agriculture* 50 (1959), 109–14.

Rowell, T. A., 'Management of peatlands for conservation', *British Wildlife* 1 (1989), 146–56.

Rowley, T., *The English Landscape in the Twentieth Century* (London: Hambledon Continuum, 2006).

Ruggles, T., 'Picturesque farming', *Annals of Agriculture* 6 (1786), 175–84

Russell Smith, J. (ed.), *The Complete Works of Michael Drayton Vol. 3* (London, 1876).

Ryle, G., *Forest Service: the first forty-five years of the Forestry Commission in Great Britain* (Newton Abbot: David and Charles, 1969).

Salisbury, E., *Weeds and Aliens* (London: Collins, 1961).

Sargent, T. D., Millar, C. D. and Lambert, D. M., 'The 'classical' explanation of industrial melanism. Assessing the evidence', *Evolutionary Biology* 30 (1998), 299–322.

Schofield, J., *London 1100–1600: the archaeology of a capital city* (Sheffield: Equinox, 2011).

Lord Justice Scott, *Report on the Committee on Land Utilisation in Rural Areas*, Command Paper 6378 (London: HMSO, 1942).

Secord, A., 'Science in the Pub: artisan botanists in early nineteenth-century Lancashire', *History of Science* 32 (1994), 269–315.

Shaw, C. E., 'Canals', in J. P. Savidge (ed.), *Travis's Flora of South Lancashire* (Liverpool: Liverpool Botanical Society 1963), pp. 71–3.

Shaw, P., 'Orchid woods and floating islands – the ecology of fly ash', *British Wildlife* 5 (1994), 149–57.

Sheial, J., *Rabbits and their History* (Newton Abbot: David and Charles, 1971).

—, 'The formation and maintenance of water-meadows in Hampshire, England', *Biological Conservation* 3 (1971), 101–6.

—, 'The impact of recreation on the coast: the Lindsey County Council (Sandhills) Act, 1932'. *Landscape Planning* 4 (1977), 53–72.

—, *An Environmental History of Twentieth-Century Britain* (London: Palgrave, 2002).

Shoard, M., *The Theft of the Countryside* (London: Temple Smith, 1980).

Short, B., 'The evolution of contrasting communities within rural England', in B. Short (ed.), *The English Rural Community: image and analysis* (Cambridge: Cambridge University Press, 1992), pp. 19–43.

Short, B., Watkins, C. and Martin, J. (eds), *The Front Line of Freedom: British farming in the Second World War* Agricultural History Review Supplement Series 4 (2007).

Shorten, M., *Squirrels* (London: Collins, 1954).

Shrubb, M., *Birds, Scythes and Combines: a history of birds and agricultural change* (Cambridge: Cambridge University Press, 2003).

Simmons, I., *The Environmental Impact of Late Mesolithic Cultures* (Edinburgh: Edinburgh University Press, 1996).

—, *An Environmental History of Great Britain: from 10,000 years ago to the present* (Edinburgh: Edinburgh University Press, 2001).

—, *The Moorlands of England and Wales: an environmental history 8000 BC – AD 2000* (Edinburgh: Edinburgh University Press, 2003).

Sinclair, D. J., 'The growth of London since 1800', in K. M. Clayton (ed.), *Guide to the London Excursion: 20th International Geography Congress* (London, 1964), pp. 13–18.

Slater, G., *The English Peasantry and the Enclosure of Common Fields* (London: Constable, 1907).

Smith, R. M., Thompson, K. and Gaston, K. J., 'Urban domestic gardens: composition and richness of the vascular plant flora, and implications for native biodiversity', *Biological Conservation* 129 (2006), 312–22.

Smout, C., 'How the concept of alien species emerged and developed in 20th-century Britain', in I. D. Rotherham and R. A. Lambert (eds), *Invasive and Introduced Plants and Animals: human perceptions, attitudes and approaches to management* (London: Earthscan, 2011), pp. 55–66.

Spooner, S., '"A prospect two field's distance": rural landscapes and urban mentalities in the eighteenth century', *Landscapes* 10 (2009), 101–22.

Rev St John Priest, *General View of the Agriculture of the County of Buckinghamshire* (London, 1813).

Stevenson, H., *The Birds of Norfolk* (London, 1870).

—, 'Ornithological notes', *Transactions of the Norfolk and Norwich Naturalists Society* 2 (1876), 306.

—, 'Ornithological notes', *Transactions of the Norfolk and Norwich Naturalists Society* 4 (1887), 125–39.

Stillingfleet, B., *Tracts Relating to Natural History, Husbandry and Physick* (London, 1759).

Stoate, C., 'The changing face of lowland farming and wildlife part 1: 1845–1945', *British Wildlife* 6 (1995), 341–50.

Straker, V., Brown, A., Fyfe, R. and Jones, J., 'Romano-British environmental background', in C. J. Webster (ed.), *The Archaeology of South West England* (Taunton: Somerset Heritage Service, 2007), pp. 145–50.

Stroud, D., *Capability Brown* (London: Country Life, 1965).

Stroud, D. A., 'The status and legislative protection of birds of prey and their habitats in Europe', in D. B. A. Thompson (ed.), *Birds of Prey in a Changing Environment* (Edinburgh, 2003), pp. 51–83.

Summers-Smith, J. D., *The House Sparrow* (London: Collins, 1963).

Sykes, N., 'The dynamics of status symbols: wildfowl exploitation in England AD 410-1550', *Archaeological Journal* 161 (2004), 82–105.

Sykes, N. and Carden, R., 'Were fallow deer spotted (OE*pohha/*pocca) in Anglo-Saxon England? Reviewing the evidence for *Dama dama dama* in early medieval Europe', *Medieval Archaeology* 55 (2011), 139–62.

Swayne, J., 'The Bustard', *Wiltshire Archaeological Magazine* 2 (1885), 212.

Switzer, S., *Ichnographica Rustica* (London, 1718).

Tallis, J. H., 'Forest and moorland in the south Pennine uplands in the mid-Flandrian period III. The spread of moorland – local, regional and national', *Journal of Ecology* 79 (1991), 401–15.

Tanner, R. A. and Gange, A. C., 'Effects of golf courses on local biodiversity', *Landscape and Urban Planning* 71 (2005), 137–46.

Tansley, A. G., *The British Islands and their Vegetation,* vol. 1 (Cambridge: Cambridge University Press, 1949).

Tapper, S., *Game Heritage: an ecological review, from shooting and gamekeeping records* (Fordingbridge: Game Conservancy, 1992).

Taylor, A. J. P., *English History 1914–1945* (Oxford: Clarendon Press, 1965).

Taylor, C., 'Post-medieval drainage of marsh and fen', in H. Cook and T. Williamson (eds), *Water Manaement in the English Landscape: field, marsh and meadow* (Edinburgh: Edinburgh University Press, 1999), pp. 141–56.

—, 'Fenlands', in J. Thirsk (ed.), *Rural England: an illustrated history of the landscape* (Oxford: Oxford University Press, 2000), pp. 167–87.

Telling, A. E. and Duxbury, R., *Planning Law and Procedure* (Oxford: Oxford University Press, 2005).

Temperley, G. W. and Blezard, E., 'The status of the green woodpecker in northern England', *British Birds* 44 (1951), 24–6.

Tennyson, J., *Suffolk Scene: a book of description and adventure* (London: Blackie and Son, 1939).

Terman, M. R., 'Natural links: naturalistic golf courses as wildlife habitat', *Landscape and Urban Planning* 38 (1997), 183–97.

Theobald, J., 'Changing landscapes, changing economies: holdings in Woodland High Suffolk 1600-1840', Unpublished MA dissertation, University of East Anglia 1993.

Thirsk, J., 'Agricultural innovations and their diffusion', in J. Thirsk (ed.), *The Agricultural History of England and Wales. Volume 6.2, 1640–1750* (Cambridge: Cambridge University Press, 1985), pp. 533–89.

—, *England's Agricultural Regions and Agrarian History 1500–1750* (London: Macmillan, 1987).

—, 'English rural communities: structures, regularities, and change in the sixteenth and seventeenth centuries', in B. Short (ed.), *The English Rural Community: image and analysis* (Cambridge: Cambridge University Press, 1992), pp. 44–61.

Thomas, B., 'Was there an energy crisis in Great Britain in the seventeenth century?', *Explorations in Economic History* 23 (1986), 124–52.

Thomas, K., *Man and the Natural World: changing attitudes in England 1500–1800* (London: Allen Lane, 1983).

Thomas, S. and Dines, T., 'Non-native invasive plants in Britain: a real, not imagined, problem', *British Wildlife* 21 (2010), 177–83.

Thompson, E. P., *Whigs and Hunters: the origin of the Black Act* (London: Allen Lane, 1975).

—, *The Making of the English Working Class* (London: Gollancz, 1980).

Thompson, F. M. L., 'The second Agricultural Revolution', *Economic History Review* 21 (1968), 62–77.

—, *English Landed Society in the Nineteenth Century* (London: Routledge and Kegan Paul, 1963).

Toms, M., 'Are gardens good for birds or birdwatchers?', *British Wildlife* 19 (2007), 77–83.

Truck, J. G., 'Note on the Great Bustard in Suffolk'. *Transactions of the Norfolk and Norwich Naturalists' Society* 5 (1891), 209–11.

Tsouvalis, J., *A Critical Geography of Britain's State Forests* (Oxford: Oxford University Press, 2000).

Tubbs, C., 'Grazing the lowland heaths', *British Wildlife* 2 (1990), 276–89.

von Tunzelmann, N., *Steam Power and British Industrialisation to 1860* (Oxford: Clarendon Press, 1978).

Turner, J. H., 'On the necessity of reducing the size and number of hedges', *Journal of the Royal Agricultural Society of England* 6 (1845), 479–88.

Turner, E. L., 'The status of birds in Broadland'. *Transactions of the Norfolk and Norwich Naturalists' Society* 11 (1922), 228–40.

Turner, M. E., 'Arable in England and Wales: estimates from the 1801 Crop Return', *Journal of Historical Geography* 7 (1981), 291–302.

—, *Volume 190: Home Office Acreage Returns HO67. List and Analysis*, 3 vols (London: List and Index Society, 1982).

Turner, R., *Capability Brown and the Eighteenth-Century English Landscape* (London: Weidenfeld and Nicolson 1985).

Turner, T., *English Garden Design: history and styles since 1650* (Woodbridge: Antique Collector's Club, 1986).

Tutsin, T. G., 'Weeds of a Leicester garden', *Watsonia* 9 (1973), 263–7.

Tutt, J. W., 'Melanism and melanochroism in British Lepidoptera', *Entomologist's Record* 1 (1891): 5–7, 49–56, 84–90, 121–5, 169–72, 228–34, 293–300, 317–25.

Upcher, H. M., 'President's address', *Transactions of the Norfolk and Norwich Naturalists' Society* 3 (1884), 564–633.

Upcher, H., 'Norfolk farming', *Norfolk and Norwich Naturalists' Society* 16 (1946), 97–105.

Upex, S. G., 'The uses and functions of ponds within early landscapes in the east Midlands', *Agricultural History Review* 52 (2004), 125–40.

Vera, F., *Grazing Ecology and Forest History* (Wallingford: CABI Publishing, 2002).

—, 'Large scale nature development: the Oostvaardersplassen', *British Wildlife* 20 (2009), 28–36.

Vesey-Fitzgerald, B., *British Game* (London: Collins, 1953).

Wade, E., *A Proposal for Improving and Adorning the Island of Great Britain: for the maintenance of our navy and shipping* (London, 1755).

Wade Martins, S., *Farms and Fields* (London: Batsford, 1995).

Wade Martins, S. and Williamson, T., 'Floated water-meadows in Norfolk: a misplaced innovation', *Agricultural History Review* 42 (1994), 20–37.

—, *Roots of Change: farming and the landscape in East Anglia, c.1700–1870* (Exeter: Exeter University Press, 1999).

—, *The Countryside of East Anglia: changing landscapes, 1870–1950* (Woodbridge: Boydell, 2008).

Walker, D., *General View of the Agriculture of the County of Hertford* (London, 1795).

Walker, K. J., 'Using data from local floras to assess floristic change', *Watsonia* 24 (2003), 305–19.

—, 'The last thirty five years: recent changes in the flora of the British Isles', *Watsonia* 26 (2007), 291–302.

Walton, I. and Cotton, C., *The Complete Angler* (London, 1853).

Warren, C. H., *This Land is Yours* (London: Eyre and Spottiswoode, 1943).

Warren, J. B. L., 'The flora of Hyde Park and Kensington Gardens', *Journal of Botany* 9 (1871), 227–38.

Warren, M., 'European butterflies on the brink', *British Wildlife* 1 (1989), 185–96.

Waterson, M., *The National Trust: the first hundred years* (London: National Trust, 1994).

Watkins, C. and Cowell, B., *Uvedale Price (1747–1829): decoding the picturesque* (Woodbridge: Boydell, 2012).

Watson, P. V., 'Man's impact on the chalklands: some new pollen evidence', in M. Bell and S. Limbrey (eds), *Archaeological Aspects of Woodland Ecology* (Oxford: British Archaeological Reports, International Series, vol. 146, 1982), pp. 75–92.

Warde, P., *Energy Consumption in England and Wales 1560–2000* (Rome: Consiglio nazionale delle ricerche, Istituto di studi sulle società del Mediterraneo, 2006).

Wauters, L. A., Tosi, G. and Gurnell, J., 'Interspecific competition in tree squirrels: do introduced grey squirrels (Sciurus carolinensis) deplete tree seeds hoarded by red squirrels (*S. vulgaris*)?', *Behavioural Ecology and Sociobiology* 51 (2002), 360–7.

Webb, D. A., 'What are the criteria for presuming native status?', *Watsonia* 15 (1985), 231–6.

Webb, N., *Heathlands* (London: Collins, 1986).

Wheeler, J., *The Modern Druid* (London, 1747)

Welch, R. C. and Hammond, P., 'Breckland coleoptera', in P. Ratcliffe and J. Claridge (eds), *Thetford Forest Park: the ecology of a pine forest* (Edinburgh: Forestry Commission, 1996), pp. 92–102.

White, G., *The Natural History and Antiquities of Selbourne in the County of Southampton* (London, 1813).

White, J., 'What is a veteran tree and where are they all?', *Quarterly Journal of Forestry* 91, 3 (1997), 222–6.

—, 'Estimating the age of large and veteran trees in Britain', Forestry Commission Information Note 250 (Alice Holt: Forestry Commission, 1999).

Whyte, I., *Transforming Fell and Valley: landscape and parliamentary enclosure in north west England* (Lancaster: University of Lancaster: Centre for North West Regional Studies, 2003).

Wilkinson, R. G., 'The English Industrial Revolution', in D. Worcester (ed.), *The Ends of the Earth: perspectives on modern environmental history* (Cambridge University Press, Cambridge,1988), pp. 80–99.

William, H. and Nisbet-Drury, I. C., 'Succession', *Journal of the Arnold Arboretum* 54 (1973), 331–68.

Williams, L. R. and McLaughlin, J., 'Tracing old hedgerows in suburban areas', *Local Historian* 18 (May 1988), 65–8.

Williams, M., *The Draining of the Somerset Levels* (Cambridge: Cambridge University Press, 1970).

Williams, R., *Key Words: a vocabulary of culture and society* (London: Croom Helm, 1976).

—, *Limekilns and Limeburning* (Princes Risborough: Shire, 1989).

Williams-Ellis, C., *England and the Octopus* (London: G.Bles, 1928).

Williamson, H., *The Story of a Norfolk Farm* (London: Faber, 1940).

Williamson, T., *Polite Landscapes: gardens and society in eighteenth-century England* (Stroud: Sutton, 1995).

—, 'Fish, fur and feather: man and nature in the post-medieval landscape', in K. Barker and T. Darvill (eds), *Making English Landscapes* (Bournemouth: Bournemouth University School of Conservation Sciences Occasional Paper, 1997), pp. 92–117.

—, *The Norfolk Broads: a landscape history* (Manchester: Manchester University Press, 1997).

—, *The Archaeology of the Landscape Park: landscape design in Norfolk, England 1680–1840* (Oxford: British Archaeological Reports, British Series, Vol 268, 1998).

—, 'Post-medieval field drainage', in H. Cook and T. Williamson (eds), *Water Management in the English Landscape: field, marsh and meadow* (Edinburgh: Edinburgh University Press, 1999), pp. 41–52.

—, 'Understanding enclosure', *Landscapes* 1, 1 (2000), 56–79.

—, *The Transformation of Rural England: farming and the landscape 1700–1870* (Exeter: Exeter University Press, 2002).

—, 'Shrubland before Barry: a house and its landscape 1660-1880', in Christopher Harper-Bill, Carole Rawcliffe and Richard Wilson (eds), *East Anglia's History: studies in honour of Norman Scarfe* (Woodbridge: Boydell, 2002), pp. 189–212.

—, *Shaping Medieval Landscapes: settlement, society, environment* (Macclesfield: Windgather, 2003).

—, 'Floating in context; meadows in the long term', in H. Cook and T. Williamson (eds), *Water Meadows: history, ecology and conservation* (Oxford: Windgather, 2007), pp. 35–51.

—, *Rabbits, Warrens and Archaeology* (Stroud: Tempus, 2007).

—, 'Archaeological perspectives on landed estates: research agendas', in J. Finch and K. Giles (eds), *Estate landscapes: design, improvement and power in the post-medieval landscape* (Woodbridge: Boydell, 2007), pp. 1–18.

—, *Sutton Hoo and its Landscape; the context of monuments* (Oxford: Windgather, 2008).

—, 'At pleasure's lordly call: the archaeology of emparked settlements', in C. Dyer and R. Jones (eds), *Deserted Villages Revisited* (Hatfield: University of Hertfordshire Press, 2010), pp. 162–81.

—, *Environment, Society and Landscape in Early Medieval England: time and topography* (Woodbridge: Boydell, 2013).

Williamson, T., Liddiard, R. and Partida, T., *Champion. The making and unmaking of the English Midland landscape* (Liverpool: Liverpool University Press, 2013).

Willis, P., *Charles Bridgeman and the English Landscape Garden*, Revised edn (London: Elysium, 2002).

Willmott, A., 'The woody species of hedges with special reference to age in Church Broughton, Derbyshire', *Journal of Ecology* 68 (1980), 269–86.

Wilson, J. H. (ed.), *Wymondham Inventories* (Norwich: Centre of East Anglian Studies, 1983).

Wilson, P. J., 'Britain's arable weeds', *British Wildlife* 3 (1991), 149–61.

Winchester, A., 'The farming landscape', in W. Rollinson (ed.), *The Lake District: landscape history* (Newton Abbot: David and Charles, 1989), pp. 76–101.

—, *England's Landscape: the North West* (London: Collins/English Heritage, 2006).

Winchester, A. and Staughton, A., 'Stints and sustainability: managing stocking levels on commons land in England c.1600-2000', *Agricultural History Review* 58 (2010), 30–48.

Rev Wood, J. G., *The Common Objects of the Country* (London, 1858).

Worcester, D., *The Wealth of Nature: environmental history and the ecological imagination* (Oxford: Oxford University Press, 1993).

Wordsworth, W., *Guide to the Lakes of Westmoreland and Cumberland* (London, 1810).

Wrigley, E. A. W., *Continuity, Chance and Change: the character of the industrial revolution in England* (Cambridge: Cambridge University Press, 1988).

Wyllie, I., 'The bird community of an English parish', *Bird Study* 23 (1976), 39–50.

Yalden, D. W., *The History of British Mammals* (London: Poyser, 1999).

Yelling, J. A., *Common Field and Enclosure in England 1450–1850* (London: Macmillan, 1977).

Young, A., *The Farmer's Tour Through the East of England*, 4 vols (London, 1771).

—, *Observations on the Present State of the Waste Lands of Great Britain* (London, 1773).

—, *General View of the Agriculture of Hertfordshire* (London, 1804).

Young, K. M. K. and Garside, P. L., *Metropolitan London: politics and urban change 1837–1981* (London: Edward Arnold, 1982).

INDEX

Page numbers in **bold** refer to figures and their captions.
NB one page may contain multiple references.